CW01500921

RECORDS OF CONVOCATION

The convocation records of the Churches of England and Ireland are the principal source of our information about the administration of those churches from middle ages until modern times. They contain the minutes of clergy synods, the legislation passed by them, tax assessments imposed by the king on the clergy, and accounts of the great debates about religious reformation; they also include records of heresy trials in the fifteenth and sixteenth centuries, many of them connected with the spread of Lollardy. However, they have never before been edited or published in full, and their publication as a complete set of documents provides a valuable resource for scholarship.

RECORDS OF CONVOCATION

I

SODOR AND MAN

1229–1877

EDITED BY

Gerald Bray

THE BOYDELL PRESS

CHURCH OF ENGLAND RECORD SOCIETY

© Gerald Bray 2005

All Rights Reserved. Except as permitted under current legislation
no part of this work may be photocopied, stored in a retrieval system,
published, performed in public, adapted, broadcast,
transmitted, recorded or reproduced in any form or by any means,
without the prior permission of the copyright owner

First published 2005
The Boydell Press, Woodbridge
in association with
The Church of England Record Society

The Boydell Press is an imprint of Boydell & Brewer Ltd
PO Box 9, Woodbridge, Suffolk IP12 3DF, UK
and of Boydell & Brewer Inc.
668 Mt Hope Avenue, Rochester, NY 14620, USA
website: www.boydellandbrewer.com

ISBN 1 84383 176 7

This volume is published with the financial assistance of
The Manx Heritage Foundation

A catalogue record for this book is available
from the British Library

Printed on acid-free paper
from camera-ready copy supplied by the editor

Printed in Great Britain by
Antony Rowe Ltd., Chippenham, Wiltshire

CONTENTS

EDITOR'S NOTE

This and the companion volume of the Manx convocation records, which contains the material covering the years from 1878 to 2003, form a subset of a wider project to publish all the unpublished records of convocation in the Church of England and in the Church of Ireland. I am deeply grateful to the present lord bishop of Sodor and Man, the Rt Rev. Graeme Knowles, for allowing me to transcribe the records, including some recently discovered ones which had not (at that time) been deposited in the Manx National Heritage Library. I am also very grateful to Roger Sims and Wendy Thirkettle, archivists at that Library, and their staff, who gave me every assistance as I prepared the different manuscripts for publication, and to Brian and Jenny Darbyshire of St Ninian's Church, for their kind hospitality to me on my frequent visits to the Isle of Man. I have also received invaluable help from Canon Hinton Bird, one of the island's leading historians, and from Mrs Brian Kelly of Peel, who is a mine of information about the diocese over the past generation. Finally, I must thank Mr Charles Guard and the Manx National Heritage Foundation for their generous grant towards publication. May God bless you all and may these volumes be used to make known the story of His marvellous works in Ellan Vannin.

Gerald Bray

19 May 2005
Convocation Day

INTRODUCTION

The Isle of Man and its church[1]

A teardrop-shaped landmass of 572 square kilometres, the Isle of Man is the only place in the British Isles from which it is possible to see England, Scotland, Ireland and Wales all at the same time. Its history is not unnaturally bound up with that of these neighbours, but what is surprising about it is the extent to which it has escaped falling under the overwhelming influence of any one of them. For the Isle of Man is *sui generis*, not a part of the United Kingdom which surrounds it, but retaining laws and forms of government unknown or else long forgotten elsewhere in these islands.

Its recorded history begins in the high middle ages, when it was an Irish-speaking Christian island under Norse rule. Archaeological evidence, and the names of the parish churches, suggest that Christianity reached Man from Ireland, though when, or in what circumstances, no-one can now say for certain. The first Manx bishops of whom we have any knowledge were suffragans of York, appointed in the eleventh century, though this link may owe as much to Viking influence in both places as to anything else. Certainly York's medieval relationship with the Isle of Man was ephemeral, and no more was heard of it after about 1100.

The Vikings arrived in Man sometime in the ninth century and after a fairly slow conquest, they managed to establish a kingdom there which was ultimately dependent on Norway. By 1100 the kings of Man were recognized as rulers of the Scottish Hebrides, and occasionally of the Mull of Kintyre also. These Scottish possessions were known to the Norsemen as the *suðre øyar* (southern islands) – 'southern' in relation to Orkney and Shetland that is – and it is from this that the name Sodor is derived. In 1134 King Olaf I (1103-53) established a bishopric in his kingdom which in 1153 became part of the ecclesiastical province of Nidaros (Trondheim) in Norway.[2]

This seems to have been the final stage in a governmental organization which encompassed every aspect of Manx life. The Norsemen divided the Isle of Man into a north and a south side, apparently because of perceived ethnic distinctions

[1]The only full-scale history of the diocese is by A. W. Moore, *The diocese of Sodor and Man* (London, 1893). It has recently been put on the internet and can be downloaded from a number of websites. A fuller history is J. D. Gelling, *A history of the Manx church 1698-1911* (Douglas, 1998). There is also W. Harrison, *The diocese of Sodor and Man*, Manx Studies Series XXIX (Douglas, 1879), but unfortunately it must be used with great caution, as much of its information is both inadequate and inaccurate.
[2]This was when the province of Nidaros was established. Before then, the diocese would have belonged in the province of Lund, but there is no mention of that anywhere.

between them. The north side was where the Viking settlements mainly were, whereas the south side seems to have remained more purely Gaelic. Each side had its own laws and law officers, and the distinctions between them were not finally abolished until 1796. At first, it was the north side which dominated island life, and vestiges of this still remain. The cathedral is situated at Peel, the north side's port, and until 1974 the bishop lived at Bishopscourt, which is in the parish of Kirk Michael, also on the north side. Until 1938 the archdeacon's parish was Kirk Andreas, near the northern tip of the island, and the Tynwald hill, where the island's government meets in formal session every summer, is not far from Peel. All three rectorial parishes in the island (Andreas, Ballaugh and Bride) are on the north side, as are three of the four ancient parishes which are in the gift of the bishop.[3]

Each of the sides was subdivided into three 'sheadings'[4] for judicial purposes, and each sheading contained two or three parishes. At first there were sixteen parishes, eight on each side, but the anomaly of having one sheading with only two parishes seems to have led to the creation of a ninth parish on the south side, by dividing Marown into two. This did not happen on the north side, however, possibly because the sheading with only two parishes (Glenfaba) was based on Peel, and both parishes were in the gift of the bishop. Until the early eighteenth century they normally shared a vicar and met for worship at Peel, which suggests that the sheading as a whole was kept under fairly tight control from the centre.

Viking rule was relatively democratic, and every year the freemen of the island would meet to hear the laws read and to voice their grievances. The *thing*, as it was called in Norse, became the ancestor of the modern Tynwald,[5] though what its functions were is hard to say. It seems that for many centuries it was more of a court than a legislature, though it was the natural forum for lawmaking and was certainly used for that purpose from the fifteenth century onwards.

The kingdom of Man and the Isles declined along with Norse power in general, and in 1266 King Magnus IV of Norway ceded it to Scotland. That subsequently led to a period of English domination (1290-1312), when King Edward I claimed the Scottish throne, but the Scots recovered it and remained in control until 1333, when King Edward III of England ordered it to be occupied on his behalf. The diocese of Sodor and Man never declared its independence from Nidaros, but in practice it became part of the Scottish church during this period and there is no sign that it had any contact with Norway after 1266. The English domination of Man did not alter this, and for a while the diocese continued to function as if the ancient kingdom of Man and the Isles still existed.

Change came only in 1387, when the Avignonese Pope Clement VII deposed the bishop, John Donegan, who supported the claims of Rome during the great schism. As Scotland supported Avignon, Donegan was driven out of Sodor and had to seek help from England, which recognized Rome. This help was forthcoming, and in 1291 Donegan was made a suffragan of London. Since that time there has always been an 'English' bishop in the Isle of Man, and he has continued to claim

---

[3]Patrick, German and Jurby. The exception is Braddan.
[4]The word rhymes with 'feedings' and derives from an old Norse term for 'division'.
[5]The word is a corruption of the Norse *thing vøllir*, or 'assembly place'.

Sodor as part of his diocese, much as the lords of Man have also retained the designation 'and the Isles' in their official title.

Under English rule, Man was governed as a fiefdom which in 1405 became hereditary in the Stanley family, who were earls of Derby from 1485. The Stanleys seldom visited the island, preferring to rule it through governors, most of whom were sent from England and had little familiarity with the place. Following a disputed succession in the Derby line, Man was taken into crown administration in 1594, only to be restored to the Stanley heir in 1610. During the commonwealth period (1652-60) the Stanleys lost their rights to Thomas Fairfax, but the structure of island government remained unaltered. When the last of the Stanleys died out in 1736, the lordship passed to the dukes of Atholl, who were forced to cede it to the crown in 1765, an event known locally as the 'revestment'. Since then, the island has been governed as a crown dependency, with full internal self-rule developing from the mid-nineteenth century onwards. Until 1840 Man retained its own currency,[6] but although this has since merged with sterling, the island retains (or has regained) its autonomy in most other spheres and now functions as a semi-independent state.

The Manx language

The Manx language is an aberrant dialect of Irish and it was the tongue of the majority of the island's population until about 1800. Centuries of separation from Ireland made it a distinct language, so that when the Bible and Prayer Book were translated into Irish in the seventeenth century, it was not possible to use the translations in the Isle of Man in the way that it was in the highlands of Scotland. The language remained almost entirely oral, and church services had to be translated by the clergy as they went along. The fact that a knowledge of Manx was necessary for ministering in the island meant that English clergy were generally kept out (or else restricted to the few towns on the island where there was an English-speaking population), and until the mid-nineteenth century this gave the diocese a homogeneity unknown elsewhere. Nevertheless, the bishops were always English or Anglo-Irish, and none of them mastered Manx to the extent needed to be able to preach in it.

The reduction of Manx to writing occurred in the eighteenth century, and was carried out by men used to English orthographic conventions. This produced a most peculiar script, which appears quite outlandish when compared with Irish or Scottish Gaelic, and increases the psychological distance between Manx and its closest linguistic relatives. Translation of the Bible and Prayer Book began under Bishop Thomas Wilson (1698-1755) and was completed under his successor, Bishop Mark Hildesley (1755-73) who was a devotee of the language, even though he did not know it himself. Manx Bibles and New Testaments continued to be printed until 1825, but by then they were no longer needed, as there were few monoglot Manx speakers left. The language decayed rapidly in the nineteenth

---

[6] A Manx pound, rather like the Irish pound before 1826, was worth about six-sevenths of a pound sterling.

century, and was not used for church services after the death of William Drury, vicar of Braddan, in 1887.[7] The last native speaker of Manx was Henry Maddrell, who died in 1974, and the language now survives only as a hobby for enthusiasts.

Church records were in Latin before the reformation and then in English, which was also the language of education from the very beginning. The clergy were thus functionally bilingual, though there is no sign that any of them was prejudiced against the Manx tongue as such. It was the growth of education and the influx of outsiders in the nineteenth century which killed off the native language of the island, not prejudice or snobbery sponsored by the church, which remained one of the language's firmest bastions as long as monoglot speakers survived.

Although the student of Manx church history has no need to learn Manx, it is useful to be aware of some features of it which help to explain the forms of personal and place names. The Manx language (like all Celtic languages) mutates initial consonants in certain positions, a feature which can be most disconcerting to the uninitiated. For example, 'Mannin' (Manx for 'Man'), becomes 'ellan Vannin' ('Isle of Man'), and an initial 'c' can disappear altogether. This has given Kirk Arbory (from Carbory) and Kirk Onchan (from Conchan). By the eighteenth century the form 'Carbory' had vanished, but 'Conchan' remained as the 'correct' form for 'Onchan'. Manx pushed this tendency to lose initial letters further than its sister languages, particularly in personal names. This explains why so many Manx surnames begin with 'c', 'k' or 'q', all of which are survivals from the more ancient (and more familiar) 'mac'. Sometimes this is fairly obvious, as in 'Clucas' (MacLucas), Kissack (MacIsaac) or 'Quilliam' (MacWilliam), but not everyone would detect that 'Qualtrough' is just the Manx for 'MacWalter' and is therefore identical with the surname 'Watterson', which appears alongside it in the records![8]

Pronunciation, as we might expect, is a constant hazard, even though Manx spelling is based on English rather than Gaelic. 'Clague' sounds like 'Clegg', 'Kermode' is stressed on the first syllable, the 'r' in 'Corlett' is silent and 'Curghey' is pronounced, as it is now spelled, 'Curphey'.

The pre-reformation church

The earliest records of the Manx church date from the thirteenth century and take the form of ecclesiastical statutes officially promulgated by Bishop Simon (1226-48) in 1229/30.[9] In their present form, they are most unlikely to have been Simon's work, though it is possible that they were developed out of statutes originally issued by him. Their content can mostly be paralleled without difficulty in English statutes of a slightly earlier date, and it is quite possible that Simon got his inspiration from the Canterbury statutes of 1213/14 or something similar. But the fourteenth statute

---

[7]Drury did not use the language much in services, but he spoke it fluently and ministered to many older members of his congregation in it.
[8]See L. Quilliam, *Surnames of the Manks* (Peel, 1989; reprinted Douglas, 1996) for the details. Mrs Quilliam, somewhat eccentrically, prefers the older spelling of the word 'Manx'.
[9]The precise date depends on whether the year was calculated from 25 March (unknown) and whether the diocesan synod was held, as much later ones generally were, in late winter.

(on weavers) recurs in a simpler and more generalized form in the Manx statutes of 1292, which makes us wonder whether the latter is not in fact the original of the two. The general style of Simon's statutes fits much better with English and Scottish statutes of the early fourteenth century than it does with the period before 1229, and leads us to conclude that in their present form at least, they probably date from that period. It is even possible that they are somehow connected to the English occupation in 1333, when they may have been written down as 'proof' of the church's ancient rights which required protection.

Bishop Mark (1275/8-1303) is the next legislator known to the Manx church, and his canons were apparently passed at a diocesan synod held at Kirk Braddan on 10 March 1292. The superscription is noticeably more precise than is the case with Simon's constitutions, and there is no reason to doubt that these canons were indeed promulgated on that date, even if some of them may have been touched up slightly at a later time. They are very extensive for their time and cover the full range of church law. Their authenticity is supported by the fact that in 1351 Bishop William Russell (1349-71) made additions to them, based to a considerable degree on already existing Scottish legislation. That means that they must have been written before 1387, when the links with the Scottish church were broken, and there is no reason to doubt that we are on firm historical ground at this point. The last of the pre-reformation documents which is relevant to our present purposes is the confirmation of the church's liberties issued by Thomas Stanley, lord of Man, in 1505. It is quite likely, in fact, that the manuscript which contains all of the above, was composed about that time and kept as a record of what the church's rights and liberties were. The diocese of Sodor and Man was thus a fully functioning part of the late medieval church, with a major stake in the island's economy and government.

From the reformation to 1698

The reformation reached the Isle of Man in 1540, when the monasteries were dissolved and their property impropriated by the lord in the name of the crown. This event was not strictly legal, since the English legislation by which it was justified did not extend to the Isle of Man, but such niceties did not trouble Henry VIII, nor was his action questioned by anyone at the time. In 1542 the English parliament legislated for the inclusion of the diocese of Sodor and Man in the province of York,[10] and in 1546 the king successfully claimed the right to confirm the appointment of the bishop. From then until 1825, the bishop of Sodor and Man was appointed by the lord of the isle (after 1765 by the duke of Atholl, who did not surrender this privilege at the time of the revestment), as were the archdeacon and twelve of the sixteen other parish clergy, but the bishop's appointment had to be confirmed by the crown. Representatives of Sodor and Man were given the right to sit in the convocation of York on the same basis as the other dioceses of the province, but this right was seldom exercised in practice.

---

[10] 33 Henry VIII, c. 31.

The bishop of Sodor and Man did not have a seat in the English house of lords, since he was not a bishop in England, but instead, as a baron of the Isle of Man, he sat (as indeed he still sits) in the legislative council of Tynwald.[11] This oddity might have made him the ideal person to chair the York convocation, which met during sessions of the Westminster parliament when the northern bishops were usually in London, but this expedient seems to have been adopted only once, and with little practical effect.[12] The bishop almost never appeared at York in person, though he sent proxies from time to time. Similarly, the archdeacon and the clergy were normally represented by a member of the cathedral establishment at York. It was only after the revival of the York convocation in 1861 that the diocese of Sodor and Man began to send its own representatives on a regular basis, and to play an active part in its deliberations.

The real reformation of the Manx church did not begin until 1570, when after an interregnum lasting nearly fourteen years, a Protestant bishop was finally appointed. Whether John Salisbury (1570-3) achieved much is uncertain, but there are grounds for thinking that he may have laid the foundations for a reformed diocese. Certainly by the time the next bishop, John Meyrick (1576-99) arrived in the island, there was a functioning system of ecclesiastical courts, with an archdeacon, two vicars-general and incumbents in most of the parishes. The confusion which envelops most of this period must be understood as part of a wider breakdown in the island's government, which was put right by the lord himself, when he paid an extensive visit to his remote domain in 1577. On 13 July of that year, Henry Stanley, the fourth earl of Derby (1572-93), presided over a meeting of Tynwald, and during his stay he reorganized both the legal system and the administration. The church cannot have escaped from this reform, and indeed there is a collection of spiritual laws which claims to date from this time and is printed in the Manx statutes accordingly.

These spiritual laws survive in two slightly different recensions, of which the shorter (with fifty-nine canons) is now regarded as the official version. It is known that these laws were approved by Tynwald in 1610, and the great Manx historian A. W. Moore therefore concluded that they probably dated from that time, rather than from 1577.[13] But the signatures attached to the laws tell a different story, since they are those of clergymen who were in post in 1577 and dead by 1610. It therefore seems most likely that the laws were indeed composed in 1577, probably in their longer form, and that the ratification which took place in 1610 was the point at which they were slightly abridged. If that is the case, the synod of 1577, which seems to have taken place in the bishop's absence, may be regarded as a proto-

---

[11]Tynwald consists of an upper house of nine councillors and a lower house of 24 'keys'. The name appears to derive from a corruption of the Manx for 'twenty-four' which is *yn kiare as feed*. It probably stuck because 'keys' seemed to be an appropriate word for those whose job it was to 'unlock' the law. For a detailed explanation of Manx government, see J. R. Dickinson, *The lordship of Man under the Stanleys. Government and economy in the Isle of Man, 1580-1704* (Douglas, 1997), especially pp. 13-74.

[12]Bishop John Philips (1605-33) was granted a commission to preside at the York convocation on 10 February 1610, but does not appear ever to have done so.

[13]Moore, *Sodor and Man*, pp. 130ff.

convocation, since it clearly met in conjunction with the civil legislature and its laws were incorporated into the civil statutes. An interesting point about this synod is that it met *before* Tynwald and not alongside it, so that it could prepare the laws for Tynwald's subsequent endorsement, a pattern different from that which obtained elsewhere but which would later establish itself as the norm in Sodor and Man.

Whatever the truth about the synod of 1577 might be, there is no doubt that convocations were meeting (under that name) early in the reign of James I (1603-25), when the island was still under direct royal government. The main purpose seems to have been judicial, which was also the case with Tynwald at that time, but the 1610 convocation apparently legislated for the church as well. The date is significant, not only because it coincides with the restoration of Stanley rule in the Isle of Man, but also because it took place at the same time as the king's attempt to introduce English forms of church government into Scotland, and preceded by only a few years the inauguration of the Irish national convocation in 1615. It is quite possible that the emergence of the Manx convocation as a legislative body formed a part, however small, of a much bigger design for the Anglican family of churches, all of which came under the supreme government of the king. If that is so, then the Manx convocation today represents the lone survivor of this attempt at English ecclesiastical imperialism, and probably the only fragment of the Jacobean church which still exists in something like its original configuration.

How often convocation met in the years after 1610 is unknown, though records survive for 1613 and 1629. We do not know whether it was supposed to convene every time there was a meeting of Tynwald, nor do we have any idea what its rules of procedure were. We can only assume that they must have been recognizably similar to what went on elsewhere, though on a much smaller scale. What does appear to be certain is that from the beginning, the Manx convocation was an assembly which included all the clergy resident in the island, making it far more representative than any other body of that name.[14]

On 30 October 1643 there was a joint meeting of both civil and ecclesiastical authorities to sort out grievances over tithes and related matters, and this agreement was ratified by both the church and the state. What happened after that is obscure, and it is not certain whether Bishop Richard Parr (1635-44), who signed the agreement, was removed from office or simply died shortly afterwards.[15] Either way, the island was left without a bishop from 1644 until the restoration, a circumstance which meant that the commonwealth government, when it finally reached the island in 1652, was less traumatic than it might otherwise have been. Cromwell's men had no need to replace the existing church structure, and it seems that relatively little was touched. The civil courts handled church business during the years 1652-60, and it seems that the archdeacon went into (voluntary?) exile, but we know of only one incumbent, John Cosnahan of Kirk Arbory, who was forcibly removed, leaving the living vacant for about four years. That matters proceeded

[14]Only the Irish convocation, which may have included up to one quarter of the beneficed clergy in Ireland, came anywhere close to this.
[15]The last document in the records signed by him is dated 20 February 1644. See the Manx episcopal wills, 10 (unfoliated), kept in the Manx National Heritage Library, Douglas.

fairly amicably can be seen from the fact that John Harrison, who was *locum tenens* for the archdeacon during this period, was appointed to the rectory of Kirk Bride when the same archdeacon returned as bishop in 1660.

Church records survive in reasonable quantity from 1660 onwards, though they are not organized as one would expect in an English diocese. The *Libri causarum* contain all kinds of extraneous material, including minutes of the convocations held in 1683 and 1685, and the impression given by this is that the latter were seen primarily as supports to the work of the ecclesiastical courts. As with the pre-1640 material, it is impossible to be sure how often the convocation met, although we do have a clearer idea of what it did. But when Bishop Levinz died in 1693 no successor was appointed, and the administration of the Manx church gradually disintegrated. In 1695 vicars-general were appointed as a temporary measure, simply to keep the wheels turning, but it was becoming clear that a new start would soon have to be made. That was to be the work of Bishop Thomas Wilson (1698-1755), the longest serving diocesan bishop in the history of the Church of England, who became a legend in his own lifetime. It is to him and his achievement that we now turn.

Bishop Wilson (1698-1755)

When Thomas Wilson arrived in the Isle of Man in 1698, he was greeted by a church which appeared to be in ruins. One of his first acts was to appoint a series of schoolmasters to the different parishes, in accordance with a benefaction made by King Charles II in 1676 but not properly acted upon before his arrival. These schools were to be of great importance for the island and for the church, since it was in them that the Manx clergy learned English and were trained for the ministry, given that hardly any of them went on to university before the nineteenth century.[16] Wilson realized that a complete overhaul of both church and state was needed on the island, and he was instrumental in sponsoring the reforms of 1704, which secured land tenure for the native farmers, increased the power of the house of keys to frame legislation in Tynwald, and defined the position of the church in relation to society as a whole.

In preparation for this, Wilson called a convocation for 3 February 1704, which became in effect a constituent assembly for the diocese.[17] It framed fourteen canons defining the responsibilities of the church, and these were duly ratified by Tynwald along with the civil reforms. Over the years, most of these regulations became outdated, but the fourteenth, which defines convocation, has remained in force to the present day. According to it, convocation must meet every year on the Thursday in Whitsun week at the bishop's chapel (at his residence of Bishopscourt) if the bishop is in the island. The date was probably chosen so that its proceedings could be reported to Tynwald at its annual meeting in the summer.

---

[16]On education in the Isle of Man, see F. H. Bird, *An island that led — the history of Manx education* (2 vols., Douglas, 1995).

[17]Manx sources often say 1703, but this is because they have neglected the fact that the old calendar, beginning on 25 March, was still in use at that time.

Wilson himself adhered fairly closely to the rules, but later on they were bent from time to time. Bishop Hildesley thought convocation was so important that he convened it either before or after the statutory date if he knew that he was going to be in England at Whitsun, and in later years there were occasional meetings of convocation at other times of the year. It was not infrequently the case that a convocation would be called a few weeks late, and meetings were sometimes held in places other than Bishopscourt, notably in St Peter's church, Peel and at Kirk Michael. Lack of evidence for much of the early nineteenth century makes it hard to say what happened during that period, but the tradition of holding an annual convocation has survived even the most negligent absentee bishops and it is now a regular event on the diocesan calendar. The sale of Bishopscourt in 1979 forced Tynwald (in 1986) to alter the statute, so that the bishop could hold the convocation anywhere in the island. It now meets at the cathedral in Peel, but apart from that, Bishop Wilson's directive remains in force to this day.[18]

Bishop Wilson's early convocations were somewhat lacklustre affairs, but his reorganization of the institution must be seen in its wider ecclesiastical context. The Canterbury convocation had recently sprung to life again, and Wilson naturally followed its progress with considerable interest. During Queen Anne's reign it seemed as if it might develop into a clerical version of parliament, and the prospect of this encouraged the Irish clergy to demand a revival of their convocation as well.[19] Constitutionally speaking, Wilson was in the vanguard of progress, and it mattered little if the actual business which convocation transacted at this time scarcely went beyond what one would expect from an ecclesiastical court. The effective silencing of the Canterbury convocation in 1717 left the Manx body as the only one to continue functioning normally, and its records preserve a vignette of eighteenth-century church life which is unique in the Church of England. Nowhere else did the parish clergy play such an important part in the government of a diocese, a circumstance which could still astonish observers as late as the 1840s.

Broadly speaking, the business handled by convocation can be divided into moral offences on the one hand, and revenue questions (tithes, rents, etc.), on the other. Of the former, by far the most important were clandestine marriages, drunkenness and swearing, all of them common complaints of the period. The first of these was not dealt with satisfactorily until the marriage act of 1757 (an imitation of the English act of 1753), whilst the latter two remain with us to this day, seemingly impervious to any kind of ecclesiastical censure.

Revenue matters were less clear cut, and they were to dog the Manx church for more than two centuries. The basic problem was that the ancient church lands had mostly been impropriated by the lord after the reformation, and had only been partially redeemed by the church in 1666. Never a wealthy diocese, Sodor and Man thus found itself in a precarious financial position and it was forced to do everything

---

[18]He must however be turning in his grave at the thought that the three-hundredth anniversary convocation, due to be held on 3 June 2004, was moved forward two days so as not to clash with the island's motorcycle races!

[19]It met again for the first time on 11 January 1704, only three weeks before the Manx convocation.

it could to extract whatever tithes and rents were due to it. Parishioners were not always disposed to pay up, and the result was a series of conflicts which could only be resolved by tiresome and expensive litigation, often before unsympathetic secular judges.

Convocation tried to rationalize the system by enforcing what it could and altering what seemed to need change. One murky area was that of corbs, a kind of death duty payable to the clergy, which was perceived as an injustice when it seriously diminished the estate of a dead man who might have several children liable to inherit his already meagre possessions. The convocation started by trying to enforce the ancient law, but later gave up and eventually accepted the abolition of a duty which could not be levied effectively. Rents due from glebe lands were pursued with greater vigour, not least because the redemption of the impropriations involved a payment of £130 every thirty years to the lord, in compensation for his surrender of the land. This agreement had been made in 1666, and so the first payment of £130 had fallen during the interregnum and had been raised only with great difficulty. The issue was a highly sensitive one, and it took some time for the bishop to organize the diocesan finances in such a way that the next payment could be made in 1726. After that, convocation agreed to adopt an annual budget which would ensure that there would be enough money available to pay in 1756, but long before then the whole agreement was called into question by the lord's officials, and the church was forced to spend the money it had saved on litigation in London.

Tithes were a more complex matter, particularly since new crops and trades had appeared in the island since the first determination of the tithe had taken place in the middle ages. The most important development was the widespread introduction of the potato[20] which was not subject to tithe. Bishop Wilson wanted to correct this oversight, especially as potatoes had become a staple crop displacing tithable ones, but the matter was extremely delicate, since they were the poor man's food and most Manxmen were desperately poor. A potato tithe was proposed and voted on, but it seems that it was never collected, and when an attempt was finally made to enforce it in the 1820s, it provoked such a crisis that the entire tithe regime was called into question. After a thorough inquiry, it was abolished in 1839, when the tithes formerly due to the clergy were commuted to an annual cash payment, which continued until it too was abolished in 1946.[21]

Convocation also undertook the management of the island's schools, as can be seen from the 1715 meeting, where the royal bounty was distributed to the parishes in question. By then political events in England were beginning to dictate a change in government policies towards the church, and before long the convocations in both England and Ireland were effectively suppressed.[22] Although this did not happen in the Isle of Man, where the king's writ did not run, it soon became

[20]Yet another of the many parallels with Ireland.
[21]The tithe act of 1946 provided for the final redemption of tithes to be completed by 30 September 1951. In fact, this date had to be extended by several months and a small amount of the tithe was found to be irrecoverable and thus was never redeemed. Tithes due to the crown because of impropriations still have a residual existence in the island.
[22]They continued to exist but were not allowed to transact business.

apparent that the anti-clerical sentiments of the Whig ascendancy were shared by the lords of Man and by the governors whom they appointed. Battles between the civil and ecclesiastical jurisdictions became common, and it was relatively easy for defendants to avoid punishment by appealing from one to the other. Matters reached a head in 1721 when Bishop Wilson suspended the archdeacon, Robert Horrobin, partly for preaching heresy and partly for refusing to discipline Mrs Jane Horne, the governor's wife, who had wrongly accused another woman of immoral conduct. The governor naturally took the archdeacon's side and tricked Tynwald into imposing a fine on the bishop and the vicars-general for their suspension of Mr Horrobin.

Bishop Wilson refused to pay as a matter of principle, and so both he and the vicars-general were imprisoned in Castle Rushen from 29 June to 31 August 1722. Wilson eventually won his case, but the price he paid for his victory was very high. His right hand was permanently damaged by rheumatism, incurred during his imprisonment (which was very strict), and he was forced to pay legal costs of about £1600 out of his own pocket, which virtually ruined him financially. On the other hand, the events of 1722 made the bishop a hero to the common people of the island, among whom Wilson's writ, and that of the ecclesiastical courts, ran unchecked until his death in 1755.

In 1721 what was to become another feature of Manx church life appears in the records – charitable donations. The poverty of Sodor and Man had become increasingly well known abroad, and influential people began to give money to help alleviate its distress. Prominent among them were the archbishop and dean of York, who seem to have felt a special responsibility towards the Cinderella diocese of their province, and the bishop of Cloyne in Ireland, who was himself a Manxman.[23] Another donor was the widow of Bishop Baptist Levinz, who was contributing to the diocese as late as 1731, nearly forty years after her husband's death.

Convocation's interest in education extended beyond the provision of schools to that of parochial libraries, which were established in the island largely through the work of Dr Thomas Bray and the Society for Promoting Christian Knowledge, which he founded in 1699. An inventory of the books given was made in 1725, and from it we can discern what the Manx clergy were reading for their spiritual sustenance. Most of the books were either aids to studying the Bible and the church catechism, or devotional works from the moderately high church school of men like Bishop John Pearson and Bishop Simon Patrick. Needless to say, the Manx clergy were also given copies of most of Dr Bray's works, as well as those of Bishop Wilson as they appeared.

Under Bishop Wilson, convocation also undertook to repair dilapidated clergy houses throughout the island, and to build ones in parishes where none had previously existed. This was the beginning of a much wider project designed to improve and secure the clergy's financial position, and it laid foundations for the future which continue to bear fruit today. Of particular importance was the clergy widows' fund, which was launched in 1731 and soon attracted significant donations from wealthy people in England. It was a cause particularly dear to the heart of the

---

[23]This was Charles Crow, who was bishop of Cloyne from 1702 to 1726. His widow continued to give to the Manx church long after her husband's death.

bishop's son, Dr Thomas Wilson, who was a student of Christ Church, Oxford, and later became rector of St Stephen's, Walbrook (London), and a canon of Westminster. Moving as he did in high financial circles, the younger Dr Wilson was able to secure the clergy widows' fund on the London market, and in 1740 he established it on a permanent, legal basis. Despite various difficulties arising from heavy commitments and the desire to extend the fund's remit to include clergy children who were left orphans, the clergy widows' fund managed to survive and it continues to exist to this day.[24]

In 1740 the convocation managed to raise money for the defence of the island against possible French attack, but that never materialized (thanks, it is said, to the French Cardinal Fleury's great respect for Bishop Wilson) and the money was eventually refunded. Considering that this occurred during the great struggle with the lord over the impropriations, it is a great testimony to the essential patriotism and spirit of self-sacrifice present among the Manx clergy at that time.

The demise of Stanley rule in 1736 and the appearance of the Atholls was a disaster for the church. The Atholls had none of the experience acquired over centuries by the Stanleys, and did not feel the same sense of obligation towards the island, which they wanted to milk for profit as much as they could. This was the problem which lay at the heart of the impropriations controversy, because the Atholls wanted to undo the settlement of 1666 and regain the revenue which the Stanleys had given up at that time. The ensuing controversy was to drag on for years, and although the church eventually won its case, the cost was so great that it kept the diocese in financial straits well into the nineteenth century. To make matters worse, the church could not rid itself of the Atholls, who continued to abuse their rights of patronage until they were bought out by the crown in 1825.

In 1744 a new note of spirituality appears in the convocation records, as the bishop enjoined frequent communion and the public reading of the psalms – in Manx. This led to greater attention being paid to confirmation, which was the necessary prerequisite for communion, and also to a serious interest in translating the Bible and the liturgy into Manx. Bishop Wilson's advancing age and declining health forced a postponement of the latter, but a start was made, and in 1748 the Gospel according to St Matthew was published in a Manx translation.

The last convocations of Bishop Wilson's time are taken up with such matters as provision for schoolmasters and the administration of the various charitable funds which had been established, and we can chart the bishop's declining powers as he progressively delegated responsibility for these things to various subordinates. The end, when it came, was peaceful, and Bishop Wilson had the satisfaction of knowing that he was handing on a relatively strong church, governed by an active convocation, to a successor who fortunately was able to appreciate his achievement and to build on it over the next eighteen years.

[24]The collection taken at the 2001 convocation was donated to it.

Bishop Hildesley (1755-73)

The arrival of a new bishop after more than half a century was bound to be a major event in the life of the Manx church, but Mark Hildesley (1755-73) turned out to be more of a successor to Bishop Wilson than might have been expected. Hildesley had a great respect for his predecessor's achievements and was determined to carry on along similar lines, particularly in the matters of education and charity. In his declining years, Bishop Wilson had been unable to pursue certain disciplinary matters as much as he would have liked, and so Hildesley had to take these in hand. The problem of clandestine marriages was finally solved, by adopting legislation in 1757 similar to that which had been enacted at Westminster in 1753. Hildesley also seems to have introduced the practice of clergy exhibiting their letters of orders and induction to a newly-appointed bishop, even though this had been a canonical requirement since 1604. At the same time, we come across the clerical postal system which was used to transmit the bishop's directives from one parish to another. Each incumbent was required to note the time of the directive's arrival and sign it when he was ready to send it on to the next man. These were perhaps small matters in themselves, but they demonstrate an increasingly professional attitude towards diocesan administration which was characteristic of Hildesley's episcopate.

On more purely spiritual matters, Hildesley continued Wilson's attempts to get the Manx laity more firmly anchored in the life of the church by insisting that those presenting themselves for matrimony, or intending to become godparents, should not only be baptized but confirmed as well, and that they should be known to be regular communicants. At a time when holy communion was celebrated at irregular intervals, this was not a particularly onerous burden, but it is revealing of the spiritual state of the laity, many of whom seem to have had little to do with the church's liturgical activities. Their relaxed attitude to worship scandalized Hildesley when he noticed that even the great fasts of Ash Wednesday and Good Friday went unobserved by most lay people, who went about their customary occupations apparently unconcerned. Hildesley's attempts to rectify this were largely unsuccessful, not least because the clergy were not persuaded of the legitimacy of his case. They pointed out that in Bishop Wilson's time even the vicars-general had ignored the major fasts, and that Manx people were accustomed to celebrate other holidays, like Lady Day, although (as Hildesley remarked) they were of far less theological significance. Here the bishop was up against longstanding local custom, which proved too strong even for his pious, reforming zeal.

He seems to have had more success in enforcing his rules for the wearing of clerical dress, but even that proved difficult in a small community where it was unnecessary most of the time. Disciplinary questions continued to occupy his tidy mind, and in 1761 he issued lengthy directions to churchwardens, instructing them as to when they should present people (including clergymen) for various infractions of church order. Schoolmasters and schoolmistresses also came under his watchful eye; they were to be licensed and supervised almost as much as the clergy themselves.

Another change which we notice in Hildesley's time is the sudden appearance of the royal family in the convocation records. Bishop Wilson had been ordained under James II, and in Ireland to boot. He had lived through the revolution of 1688-

9 and the subsequent uncertainties surrounding the succession. He was certainly no Jacobite, and his relations with George I were cordial, but he instinctively kept his distance from secular authority and was quite prepared to tackle it when he felt that the interests of the church were in danger. His relations with the successive lords of Man were initially good, but that changed when his own authority was challenged, and after 1714 he was engaged in semipermanent controversy with the secular government. Hildesley, by contrast, was a child of the Hanoverian age and shared in the general rise of popular support for the monarchy which followed the defeat of Bonnie Prince Charlie in 1745-6. He was also no doubt aware that the days of Manx 'independence' were numbered, and that sooner or later the crown would reclaim its ancient rights over the island.

In 1761 Hildesley called a special convocation of the clergy to present a loyal address to the new King George III, a practice which had become common in both Canterbury and Ireland after 1689 but which was hitherto unknown in Sodor and Man. The address was printed in the *London Gazette*, a copy of which was duly pasted into the convocation records! Later he had a similar address sent to the duke and duchess of Atholl when they succeeded to the lordship in 1764, an exercise in flattery which must have sent Bishop Wilson spinning in his grave. When the revestment came in 1765, Hildesley did nothing immediately, but when the governor came to open the first Tynwald of the new era in 1770, he was ready with yet another loyal address, which was also printed in the *London Gazette*.

The 1761 convocation also marks the beginning of what would be the chief project of Hildesley's episcopate – the translation of the Prayer Book and of the Bible into Manx. Though not a Manx speaker himself, Hildesley believed very strongly that it was necessary to preach and teach the Christian faith in the language of the people, and that many of the pastoral defects of the Manx church could be put down to their lack of understanding of spiritual matters which was available only through the medium of English. With his characteristic energy, he deputed his clergy to carry on the work of translation, and the convocation records tell us in considerable detail how this was actually carried out. Portions were assigned to individual clergy and then their work would be reviewed by a committee. When the latter preferred another reading, the original translator would be consulted and efforts would be made to come to a common mind.

Hildesley's persistence and his organizational genius were such that in only ten years a Manx Prayer Book and Bible of high literary quality were in existence. Printing the latter took some time and Hildesley did not live to see it completed, but there can be no doubt that this achievement was his, and his alone. It came too late to save Manx as a living language, and a century later these translations would no longer be required, but Hildesley could not have foreseen this, and without his efforts our knowledge of the Manx language would be considerably poorer than it is. As a further aid towards understanding the Christian faith, he also had *The Christian Monitor*, a devotional book written two generations before by an obscure person called John Rawlet, translated into Manx and published in a bilingual edition. It is illustrative of the way in which minds did not meet on this issue, that the printer put the English text first and appended the Manx to it, whereas Hildesley had wanted it the other way round. Nevertheless, distribution figures for this volume, which are preserved in the records, give us a good idea of how far the bishop's programme met the needs of the church at grass roots level, and it must be said that at the time, there was a considerable demand for further copies, something which was evidently not expected when they first went to print.

In other matters, Bishop Hildesley carried on the work of his predecessor, though as always, the hand of the efficient administrator can be detected at every turn. The parochial libraries were inventoried, the charitable funds were audited and potential donors were assiduously courted, with modest success. The clergy widows' fund got into difficulties because there were more widows than could be supported as the trustees of the fund had originally desired, but Hildesley did not hesitate to revise the terms of the grants made, so that each widow would receive a fair proportion of the (static) revenue until such time as the fund's capital could be increased (as it eventually was).

Things might have gone on like this indefinitely, but towards the end of Hildesley's episcopate there were two unforeseen developments which between them spelled the end of Man's model spiritual commonwealth. The first of these was a lawsuit over the fish tithe, which began almost immediately after the revestment and came to a head in 1767. The clergy had long been accustomed to receiving a portion of the herring catch every year, and their rights were explicitly recognized by Tynwald in 1577. But the fishermen of Kirk German decided, for reasons which are not stated, to withhold the annual tithe and attempted to challenge the clergy's rights in a lawsuit which eventually reached the highest courts of appeal in London. On paper, the clergy's rights were clear and the fishermen lost their case, a disaster which bankrupted them, but the church also lost. Collecting the fish tithe was not worth the animosity which was being created by the protracted lawsuit, and when it was all over, the fish tithe had to be abolished for peace to be restored to the island.

What was it that caused the fisherman to revolt? Many factors were undoubtedly involved in this. The 1760s were a hard time economically, and there was growing unrest among labourers in England during these years. Man was remote but not unaffected, and it is possible that the fishermen knew of successful attempts made elsewhere to deny traditional authority. Then too, the clergy had come to rely increasingly on proctors to collect the tithe for them, so that the personal bonds which had previously led the fisherman to pay their minister no longer functioned to the same extent. But probably the greatest single factor was the effect of the revestment in 1765. This had occurred mainly because the island had become a haven for smuggling, and the authorities in London felt that they had to stamp this out. This was an economic disaster for the island, of course, and the fishermen, who had done most of the smuggling, felt the blow most of all. There had been no problem about parting with herring when their income was hugely supplemented from elsewhere, but their sudden poverty made them more possessive of what they had left, and so they resisted the payment of tithe. The interesting thing about the case is that both sides in the dispute must have understood this perfectly, and yet there is not a word about it anywhere in the surviving documentation. One is left with the impression that Bishop Hildesley turned a blind eye to smuggling, as long as it did not occur on Ash Wednesday or Good Friday!

The second development is not mentioned in the convocation records until after Hildesley's death, but it was already in evidence before that. This was the appearance in the island of sectarian preachers, who offered the people a new kind of religious experience and posed a challenge to the clergy far greater than anything a few fishermen could achieve. In this respect, Hildesley died just in time. Had he lived even two or three years more, he would have been embroiled in a controversy which would ultimately destroy everything which he and his predecessor had striven so hard to build.

The convocation from 1773 to 1836

Hildesley was succeeded by Richard Richmond (1773-80), who to all intents and purposes intended to carry on his predecessor's work. He was assisted in this by the duke and duchess of Atholl, who agreed to sell their rights to the impropriated tithes at a reduced rate. The Atholls had retained their ecclesiastical patronage at the time of the revestment, and as long as the duke of Atholl lived (he died in 1774) it seems that things went reasonably well for the church. After the expenses of the fish tithe dispute, the financial relief was very welcome, as were the fresh donations which appeared for the charities in the bishop's control. Bishop Richmond repeated the exercise of having the clergy exhibit their letters of orders and institution, and he was equally flattering to the authorities. On 23 October 1775 he and the clergy sent an address to George III supporting him against the rebellious Americans, although (as they pointed out) they were unable to offer him any material assistance. But of more immediate importance to Richmond was rebellion closer to home, this time in the form of unauthorized preaching and teaching in his diocese.

The appearance in the island of the evangelical revival, against which Richmond set his face, could not have come entirely as a surprise to him. John Wesley (1703-91), whose own spiritual background and education was very similar to that of Bishop Wilson and his son, who was Wesley's exact contemporary, dated his conversion to 24 May 1738, and within a few years he and several others who had been similarly moved were preaching all over England. They were not anti-establishment in principle, but the church authorities generally regarded them as a threat and treated them accordingly. Wesley and his fellow revivalists had no choice but to organize a pastoral network of their own, and the people who identified themselves with them came to be called 'methodists', because of the methodical and serious way in which they practised their faith.

Why did methodism pose such a threat to the established order when its leaders had no desire to do that? Curiously enough, the convocation records of Sodor and Man give us a very clear answer to this question, even though it has to be sought indirectly. If we look at the activities of Bishops Wilson and Hildesley, it becomes clear that they regarded the church as if it were a school. The bishop was the headmaster, his clergy were the teaching staff and the laity were the pupils. The staff were entrusted with the pupils' education, which would fit them for life both in this world and in the next. As in any school, the pupils showed a wide range of ability, but there could be no question of neglecting the weak or the recalcitrant. On the contrary, Christian love demanded that special attention should be given to them, and so remedial learning (otherwise known as church discipline) became a major part of the curriculum. A certain amount of indiscipline was only to be expected of course, and a good schoolmaster (which Bishop Wilson undoubtedly was) showed no partiality in dealing with it. If the governor's wife was delinquent (as Mrs Horne was) she had to be dealt with on the same basis as anyone else. Similarly, if his staff refused to obey orders, they too would be disciplined. Wilson got into trouble for this, but it is indicative of what was expected of him that this only served to increase his popularity with the masses, who praised him for his impartiality and regarded him as the very model of an apostolic bishop.

The evangelical revival challenged all this at the root — by effectively redefining what the church should be doing to achieve its aims. The evangelicals did not dispute the church's educational programme and they were generally in full agreement with the educational aims of the school-church. Where they disagreed with it was in their belief that the only way the pupils would ever really learn their subject was by an internal change of heart and mind. Attempts to abolish drunkenness by legislation were as foolish as they were unproductive, because they did not get to grips with the root cause of the problem — human sinfulness. This could not be legislated out of existence, nor could it be successfully controlled by the church authorities, however well-intentioned they might be. Only the Holy Spirit could do this by a process of spiritual death and rebirth which was illustrated in baptism and taught in the Gospels, but which could only be experienced by a personal conversion, something which could not be engineered by sacramental or other external means. Furthermore, the sovereignty of God in the process of conversion meant that it could happen to anyone anywhere at any time. Where Bishop Hildesley quite seriously believed that regular communion and observance of days like Good Friday would bring people closer to God, evangelicals rejected all this as legalism. Furthermore, even when we make allowances for exaggeration, hypocrisy and backsliding, there is no doubt that the evangelical message worked — hundreds of lives were dramatically changed for the better, and in a generation the whole moral climate of Manx society had been renewed. The church courts could never have achieved as much, but it took time before that fact was generally accepted. The two ways of thinking were diametrically opposed, so that when evangelical preaching appeared in the Isle of Man it was inevitable that those who believed in the school-church system would feel bound to oppose it.

Fortunately for the church, there were those in its service who understood that evangelicalism was nothing other than true, primitive Christianity. When John Wesley visited the island in 1777 there were some clergy who befriended him and accepted his message, in spite of the bishop's opposition. It took a generation for this to have much impact, but by the middle years of the nineteenth century, the majority of Manx clergy were evangelicals, a circumstance which not only helped to stem the drift into nonconformity (though it came too late to stop it entirely) but which gave the church a new self-understanding at the very moment when the laws and structures which had made the old school-church possible were being abolished. Bishop Wilson, for all his virtues, could not have functioned in the late nineteenth-century church, but the evangelical clergy of that time not only could but did — with considerable success. What had appeared to be a terrible threat in 1776 had taken over the church a century later, and transformed it in a way which made it possible for it to continue and expand its mission in a changing society.

After Bishop Richmond's death the Manx church went through a dark period. His successor, George Mason (1780-4), revamped the church's administration in the hope of reinvigorating its disciplinary structures, but he died after only three years and his project collapsed. The next bishop, Claudius Crigan (1784-1813), was appointed by the dowager duchess of Atholl as a stopgap until her own son could succeed to the bishopric, but Crigan surprised everyone by outliving them both. It was during this time however, that the negative consequences of leaving ecclesiastical patronage in the hands of the Atholls became increasingly apparent. No longer responsible for the island's government, the Atholls could afford to be irresponsible in their church appointments, and their lesser family members began to make an appearance as archdeacons. Naturally, the Murrays[25] were disinclined to live on the island any more than they had to, and church life suffered as a result. Convocation continued its traditional functions, but the minutes start to tail off and it is clear that less and less attention was paid to it. The last record of any serious activity dates from 1796, and after 1798 there is silence, broken only by two lists of clergy whose attendance was registered in 1822 and 1834, though in both cases it was at a convocation which met on a day other than the officially appointed one (which may be the reason why the lists have survived), and by some isolated material from 1829. What the clergy did when they met is completely unknown, and it is not even certain that the convocations took place at all for many years, even though they were required to do so by statute. After nearly a century of vibrant activity, it seemed as if the Manx convocation had finally slipped into the torpor which characterized the convocations of Canterbury and (especially) York, with no future before it other than eventual and long-overdue abolition.

The convocation from 1836 to 1877

That this did not happen is probably due to a quite unforseen circumstance. The reforms of 1828-32 in England brought a new spirit into church affairs. Things which had lain untouched for centuries suddenly became objects of inquiry, with a view to modernizing what had in many respects become a creaky and outdated system. At the diocesan level, it was becoming clear that the pattern established by Henry VIII in 1540-2 could no longer continue as it was. Some dioceses were much too large, others were misshapen, and a few were too small. Needless to say, Sodor and Man, always the smallest diocese in the Church of England, was too small — much too small. The remedy for this anomaly, so it was thought, was to tie it up with another small diocese (Carlisle), and thereby create, on paper at least, a functionally viable unit. It must have sounded like an ideal solution to the ecclesiastical commissioners whose responsibility it was to draft the proposal, but it ignored several important facts. First of all, Carlisle had no connection with the Isle of Man, and a bishop based there would find it highly inconvenient to visit such a remote part of his diocese. Secondly, Carlisle was a parvenu diocese in English terms. It may have been founded in 1133, almost exactly at the same time as Sodor and Man came into being, but the Manx did not see it that way. As far as they were concerned, their diocese was much older, going back to the Irish mission of St Patrick in the mid-fifth century. The historical basis for such a claim was weak, but

[25]The family name of the Atholls.

the Manx were on much stronger ground when they insisted that Man was not, and never had been, a normal part of the Church of England. Small it might be, but it was still another country, with its own laws, its own language and its own governmental traditions which were quite different from those of any English diocese.

The Manx convocation was one of these distinctive features, and it was this apparently moribund body which quickly sprang to life as the great defender of the Manx church. When the proposal to unite the diocese with Carlisle became known, the bishop wrote a long letter opposing the move, and the clergy quickly followed suit. Fortunately, the Atholls had sold their remaining rights of patronage to the crown in 1825, and there had been time to install a more committed church leadership. Long used to acting in concert, the Manx clergy knew how to organize their opposition, and their close links with the islanders ensured that a wide body of public opinion would rally to their support. For once, parliament listened, and in January 1838 it voted to exclude Sodor and Man from the provisions of the established church act of 1836, which had decreed the union of the diocese with Carlisle on the demise of the incumbent bishop.[26]

Suddenly it began to seem as if convocation might have a place in the new order of things after all. In England, agitation to revive the convocations of Canterbury and York was about to begin, and the notion that the church should be free to govern itself was gathering support in many quarters. Sodor and Man was unique in that it already had a convocation in place, which could serve as a model for others as they sought ways and means of restoring a semi-defunct institution. The man who saw the potential for this was Bishop Thomas Vowler Short (1841-6). Almost singlehandedly, he revived the convocation, not as a court of judgment but as a platform for diocesan policy. He was helped in this by the provisions of the tithe commutation act of 1839, which had made convocation the forum in which the annual payments, due under that act from 1842 onwards, were made and ratified. That gave the annual meetings a purpose which they had not previously had, and ensured that they would be held with greater regularity than had sometimes been the case in the past. We also possess something else – the bishop's charge, which Short had printed, so that it could be widely distributed. There is no record of any bishop having delivered a charge before 1842, and it seems to have been an unknown practice in Hildesley's day. Short may well have invented it, but if he did not, he certainly put it on the diocesan map for the first time, and used it as a vehicle for promoting his own vision of what the church should be. This was not always a happy exercise – he took the opportunity to criticize the Methodists for sheep-stealing, for example – but there is no doubt that on matters like church planting, preparation for confirmation, and so on, he was determined to stir up his clergy to achieve the transformation which evolving island society demanded.

Short's immediate successors do not seem to have shared his vision for the convocation, which appears to have slipped back into something like its earlier torpor, but the advent of Bishop Horatio Powys (1854-77) restored his fading vision, at least to some degree. From 1855 episcopal charges became an annual

---

[26]Bishop William Ward died on 26 January 1838, so the relief came just in the nick of time.

event at convocation, and through them it is possible to follow the ups and downs of diocesan politics during this period. Unfortunately, Powys was a legalistically-minded high churchman, quite unsuited to be a diocesan bishop, particularly in Sodor and Man, which by this time was largely evangelical, and he provoked controversies with his clergy and with prominent local laymen which could and probably should have been avoided.[27] Convocation was often the bishop's chosen platform for his attacks, and for the first time in its history it became a regular theatre of combat between opposing forces *inside* the church. Such a situation could not long continue in a very small diocese, where co-operation and mutual respect had always been taken for granted, and the appearance of internal conflict posed a greater threat to convocation than any which it had thitherto experienced.

Powys also had the misfortune to be bishop for along period at a time of rapid and unprecedented change, both on the island and in the Church of England at large. It was during his episcopate that the number of chaplaincies on the island came to exceed the number of the ancient parishes, a development which quickly created tension between the old and the new style of worship centre. The chaplaincies were generally more susceptible to extremes of churchmanship and tended to be staffed by men from off the island, giving the Manx church more of an English flavour than it had previously had. This was not popular with the native Manx clergy, many of whom felt that such an influx was bound to dilute the church's special character. The real struggles over this lay in the future, but Powys' time saw the seeds of that conflict being sown. On the mainland, the York convocation, to which Sodor and Man officially belonged, was revived in 1861, and before long the diocese was sending representatives to it. Meetings of the Manx convocation now became, at least in part, a forum for the local discussion of wider church business, and this in turn exposed the Manx church to both problems and opportunities, from which it had previously been sheltered by its isolated position. Sodor and Man would have to come to terms with the Church of England in more than a purely formal way, though it was to take some decades before the full impact of the revival of the York convocation made itself felt in the diocese. It was also clear that the ancient ecclesiastical jurisdiction over matrimony and probate, which had been ended in England in 1858, could not long continue in the Isle of Man, and that its demise would greatly reduce the activities of the vicar-general and the episcopal registrar, if not end them altogether.

That change was in fact delayed until 1884, but everyone could see that a new type of church was emerging, and that Bishop Powys was unlikely to be able to lead it successfully. In the event, he fell seriously ill in 1874 and left the island to seek a cure. He never returned, dying in England — but still in office — in 1877. During those years, the Manx convocation did not meet, and church business ground to a halt. The tithe agent and the vicar-general carried on as usual, of course, but they were unable to link up with the clergy in the accustomed way and many things were allowed to go by default. It was a hiatus which the church could ill afford, particularly as its administrative needs were increasing every year. To make matters even worse, the very existence of the diocese came under threat a second time, as

[27]On Powys, see Gelling, *Manx church*, pp. 104-55.

it was proposed to extend it to include the area around Liverpool, giving the great port city a diocese of its own. As things turned out, a new diocese of Liverpool was created in 1880, sparing Sodor and Man once more, but in the process underlining the diocese's urgent need to change in the face of new challenges. For this to happen, the Manx convocation needed an inner reform, which would make it a more stable administrative body. That reform was to come in the years after 1878, under the energetic leadership of Bishop Rowley Hill (1877-87), who in some senses can claim to have been convocation's second founder, as he stepped into the role so famously carved out by Bishop Wilson. How that was achieved forms the theme of the second volume, which takes the story of the Manx convocation down to the present day.

The sources and this edition

Most of the Manx convocation material is available, one way or another, in the Manx National Heritage Library, which is an extension of the Manx Museum in Douglas, and the precise source of each document is given in the main body of the edition. The pre-reformation texts are in a single manuscript, which dates from about 1505, but it appears that most of the material from 1577 to 1660 survives today only in printed form. From 1660 to 1704 the material is in the *Libri causarum* and it is only after that that convocation records in the strict sense of the term can be said to begin. Even then, the material for the period from 1704 to 1773 has been put together, not always very well, from loose papers of the period, and the content is not always strictly relevant to convocation.

From 1773 there is a convocation book which was intentionally kept as a record, but it peters out in 1798, and apart from a few loose papers, there is nothing substantial until the convocation charges begin to appear in 1842. From then until 1877 there is some primary material in the archives, and contemporary newspaper reports enable us to fill in the rest of the story. News of the convocation was usually printed in the weekly *Manx Sun*, which appeared on the Saturday immediately following the meeting. For this edition, these newspaper reports have been condensed and printed in italics.

This volume reproduces all the manuscript material available up to 1877, and such printed material as is required to supplement it, though not the convocation charges of 1842-74. The manuscript texts have generally been reproduced as they stand, with only minor editorial revisions. Most of the loose papers carry a superscription giving the date and place where they were composed, but these have usually been omitted, unless they are in some way exceptional. Similarly, the clergy lists all state the parishes or charges where the clergymen were serving at the time and these too have been omitted, except in unusual cases. Further information about them will be found in the clergy index at the end of this volume.

The presentation of accounts has been slightly altered to make them more readable today; in particular, sums of money, when they occur in tables, are given as pounds/shillings/pence (0/0/0) and not as the more cumbersome £0 0s. 0d., or the (even worse) £00 00s. 00d., a form which is not infrequently found in the sources. In addition, the format has been standardized, so that the information can be read as a table without undue inconvenience or confusion. A few spellings have been quietly modernized (e.g. 'Manx', not 'Manks'), and the word 'register' has been replaced, wherever appropriate, by 'registrar', which is more faithful to the underlying Latin and avoids unnecessary confusion between the person and the thing.

PRE-REFORMATION STATUTES

These are all to be found in a single manuscript in the Manx National Heritage Library, M 2042A, fos. 1r-14r. This MS formerly belonged to John Selden, and is almost certainly the text used by Sir William Dugdale in his *Monasticon Anglicanum* (6 vols., London 1665), I, 711-17; 2nd edn. (8 vols., London, 1817-30), V, 253-6. The texts are also found in Bodleian Library, Oxford, MS Add. C 64, fos. 55r-57r, 58r-66v, 113r-116r, which seems to have been the basis for David Wilkins' edition in the *Concilia Magnae Britanniae et Hiberniae* (4 vols., London, 1737). A third MS containing them is in Gonville and Caius College, Cambridge, MS 793 (P 28), pp. 53-79. However, it appears that both the Oxford and the Cambridge manuscripts depend (independently of each other) on the first, and are therefore valuable mainly for occasional conjectural emendations. On the history of the canons, see C. R. Cheney, 'Manx synodical statutes, A. D. 1230(?)-1351. Part I: Introduction and Latin texts', *Cambridge Medieval Celtic Studies*, VII (Summer 1984), pp. 63-89 and 'Part II: Translation of Latin texts', *ibid.*, VIII (Winter 1984), pp. 51-63.

The statutes of Bishop Simon, 1229[28]

[1r] Haec sunt statuta synodalia et constitutiones dioecesis in insula de Mann, per reverendum patrem Simonem Sodorensem episcopum ibidem[29] confecta et constituta anno Domini millesimo ducentesimo vigesimo nono.

1. *De probationibus testamentorum*

Pro probationibus testamentorum ultra summam triginta duorum denariorum nihil penitus exigatur, sed de eadem summa secundum bonorum quantitatem aliquid pauperibus subtrahatur.

2. *De bonis intestatorum discedentium*[30]

Bona intestatorum ad arbitrium episcopi dioecesani vel, eius in absentia, sui generalis vicarii ministrentur.

3. *De mortuariis*

In mortuariis principale animal ecclesiae persolvatur, vacca vel bos vel equus si fuerit ad valorem sex solidorum aut minus. Et quantum ad vestes, si homo mortuarium persolverit, ad arbitrium ecclesiae stabit an vestes aut tres solidos et sex denarios habere maluerit. Et si pauper fuerit, et nullum mortuarium persolverit, accipiantur vestes sicuti sunt, et quintus quique denarius ex liberis [bonis]. Et de *gilbogo*[31] in bonis possesso ad mortuarii valorem [1v] se extendentibus mortuarium ecclesiae persolvatur. Quod si bona sua ad hoc minime se extendant, tunc quintus quisque denarius de liberis bonis ecclesiae persolvantur.

Et si quaeratur, quid est *gilbogus*, dicendum est quod *gilbogus* est quis, si unius tantum noctis aetatis extiterit, et ad habendum bona ordinatus, aut in bonis possessus existat. Si ut dictum est obierit, ecclesia tamen suum debitum obtinebit. Item praefatus *gilbogus*, licet mortuarium persolverit, ultra hoc tamen, tam presbytero et clerico, quam etiam ecclesiae sua debita contenentur. Et si nullum mortuarium persolverit, nihilominus cum eis concordet.

---

[28]*I.e.*, sometime between 25 March 1229 and 24 March 1230. Most of the statutes recorded here, and especially those dealing with the probate of wills, mortuaries, etc., appear to be far too detailed in their content to date from as early as 1229-30, and would fit much better about a century or so later.

[29]Simon was bishop of Sodor and Man from 1226 to 1248.

[30]A similar provision is found in the statutes of Worcester II, 1229, c. 66 (PC, 181).

[31]Most likely a compound of *gilla* ('boy') and *boc* ('young', 'tender'). See Cheney, 'Manx synodal statutes', I, p. 70 for a discussion of this term, which seems to mean a 'minor'.

The statutes of Bishop Simon, 1229

These are the synodal statutes and constitutions of the diocese of Sodor in the Isle of Man, made and ordained there by the reverend father Simon, bishop of Sodor, in the year of our Lord 1229.

1. *On the probate of testaments*

For the probate of testaments no more than thirty-two pence may be charged, but the amount shall be reduced for poor people, according to their means.

2. *Of the goods of those who die intestate*

The goods of those who die intestate shall be administered at the discretion of the bishop, or in his absence, at that of the vicar-general.

3. *Of mortuaries*

With regard to mortuaries, the best animal shall be paid to the church if there is a cow, ox or horse worth six shillings or less. As for clothes, if a man pays a mortuary, the church shall decide whether it prefers to have clothes or three shillings and sixpence. And if the man is poor and pays no mortuary, the clothes shall be taken as they are, as well as every fifth penny from his free goods. And a mortuary shall be paid to the church for a *gilbogus* who possessed goods to the value of a mortuary. But if his goods are less than that amount, every fifth penny shall be paid to the church out of his free goods.

And if it is asked what a *gilbogus* is, it shall be said that a *gilbogus* is anyone who, even if he lives only one night, is entitled to have goods, or is seised of goods. If someone like that dies, the church will take its due. Also, if the aforesaid *gilbogus* has paid a mortuary, his dues to the priest and to the clerk, as well as those to the church, shall be paid. Even if he pays no mortuary, he must still settle with them.

4. *De debitis clerico persolvendis*

Debita clerico persolvenda sunt haec. Si homo mortuarium persolvat, clericus habeat ipsius hominis caligas, calceamenta ad pretium sex denariorum, et capitum pileum, aut capellum pretii maioris vel minoris, sicut ipse homo in die Natalis Domini ambulaverit; item camisiam, zonam ad unius denarii valorem; bursam ad unius denarii valorem. Et cultellum ad unius denarii valorem.

5. *De aucis, porcis, buculis, vitulis et pullis*

Aucae apud festum Sancti Michaelis aut post capiantur. Et porci, buculi, vituli et pulli apud festum Sancti Martini in liberos recipiantur, et apud Pascha exigantur,[32] rectore ecclesiae de [2r] praedictis porcis, pullis ac buculis in periculo persistente. Excepto quod si oeconomi[33] buculos desideraverint habere ad suas efficiendas vaccas lac praebere, ipso rectore oeconomum causante ad custodiendum illos ac si proprios.

6. *De defunctis nulla bona habentibus*

Si vir aut mulier obierit, et nulla bona ad contentandam ecclesiam pro sua sepultura habuerit, tunc ei qui eorum bona habere voluissent, si divites existissent, videlicet de eorum sanguine propinquiores, ecclesiae presbytero et clerico, ad illorum humationem contentabunt.

7. *De lacticiniis*

Si lacticinia in ecclesiam conformiter iuxta consuetudinem non portentur, de una vacca duo denarii, de quatuor capris duo denarii, et de octo ovibus octo denarii persolvantur.

8. *De electione et collectione agnorum decimalium, buculorum, porcorum et pullorum*

Cum ad congregandos agnos decimales, buculos, porcos vel pullos procuratores pervenerint, oeconomus duos et procuratores tertium eligant.

9. *De removentibus domicilia ac bona sua ab una parochia in alteram*

Si vir vel mulier forte ab una parochia in aliam [2v] domicilium suum permutaverit, et bona sua secum abduxerit, si vir nil[34] praeter uxorem suam,

---

[32]MSS: 'erigantur'.
[33]In England this word meant 'churchwarden' but in the Isle of Man it seems to have referred to a householder or tithe-payer.
[34]MS: 'vel', corrected by the derivative MSS to 'nihil'.

4. *Of dues to be paid to the church*

Dues to be paid to the church are these. If a man pays a mortuary, let the clerk have his stockings and shoes to the value of sixpence, and a hood or cap or hat of greater or lesser value, such as the man would wear on Christmas Day; also a shirt, a belt worth a penny, a purse worth a penny, and a knife worth a penny.

5. *Of geese, swine, bullocks, calves and colts*

Geese shall be taken at Michaelmas or later, and pigs, bullocks, calves and colts shall be registered at Martinmas and taken at Easter. The rector of the church shall be answerable for the aforesaid pigs, colts and bullocks, except that if householders want to keep the bullocks in order to make their cows give milk, the rector shall oblige [each] householder to keep them as his own.

6. *Of those who die without possessions*

If a man or woman dies leaving no goods to pay the church for their burial, then those who would have claimed their goods had they been well off – that is, their nearest blood relations – shall pay the church, the priest and the clerk for their burial.

7. *Of dairy produce*

If dairy produce is not brought to church according to the custom, two pence shall be paid for a cow, two pence for four goats, and eight pence for eight sheep.

8. *Of the choice and collection of tithe lambs, bullocks, pigs and colts*

When the [rector's] agents come to collect the tithe lambs, bullocks, pigs or colts, the householder shall choose two and the agent the third.

9. *Of those who transfer their residence and property from one parish to another*

If a man or woman happens to have transferred his residence and moved his property – if a man has taken nothing with him except his wife and children,

pueros, lectum, gallum, gallinam, craticulam, et mensulam pistoralem secum asportaverit, et ibidem nisi per tres noctes perseveraverit antequam ab hac luce decesserit, in illa parochia in quam nuper accessit, debita ecclesiastica persolvantur, quamvis bonorum suorum maior portio in altera parochia relinquatur.

10. *De granis decimalibus*[35]

In antiquo statuto oeconomi grana decimalia, ac si propria arconizabant, et ad sua foenilia ducebant ac custodiebant, quousque rector, vel eius procurator ob ea commodius venire posset, forte usque festum Omnium Sanctorum; modernis vero diebus rectores grana decimalia in arconiolis[36] accipiunt ob maiorem oeconomorum commoditatem.

11. *De cervisiae vendentibus*[37]

Si vir vel mulier cervisiam vendendam pandoxaverit, sive communis pandoxator vel pandoxatrix fuerit, sive non, si duos denarios et obolum de unaquaque pandoxatione accipiat, lagunculam decimalem ecclesiae persolvat.

12. *De textoribus sive textricibus*[38]

Si textor vel textrix tres telas a suis telariis descindat vel decidat, et pro earundem textura solutionem recipiat, duos denarios ecclesiae annuatim inde persolvat, et si centum descindat vel decidat, amplius non persolvat.

13. [3r] *De sumptori debitis*

Sumptor de iure antiquo et statutis veteribus, ab omnibus oeconomis garbam de trium ligarum longitudine scilicet frumenti, ordii et avenae annuatim recipere debet, et ad omnem caseorum decimationem et collectionem, unum agnum electum habere debet, et ad lanae decimationem unum vellus electum debet obtinere.

---

[35]This appears to be a much later gloss inserted here, quite out of place. The old statute referred to may be 1292/15 below.
[36]MSS: 'arconomolis'.
[37]This and the following canon appear to be an elaboration of c. 6 of the statute of Archbishop Boniface of Canterbury on tithe, which he published sometime between 1249 and 1269 (PC, 796).
[38]Cf. 1292/19 below, which appears to be less precise than this.

a bed, a cock and a hen, a gridiron and a kneading board – and if he dwells there only three nights before he dies, then the church dues shall be paid in the parish in which he has just arrived, even if the greater part of his possessions remains in the other parish.

10. *Of the corn tithe*

According to an old statute, householders treated tithe sheaves as if they were their own, and took them to their barns and stored them until it was convenient for the rector or his agent to come for them, perhaps not before All Saints' Day. But in more recent times, rectors receive their tithe grain in the shocks, for the convenience of the householders.

11. *Of beer-sellers*

If a man or woman brews beer for sale and gets twopence halfpenny from each brewing, they shall pay the church every tenth bottle, whether they are brewers by trade or not.

12. *Of weavers and websters*[39]

If a weaver or webster cuts off or detaches three lengths of cloth from their loom and receives payment for weaving them, they shall pay the church two pence a year for this. Even if they cut off or detach a hundred lengths, they shall pay no more.

13. *Of the sumner's dues*

According to the old law and statutes, the sumner should receive a sheaf of three straws' length, that is of wheat, barley and oats, from every householder; and at the tithing and collection of cheese, he should get one lamb of his choice, and at the tithing of wool, one fleece of his choice.

[39] A 'webster' is a female weaver; cf. 'spinster' as a female spinner.

The constitutions of Bishop Mark, 10 March 1292

Incipiunt constitutiones synodales Sodorensis ecclesiae, in synodo ordinatae, celebratae et statutae in ecclesia Sancti Bradani in Mannia, sexto Idus Martii anno Domini millesimo ducentesimo nonagesimo primo, cui praefuit venerabilis pater Dominus Marcus Sodorensis episcopus.[40]

1. De infirmis visitandis[41]

Statuimus ut singuli capellani prompti sint ad infirmos visitandos cum vocati fuerint, ne per eorum negligentiam, aliquos contigerit sine sacramentis ecclesiasticis mori.[42] Et cum ad eos accesserint induti superpelliciis, reverenter corpus Dominicum deferant, in pixide ad hoc deputata, lintheo albo vel serico cooperto, et tintinnabulo praecedenti in villam ecclesiae, vel in locos prope ecclesiam constitutis. Ad loca vero remota corpus Dominicum non deferatur nisi per capellanum ecclesiae, capa clausa indutum. Et cum adeo infirmos [3v] accesserint, moneant eos salubriter, et inducant ad veram confessionem et paenitentiam, et testamentum rite faciendum, nec aliquos sine candela accensa de cera communice[n]t. Et ipsos ad fabricam parochialis ecclesiae iuxta facultates suas, ut aliquid relinquant, diligenter moneant, ad quae colligenda et reservanda duo fideles parochiae iuxta providentiam rectorum ecclesiarum deputentur.

2. De indumentis capellanorum[43]

Statuimus ut singuli capellani capis clausis utantur, et aliis indumentis suis ordinibus convenientibus; sed mantellam capellanis omnino interdicimus. Et praecipimus quod capellani omnes, diebus festivis et solemnibus, maxime capis clausis utantur, et etiam cum ad capitula, vel ad synodum accesserint. Quod si secus fecerint, illud aliud indumentum inhibitum quod portaverint, fabricae ecclesiae Sancti Germani sine aliqua redemptione applicetur.

3. De honestate sacerdotum

Praecipimus quod omnes capellani caveant ne aliquo modo ad tabernas accedant, vel in suis domibus tabernas teneant, quo[d] non sint ebriosi, luxuriosi, litigiosi, sed parati verbo et opere exempla bonae vitae, et laudabilis conversationis

---

[40]Mark was bishop of Sodor and Man from about 1276 until 1303.
[41]Cf. Robert Grosseteste's statutes for Lincoln, c. 1239, cc. 2-3 (PC, 268) and with Scottish statutes, c. 1242-9, cc. 61-2 and 72. See *Concilia Scotiae*, ed. J. Robertson (2 vols., Edinburgh, 1866), II, 34-5, 39; trans. *Statutes of the Scottish Church*, ed. D. Patrick (Edinburgh, 1907), pp. 35-6, 41.
[42]MS: 'mors'. The other MSS have emended this to 'mori'.
[43]Cf. Carlisle diocesan statutes, c. 1258-9 (PC, 630).

The constitutions of Bishop Mark, 10 March 1292

The synodal constitutions of the church of Sodor ordained, celebrated and proclaimed in the synod [held] in the church of St Brendan in Man on the sixth of the ides of March 1291, at which the venerable father Lord Mark, bishop of Sodor, presided.

1. *Of visiting the sick*

We ordain that every chaplain [*i.e.* resident priest] shall be prepared to visit the sick when summoned, lest by their negligence some should happen to die without the sacraments of the church. And when they go to them, wearing surplices, they shall carry the body of Christ reverently in a pyx set aside for that purpose, covered with a white linen or silk cloth, preceded by a bell, within the village or in nearby places. The body of Christ shall be carried to distant places only by the chaplain, wearing a closed cloak. And when priests visit the sick, they shall earnestly admonish and persuade them to make true confession and penance, and to make their wills properly, and they shall not give them communion without lighting a wax candle. They shall also make sure that they admonish them to leave something for the fabric of the parish church, according to their means, and two trustworthy parishioners shall be appointed, at the rectors' discretion, to collect and store this.

2. *Of priests' clothing*

We ordain that all priests shall use closed cloaks and other attire suitable to their order, and absolutely forbid them to use mantles. And we order that all priests shall use closed cloaks on feast days and solemn days, and also when they attend chapters or synod. If they transgress, the forbidden garment which they wore shall be applied to the fabric of St German's church, with no hope of recovering it.

3. *Of priest's good behaviour*

We order all priests to take care not to enter taverns or to have taverns in their homes, and that they shall not be drunk, loose-living, or litigious, but be ready to set an example of good life and praiseworthy behaviour, both in word and

transmittant in subditos suos.[44] Et quod unusquisque secundum quod sapit, de Evangelio et Sacra Scriptura, articulos quoque fidei plebi suae exponat; necnon diligenter moneant parochianos suos, ut pueros suos instruant symbolum apostolorum et [4r] orationem Dominicam, cum salutatione Beatae Mariae Virginis.[45]

4. De baptismo[46]

Capellani caveant ne per negligentiam aliquis infans sine baptismo, quod absit, moriatur, et etiam sub poena excommunicationis inhibemus, ne aliquis capellanus pro baptizandis infantibus vel infirmis[47] visitandis aut mortuis sepeliendis praemium aut munus exigat aut recipiat nisi quantum de iure exigendum, et quod nullus capellanus tunicas seu chrismalia baptizatorum in alios usus convertat [quam] in usus ecclesiae, nec mutando tunicam seu chrismale unius pueri nec alterius pueri, denuo recipiat sub poena excommunicationis.

5. De castitate sacerdotum[48]

Statuimus quod nullus capellanus focariam et concubinariam alterius capellani vel cuiuscunque adulteram in parochia sua permittat, nisi tribus monitionibus praemissis parochiam suam deserat, aut nominatim excommunicet. Quod si non fecerit, sciat se poenae excommunicationis subiacere.

6. De poena transgressorum[49]

Districtius inhibemus ne ecclesiarum rectores, vicarii, sacerdotes, vel clerici in sacris ordinibus constituti, publice vel privatim habeant focarias, unde sinistra poterit oriri suspicio;[50] quod si facere praesumpserint beneficia clericorum taliter vivientium in nostra manu capiantur, eisque interdicantur ingressus ecclesiae, quousque paenituerint de commisso, et ad nos accesserint paenitentiam canonicam acceptum. Hanc autem destrictionem non tantum de capellanis parochias regentibus, [4v] sed etiam de quibuscunque aliis praecipimus inviolabiliter observari. Personae vero ecclesiarum qui ausu temerario, vel capellanos[51] in ecclesiis publice concubinarios retinent ministrantes, seu ministraturos, vel in parochiis sustinuerint, ad arbitrium nostrum puniantur.

---

[44]Cf. statutes of Canterbury I, 1213-14, c. 7 (PC, 26).
[45]Cf. council of Lambeth, 1281, c. 9 (PC, 900-5).
[46]The text is faulty. Cf. Durham diocesan statutes (c. 1241-9), c. 18: 'Panni etiam chrismales in usus saeculares nullatenus convertantur... Nec uni parvulo nisi propter necessitatem aut pauperiem pannus alius deputetur per avaritiam aut incuriam sacerdotis' (PC, 427).
[47]The MS transposes 'infantibus' and 'infirmis' but this was corrected in the copies.
[48]Cf. statutes of Canterbury I, 1213-14, c. 4 (PC, 25-6).
[49]Cf. statutes of Canterbury I, 1213-14, c. 3 (PC, 25).
[50]MSS: 'suscipio'.
[51]MSS: 'capellani, qui'.

deed, to their subordinates. Each of them shall instruct his parishioners in the articles of the faith according to his knowledge of the gospel and of Holy Scripture. He shall also take care to admonish his parishioners to teach their children the Apostles' Creed, the Lord's Prayer, and the *Ave Maria.*

4. *Of baptism*

Priests must take care to ensure that no child dies without baptism, which God forbid! We also prohibit priests, under pain of excommunication, to exact a fee or take a present for baptizing children or for visiting the sick or burying the dead, beyond what the law requires. And no priest shall convert the tunics or chrism cloths of the baptized to other than church purposes, nor allow those used for one child to be used for another, under pain of excommunication.

5. *Of the chastity of priests*

We ordain that no chaplain shall allow the housekeeper and concubine of any other priest, or any adulteress, to be in his parish, unless she leaves the parish after three warnings, or he shall excommunicate her by name. If he does not do so, let him know that he shall come under pain of excommunication.

6. *Of the punishment of transgressors*

We strictly forbid rectors of churches, vicars, priests and clerks in holy orders to keep householders publicly or in private, which might give rise to negative suspicion. If they presume to do so, the benefices of clerics who live this way shall be sequestered by us, and they shall be forbidden to enter the church until they repent of their conduct and come to us for canonical penance. We want this punishment to be inviolably observed, not only with respect to priests in charge of parishes but to all others also. Incumbents of parishes who dare either to tolerate notoriously unchaste priests to minister in their churches, or to allow them in their parishes, shall be punished at our discretion.

7. *De ministerio clericorum*[52]

Statuimus idem quod omnes capellani, diaconi et ceteri ministri altaris honeste et devote sine murmuratione non caputiis in capitibus nec tenis vel piliis aut cerothecis in manibus aut in pede calcaribus, cum tonsura et corona decenti iuxta gradus sui dignitatem, ad divinum officium accedant.

8. *De ieiuniis iniungendis*[53]

Et praecipimus quod singuli capellani in suis parochiis ieiunia quatuor temporum et rogationis, apostolorum vigilias, sanctorumque festivitates consuetas in Dominicis praecedentibus rite denuntient.

9. *De vicariis, ut respondeant de ornamentis ecclesiae*

Statuendo praecipimus quod omnes vicarii tam de custodia vestimentorum et ornamentorum quam de omnibus aliis ecclesiae pro rata sua portione respondeant.

10. *De purificatione post partum*

Praecipimus ut singuli capellani moneant parochianas suas et[54] inducant post puerperium ad ecclesias accedere cum candelis et oblationibus tempore purificationis statutae, ut infra quindenam minime purificentur.

11. *De mortuariis discedentium*

Statuendo pronuntiamus quod de bonis cuiuslibet discedentis ecclesia [5r] habeat optionem de omnibus, iuxta consuetudinem vicinarum provinciarum, excepto uno, cum omnibus indumentis suis et fulcro vel culcitra. Quod si non habeat pirottum[55] vel culcitram, septem dentur denarii. Et cum quolibet mortuo iuxta facultates fiant oblationes, tam in denariis quam in candelis in ecclesia sua parochiali. Et sub poena excommunicationis inhibemus ne aliquis mortuus alio loco deferatur sepeliendus, donec missa pro eo fuerit celebrata in ecclesia sua parochiali.

---

[52]Cf. statutes of Canterbury I, 1213-14, c. 8 (PC, 26); Salisbury I, 1217-19, c. 11 (PC, 63).
[53]Cf. statutes of London II, 1245-59, c. 25 (PC, 638).
[54]MSS: 'ut'.
[55]MSS: 'pirettam'.

7. *Of the ministry of the clergy*

We ordain that all priests, deacons and other ministers of the altar shall attend divine service decently and devoutly, not whispering, without wearing hoods, coifs or caps, or gloves on their hands or spurs on their feet, with a tonsure and crown befitting their station.

8. *Of enjoining fasts*

We also order that priests shall duly announce the ember and rogation days, the vigils of the apostles and the customary feasts of the saints in their parishes, on the preceding Sundays.

9. *The responsibility of vicars for church ornaments*

We order and appoint that all vicars shall be responsible for the care of vestments and ornaments, and for all other church furniture, according to their prescribed portion.

10. *Of purification after childbirth*

We order every parish priest to admonish his women parishioners and persuade them to go to church after childbearing with candles and offerings at an appointed time of purification, as long as they are not purified in less than a fortnight.

11. *Of the mortuary fees of the deceased*

We ordain and appoint that the church shall have the choice out of the effects of every deceased person of any except one, according to the custom of neighbouring provinces, with all his garments and a bed or a mattress. But if he has no bed or mattress, seven pence shall be paid. And with each deceased person, offerings of money and candles shall be made to his parish church, according to his means. And under pain of excommunication, we forbid any dead body to be carried elsewhere until mass has been celebrated for the deceased in his parish church.

12. De intestatis

Item stauimus ut cum aliquis intestatus decesserit, quod omnia bona sua sequestrentur in manu episcopi per loci rectorem vel vicarium, donec per episcopum quid debeat fieri fuerit ordinatum. Et nullus executorum bonis discedentium se ingerat, donec coram rectore aut officiali vel archidiacono de ultima voluntate doceantur.

13. De vicariis religiosorum

Statuimus ut in ecclesiis religiosorum ad proprios usus appropriatis, secundum concilium Lateranense[56] vicarii ordinentur.

14. De periculo parvulorum[57]

Inhibemus sub poena excommunicationis, ne aliqua[e] mulier[es] vel uxores parvulos suos in lectulis suis secum collocari permittant antequam aetatis suae tertium [annum] compleverint. Quod statutum ad minus semel in anno, [a] singulis sacerdotibus volumus promulgari.

15. De decimis, primitiis et oblationibus

Sub poena excommunicationis statuimus quod omnes dioecesani nostri [5v] decimas omnium bonorum suorum quae eis de anno in annum renovantur integre, plenarie sine deductione, diminutione[que] aliqua solvant, sicut in Veteri et Novo Testamento praecipitur, videlicet de omni genere bladi, leguminum, pomorum[58] et fructuum, tam in hortis quam in rure crescentium. Decima autem bladi [et] leguminis deferatur per parochianos ad domos vel grangias suas, et eadem [di]ligentia eam custodiant qua suam partem, donec rectores ecclesiae vel sui procuratores de toto decimam recipiant.[59] Item de blado suo non decimato nihil praeparent nisi quantum rectores ecclesiae vel suos procuratores scire fecerint.

Item statuimus ut de qualibet domo dentur in aestate octodecim casei de melioribus et octodecim in auctumno facti, mundi, salsi et bene praeparati. Item, in domibus in quibus fit butirum, detur decima butiri sine aliqua fraude vel diminutione lacti[s]. Si vero lac diminuatur vel in alios usus distribuatur, fiat recompensatio de caseo vel butiro. Quod si aliis temporibus anni caseum vel butirum contingat fieri, de hoc decima integra sine aliqua fraude persolvatur.

Item statuimus de lana, agnis, haedis, vitulis, porcellis, pullis equorum, aucarum, de ovis gallinarum, de lino, canabo, foeno, decima integra persolvatur.

---

[56]Lateran IV (1215), c. 61. Cf. council of Oxford, 1222, c. 14 (PC, 110).
[57]This inhibition is very common in diocesan statutes, but only those of Coventry (c. 1224-37), c. 21, mention a specific age.
[58]MS: 'perrorum', corrected to 'porcorum' in the copies.
[59]Cf. 1229/10 above.

12. *Of intestates*

We also ordain that when a person has died intestate, all his effects shall be sequestered into the bishop's hands by the rector or vicar of the place, until the bishop has given an order regarding their disposal. And no executor shall concern himself with the effects of a deceased person until he is instructed about his last will, in the presence of the rector, the official or the archdeacon.

13. *Of vicars of the religious*

We ordain that in churches appropriated to religious houses, vicars shall be appointed, according to the Lateran council.

14. *Of danger to little children*

We forbid all women and wives, under pain of excommunication, to let their little children be placed beside them in bed before they are three years old. We want this statute to be published by every priest at least once a year.

15. *Of tithes, first-fruits and offerings*

Under pain of excommunication, we ordain that all persons in our diocese shall pay tithe on all fruits recurrent in each year, wholly, fully, without any deduction or diminution, as is commanded in the Old and New Testaments, that is, of all manner of corn, vegetables, fruit trees and other fruit growing in gardens or in the countryside. Tithe of corn and vegetables shall be brought by parishioners to their dwellings or barns, and stored with the same care as their own portion, until the rectors or their agents receive all their tithe. Also, they shall do nothing with untithed corn without informing the rectors or their agents of the amount.

We also ordain that during the summer eighteen cheeses of the better sort shall be paid from every house, and eighteen made during the autumn – clean, salted and well prepared. And in houses where butter is made, tithe of butter shall be paid, without cheating or stinting of milk. But if the milk is reduced or turned to other uses, then compensation shall be provided with cheese or butter. Should cheese or butter happen to be made at other times of the year, tithe shall be paid in full for it, without cheating.

And we ordain that tithe is to be paid in full from wool, lambs, kids, calves, piglets, colts, geese, hen's eggs, and of flax, hemp and hay.

Et ubi decem animalia decimanda sunt, habeat possessor optionem de duobus, ecclesia vero de reliquis; et ubi sunt nisi novem, detur nonum animal eodem modo sicut prius. Et si fuerit undecim detur nisi unum. Quod si fuerint unum vel duo, seu tria aut [6r] quatuor, pro singulis capitibus vitulorum et pullorum, detur denarius;[60] pro agnis vero et haedis quadrans, pro porcellis obolus. Quod si fuerint quinque vel sex, vel citra novem, tunc quintum animal aestimetur et dividatur inter rectorem et possessorem; et in optione rectorum sit an velit redimere, aut dimidium pretii recipere. Item de uno agno vel duobus detur obolus, de tribus vel quatuor detur denarius; si fuerit quinque vel citra novem, aestimetur prout dictum est. De sex vero, septem vel octo fiat sicut dictum est, de uno, vel duobus vel tribus vel quatuor. Si vero undecim vel novem, animal solvatur. De porcellis, si decem vel quinque fuerint, fiat decimatio sicut statutum est de vitulis. Quod si pauciores quinque vel citra novem, pro singulis detur obolus.

16. *De molendinis, piscaturis et aliis minutis decimis*

Item de molendinis[61] et piscaturis, tam aquarum dulcium quam salsarum, decima integra persolvatur. Item si contingat aliquem oves suas bis in anno tondere, bis decima solvatur. Item de agnis decimatis in sequenti anno tonsis, sine aliqua contradictione decima solvatur. Item de pellibus agnorum, haedorum, vitulorum et aliarum bestiarum, omnium immortuarum et interfectarum, decima integra persolvatur. Item ubi animalia alicuius pascuntur et cubant, tota decima solvatur ecclesiae loci illius. [6v] Quod si loca communibus pasturis sint deputata, tunc decima ecclesiae parochiali solvatur. Quod si pascant in una et cubent in alia, decima casei et butiti dividatur. Quod si pascantur in una et cubent in alia, tunc si in aliena parochia tondeantur et agnos pariant, tunc inter alienam parochiam et propriam parochiam decima dividatur, tam de lana, quam de agnis.

17. *Inhibitio ne vendant animalia ante decimationem*

Inhibemus sub poena excommunicationis ne aliqui agnos, procellos, pullos, haedos, vitulos vel aliqua alia animalia decimanda vendant, vel eorum decimam aliquo modo in alios usus transferant, ante legitimam decimationem. Quod si ausu temerario hoc fecerint, statuimus omnes sic alienantes ad decimam teneri, et novimus poenae excommunicationi subiacere.

---

[60]MS: 'denarium'; error corrected in the copies.
[61]MSS: 'molendinariis'. Corrected by Dugdale.

And where ten animals are to be tithed, the owner shall choose two and the church shall choose from the others. And where there are only nine, the ninth animal shall be given in the same way. And if there are eleven, only one shall be given. But if there are one, two, three or four, a penny shall be given for each head of calves and colts, a farthing for lambs and kids and a halfpenny for a piglet. But if there are five or six, or a number less than nine, the fifth animal shall be valued and divided between the rector and the owner, and the rector shall decide whether he will redeem it or accept half its value. For one lamb or two a halfpenny shall be paid; for three or four, a penny. If there are five or a number less than nine, an estimate shall be made for six, seven or eight, as is said of one, two, three or four. But if there are eleven or nine, one animal shall be given. For piglets, if there are ten or five, tithe shall be paid as for calves. But if there are fewer than five, tithe shall be paid as for calves. But if there are under five, or under nine, a halfpenny shall be paid for each.

16. *Of mills, fisheries and other small tithes*

Tithe shall be paid in full on mills and fisheries, whether they are freshwater or saltwater. If anyone shears his sheep twice a year, tithe shall be paid twice. Also, when lambs which have been tithed are sheared in the next year, tithe shall be paid without question. Also, tithe shall be paid fully on fleeces of lambs, kids, calves and other animals which die or are killed. And where animals graze and sleep, the whole tithe shall be paid to the local church. But if places are set aside for common pastures, tithe shall be paid to the parish church. But if they graze in one and sleep in another, the tithe of cheese and butter shall be divided. But if they graze in one and sleep in the other, and are shorn in the second parish and produce young, the tithe of both wool and lambs shall be divided between the two parishes.

17. *Prohibition of selling animals before tithing*

We forbid anyone to sell lambs, piglets, colts, calves or other animals subject to tithe, or to convert their tithe to any other use before the lawful tithing under pain of excommunication. Should anyone dare to do so, we ordain that such alienators shall be liable for the tithe and shall suffer a canonical penalty.

18. *De piscatoribus applicantibus in alienam parochiam*[62]

Statuimus quod si piscatores applicuerint cum piscaturis in parochiam alienam, vel cimbam alterius parochiae causa piscandi acceperint, tunc decima dividatur. Quod si duo vel tres in aliam parochiam causa piscandi accesserint, pro rata portione eorum decima dividatur.

19. *De textoribus et textricibus*[63]

Item statuimus quod textores vel textrices qui non solvunt decimam de aliis rebus, solvant quatuor denarios; alii vero quinque denarios, quod si plus lucrentur, conscientiae eorum relinquatur.[64]

20. [7r] *De mercatoribus et ceteris operariis*

Statuimus quod mercatores, negotiatores et laboratores ceterique de omni lucro suo decimam solvant. Similiter et servientes qui conducti fuerint ab aliis, decimam solvant de stipendio suo.

21. *De diminutione lactis*

Statuimus ut hi qui propter paucitatem animalium nec caseum nec butirum facere possunt, pro decima vaccae vitulatae solvant duos denarios [et] obolum. Pro non vitulata, lac tamen faciente, unum denarium [et] obolum. Similiter de ovibus octo tantum reputentur pro vacca.

22. *De fabris et aliis artificibus*

Item aurifabri, fabri, fabricatores, ferrarii, falcatores, carpentarii, cementarii, de lucro suo decimam solvant, quarum solutio proprio sacramento relinquatur.[65]

23. *Sequitur de oblationibus*[66]

Ordinamus et sancimus quod omnes parochiani et parochianae ter in anno singuli, singulis vicibus offerant obolum, videlicet ad festum Nativitatis Domini, Paschae, Pentecostes vel ad festum dedicationis ecclesiae. Et quod unusquisque habens domicilium et certa bona solvat in Quadragesima duos denarios et

---

[62]MS: 'in aliqua parochia', corrected to 'in aliam parochiam' by the Bodleian copy.
[63]Cf. 1229/12 above, which appears to be more precise than this.
[64]MS: 'relinquetur'; corrected in the copies. Cf. PC, 819, n. 1 for the custom in the diocese of York.
[65]See the note on c. 19 above for a reference to this practice in York.
[66]Cf. PC, 180, n. 3 for customary offerings in York diocese.

18. *Of fishermen who come ashore in another parish*

We order that if fishermen come ashore with their catch in another parish, or if they use a boat of another parish for fishing, the tithe shall be divided. But if two or three go into another parish to fish, the tithe shall be divided according to their portions of the catch.

19. *Of weavers and websters*

We also ordain that weavers and websters who pay no tithe on other things shall pay four pence; others, five pence. If they earn more, the amount shall be left to their conscience.

20. *Of merchants and labourers*

We ordain that merchants, tradesmen, labourers and others shall pay tithe on all their profit. Likewise, hired servants shall pay tithe on all their wages.

21. *Of lack of milk*

We ordain that those who cannot make cheese or butter because their herd is small, shall pay twopence halfpenny for the tithe of a calved cow, and a penny halfpenny for a cow that has not calved, yet is producing milk. Likewise for sheep, reckoning eight sheep for one cow.

22. *Of smiths and other craftsmen*

Goldsmiths, smiths, artisans, farriers, scythe-makers, carpenters and masons shall pay tithe on their profit. The amount shall be left to their own self-assessment.

23. *Of offerings*

We order and decree that every parishioner shall offer one halfpenny three times a year, at Christmas, Easter and Whitsun or the patronal festival of the church, and that everyone who owns a home and certain effects shall pay twopence

obolum ad luminaria ecclesiae. Si vero morantur in aliis domibus dum tamen habeant in bonis ad valorem sex solidorum, solvant duos denarios iuxta consuetudinem vicinarum provinciarum.

24. *De excommunicatione quater per annum*[67]

Ut in singulis ecclesiis quoruncuncque religiosorum seu saecularium, statuimus quater in anno, videlicet in Dominicis proximis post observa[7v]tionem quatuor temporum, et etiam in synodo, in genere excommunicentur omnes sortilegi, venefici, incendiarii, ecclesiarum f[r]actores, falsarii, usurarii manfesti,[68] impedientes testimonia[69] legitime facta. Laici[70] invadentes, detinentes, defraudantes, et auferentes possessiones seu quaecunque [iura] ecclesiastica aut libertates et omnes illi[71] qui se in beneficio ecclesiastico intruserint et testes scienter[72] periuri, unde amittitur ab aliquo haereditas sua, aut beneficium seu terrenum; raptores etiam publici et notorii et omnes fures et latrones, vel eos qui manuteneant vel pro eis fidem dabunt cum dicta causa revelatur.[73] Item omnes qui in causa matrimoniali falsum testimonium perhibent, vel falsas exceptiones opponunt malitiose, vel opponi procurant, [vel] in causa matrimoniali testes subornant, et omnes impedientes ordinarios, quominus de bonis discedentium ab intestatis, secundum consuetudinem Ecclesiae Scoticanorum et nostrae valeant ordinare excommunicationis sententiae volumus subiacere. Item excommunicamus omnes conspiratores contra episcopos proprios vel alienos regni, seu contra tales praelatos et omnes conspiratoribus consentientes, ita quod omnes tales schismatici sunt et infames. Item auctoritate huius sacrae synodus [*sic*] nostrae excommunicamus omnes illos qui pacem regis et regni perturbant, et omnes illos qui causa odii vel lucri aliis falsa crimina imponunt, pro quibus mors, exilium, membrorum mutilatio, exhaeredatio vel bonorum spoliatio [8r] aut bonae famae amissio sequi debeat, si iudicialiter convincantur.

25. *De confessionibus*

Inhibemus ne aliquis religiosus infra terram vel extra venientium sine nostra licentia confessionem audiat, pueros baptizet, infirmos communicet, vel aliqualiter alia sacra[menta] ecclesiastica exerceat.[74] Item inhibemus ne aliquis parochianus extra ecclesiam suam parochialem, causa confessionis vel alicuius alterius sacramenti

---

[67]An amalgam of three Scottish statutes *c.* 1242-9 (c. 51, 47, 52). See Robertson, *Concilia Scotiae*, II, 24, 26-7; Patrick, *Statutes*, pp. 24, 26-7.
[68]Perhaps this should read: 'usurarii, malitiose'.
[69]I.e., 'testamenta'.
[70]MS: 'laicos', corrected in the Bodleian copy.
[71]MSS: 'illos'; emended by Dugdale.
[72]MSS: 'scientes'; emended by Dugdale.
[73]Perhaps this should read: 'fidem dent cum ex dicta causa querelantur' as in the Scottish statutes, *c.* 1242-9, c. 51.
[74]MS: 'exerceatur'; corrected in the copies.

halfpenny in Lent for the lighting of the church. If they do not have homes of their own, but possess effects to the value of six shillings, they shall pay two pence, according to the custom of neighbouring provinces.

24. *Of excommunication four times a year*

We ordain that in all churches, regular and secular, four times a year, on the Sundays next after the ember days, and in synod, every kind of sorcerer, poisoner, arsonist, breaker into churches, forger, usurer, malicious obstructor of the execution of lawfully made wills, layman who encroaches on or seizes or fraudulently acquires or removes church property or any ecclesiastical goods or rights, intruder into an ecclesiastical benefice, conscious bearer of false witness by which someone loses his inheritance, benefice or land, notorious abductor, thief, robber or person who stands security for them when they are prosecuted on this account, shall be excommunicated. Also, we order that all those who bear false witness in marriage suits, or who maliciously put forward, or cause to be put forward, false exceptions, or who suborn witnesses, as well as all who prevent ordinaries from administering the effects of intestates according to the custom of the Scottish church and of ours, shall be subject to excommunication. Also, we excommunicate all conspirators against their bishops or other bishops of the realm or any such prelates, and all who support such conspirators, shall be deemed schismatic and infamous. And by authority of this our sacred synod, we excommunicate all who disturb the peace of the king and kingdom, and all who out of hatred or for profit falsely impute crimes to others, whereby death, exile, mutilation, disinheritance, loss of property or of good name must ensue were the accused judicially convicted.

25. *Of confessions*

We forbid any member of a religious order in the land, or any who come from elsewhere, to hear confessions without our licence, or to baptize children, or to give communion to the sick, or to celebrate any of the other sacraments of the church in any way. We also forbid any parishioner to go outside his own parish church to another parish or to any secular or religious establishment for confession or any

ecclesiastici [habendi], ad alienam parochiam sive ad quemcunque alium locum saecularem, vel religosorum accedere praesumat, et si ter monitus fuerit, excommunicetur. Et quod nullus capellanus alterius parochiae eius confessionem audiat vel ipsum communicet, vel sacra[menta] alia ecclesiastica ministret, nisi in articulo mortis, vel de licentia proprii capellani.

26. *De legatis in testamento*

Inhibemus ne aliquis vicarius vel capellanus in fraude[m] ecclesiae vel aliquis alius legatarius aliquod legatum exigat aut recipiat, nisi prius debito ecclesiae declarato et soluto. Quod si secus fecerint, poena[m] excommunicationis incurrant. Item praecipimus quod si aliquis adhuc in vita existens causa donationis vel alia ex causa in filios, alumnos, vel in alias personas, aliquid de bonis suis transferri voluerit, hoc publice in ecclesia faciant, vel saltem coram rectore [8v] ecclesiae, vel eius attornato, vel coram bonis testibus et fidedignis.

27. *De matrimonio*

Inhibemus ne aliquis sacerdos a Quadragesima usque ad octavas Paschae inter aliquos matrimonium celebrare praesumat,[75] nisi de nostra licentia, vel officialium nostrorum, et ne aliquis saecularis vel clericus infra illud tempus aliquod sacramentum iudiciale aut in diebus festivis vel solemnibus praestare vel subire praesumat. Item quod nullus capellanus clandestinis sponsalibus interesse praesumat, vel clandestine[76] per annuli benedictione[m] aliquos contrahi permittat, sed matrimonium[77] secundum quod moris est, tribus denuntiationibus prius factis in ecclesia, publice et solemniter ad missae celebrationem per debita intervalla praemissis, contractum faciat.[78] Item quod capellanus inter aliquos matrimonium vel sponsalia facere [non] praesumat, nisi tribus denuntiationibus prius factis in ecclesia, quaerendo tam ubi vir manet, quam mulier, nisi ambo in una parochia fuerint. Et si qui postea contra matrimonium taliter contractum, aliquid alicui obiicere voluerint, qui tempore contractus[79] in eadem parochia fuerint quod ad eorum notitiam verisimiliter[80] sit tales denuntiationes [devenisse], nullatenus audiantur.

28. *De iuramento cum contractu*

Item statuimus quod quilibet capellanus iura[re] faciat, non solum ipsos contrahentes, verum etiam tres vel quatuor aut quinque de senioribus et fidedignioribus utriusque parentelae contrahentium quorum [9r] nomine redigantur

---

[75]MS: 'praesumant'; corrected in the copies.
[76]MS: 'clandestinate'.
[77]MSS: 'ea'.
[78]The text here is corrupt and obscure.
[79]MS: 'vel' added here unnecessarily.
[80]MS: 'verisimiles'.

other sacrament. Should he do so, he shall be excommunicated after three warnings. No priest of another parish shall hear his confession or give communion or administer other ecclesiastical sacraments unless at the point of death or by leave of his own parish priest.

26. *Of bequests in a will*

We forbid any vicar or parish priest or any other legatee to demand or accept any legacy to the defrauding of the church, unless the debt to the church has previously been declared and paid. Should they do otherwise, they shall incur the penalty of excommunication. Also, we order that if anyone wants to transfer, during his lifetime, any of his effects as a gift, or for any other reason, to his children, wards or other persons he shall do so publicly in church, or at least in the presence of the rector or his attorney, with good and trustworthy witnesses.

27. *Of marriage*

We forbid any priest to presume to celebrate marriage between a couple from the beginning of Lent to the octave of Easter, without a licence from us or from our officials. During that season, and also on feast days and solemn days, no layman or cleric shall presume to give or subscribe to any judicial oath. Also, no parish priest shall presume to attend a clandestine betrothal or allow a couple to be joined together by a clandestine blessing of a ring, but he shall arrange the contract, as is customary, after the banns have been called three times publicly and solemnly at due intervals, when mass is being celebrated. Nor shall a priest presume to perform a marriage or a betrothal between any persons if banns have not been called three times in church, asking in the home parish of both the man and the woman, if they are not both from the same parish. And if, after a marriage so contracted, anyone wishes to object to either, if the objectors were in the parish at the time of the contract, so that the banns presumably came to their notice, they shall not be listened to.

28. *Of oaths with the marriage contract*

We also ordain that every priest shall cause oaths to be taken, not only by the contracting parties, but also by three, four or five of the elder and more trustworthy

in scriptis, quod inter eosdem nesciunt aliquod impedimentum, quominus possint legitime copulari. Similiter et ab omnibus circumstantibus sub periculo animarum suarum diligenter inquirant. Et hoc ab omnibus capellanis nostrae dioecesis in matrimoniali contractu sub poena suspensionis triennalis praecipimus observari. Et nullus de causis matrimonialibus cognoscat nisi qui iura noverit et finem in causis matrimonialibus in scriptis proferat.[81] Item statuimus quod secundum iura canonica omnes causae matrimoniales et testamentariae viduarum, pupillorum, cruce signatorum et miserabilium personarum, ad examen ecclesiae pertineant.

29. De laicis vel clericis arma in ecclesia portantibus

Inhibemus ne quis laicus vel clericus decetero in ecclesiis nostrae dioecesis aliqua arma ferre vel aliquem tumultum seu perturbationem, et maxime tempore celebrationis missae, in eis facere praesumat. Quod si aliquis post trinam monitionem in huiusmodi crimine incorrigibilis inventus fuerit, per censuram ecclesiasticam prout nobis videtur, puniatur.

30. De saecularibus placitis festivis diebus non tenendis[82]

Statuimus[83] quod decetero saecularia placita in Dominicis diebus aut festivis solemnibus minime teneantur in ecclesiis, in coemeteriis vel aliis locis Deo dicatis, et maxime causae sanguinis,[84] aut criminales, er quoscunque iudices saeculares locis aut temporibus praedictis [9v] agitentur. Quod si necesse fuerit edicta regalia vel aliqua ex parte principis forte coram populo proferre, non infra missarum solemnia, sed sive ante sive post, ubi commodius potest fieri, extra tamen ecclesiam, ne praepediantur divina, praecipimus et permittimus.

31. De testamentis condendis

Praecipimus et statuimus quod quilibet languens in extremis agoniis cum testamentum condere voluerit, vocet capellanum ecclesiae et clericum, et ipsis praesentibus, duobus vel tribus viris adhibitis bonis et fidedignis, testamentum suum ore suo ordinet. Et ipse sacerdos substantiam suam diligenter exquirat, et si in aliquibus creditoribus sit obnoxius[85] vel de aere[86] alieno oneratus. Quod si non fecerit tanquam intestatus reputatur. Quod statutum volumus ut singuli capellani in

---

[81]MSS: 'proferantur'.

[82]A Scottish statute c. 1242-9 (c. 29). See Robertson, *Concilia Scotiae* II, 19; Patrick, *Statutes*, p. 19. See also Canterbury statutes I, 1213-14, c. 60 (PC, 35-6).

[83]The word order has been rearranged by Dugdale. All the MSS read 'quod solemnibus statuimus...'

[84]MS: 'sanguinum'; corrected in the copies.

[85]MS: 'sint obnexis'; corrected by Dugdale.

[86]MS: 'ore'; corrected by the Bodleian copy.

relatives of each party, whose names should be recorded in writing, to the effect that they know no lawful impediment why the couple should not be joined in marriage. Similarly, the priest shall inquire carefully of all bystanders, on peril of their souls. And we order this to be observed by all priests of our diocese in the contracting of marriage, under pain of three years' suspension. And only those who have knowledge of the law shall take cognizance of matrimonial cases, and pronounce the resolution of their case in writing. We further ordain that in conformity with canon law, all cases concerning marriage, wills, widows, orphans, crusaders and 'miserable persons' shall come under ecclesiastical jurisdiction.

29. *Of laymen or clerics who carry weapons in church*

We forbid any layman or cleric from henceforth to carry arms within the churches of our diocese, or to presume to make any nosie or disturbance in them, especially during mass. If, after three warnings, anyone is found to be incorrigible in so offending, he shall be punished by ecclesiastical censure at our discretion.

30. *Of not holding secular lawsuits on feast days*

We ordain that from henceforth lay pleas shall not be heard on Sundays or on solemn feast days in churches, cemeteries or other consecrated places. In particular, blood cases are not to be heard by lay judges of any kind in such places or at such times. But if it is necessary to proclaim royal edicts or other announcements from the prince to the people, we order and permit it to be done, not during mass, but either before or after it, whatever is more convenient, and not inside the church, lest it hinder divine service.

31. *Of making wills*

We decree and ordain that anyone on the point of death who wishes to draw up his will shall summon the priest and the clerk, with two or three trustworthy men, and shall dictate his will in their presence. And the priest shall carefully enquire into the testator's property, and whether he is under any obligation to creditors, or burdened with debt. If the dying man does not do this, he shall be deemed to have died intestate. We desire all priests to proclaim this ordinance in their churches.

ecclesiis suis publicent. Item statuimus, ut quicunque amodo se[87] creditorem alicuius dixerit defuncti vel aliquem cum eo iniisse[88] contractum, et in eadem parochia manens, vel ita prope quod de infirmitate eius constare poterit, non in vita sua, nec hora testamenti, vel tempore infirmitatis illius, super hoc quaestionem moverit,[89] vel mentionem fecerit coram viris fidedignis, post mortem defuncti nullatenus audiatur.[90]

32. De communicatione cum excommunicato[91]

Inhibemus quod nulli cum publice excommunicatis et maxime capellani [10r] communicent. In quo delicto si capellani rei inventi fuerint, ultioni gravissimae subiacebunt.

33. De campanis pulsandis

Statuimus quod campanari[i] ecclesiarum, cum episcopus ad ecclesias accesserit, vel prope transierit, campanas pulsent, quod si non fecerint ad arbitrium episcopi clerici punientur.

34. De oleo et chrismate

Statuimus quod quilibet capellanus chrisma, oleum sanctum et oleum infirmorum semel in anno[92] recipiat in vasis mundissimis bene ceratis. Tempore receptionis singuli eorum quatuor denarios reddent.

35. De visitatione archidiaconi et ornamentis ecclesiae[93]

Item statuimus quod archidiaconus secundum apostolum non quae sua sunt quaerat, sed quae Iesu Christi. In sua visitatione provideat quod canon missae emendetur et quod sacerdotes rite proferre sciant dicta canonis et baptismatis,[94] et doceant laicos in qua forma baptizare debeant in articulo necessitatis, ut[95] saltem hoc sciant facere in suo idiomate. Habeat etiam archidiaconus omnia ornamenta ecclesiarum in scriptis redacta et utensilia, earum vestes et libros, et singulis annis suo conspectui faciat praesentari, ut videat quae adiecta fuerint per diligentiam

---

[87]Dugdale. All the MSS have 'ad'.
[88]MSS: 'missa' for 'eo iniisse'.
[89]Dugdale. The MSS have 'noverit'.
[90]Dugdale. The MSS have 'audiantur'.
[91]Although there are frequent commands in English statutes not to have dealings with excommunicates, there does not seem to be any one which specifically forbids the clergy from having such contact.
[92]This was normally Maundy Thursday, although no day is specified by this canon. Cf. 1268/21 (PC, 769-70).
[93]Cf. council of Oxford, 1222, c. 29 (PC, 115).
[94]Corrected from the Oxford canon. The MSS have 'baptisterii'.
[95]Corrected from the Oxford canon. The MSS have 'vel'.

We also ordain that anyone hereafter who says that he was the creditor of a deceased person or had made a contract with him, and who did not raise the question of his debt in the presence of trustworthy persons during his lifetime, when he made his will or when he was ill, though dwelling in the same parish or so near as to be aware of his illness, shall not be listened to after the death of the deceased.

32. *Of association with an excommunicate*

We forbid everyone, and especially priests, to associate with excommunicates. If priests are found guilty of this offence, they shall be subject to a very heavy penalty.

33. *Of bell-ringing*

We order the bell-ringers of churches to ring the bells when the bishop visits the church or passes by. If they fail to do so, the [parish] clerks shall be punished at the bishop's discretion.

34. *Of oil and chrism*

We ordain that every priest shall receive chrism, holy oil, and oil for the infirm, once a year in vessels which are very clean and securely locked. On receipt of them he shall pay four pence.

35. *Of the archdeacon's visitation and of church ornaments*

We ordain that the archdeacon shall, as the apostle says, seek not his own, but what is due to Jesus Christ. On his visitation, he shall ensure that the canon of the mass is correct, and that priests know how to pronounce the words of the canon and of baptism correctly, and that they teach lay people in what form they should baptize in case of need, so that at least they know how to do this in their mother tongue. Also, the archdeacon shall have all the church ornaments, vessels, vestments and books put down in writing and shown for his inspection every year, so that he may see what have been added by the parishioners' diligence, or what have been

parochianorum vel quae medio tempore per negligentiam vel malitiam vicariorum deperdita,[96] vel per incuriam eorum aliquo modo diminuta, [10v] quid per clericos, quid per laicos.

36. De missis celebrandis[97]

Districtius inhibemus ne aliquis sacerdos missarum solemnia bis in una die celebret, exceptis diebus Paschali et Natalium Domini, et in obsequiis mortuorum, videlicet, cum corpus alicuius defuncti eo die fuerit in ecclesia tumulandum. Et hoc si in diebus Dominicis et festivis contigerit, tunc caveat sacerdos cum ipse resincerat manus suas et calicem cum aqua et vino post communionem, ne sumat ablutionem, sed reponat illam in vaso mundo usque ad finem alterius missae, et tunc sumat utramque ablutionem, quia propter reverentiam sacramenti non debet aliquis celebrare nisi ieiunus.[98] Si ablutionem illam sumpsisset quae est pura aqua vel purum vinum, tunc ieiunus non esset. Item districtius inhibemus ne aliquis sacerdos duabus matricibus ecclesiis deservire praesumat, et provideat sacerdos quod ab incohatione missae usque ad finem, lucerna cerea ardeat.

Expliciunt statuta synodalia.

---

[96]MS: 'depraedata'; corrected in the copies.
[97]Council of Oxford, 1222, c. 11 (PC, 109).
[98]Cf. statutes of Salisbury I, c. 1217-19, c. 61 (PC, 80) and of Worcester II, 1229, c. 16 (PC, 173).

lost in the interval through the negligence or fraud of the vicars, or diminished in any way by their carelessness, and what was due to the clergy, and what to the lay people.

36. *Of celebrating masses*

We strictly forbid any priest to celebrate mass twice a day, except on Easter and Christmas Days, and at burials, on a day when a body is to be buried in the church. And should this happen on Sundays and feast days, the priest shall take care, when he rinses his hands and the chalice with water and wine after communion, not to drink the ablution, but to place it in a clean vessel until the end of the second mass, and then let him drink both ablutions. For out of reverence for the sacrament, no-one should celebrate unless he is fasting; were he to drink of the first ablution, whether pure water or pure wine, then he would not be fasting. And we strictly forbid any priest to presume to serve two mother churches, and the priest shall ensure that a wax candle is burning from the beginning of the mass until the end.

Here end the synodal statutes.

The additions to the above constitutions made by Bishop William Russell, 23 February 1351

Hae sunt additiones additae per venerabilem patrem Dominum Willielmum Russell Sodorensem episcopum[99] una cum toto clero Manniae, anno Domini millesimo tricentesimo quinquagesimo in ecclesia Sancti Michaelis Archangeli, septimo Kalendas Martii.

[1. *Preface*]

[A]d pastorale spectat officium circa statum [11r] ecclesiarum et animarum salutem pastori provido commissarum curam impendere pervigilem, ut [de] grege sibi commisso rationem redditurus, de talento sibi credito lucrum reportare valeant indeficiens. Inde[100] est quod ex his quae ab antiquis patribus prius statuta sunt, quaedam ad praesens ad memoriam revocamus, pauca de novo ad haec adiicientes, ne regimen commissum sub dissimulatione (quod absit) negligere videamur.[101]

Cum regimen animarum sit ars artium[102] et sancta et salubris est operatio pro defunctis exorare; imprimis deliberato cleri nostri consilio, duximus statuendum ut quotiescunque aliquis rector, vicarius, vel capellanus ecclesiae nostrae Manniae vel aliqua alia honesta persona, orationum nostrarum suffragiis commendata, et ad similia suffragia commendata et nobis obligata ab hoc saeculo migrare contigerit, ad locum et diem sepulturae eius, omnes alii superstites, absque quocunque figmento vel colore, conveniant, et defuncto corpori congruum honorem impendant. Et si poterint, singuli missas celebrare faciant cum aliis suffragiis ad hoc consuetis. Et ab ipso die sepulturae eius quilibet praedictorum triginta missas sine morae dispendio, per se seu per alium faciat celebrari, et triginta diebus proxime sequentibus, officium defunctorum cum novem lectionibus et consuetis p[s]almis sine dierum interruptione per quemlibet superstitem continue decantetur, cum decenti devotione, iniungentibus nostris officialibus et decanis, ut de[103] nostra ordinatione diligenter inquirant, [11v] ne quis inveniatur negligens vel remissus in praemissis. Et de quolibet dictam nostram ordinationem[104] infra sexaginta dierum spatium a die sepulturae non persolvente poena dimidiae marcae[105] levetur absque personarum exceptione per dictos officiales nostros, et de ipsa pecunia

---

[99]William Russell was bishop of Sodor and Man from 1349 to 1374.

[100]MS unclear; copies have 'idem'.

[101]MSS: 'videamus'. This preamble is found in statutes of David of Bernham, bishop of St Andrews from 1239 to 1253 (Robertson, *Concilia Scotiae*, II, 53; Patrick, *Statutes*, p. 57), and to some extent it resembles a mandate of Robert Grosseteste, bishop of Lincoln, to his archdeacons in 1235 or 1236 (PC, 203).

[102]Pope Gregory I (590-604), *De cura pastorali* I,1. The quote is a commonplace in medieval canons.

[103]MSS: 'dicta'.

[104]MS: 'de qualibet dictarum nostrarum ordinatione...'

[105]6s. 8d.

The additions to the above constitutions made by Bishop William Russell, 23 February 1351

These are the additions made by the venerable father, Lord William Russell, bishop of Sodor, with all the clergy of Man, in the year 1350 [1351], in the church of St Michael the archangel, on the seventh of the calends of March.

[1. *Preface*]

It belongs to the pastoral office of a provident shepherd to exercise ever-watchful care over the state of the churches and the salvation of the souls committed to him, so that in giving account of his flock, he may be able without fail to return profit on the talent with which he has been entrusted. So now we recall to memory certain precepts of the early fathers, adding to them a few new rules, so that we may not appear to be neglecting our responsibility by dissembling.

Since the direction of souls is the art of arts, and it is a holy and wholesome work to pray for the dead, having taken counsel with our clergy, we first ordain that whenever any rector, vicar or priest of our church of man, or any other worthy person commended to the suffrage of our prayers and bound to us by similar undertakings, dies, all who survive him should without any pretence or excuse assemble at the place and on the day of his burial, and show fitting honour to the body of the deceased. And if they can do so, they should celebrate mass with the other customary prayers. And after the day of his burial, each of them should celebrate thirty masses, or cause them to be celebrated, without delay, and in the thirty days next following, without any interval, let each of them reverently chant the office of the dead, with nine lessons and the customary psalms. We enjoin our officials and deans that they should enquire carefully about compliance with our ordinance, lest anyone should be negligent or remiss in the foregoing. Anyone who does not perform these services within sixty days of the burial shall be fined half a mark by our officials, without respect of persons. With this money, if the bishop

tot missas vel plures, si episcopus absens fuerit, in suarum animarum periculum faciant celebrari, responsuri episcopo cum ad partes venerit singulis praemissarum.

2. *De capellanis qui tenentur fidem Catholicam plebi exponere*[106]

Statuimus etiam quod omnes rectores, vicarii seu capellani in ecclesiasticis officiis constituti populo suo omnibus Dominicis diebus et festivis, Verbum Dei et fidem Catholicam et apostolicam firmiter et indesinenter exponant,[107] et suos subditos in articulis[108] fidei diligenter instruant, et ad informandum in lingua materna symbolum apostolorum moneant ipsos et adinducant, et suis liberis eandem fidem exponant et articulos doceant. Item statuimus quod ecclesiastica sacramenta de devota reverentia celebrentur, sub certa forma a sanctis patribus in scripturis tradita, quam formam Catholica fide approbatam, nullus audeat in aliquas novitates commutare, et summopere praecaventes ne vinum quo celebretur sit corruptum, vel in acetum commutatum, et quod potius sit rubrum quam album. In albo tamen bene conficitur sacrum, et non de aceto, cum in aceto mutatur [12r] omnes substantiales vires vini amisit. Et aqua in tam modica quantitate apponatur, ut non vinum ab aqua sed aqua a vino absorbeatur. Hostia de frumento sit rotunda, et integra et sine macula, quia agnus extitit sine macula, et os non fuit comminutum ex eo. Unde versus:

Candida triticea tenuis non magna rotunda
Expers fermenti non mixta sit hostia Christi
Inscribatur aqua non cocta, sed igne fit assa.[109]

Renovetur[110] hostia infirmis danda singulis Dominicis diebus, et ponatur in loco honesto, scilicet in pixide ad hoc deputato corporali cooperto, et nusquam sine corporali recondatur.[111] Aliis autem diebus ex necessitate poterit innovari. Et quando conficiuntur plures hostiae, habeat conficiens intentionem ad omnes et non ad unam solam. Et ipsis sacerdotibus firmiter iniungimus [ut] sacrosanctum conficiendo damnabiliter non se ingerant quamdiu sentiant se in quacunque macula mortali irretitos.

---

[106]Cf. Scottish statutes *c.* 1242-9, cc. 3-4 (Robertson, *Concilia Scotiae*, II, 10; Patrick, *Statutes*, pp. 9-10).

[107]Dugdale. The MSS have 'expositatis'.

[108]Dugdale. The MSS have 'artem'.

[109]These verses are found in various collections in England and on the continent from the thirteenth century onwards; see Hans Walther, *Initia carminum ac versuum medii aevi* (München, 1959), no. 2350.

[110]MS: 'renovatur'; corrected in the Bodleian copy.

[111]MS: 'recondatur'; correcte din the copies.

is absent, they shall have as many masses, or more, celebrated, on peril of their souls, and they shall be answerable for all these matters to the bishop when he arrives in those parts.

2. *Of the obligation of priests to expound the catholic faith to the people*

We also ordain that all rectors, vicars and priests appointed to ecclesiastical office shall preach the Word of God and the catholic and apostolic faith every Sunday and feast day steadfastly, and without intermission, to the people, and instruct their subjects diligently in the articles of the faith, and admonish and persuade them to learn the Apostles' Creed in their mother tongue, and to expound the faith to their children and teach them the articles. And we ordain that the church's sacraments shall be celebrated with devout respect in the set form handed down by the holy fathers, which form, approved by catholic doctrine, no-one shall presume to alter into any new forms, taking special care that the wine for the celebration is not corrupted or turned to vinegar, and that it is red rather than white. The sacrament may indeed be prepared with white wine, but not with vinegar; when it has changed into vinegar, it has lost all the substantial qualities of wine. And water shall be added in so moderate an amount that the wine is not absorbed in the water, but the water in the wine. The host shall be made of wheat, round, whole and unblemished, for the Lamb was without blemish and not a bone of him was broken. Whence the verse:

White should be the host of Christ,
Wheaten, thin, small and round,
Unleavened, unmixed, inscribed,
Baked and not boiled.

The host given to the sick shall be renewed each Sunday and kept in a proper place – in a pyx set aside for this use, covered with a corporal – and never put anywhere without a corporal. But if need be, it may be renewed on other days. And when several hosts are prepared, the celebrant shall maintain his intention for all, and not for one only. And we strictly enjoin priests that they shall never culpably engage in preparing the sacrament when they are conscious of struggling with some mortal sin.

3. *De reparatione cancelli et navis ecclesiae*[112]

Item statuimus ut ecclesiae parochiales et coemeteria earum pro modo facultatum parochianorum per ipsos parochianos, et cancelli per rectorem in omnibus necessariis honeste construantur; et altaria de ornamentis, libris et lumine, calice argenteo [12v] vel aureo, non ligneo nec vitreo nec aereo, sed de solo argento vel auro, vel necessitate urgente de puro stanno, et aliis ornamentis disposite ornentur, et postea per episcopum consecrentur. Ecclesia vero, et omnia ornamenta illius, tam in libris quam in vestibus et aliis necessariis, munda et honesta, una cum fonte, chrismatorio, et loco in quo conditur sacramentum altaris, per vicarium ecclesiae propriis sumptibus diligenter custodiantur. Qui quidem vicarius de omnibus quae geruntur in ecclesia et eius ambitu, domino episcopo et eius ordinariis est rationem redditurus, et de lumine purificationis Beatae Mariae ubi rectores non resident. De quo lumine volumus quod ministrentur ecclesiis honeste in missis celebrandis, et fiant duo cerei ad elevationem sacramenti altaris, et cereus paschalis, quos nihilominus nolumus[113] deficere in quacunque ecclesia nostrae dioecesis ad illud in festivis diebus. Et si illud ad hoc non sit sufficiens, rector apponat ut in statutis praedecessorum nostrorum continetur.[114]

Item statuimus quod nulla ecclesia, sive oratorium sine consensu nostro in nostra dioecesi construatur, vel constructa sine nostra auctoritate divina aliqua temeritate celebrent[ur], quin potius secundum canones profanantur.

4. *De aedificio in solo ecclesiae*[115]

Item quod quaelibet[116] parochialis ecclesiae rector habeat mansionem prope se honeste [13r] constructam in qua episcopus, archidiaconus, et eorum ordinarii recipi valeant, et procurari. Et maxime in ecclesiis, domibus exemptis, appropriatis iurisdictione ordinariorum infra annum debere fieri a die publicationis praesentium, tam in expensis rectorum quam vicariorum solventium procurationes pro rata suarum portionum. Et ad hoc ipsi rectores et vicarii compellantur, per sequestrationes fructuum beneficiorum suorum tempore praefixo revoluto.

5. *De clericis extraneis et aliunde venientibus*[117]

Frimiter praecipiendo inhibemus sub interminatione anathematis ut nullus sacerdos alienae dioecesis ad nostram veniens, inibi residentiam praesumat facere, vel

---

[112]Scottish statutes *c.* 1242-9, cc. 4-5 (Robertson, *Concilia Scotiae*, II, 10-11; Patrick, *Statutes*, p. 10).
[113]MSS: 'volumus'.
[114]No such statutes are extant.
[115]Cf. Scottish statutes, *c.* 1242-9, c. 12 (Robertson, *Concilia Scotiae*, II, 13; Patrick, *Statutes*, p.12).
[116]MS: 'quilibet'; corrected in the copies.
[117]Scottish statutes, *c.* 1242-9, c. 14 (Robertson, *Concilia Scotiae*, II, 14; Patrick, *Statutes*, p. 13).

3. *Of repairing the chancel and nave of the church*

Also, we ordain that parish churches and their cemeteries shall be decently constructed in all the necessary particulars, according to the parishioners' means, and the chancels by the rectors, and the altars properly furnished with ornaments – books, lights, chalice and other ornaments – the chalice of silver or gold, not of wood, glass or brass, but only of silver or gold, or if need be, of pure tin, and then the altars shall be consecrated by the bishop. But the church and all its ornaments, including books, vestments and other necessary things, with the font, the chrismatory and the place where the sacrament of the altar is reserved, are to be kept clean and decent by the care of the vicar, at his own expense. The vicar is answerable to the lord bishop and his ordinaries for all that goes on in the church and its precincts, and also, where the rectors are not resident, for the light for Candlemas. With regard to lights, we want decent provision to be made in churches at the celebration of mass, and two wax candles for the elevation of the sacrament, and a wax paschal candle. We do not want to be lacking lights for this in any church of our diocese on feast days. And if this is not enough, the rector shall help, as is set out in the statutes of our predecessors. We also ordain that no church or chapel shall be built without our consent, nor, if it is built, shall any services be rashly celebrated without our authority, for according to the canons, this is profanation.

4. *Of building on church land*

Also every parish church shall have a properly built dwelling nearby, in which the bishop, archdeacon and their ordinaries can be received and entertained, and above all, this should be done in churches appropriated to religious houses exempt from the jurisdiction of the ordinaries, within a year of the publication of the present statutes, at the expense of rectors and vicars, who shall pay procurations according to their portions. And rectors and vicars shall be compelled to do this by the sequestration of the fruits of their benefices after a set time limit.

5. *Of outside clerics who come from elsewhere*

Under pain of anathema, we strictly forbid any priest of another diocese who comes into ours, to presume to make his abode here or to contract with anyone to

cuiquam ad celebrandum pro vivis vel defunctis se ibidem obligare, nisi prius nobis vel nostris ordinariis in nostra absentia honeste et rite pervenerit, ostendens nobis vel nostris deputatis instrumenta publica vel testes idoneos de veritate suae ordinationis et conversationis. Et quia nolumus poena istius statuti ligari [ignorantes] decrevimus vicarios sacerdotes ad quos tales declinaverint, eis ostendere praesens statutum, et certificare debere, ne de praemissis se ignorantia excusent. Hoc idem statuimus de quaestoribus aliunde venientibus, ut non ad[13v]mittantur sine nostris literis specialibus et commendat[it]iis in quacunque parte nostrae dioecesis, sub poena decem solidorum sterlingorum. Et si nostri vicarii negligentes inveniantur in ostensione nostri praesentis statuti facienda praemissis personis infra octo dies postquam ad eos pervenerint, suspendantur a divinis, quousque congrue satisfaciant de negligentia et violatione nostri mandati, his adiicientes ut clerici, maxime in sacris ordinibus constituti, nisi causa peregrinationis, vel alia urgente necessitate non[118] in tabernis comedant aut ultra unam vicem stantes bibant, nec intersint publicis morando potationibus aut societatibus, vel aliis ioculationibus utendis locis publicis. Quod si fecerint ab ingressu ecclesiae et divinis extunc se noverint virtute istius constitutionis fore suspensos per tres menses sequentes, nisi nobis vel ordinariis nostris de tali transgressione reatum suum infra dictum tempus ostenderint, [et] congruam poenam inde peregerint.

6. *Poena absentium ab ecclesiis diebus Dominicis*

Item statuimus ut in qualibet parochiali ecclesia pronuntietur[119] parochianis ut de qualibet domo vir vel mulier vel uterque eorum quolibet die Dominica veniant ad ecclesiam audituri divina [14r] et praecepta ecclesiae, nisi rationabiliter sint excusandi, quam excusationem non requisiti ostendant rectori vel eius vices gerenti, in primo suo adventu ad eandem, sicuti catholicam voluerint evitare ultionem, et nihilominus pro qualibet transgressione levetur [poena] trium solidorum et quatuor denariorum de quolibet qui consuetudinarie[120] sic se absentando subtraxerit a proprio ovili ut inter existentes ibi adhibeatur omnis humanitas, prout tangitur in concilio Lugdunensi 'De immunitate[121] ecclesiarum', capitulo 'Domum tuam decet sanctitudo', libro sexto.[122]

Expliciunt additiones Willelmi Russell.

---

[118]MSS: 'etiam'.
[119]Dugdale. The MSS have 'pronuntiatur'.
[120]MSS: 'consuetudinem'.
[121]MSS: 'eminitate'.
[122]Lyon II, 1274, c. 25; VI, 3.23.2 (Fr II, 1061-2).

celebrate for living or dead persons unless he has first approached us, or in our absence our ordinaries, properly and duly, producing before us or our deputies public instruments or appropriate witnesses of his ordination and good character. And since we do not want men who are unaware of this statute to be bound by its penalty, we have decreed that vicars who are visited by such persons should show them this statute, and make it clear to them, lest they should excuse themselves as ignorant of these matters. We also ordain this about collectors of alms coming from elsewhere, that they are not to be admitted in any part of our diocese without our special letters of recommendation, under penalty of ten shillings sterling. And if our vicars are found to be negligent in showing this our statute to these people within eight days of their arrival, they shall be suspended from divine office until they have made appropriate satisfaction for their negligence and violation of our mandate. We add that clerks, especially those in holy orders, are not to eat in taverns unless they are on a journey or for other pressing need, nor linger there to take more than one drink, nor attend public drinking parties, assemblies or merry-makings in public places. If they do so, they shall know that they will be suspended from entering the church and from divine office for three months following, by virtue of this statute, unless within that period they confess their guilt and do appropriate penance for their fault to us or to our ordinaries.

6. *The penalty for those who absent themselves from church on Sundays*

We also ordain that in every parish church it shall be announced to the parishioners that the husband or wife of every household, or both of them, should come to church every Sunday to attend divine service and hear the teaching of the church, unless they have reasonable excuse, which excuse they must disclose, unasked, to the rector or his deputy when they next come to church, if they wish to escape the vengeance of the catholic church. Nevertheless, a fine of three shillings and fourpence shall be imposed for each offence on anyone who by habitual absence withdraws from his own sheepfold, just as among the churchgoers every kind of loving kindness may be practised, as is mentioned in the council of Lyon on the immunity of churches, in the chapter: 'Holiness becomes thy house', in the sixth book of the decretals.

Here end William Russell's additions.

Confirmation of the church's liberties by Thomas, earl of Derby, Lord Stanley, 28 March 1505

[14v] Confirmatio ecclesiarum et terrarum atque libertatum data, concessa et facta per nobilissimum Dominum Thomam, comitem Derbei, Dominum Stanley, ac dominum Insulae de Mann et insularum, Huano Sodorensi episcopo suisque successoribus.[123]

Universis sanctae matris ecclesiae filiis, praesentes literas inspecturis vel audituris, Thomas Dei gratia rex Mannae et insularum, comes Derbei and Dominus Stanley, salutem in Domino sempiternam. Universitati vestrae innotescimus, quod nos pro salute animae nostrae et animarum antecessorum nostrorum atque omnium fidelium defunctorum, concessimus et dedimus dilecto nobis in Christo, reverendo in Christo patri ac domino, Domino Huano permissione divina Sodorensi[124] episcopo moderno, in puram et perpetuam eleemosynam ad mensam suam episcopalem, omnes ecclesias, terras, decimas, ac possessiones quas antecessores nostri reges et domini Mannae, ecclesiae Sodorensi et episcopatui eiusdem dederunt, concesserunt et confirmaverunt. Videlicet:

ecclesiam cathedralem Sancti Germani in Holme Sodor vel Peel vocatam,

ecclesiamque Sancti Patricii ibidem et locum praefatum in quo praefatae ecclesiae sitae sunt,

et etiam ecclesiam Sancti Bradani

et ecclesias Sancti Patricii de [15r] Jurby

cum ecclesia Sancti Croriae

cum omnibus et singulis ecclesiarum praedictarum decimis, primitiis, fructibus, emolumentis, obventionibus, libertatibus, commoditatibus et pertinentiis universis, et tertiam partem decimarum de omnibus ecclesiis de Manne, confirmantes eis:

tertianam plenae villae de Kirkby,

propinquiorem ecclesiam Sancti Bradani cum terra Sancti Bradani,

et tertianam plenae villae de Kirkmarona [Kirk Marown],

terras de Cullusshy,

de Glenfaba,

de Fotysdeyn,

de Balymary,

de baculo Sancti Patricii

et de Holme Town, cum piscariis, braciniis, consuetudinibus, ancoragiis et vertenariis;

tertianam de Balycem,

de Knokcroker,

---

[123]Thomas III, Lord Stanley was lord of Man from 1504 to 1521. The bishop was Hugh Blackleach (1487-1512?). The place names are those identified by J. Kneen, *The place-names of the Isle of Man* (Douglas, 1925), as modified by G. Broderick, *Placenames of the Isle of Man* (multivolume, Tübingen, 1994-).

[124]MS: 'Sodoriensi'.

Confirmation of the church's liberties by Thomas, earl of Derby, Lord Stanley, 28 March 1505

The confirmation of the liberties of churches and lands given, granted and made by the most noble Lord Thomas, earl of Derby, Lord Stanley, and lord of the Isle of Man and of the isles, to Hugh, bishop of Sodor and his successors.

To all the children of holy mother church who shall read or hear the present letters, Thomas, by the grace of God king of Man and the isles, earl of Derby and Lord Stanley, eternal greeting in the Lord. We make known to all of you that for the salvation of our soul and of the souls of our predecessors, and of all the faithful departed, we have granted and given to our beloved in Christ, the reverend father in Christ and lord, Lord Hugh, by divine permission the present bishop of Sodor, as a pure and perpetual offering to his episcopal table, all the churches, lands, tithes and possessions which our predecessors the kings and lords of Man gave, granted and confirmed to the church of Sodor and its bishopric. To wit:

the cathedral church of St German in Holme Sodor, or Peel,

and the church of St Patrick there and the aforesaid place in which the aforesaid churches are situated,

and also the church of St Braddan [Brendan]

and the churches of St Patrick of Jurby

with the church of Keeil Crogh [in Kirk Patrick]

with all and several the tithes of the aforesaid churches, first-fruits, revenues, emoluments, receipts, liberties, commodities and everything belonging to them, and a third part of the tithes of all the churches of Man, confirming to them:

a third of the whole town of Kirkby [in Kirk Braddan],

the nearer church of St Braddan with the land of St Braddan,

and a third of the entire town of Kirk Marown,

the lands of Cooillingill [in Kirk Marown],

of Glenfaba,

of Bawshen [in Kirk Marown],

of [Ballamore in Kirk Patrick],

of the staffland of St Patrick

and of Holme Town, with its fisheries, malthouses, customs, anchor fees and tolls,

a third of Ballacurn [in Ballaugh],

of Cronk y chrogherey [in Kirk Michael],

et de Balybruste,
de Jurby,
de Balycane,
de Brottby
et de Ramsey.
Terris etiam ecclesiae Sanctae Trinitatis in Lezayre,
Sanctae Mariae de Balylagh [Ballaugh],
Sancti Maghaldi [Maughold] et Sancti Michaelis adiacentis,
et unciatam terrae Sancti Columbae quae vocatur Here [Arbory].

Necnon omnimodas libertates antiquitus eidem ecclesiae concessas, curiam suam de vita et membris, de furto, homicidio, et omnibus sceleribus; et quod habeant incarcerationem et incarceratorum evasionem, et furcas seu patibulum super terram suam, et quod tam clerici quam laici [15v] in praediis et tenementis ecclesiasticis commorantes in curia domini episcopi in foro ecclesiastico agant et respondeant, et quod liberi sint ab omni servitio saeculari, exactione et demanda, ac forisfactura seu merciamento. Et si aliqua causa non ecclesiastica inter homines nostros et homines dicti episcopi seu successorum nostrorum vertatur, actor forisfactus rei forum sequatur. Dedimus etiam et confirmavimus eidem episcopo et successoribus suis omne genus 'le wreke' et terram ubicunque et undecunque episcopo per Mannam venientibus, una cum villa de Kyrcrest iuxta Ramsey integre cum clericis et laicis, braciniis et aliis pertinentibus, sine aliquo retinemento, una cum medietate piscariae ibidem in Mirescogh. Et quod idem episcopus, successores sui, clerici et firmarii reredituum ecclesiasticorum habeant liberam potestatem de decimis suis, et ceteris rebus clericorum et laicorum in terris ecclesiasticis commorantium, vendendis, disponendis, ubicunque viderint expedire, tam infra terram nostram de Mann quam extra, sine contradictione nostra, seu haeredum nostrorum vel successorum nostrorum, ac etiam minera plumbi vel ferri quam invenire poterit per totam terram suam in Mann; habenda et tenenda et possidenda praedicto Huano suisque succe[16r]ssoribus episcopis Manniae in perpetuum, adeo libere, quiete et honorifice sicut aliqua eleemosyna liberius et quietius ad quamcunque mensam episcopalem confertur et appropriatur, per reges vel dominos quoscunque, temporibus perpetuis duratura. In cuius rei testimonium praesentes literas sigillo nostro signatas fieri fecimus patentes. Datum apud Lathum vicesimo octavo die mensis Martii anno Domini millesimo quingentesimo quinto.

and of Ballabrooie [in Lezayre],
of Jurby,
of Ballacain [in Ballaugh],
of Brottby [in Kirk German],
and of Ramsey.
Also the lands of the church of the Holy Trinity in Lezayre,
of St Mary in Ballaugh,
St Maughold and Keeil Vichal alongside it,
and a twelfth of the land of St Columba which is called Arbory.

Likewise all the liberties anciently granted to the same church, its own court for its life and members, dealing with robbery, homicide and all crimes, and the right to imprison and release the imprisoned, the right to dig or plough their land. Likewise, both clergy and laity who dwell on church farms and tenancies shall act in and be answerable to the ecclesiastical court, and they shall be free of any secular service, exaction and demand, as well as any forfeiture or amercement. And if any case which is not ecclesiastical arises between our men and the men of the said bishop, or of our successors, the defendant shall follow the jurisdiction in the matter. We have also given and confirmed to the same bishop and his successors every kind of wreck and land throughout Man, wherever and from wherever they may come to the bishop, along with the town of Kyrcrest by Ramsey, complete with the clergy and laity, its malthouses and other things belonging to it, without any exception, along with half the fishery there in Mirescogh [Mooragh?]. And that the same bishop, his successors, clerics and lessees of church revenues shall have full power over their tithes and other things belonging to clergy and lay people on church lands, to sell them or dispose of them as they see fit, both within our land of Man and elsewhere, without any veto from us or our heirs and successors, and also whatever lead or iron ore which may be found anywhere on their lands in Man shall be had, held and possessed by the aforesaid Hugh and his successors the bishops of Man for ever, to remain for all time freely, peacefully and honourably, as an offering more freely and peacefully given and set aside for any bishop's table whatsoever. In witness whereof we have caused these our letters patent to be signed with our seal. Given at Latham the twenty-eighth day of March in the year of our Lord one thousand five hundred and five.

THE BOOK OF SPIRITUAL LAWS AND CUSTOMS, 1577[125]

I. The clergy's right to a fishing boat

1. First, that the bishops shall have their herring scout and their fishing boat, freely and frankly, without any tithes paying, wheresoever they land in this isle. In like manner had the abbot, the priors, the archdeacon.

2. Also, all parsons, vicars of the thirds or pension instituted, shall always choose their fishing boat at Easter time, and their scout at herring fishing time, whether their fishing be about this land or elsewhere.

II. Probate of wills and administration of the goods of those who have died intestate

3/2. Also, that everyone that dieth intestate, that the bishop or his vicars-general shall constitute, and ordain his children legitimately begotten, to be jointly executors, provided always those being unmarried, and those that are married, their dowry cutteth them off from having any further portion of goods.[126]

4/3. Also, if any make their testament and leave not six pence legacy unto their children unmarried (legitimately begotten) or the value thereof, that then the ordinary may lawfully make him or her executors with the rest.[127]

5/4. Also, if any die intestate, having no children legitimately begotten, but only base children, then the ordinary shall make and ordain his next of kindred, both of father's and mother's side, to be lawful executors, and the base begotten to be rewarded of charity, at the discretion of the ordinary.[128]

6/5. Also, that every man and wife which depart this life upon the south side of the isle do stand in one effect, that is to say, the man to have the one half and the wife the other half, provided always that the debts temporal be paid out of the whole, and the debts spiritual out of the dead his part.[129]

---

[125]M. A. Mills, *The ancient ordinances and statute laws of the Isle of Man* (Douglas, 1821), pp. 46-54; John F. Gill, ed., *The statutes of the Isle of Man* (6 vols., London, 1883), I, 40-7; Manx National Heritage Library, MS 151A, pp. 1-21. The last of these texts contains additional material which was not included in the official statutes, and also numbers them differently. Both the numbers and the extra material are indicated by the use of *italics*. These statutes seem to have been compiled by a church synod which met in conjunction with the session of Tynwald on 13 July 1577. They were all finally repealed (except 54) by the pre-reversement written laws (ascertainment) act, 1978.

[126]Repealed by statute of 1777, c. 14.

[127]Repealed by the wills act, 1869, s. 26.

[128]Repealed by the statute of 1777, c. 14.

[129]Repealed by the statute of 1777, c. 13.

7/6. Also, upon the north side of the isle, in case a man or wife depart this life having no children or issue, the wife hath the one half and may bequeath it to whom she will; and in like manner it is upon the south side of this isle. But in case there be any issue or children, lawfully begotten, then if the man depart, the goods movable are divided into three parts, viz., one part to the executors, another part to the dead, and the third part to the wife. And of all goods movable, not having any life, the wife hath the half on the north side.[130]

8/7. Also, if either father or mother depart, having children, if the said children be of years of discretion, that is to say, fourteen years of age, they may divide goods either with father or mother, and may repair to whom they will.[131]

9/8. Also, if there be but one child betwixt man and wife, the father's kindred that have the custody of the aforesaid child and goods until fourteen years of age, except the father make any other order by his last will, and leave the custody of the said child and goods unto the tuition of any other, then that to be observed. And if there be two children, the mother shall have the one, that is to say, the eldest; and if the mother die before the child come to years of discretion, she may leave the custody of the said child to whom she thinketh good, and the next of kin of the father's side and of the mother's side supervisors.

10/9. Also, if either father or mother depart, having children not come to years of discretion, having left executors, and if any of them depart, the ordinary shall make the rest, being alive, executors; and in case all die under age, then the goods shall return to the kindred next from whence it came.[132]

11/10. Also, if any man marry a wife and the wife depart before a twelvemonth and a day, the man shall have none of the marriage goods, and in like manner, if the man depart before a twelvemonth and a day, the wife can have no part or portion of his goods, except it be given by gift or bequeathed by the will of either party; if there be no will or testament made, then the goods to return to the next of kin.[133]

12/11. Also, if any do remove from one parish to another, and if the cock crow thrice, they remaining there three nights and three days after removing, that then the person departed shall pay all spiritual duties to that same church within the same parish he doth remove unto.

13/12. Also, the ordinary hath for the probation of a rich man's will twelve pence, and for a poor man's will four pence, as is expressed in the perpetual indentures betwixt the clergy and the temporalty. But whereas rich men do depart intestate, and the ordinary to make a perfect will according to the custom of the country, it hath been accustomed, the ordinary to have three shillings four pence for his pains.[134]

---

[130]Repealed by the statute of 1777, c. 13.
[131]Repealed by the statute of 1777, c. 14 and by the act of 1852.
[132]Repealed by the statute of 1777, c. 14 and by the act of 1852.
[133]Repealed by the statute of 1777, c. 13.
[134]Repealed by the statute of 1748, c. 3.

14/*13*. Also, as concerning corse-presents or mortuaries are taken as it is expressed in the indenture betwixt the clergy and the temporalty; which indenture is agreed to stand for ever, and all under fourteen years of age pay no corse-presents.[135]

15/*14*. Also, legacies are to be paid within fourteen days after the probation of the will.

III. Tithes

16/*15*. Also, that all tithe corn be received by the tenth stoke for casting the tenth sheaf in the rean or furrow was never used nor heard of, and for carrying of the tithe corn away, the parson or proctor is at liberty to carry it the next way, keeping the husbandman harmless, making the ditch in the same sort, or as able as it was, or as he found it.[136]

17/*16*. Also, that no husbandman do lead any corn or hay before sufficient warning and knowledge be given to the parson, vicar or proctor, when that the corn is sufficient dry and able to be stacked, and the hay also.[137]

18/*17*. Also, if any man convey, purloin or hide any corn in houses or elsewhere to defraud the tithes, that then the parson, vicar or proctor to be restored threefold; but in case they need to thresh any corn for their necessity or need, then to take with them two honest men, which will testify the tithe thereof to be truly paid.[138]

19/*18*. Also, if any do lead or stack their corn in contumation, or not agreeing with the parson, vicar or proctor, for the tithe thereof, that them the sumner at the appointment of the ordinary, with two honest neighbours or more, have used to cast down their stacks and take forth their tithes; and the said husbandman shall make all charges for casting down the stacks and making up again; and further to be punished at the discretion of the ordinary for their crime.[139]

20/*19*. Also, all tithe flax and hemp is to be brought to the parish church, with the seed thereof.[140]

21/*20*. Also, that everyone do bring into their parish church their tithe cheese and their butter truly; that is to say, once every month the twenty-four hours milk made in a cheese or butter, beginning in the month of May, and so of the months of June, July, August, September and October; and in case any do make cheese or butter and do not bring it in as aforesaid, in case they be searched to be found withal, then to forfeit all the cheese and butter that is so taken.[141]

---

[135]Repealed by the act of 1643, s. 5.
[136]Tithes payable to the bishop and clergy, and certain impropriate tithes, commuted by the act of 1839.
[137]Ditto.
[138]Ditto.
[139]Ditto.
[140]Ditto.
[141]Repealed by the act of 1643, s. 6.

22/21. Also, those that depose that they have neither butter nor cheese made within any of the said months, that then if they have one milk cow, to pay two pence, out of every farrow cow four pence, out of eight sheep two pence, and out of four goats, two pence.[142]

23/22. Also the sumner hath for his pains and duty doing one principal cheese; in like manner hath the parson, clerk, vicar or curate, for writing all things orderly belonging to the tithe cheese.[143]

24/23. Also, that everyone do bring into their folds all their sheep and lambs at such time as the parson, vicar or proctor shall appoint, either in the latter end of the month of May or else in the month of June, to pay truly their tithe lamb and wool without any fraud or deceit; that is to say, out of eight one lamb, and so out of nine, ten, eleven or twelve, but one lamb; provided always that if the husbandman pay one lamb or more, he shall have choice of two lambs, and then the proctor where he pleaseth, of the rest.[144]

25/24. Also, in case the husbandman hath but five lambs, then the husbandman shall choose one, and the next to the best; the proctor shall praise and the husbandman shall give or take; and if there be but two or three lambs, then Ob.[145] out of every lamb.[146]

26/25. Also, everyone that hath wild sheep or lambs that cannot be brought to fold, then the proctor hath used to depose them upon a book what wool and lambs they have, and so to pay truly the tithe thereof.[147]

27/26. Also, whoever doth convey or hide his lambs from place to place and from parish to parish, for deceiving of the church, if it can be so proved, then restitution to be made threefold.[148]

28/27. Also, that all proctors ought at Martinmas time [11 November] to put in a book all small tithes within the parishes, that is to say, purrs, calves and colts, and to receive them from the husbandman at Easter time, and out of eight, nine or ten, one purr, and out of twelve but one purr; and in like manner of calves and colts, provided always that the husbandman shall choose one or two out of the whole of the best when he payeth one or more, either purrs, calves or colts.[149]

29/28. Also, when any man hath but five purrs, calves or colts, then the husbandman shall have one choice, and then the proctor to praise the next, and the husbandman to take or give; and if the husbandman have but three calves, he shall

---

[142]Ditto.
[143]Ditto.
[144]Tithes payable to the bishop and clergy and certain impropriate tithes commuted by the act of 1839.
[145]'Obolus', halfpenny.
[146]Commuted by the act of 1839.
[147]Ditto.
[148]Ditto.
[149]Ditto.

pay out of every one Ob.,[150] out of three colts, 5d. And whereas the proctor hath not had for six or seven lambs but half a lamb, then he may take out of four lambs half; in like manner of purrs, calves and colts.[151]

30/29. Also concerning tithe geese, they are to be taken after the same order, and most commonly taken in the month of December.[152]

30. And as for tithe eggs, they are to be taken at Easter, and are the beginning of the annual fruits next ensuing; for every hen one egg, and for the only cock, two eggs.[153]

31. Also, concerning honey and tithe wax; if there be eight, nine or ten hives of that year, then the husbandman shall have two choices, or out of twelve; and the proctor shall have the third choice hive for tithe. And if in case there be but five hives, the husbandman shall have one choice, and the proctor shall praise the next choice, and the husbandman to give or take; but when there is but two or three hives, then after the wax and honey is purified, they shall take the tithe thereof justly and truly. And whereas the proctor hath not had out of six or seven hives but half a hive; then he may take out of four hives half a hive.[154]

32. Also, every master of every fishing boat shall cause all the fish to be bought above the full sea mark, and there pay truly the tithe. And if they will not truly pay, then the master shall make five shares of all his fish, and the proctor shall appoint to be divided what share he will; the master must divide; the proctor shall choose in that order, because it hath no life.[155]

33. Also, when herring fishing is, the proctor shall take his tithe where the boat doth ground and land; if the boats land in another parish than their own, they pay half tithe there for the landing, except it be of such boats as are in the first article specified. Bishop, archdeacon, or parson instituted, their boats are free, and pay no tithings.[156]

34. And if there be any salmon fishes taken, either in salt water or fresh water, the tithe thereof is to be paid.[157]

35. Also, all those boats that fish, either in England or in Ireland, either for herring or gray fish, is to agree for half the tithe at their coming home, with their own parson, vicar or proctor; and in case they bring any fresh herrings, not having paid half tithe there, they must pay whole tithe here.[158]

36. Also, whereas the sumner, parson and clerk take pains in gathering wool and lamb, having with them one horse apiece, and in like manner one sack for carriage of the wool; then either of them to have one choice lamb and one fleece of wool paid out of the tithe.[159]

---

[150]'Obolus', halfpenny.
[151]Commuted by the act of 1839.
[152]Ditto.
[153]Ditto.
[154]Ditto.
[155]Ditto.
[156]Ditto.
[157]Ditto.
[158]Ditto.
[159]Ditto.

37. Also, as concerning the sumner's duty of corn, he must have a band of three lengths of three principal corns' portion alike paid from every husbandman, and he must call within the church with the advice of the vicar or curate all such things as he is requested of the parish that is gone or lost, and ought to stand at the chancel door at time of service to whip and beat all the dogs.

IV. Legal fees and rights

38. Also, when the sumner is required by the ordinary to bring any offender to prison, he hath for his pains fourpence, and in like manner the porter fourpence of the same offender; and when any is irregular or disobedient unto the sumner and ordinary, then the ordinary hath used to send for aid unto the constable of the castle or of the Peel, who presently ought to send a soldier to bring such offender to the bishop his prison; and the same soldier to have for his pains of every such offender at the discretion of the ordinary.[160]

39. Also all fornicators and such as are presented by the chapter-quest, the ordinary doth receive a penny a piece for entering and putting down the names, and all such as are found guilty are punished and enjoined to penance at the discretion of the ordinary; all such offenders found guilty have been accustomed to be taken bound in a penalty of monies according to the ability of the offender, for ever committing fornication afterwards. And if the said penalty be lost, then to be used at the discretion of the ordinary, weighing the ability of contrition of the party; provided always that adulterers shall be sharply punished at the discretion of the ordinary.

40. Also if any Scottish man or Irishman or such alienate persons do dwell within this isle, not being sworn to the lord and the country, and so depart this life, they have no authority to make any will or bequeath any goods to any man, for my lord is wholly their executor, and my lord to pay all spiritual duties.

39/41. Also, if in case any do bequeath a corb or heirloom for a legacy, the same shall not be given, but the value thereof with discretion.

V. Other dues

40/42. Also, it is accustomed that all men of occupation, what science soever they be of, is to pay for the tithe of the same twopence yearly, although he use it but three times in the year; provided always that all apprentices, during the time of their apprenticeship, pay nothing.

41/43. Also, all persons that are married and unmarried, that have received the communion before, pay twopence every Easter for four offering days; but in case that be the first time that any person doth receive, he payeth but an Ob.,[161] which the curate must have, and he shall examine all such of their belief.

---

[160]Repealed by the statute of 1813, c. 2.
[161]See footnote 150.

VI. Parish clerks

42/*44*. Also, every parish that hath a liberty, that they may choose their clerk,[162] but the ordinary must authorize, accept and allow of him to be sufficient and able for that office; and in every time of visitation and other business, first the parish must send to the clerk, and the clerk come to the priest and wait upon him.

43/*45*. Also, the clerk's due his standing wages is a groat out of every plough, if the ploughs plough but three furrows within the year, and those that have no ploughs and keep smoke, payeth annually twopence.

44/*46*. Also, the clerk must have of every man that departeth this life, being able to pay, a whole corse present twenty-one pence or else his apparel, as was used in old time; and of a woman seventeen pence or else such duties as were used in old time; and of the poor, all debts being paid, to be reasonably agreed withal.

45/*47*. Also, the clerk's silver on the south side of the isle is eleven pence and the headpenny, of the which twelve pence the curate hath seven pence, the parish clerk threepence and the parson's clerk twopence, and on the north side fifteen pence.

46/*48*. Also, in case a poor man or woman depart and there is not wherewithal to pay the clerk's silver, then the clerk shall have no duty, but the duty to be sold to pay the headpenny and clerk's silver; and if any want, the next of kin, both of father's and mother's side, legitimately begotten, is to make it out; because if the party which departed were wealthy and made no will, they should be his executors.

VII. Glebe lands

47/*49*. Also, all glebe lands pertaining to spiritual men, that is to say, bishop, archdeacon, parson, vicar, curate or clerk, if the executors or assignees do sow any of the said glebe land before Easter day, they shall have all such corn as is sown, with the profit thereof, and shall be at liberty to reap the said corn and carry it away.[163]

48/*50*. Also, if either bishop, archdeacon, farmer, parson or vicar, having leases, do depart this life after twelve of the clock past upon Easter day, their executors or assignees have ever been accustomed to have and enjoy all the profits of that year until Easter day next ensuing, and shall find and see the cure served and discharged.[164]

49/*51*. Also, whereas parsons and proctors having tithes being far off, and cannot conveniently bring them home, it hath been accustomed to draw and stack the same in the husbandman's haggard without any trouble or let.

---

[162]Repealed by the church act, 1880, s. 34.
[163]Repealed by the act of 1844.
[164]Ditto.

VIII. Witchcraft

50/52. Also, all those which are suspected of sorcery or witchcraft and are presented by the chapter-quest, then the ordinary doth examine all such causes; and finding any suspicion, shall appoint another jury of honest, probable men within the same parish, and doth commit the party suspected in the meantime to the bishop his prison; and all the offences and crimes the jury do find or can prove, the ordinary shall write; and if the jury can bring or prove any notorious fact or crime done by the said person, then the ordinary doth deliver the same person out of the bishop's prison to my lord's gaol and court.

IX. Legal fees

51/53. Also, it hath been accustomed the ordinary to take for every citation sixpence, for every suspension eighteen pence and for excommunication two shillings sixpence;[165] and if the excommunicated will not appear, it hath been used to send for a soldier to bring the offender to the bishop's prison.

52/54. Also, when any great offence is worthy of excommunication, then the ordinary hath been used to take for the excommunication, absolution and receiving all such persons into the church again, tenpence.[166]

X. Dilapidations

53/55. Also, all parishioners are bound to maintain and keep up the body of the church within and without, with all ornaments, books and other necessaries; and the person is bound to repair and keep in good order the chancel.

XI. Churchwardens

54/56. **Also, all churchwardens must** be appointed and sworn once a year to **see good orders kept in the church and churchyard,**[167] their churchyard ditch to be well made, and to make a true and just account to their parishioners four times in the year.

---

[165]Repealed by the statute of 1748, c. 3.
[166]Repealed by the statute of 1743, c. 3.
[167]The words in bold type are still in force (2002). The other words in this section were omitted by the statute law revision measure (Isle of Man) 1994, schedule 2.

XII. Imprisonment of Irishmen and Scots

55/57. Also, when any Irishman or Scotchman is found irregular, or hath committed any notorious crime, they shall not be committed to the bishop his prison within the Peel, but shall be committed to the Moar's[168] Tower within the castle, or elsewhere by discretion.

XIII. Parish administration

56/58. Also, all curates hired from Easter to Easter, or longer, shall give a quarter of a year's warning before Easter day to his master, in case his will be to depart and go away from him; and in like manner the master shall give a quarter of a year's warning to his curate in case he will put him away; provided always that the ordinary shall place and displace all such curates at his discretion.

57/59. Also, it hath been accustomed when the ordinary sends any citation abroad for the keeping of spiritual courts, chapters or any other weighty matters, then the ordinary to send to the general sumner, and he with all speed to send them abroad.

60. Also it is accustomed that at the appointment of the ordinary, the general sumner or his factor shall take up all stresses for matters spiritual as just occasion shall require.

58/61. Also, if any parson, vicar of the third or pension do depart, and no other be installed within six months from Easter next ensuing the departure, the bishop or ordinary shall take it in lapse, if it be not in the gift of the lord of this land or isle.

59/62. Also, it was accustomed that all instituted vicars of pension, heretofore having five marks stipend, should have four nobles in tithes of the old sum at the least.

63. Also if any spiritual man in orders do depart they ought to pay no spiritual duties, neither corpse present, clerk-silver or clerk duties.

Compiled by:[169]

Hugh Holland, archdeacon.[170]
Henry Gell, vicar-general.[171]
John Moore, [vicar-general], parson, [rector of Bride].[172]
Donald Crahan, vicar [of Michael].[173]
Edward Baguley, vicar [of Santan].[174]

---

[168] A moar was a local parish officer who acted as a bailiff. It was he who collected rents from tenants and delivered them to the lord's receiver. See Dickinson, *Lordship of Man*, pp. 51-2.
[169] Preserved in Manx National Heritage Library, MS 151A, p. 22.
[170] (1577-87).
[171] Vicar of Onchan (1575-80).
[172] (1576-82).
[173] (1571-85).
[174] (1576-97).

William Crow, vicar [of Braddan].[175]
Alexander Stevenson, vicar [of Patrick].[176]
John Christian, vicar [of Jurby].[177]
William Norris, curate [of Lezayre].[178]
Philip Hogget, vicar [of German].[179]
John Cosnahan, clerk.
Edward Callow, clerk, [vicar of Arbory].[180]
Stephen Donald Callow, curate [of Ballaugh].[181]
Thomas Casement, clerk.
John Stevenson, clerk, [vicar of Maughold].[182]

Explanation of the sixty-first statute:[183]

Being required by the lieutenant to explain the sixty-first statute in the presence of the subscribed persons, we say that there is no lapse against the lord, for the words of the statute extendeth not to any church that is in the lord's gift.

William Norris, vicar-general.
William Crow, vicar-general.

[175](1577-94).
[176](1576-85).
[177](1577-1609).
[178](1575-1603).
[179](1575-85).
[180](1577-80).
[181](1577-80).
[182](1576-80).
[183]These laws were confirmed at Castle Rushen on 2 April 1610 (Manx National Heritage Library, MS 151A, pp. 23-4), when this addition was made.

SPIRITUAL ORDINANCES OF 1594[184]

Delivered the twenty-fourth of June 1594 at the Tynwald then holden, to the vicars-general, by Randolph Stanley, esquire, the captain of this isle; which articles are to be inquired of at the next consistory court to be holden within this isle.

1. First, that they impanel in the several sheadings jurors to inquire into all offences committed against the spiritual laws, and the same jurors to be chosen of such as be of the best ability and of most sufficiency to discharge the same well.

2. Item, that they take order the queen's majesty's injunctions to be read in their churches.

3. Item, that they inquire [of] and present, if there be any in the isle do use witchcraft and sorcery.

4. Item, that they inquire of and present all adulterers, fornicators, blasphemers, drunkards and such like.

5. Item, that they inquire of and present all such as carry bells or banners before the dead, or pray upon the graves of the dead.

6. Item, that they inquire of and present all such as shall keep any market upon the Sabbath Day, or otherwise profane the same.

7. Item, that they inquire of and present if there be any person or persons within this isle that refuse to come to the church to hear divine service, or to receive the blessed sacrament of the Lord's Supper.

[184]Gill, *Statutes*, I, 66.

THE CUSTOMARY LAWS OF 1598[185]

24 July 1598. Names of the subscribers:

Thomas Samsbury, deemster.[186]
William Lucas, receiver.[187]
Henry Halsall.[189]
John Stevenson.
John Norris.
George Stanley.
John Lucas.
Christopher Bridson.
Charles Moore.
Thomas Norris.
John Tumman [Taubman].

James Banks.
Ewan Christian, Little Milntown.[188]
Edward Fletcher.
Nicholas Moore.
John Curghey, deemster.[190]
Charles Tumman [Taubman].
Robert Stevenson.
Thomas Moore.
Cath Moore.
Robert Lucas.
Robert Clarke.[191]

1. Of prescription and tithe exempt

All demesne chattels in the demesnes [and] granges which abbeys keep for their own provisions and glebe, are not tithable.

No customs can prevail for tithing for other farmers.

A prescription if it be just, of time out of mind, without interruption or alteration, bonae fidei, it must prevail.

The statute law of England is no rule to direct us in judgment here, except such as the lord and the whole body of the island hath received for laws. For if so, then things of greatest importance for the inheritor were altered. At the suppression, men to whom the statute did pertain and knew of it must have been put to prove time out of mind after the suppression, but now to put them to prove it, which they had no cause to take knowledge of it, is an impossibility in my opinion. John Sodorensis.[192]

---

[185]Douglas, Manx National Heritage Library, MS 151A, pp. 25-31. The text contains various additions down to 1623.
[186](1585-1626). There were two deemsters, representing the north and south sides of the island respectively. They acted as justices of the peace. See Dickinson, *Lordship of Man*, pp. 43-5.
[187]Receiver at Castle Rushen from 1594 to about 1613.
[188]In kind. He was a deemster from 1605 to 1655.
[189]Lord's attorney (*c.* 1579-1600).
[190](1595-1605).
[191]This name is followed by the incomplete note: 'The old rent of this tithe the gra...'.
[192]John Meyrick was bishop of Sodor and Man from 15 April 1576 until his death on 7 November 1599.

2. *Of the fifteen episcopal causes*

Episcopal causes merely belonging to the ordinary's jurisdiction to be censured, being fifteen in number, exempt from the archdeacon's jurisdiction by ancient laws of this isle as anciently the vicars-general have received them from one another, from time to time, to be preserved, and now set down by William Norris, vicar-general.

1. The censuring of any of the clergy for any default.
2. Adultery.
3. Excommunication against any offender.
4. Mitigation of fines.
5. All licences of marriages.
6. All divorcements betwixt married couples.
7. The granting of administration and the punishment of adultery.
8. Incestuous persons.
9. Witchcraft.
10. The calling a man a dog or a woman a bitch.
11. The censuring of fornication upon relapse and the second or third time; also all other offenders upon relapse.
12. The effusion of blood in church or in churchyard.
13. Profanation of the Sabbath or holy days.
14. The censuring of parties for not receiving the communion in or at their parish church, upon any contempt.
15. The committing of any offender into Saint German's prison, it being the lord bishop's own prison.[193]

3. *Children taking away their parents' goods*

Apud ecclesiam Sanctae Trinitatis in Lezayre, 28 February 1602 [1603].

Whereas heretofore it hath been used that if any manchild did take away any part of his father's or mother's goods deceased, wilfully before the chapter court day, the customary and ordinary of law of this isle was and is solely to restore the same, upon his corporal oath, without suit or trouble.

4. *Negligent churchwardens*

Churchwardens or chapter-quest, neglecting presenting palpable and open crimes, to stand at the market cross in the four towns of this isle upon the market days or court days, with a paper upon their breasts showing the cause.[194]

---

[193]The crypt of St German's cathedral was used for this purpose until 1780.
[194]The following note is appended: 'See this at large in the book of causes anno 1601 until 1610.'

5. *Glebes tithe-free*

24 July 1598.

It hath been accustomed time out of memory in this isle that no manner of glebe or spiritual lands whatsoever is to answer tithe corn or any other tithe growing thereof, to no proctor, steward or collector. John Sodorensis. William Crow, William Norris.

6. *The ordinary at discretion to mitigate fines*

The mitigation and moderation of the forfeited fines in the ecclesiastical courts to be used at the ordinary's discretion, weighing the ability and contrition of the party. William Crow, Richard Thompson, John Cannell.

7. *Of corbs*

Corbs for a vicar of third. A pair of bedstocks, a portassis, his board and tressel, a chair, form, a spoon if he have it, a pot or pan, a broach, a pair of goulers of iron and a rachentree, if it be to be had.

Corbs for a man

A pan or the best pot, a jack or a sallatt, a bow and arrows and buckler. The best board and best stool, a coulter and racken-tree, his best cup if it be of wood and bound with silver and gilt, the best chest.

Corbs for a woman

The best wheel and cards, a racken-tree, a soock or else a Manx spade, the best beads of jet or amber, the best broach or Agnus Dei, or else the best cross and the best pot or pan.

Corbs of spiritual men are made by consent of the patron, advice of the deemster and verdict of twelve men, six clergy and six lay. The free beneficed men are not subject to the payment of corbs, but if there be corbs extant they are to be paid.

It may be that some will allege that the episcopal jurisdiction in decision of tithes is but from Easter to Easter. The church her liberty is from one Easter to another, but we have the tithe corn due in September before Easter and the deciding of the tithe corn appertaineth to the spiritual jurisdiction, until September next following, which we account twelve months and one day. 17 March 1622 [1623]. William Crow.

8. *Neglectors of inventories*

The accustomed laws concerning either male or female that did neglect to bring into our records a true inventory of all the goods moveable and immoveable of any decedent's possession, the same negligent person either man or woman were always enjoined by our court to make restitution to the suppliant as he was found in his possessed ability.

William Crow, official;
William Norris, vicar-general.

EARLY SEVENTEENTH-CENTURY CONVOCATIONS

The convocation of 1607[195]

At a convocation and court holden before the reverend father in God John Philips, lord bishop of Man, the third day of December 1607, in Church Peelers in Holland,[196] it is decreed as followeth:

> Whereas there is a reference from the king's majesty unto the reverend father in God, John, lord bishop of this isle, as appeareth under Sir Julius Caesar his hand,[197] for the hearing and determining of the controversy depending between Sir Nicholas Thompson and Sir Christopher Yonge, clerks, concerning the rectory of Ballalaighe [Ballalagh]. And forasmuch as the said Christopher Yonge is absent and now in England, it is therefore decreed by the said reverend father, that he the said Christopher Yonge shall have time to come in and make his personal appearance in Ballalaighe [Ballalagh] church, before the said reverend father, on Friday in Easter week next coming, being the first day of April 1608 [1 April 1608] between the hours of nine[198] and eleven in the forenoon the foresaid day, to the end, he the said Sir Christopher Yonge may there and then allege for himself what he can in that cause, and that the said reverend father may proceed to a final determination thereof, according to his majesty's good pleasure.

Thereupon a process given and granted by the foresaid reverend father after the manner of this isle, according to the decree for his appearance. Concordat in decreto. Iohannes Cosnahan, registrarius.

Yonge apparently did not appear and Thompson was confirmed in the living, with Yonge ordered to pay damages to him, on 21 September 1608.

---

[195]Douglas, Manx Heritage Library, MS 10216 (part 1).
[196]The cathedral of St German in Peel, also called Holme Town.
[197]The case of simony against Nicholas Thompson was pursued as far as the king, and Sir Julius Caesar's letter committing the matter to the determination of the bishop, was dated at Greenwich, 26 June 1605. The matter was further heard by the bishop at Ballaugh on 21 September 1608.
[198]MS: 'neene'.

The convocation of 1610[199]

At a convocation holden the 23 of January 1609 before the reverend father in God John, lord bishop of Man, in Church Peelers in Hollandtown.

It is decreed that Sir Nicholas Thompson and Sir Christopher Yonge, clerks, shall make their personal appearance in St Mary's church in Ballalaighe [Ballaugh] before the ordinary, the sixth day of February being Tuesday [6 February 1610] between the hours of nine and eleven of the clock in the forenoon the foresaid day, and there and then to know his further pleasure and not to fail, sub poena suspensionis.

Thereupon a process given and granted by the foresaid reverend father for their appearance according to the decree. Concordat in decreto.

Also, it is decreed the said day those ministers whose names are underwritten shall preach before the ordinary every Sabbath in the Lent, viz., Sir Hugh Cannell, the first Sunday, Sir William Cosnahan the second Sunday, Sir Nicholas Thompson the third Sunday, Sir Thomas Farchir the fourth, Sir Thomas Norreys [Norris] the fifth and Sir Silvester Crowe the sixth.

At the same convocation, Sir Robert Moore, vicar, committed to Church German's prison forty days, and to be released upon sureties that he come not in any unlawful manner in the company of Jane Kerwell, neither in any place frequent her company, unless it be accident in church and market. Parson Crowe please for her [...] said Jane Kerwall but as above written [...] to appear personally [...] *The rest is no longer legible.*

The decrees

1. Imprimis, that all members in their several churches do diligently catechize on the Sundays and holy days according to the Book of Common Prayer, provided that some part of the parish come one day and some another day at the appointment of the minister till he have gone through them all, and so from time to time to hold on that course, and let every minister between the morning prayer and the high service question some point of the catechism with the clerk or some other in the vulgar tongue for the better edifying of all degrees.

2. That beneficed persons that are not allowed to preach themselves take order that certain sermons be preached within their cure yearly by such as be allowed by the ordinary to preach, viz., that parsons and vicars of thirds do provide six sermons at the least by the year and the vicars of pension four sermons.

3. That the minister go not a visitation without the clerk or deputy allowed by the ordinary for the testification of wills if they be made; and of this let there be made a publication the next Sabbath in every several parish of the minister.

4. That there be a register book kept by every minister within his several charge, of the christenings, marriages and burials, and that none be churched in houses but in case of necessity and that upon special licence from the ordinary, so that no

[199]Douglas, Manx Heritage Library, MS 10216 (part 1). The decrees are in A. W. Moore, *Diocesan histories. Sodor and Man* (London, 1893), pp. 131-2.

minister be present at any private contract of youth, never before married unless the parents, guardians, or such have charge over them be present and give consent thereunto.

5. Let reparation be carefully made of the chancel and church houses upon the glebe lands within two years at the furthest, and some preparation towards it in the meantime be done.

6. And all the premises to be accomplished upon pain of suspension and sequestration according to law, unless the ordinary see just cause to give further time.

The convocation of 1613[200]

The parson, vicar or minister of the parish where the herring fishing is gotten is to repair to the harbour every morning and evening to read them divine service and to deliver them good admonition, which if he neglect or refuse to do he is to forfeit his tithe fish the ensuing night, which is to be given to the poor at the admiral's discretion. And if any person shall neglect to come to the place where such service is to be read, the admiral or his vice-admiral sets out his flag (which is the sign or token when they are to observe that duty), to offer their prayers and praises for such blessings, such upon knowledge thereof is to be excluded from the benefit of the fishing that night.

The convocation of 1629[201]

...the spiritual officers to keep our ecclesiastical courts hereafter in due time as we shall forthwith direct you without innovation or broaching of novelty. Also we command you our registrars to have a special care to keep several all the wills, decrees and acts every half year due and belonging to the said several jurisdictions as of ancient time hath been accustomed.

[200]Moore, *Sodor and Man*, pp. 132-3.
[201]*Ibid.*, p. 133.

SPIRITUAL ORDINANCES AND CUSTOMARY LAWS, 1643[202]

Apud Castrum de Rushen, tricesimo die Octobris 1643 [30 October 1643].

Whereas before this time, at Peel Town, the eighteenth day of July 1643, before the right honourable James, earl of Derby, lord of the said isle, etc., the officers spiritual and temporal, with the twenty-four keys of the said island, and four men of every parish, were assembled together to advise and consider of certain grievances of the church and commons of the said isle, laid down and expressed in and by their several petitions and complaints unto his lordship, and to study and devise such convenient remedy and redress therein as might or may best stand with the maintenance and preservation of his lordship's royalties, rights and prerogatives of and within the said island, the good and welfare of the church and commons of the same, and the peace and safety of the whole state in general; at which place and day it was mutually condescended and agreed unto by all parties, as well complainants as defendants, and it was their humble desires, that his lordship should chancelarize, order and decide all and every their matters of business and complaint or aggrievance whatsoever, as in his honour's wisdom shall be thought meet and convenient. To which order, doom and decree every of them, viz., the reverend father in God Richard, lord bishop of this isle, with his officers spiritual and the body of the clergy, the said twenty-four keys of the island, with the four men of every parish, in the name of themselves and of the whole commons of the isle, by whom they were chosen and thither sent for that purpose, did condescend and agree for them, their heirs and successors, to stand, to perform, and abide such his lordship's order, doom and decree therein, as should be thereafter published and declared under his honour's hand and seal.

To which end and purpose, and for the more perfect, more ready and good performance of the business, according to justice and equity, his honour (being willing to understand the true state of all their causes and grievances) was graciously pleased to give order that a select jury and grand inquest of twenty-four men, newly chosen, whereof twelve of the twenty-four keys to be part, and twelve of the four men of the parishes[203] there present, should be impanelled and sworn to find out and present all such wrongs and abuses as have been committed or acted against his lordship's prerogative, the laws of the island, or the good of the

---

[202]Gill, *Statutes*, I, 92-9. Repealed in full by the pre-revestment written laws (ascertainment) act, 1978.

[203]The four men of the parishes constituted a semi-official body, which probably went back to Viking times, which was called together when matters of great importance were to be discussed and enacted. This was the last occasion on which they were so summoned and the custom died out after 1660. See Dickinson, *Lordship of Man*, pp. 61-2.

commonalty, as by the tenor, form and effect of the oath then administered unto them by Ewan Christian esquire, one of the deemsters of the said isle, more plainly appeareth; which oath was verbatim as followeth:

> You shall truly and faithfully proceed and prevent all such wrongs and abuses as have been committed and acted against the lord's prerogatives, the laws of the island, and the good of the commonalty; all which you shall, by virtue of your oath, maintain and defend. You shall, without malice, favour or affection, give in a true answer according as cases shall (by sufficient proofs and testimonies, records or any other legal manner) be made appear. So God you help, and his holy Word contained in this blessed book.

The names of the said twelve chosen out of the twenty-four keys are:

John Stanley	William Tyldesly	Samuel Radcliffe
Thomas Crellin	William Cloage	William Standish
Thomas Huddleston	John Moore	John Teare
Henry Calcott	William Craine	John Caine

The names of the said twelve chosen out of the four men of the parishes are:

William Moore	William Qualtrough	Edward Shimin
William Brew, jr	William Teare	Henry Gawne
Robert Crow	Dollin Clark	William Caighan
Richard Cowle	Nicholas Moore	Finloe Kelly

All which as one grant inquest or jury of presentment do find and present upon their oaths certain proofs and examinations, which they had taken upon the petitions of the several parishes, the most of which did concern particular abuses of the clergy by particular ministers and proctors, in the collecting of their tithes and duties to the church, contrary to the known laws and orders of the island; whereupon his lordship gave order that the clergy and proctors should make their answers and plead their defence against such the complaints of the country, which accordingly they have done, and have given his lordship such satisfaction therein, with promise of reformation for future time, and have made and offered also to his lordship such feizable [sic] reasons of their just grievances against the commonalty, that his lordship (for preservation of love and unity betwixt the clergy and commonalty for time to come) thinks fit that those matters of particular grievances on both parts shall be no more remembered; nevertheless, if any of the parties grieved think good hereafter to prosecute their grievances and put them to a trial, his honour will take pains to give his especial order therein for relief of the wronged party.

And whereas amongst other the complaints of the country, some particular matters concerning the general goods are most considerable of reformation and determination, his honour was graciously pleased to assemble the clergy and twenty-four keys of the island, with the four men of every parish, to meet this day, being the thirtieth day of October 1643 [30 October 1643] as aforesaid, at his castle of Rushen, where accordingly they did appear, and then and there upon their ensuing business (agitated and disputed before his lordship) betwixt the clergy and proctors upon the one part, and the said twenty-four keys and four men of the parishes in behalf of the country upon the other part, his lordship doth order and declare as followeth:

1. First, that whereas there are divers children left under age and executors by their dead parents' wills, if any of them shall die before he or she comes to the age of fourteen years (which is the full age the law requires before such infant can dispose of his goods by will or otherwise), the goods of such infant falls by law to the rest of its brothers and sisters; yet notwithstanding, the church have used to make a decree of this child's goods, and for the same takes a fee of three shillings four pence for decreeing the goods to its brothers and sisters, which is needless (as is argued by the country), the same falling upon them by law as aforesaid, without any decree, his lordship therefore hereby ordereth that the church shall take no more than sixpence for the taking notice of, and making of the decree for and concerning such a child's goods, being under age as aforesaid.[204]

2. Item. Whereas it is a complaint of the country that the lord of the island makes clerks of the parishes by his special grants, whereas the parishioners pay the clerk his dues, his lordship is graciously pleased that the parishioners and the parson or vicar of the parish shall have the nomination of the clerk, and the bishop or ordinary to have the allowance or approbation of him for his sufficiency and ability to perform the place, and this order to take effect after the time of the grants in being be expired, which have been heretofore made by his lordship or his ancestors.[205]

3. Item. Whereas it is complained of that the ministers of the parishes have taken twelve pence for the writing of a decedent's will, whereas the party himself, or his friend for him, would have written it for little or nothing; and that the church have sometimes refused to accept of and prove such wills, except they were made and written by the minister's hand, his lordship's order is that every man may make or cause to be made his own will by whom he shall please to direct, and if he desire the minister to make it, that he shall agree with the minister as he can for the writing thereof, and not otherwise.

4. Item. Whereas when a man dies intestate his goods, by the law, ought to fall to his children unmarried equally amongst them; yet, contrary to this, the church sometimes use to decree the whole team of oxen and the crop of corn to the eldest son, which commonly is more worth than all the rest of the goods; it is therefore ordered by his lordship that if the church shall hereafter make any such decree in favour of the eldest son, to the wrong of the rest of the younger children, that decree shall be void and the goods to go equally amongst all the children according to the law.[206]

5. Item. Whereas it is a great complaint of the country that the clergy and proctors use to take eight shillings for a cors-present sent out of a decedent's goods

---

[204]Repealed by the statute of 1813, c. 2.
[205]Repealed by the church act, 1880, s. 34.
[206]Repealed by the statute of 1777, c. 14.

of the value of four pounds, and proportionably after that rate forth of goods under that value, it is ordered by his lordship that no cors-present shall be hereafter taken by the clergy or proctors of spiritual livings of any decedent's goods under the value of six pounds, thirteen shillings and four pence; and of that value, and under the value of twenty pounds they shall take but twenty pence for the cors-presents, and if the goods be of the value of twenty pounds and under the value of forty pounds, they shall take for the cors-presents but two shillings four pence, and out of the goods of the value of forty pounds or above, they shall take six shillings four pence and no more, be the goods of what value soever they may be; and that none shall pay a cors-present but such as at the time of his or her death were housekeepers and masters of a family, and that no infant or child under the age of fourteen years, nor no woman under the covert baron, shall pay any cors-present; and if any clergyman or proctor take any more for a cors-present, or otherwise than as aforesaid, he shall forfeit so much in value as he shall take above the sum before limited, and also six shillings eight pence to the party grieved, to be recovered by accon [sic] of debt at the common law; but it shall be lawful for any spiritual person to take any sum, or other thing, which by any person dying shall be given or bequeathed unto him.

6. Item. Whereas it is a great complaint of the country that by the spiritual laws here they are forced to pay tithe butter and tithe cheese, which is called the milk tithes, and in the payment thereof there is an undecent order in paying it on the Sabbath Day upon the altar in the church, where there often falls out great contention betwixt the minister and proctors on the one part and the people that pay the same on the other part; and sometimes the people are put to their oaths for such things upon trivial matters, which kind of tithing is much out of use in most parts of the king's dominions; his lordship therefore orders that from henceforth, no more tithe butter or cheese shall be paid in manner as aforesaid, but in lieu thereof the farmers, cottiers and all others who ought to pay such tithes shall at Easter, when the account for their other duties to the church, pay four pence for every cow which has a calf that year, and two pence for every farrow cow which had no calf, but gave milk since the Easter before, and one penny out of every four milk sheep, and one penny out of every two milk goats; the vicars of thirds and pensioners who were used to have a choice cheese, they have in lieu thereof the monies due for the tithe cheese, and butter of a choice house in the parish, and the sumner likewise.[207]

7. Item. Whereas there hath been, and it is a great complaint made by the country, for the losses they have suffered by the ministers and proctors not coming in due time to take the tithe of their corn, whereby the farmers have sometimes lost their own corn, not daring to draw or lead the same before the proctor or minister come to take away their tithe; his lordship therefore, for prevention of such inconveniences, doth order and decree that from henceforth the parson, vicar and proctor of every parish shall acquaint the several farmers of the parishes with the names of his or their under-proctors or deputies, who are to receive their tithes; and this shall be done in the month of July before the harvest begin; and when the time of harvest is come, the farmer shall give notice to him or them who are to have and

---

[207]Repealed as relates to bishops and clergy and certain impropriate tithes by the tithe commutation act of 1839.

receive their tithe corn the evening or day before such farmer intends to lead his corn; and then if the parson, vicar or proctor, or his or their under-proctors, come not to take the tithe of the farmer's corn according to the warning given, the farmer to take two neighbours to justify with him that he hath left his due tithe; this warning to be given by the farmer as aforesaid, shall be given at the parsonage, vicarage or proctor's house, who is to receive the tithes, if there be any such in the parish; and if it be a stranger of another parish, or layman of the same parish, such stranger of another parish or layman of the same parish shall, before the time of harvest, acquaint the farmer at what house in the same parish the farmer shall give or leave such notice, that his corn is ready for leading, or that he intends to lead; and the like order for tithe hay is to be observed.

8. Item. Whereas it is complained of by the commonalty against the ordinary and his spiritual officers that orphans' goods and just debts to creditors are not, and have not been sufficiently secured by their court; by means whereof divers poor people being left orphans, and many others who had just debts owing to them by the decedents, have mightily suffered in their estates; his lordship therefore doth order that the goods of the decedent, according to the inventory, shall be made good by the ordinary or his spiritual officers, if he or they, upon the proving of the will, or making of the decree where no will was made, do not, or shall not take sufficient security for the same.

9. And whereas there is a controversy betwixt the clergy and proctors upon the one part, and the commonalty upon the other part, concerning the payment of some other tithes and duties, as tithe wool, tithe fish, clerk silver, fees for probation of wills and the sumner's dues, and this upon a pretended record produced by the commonalty of the year 1541, which record hath this day been in open court deliberately discussed and argued pro et contra by both parties, before his lordship, and there adjudged of no validity, upon divers good reasons; his lordship doth therefore order and declare that the said record be of no force or effect hereafter to be pleaded in way of bar to the book of the spiritual statutes enrolled in the statute book of the island; and therefore that the laws and orders positively made and in that book recorded, shall be from henceforth duly and truly observed in all things, till some other law, statute or ordinance shall be agreed upon to the contrary.[208]

10. And whereas there is an undecent and irreverent use in this island by the proctors and clergy when they collect their small tithes and offering money at Easter, they demand the same at the time the people are to receive the communion, and sometimes will stop the people from receiving the blessed sacrament because they have not paid their duties; his lordship therefore ordereth that the proctors and ministers to whom such small tithes and oblations belong shall sit in the parish church upon Monday and Tuesday in Easter week after the people have received the communion, there to receive their dues; and whosoever shall not pay their dues to them upon one of those days, the ministers and proctors shall proceed against them by way of citation before the ordinary or his officers; and his lordship thinks fit that the minister or proctor in such cases of wilful neglect by the people in not

---

[208]Ditto.

paying their dues shall have the speediest and strictest course that may be from the ordinary for the recovery thereof.[209]

In witness the said James, earl of Derby hath hereunto put his hand and seal of arms the day and year first above written. James Derby.

Consented unto and witnessed by us whose names are subscribed:

Richard Sodor and Man.[210]   John Harrison.[211]
Hugh Cannell.[212]   John Greenhalgh.[213]
Robert Parr.[214]   Ewan Christian.[215]
Robert Allen.[216]   Robert Quayle.[217]
James Moore.[218]   John Sharples.[219]
Robert Norris.[220]   William Smith.[221]
John Cosnahan.[222]   John Cannell.[223]
Thomas Parr.[224]   John Christian.[225]

Twenty-four keys:[226]

John Stanley	William Christian	William Clague
John Curghey	John Garrett	John Caesar
Thomas Huddleston	John Christian	David Christian
Henry Calcott	William Standish	William Craine
Thomas Crellin	William Tyldesly	John Craine
Philip Moore	Thomas Banks	Robert Quayle
Richard Stevenson	John Moore	Robert Barry

[209]Ditto.
[210]Richard Parr was bishop of Sodor and Man from 10 June 1635 until sometime after 20 February 1644.
[211]Vicar of Patrick from 1633 and of Bride in 1660.
[212]Vicar of Kirk Michael from 1609 to 1672 and vicar-general at this time.
[213]Governor (1640-51).
[214]Rector of Ballaugh (1640-70).
[215]Deemster (1605-55).
[216]Vicar of Maughold (1642-66).
[217]Deemster (1636-44).
[218]Vicar of Lonan (1627-53).
[219]Comptroller from about 1630 to 1652.
[220]Vicar of Arbory (1628-50).
[221]Receiver (1643-8).
[222]Vicar of Santan (1618-56).
[223]Water bailiff (1641-3) and then deemster (1644-52).
[224]Vicar of Malew (1641-?).
[225]Assistant deemster (1627-55).
[226]The absent members were Samuel Radcliffe, John Teare and John Caine, all of whom were members of the committee of twelve mentioned above.

Four men of the parishes:[227]

Rushen:	Henry Gawne	William Gawne[228]
	Nicholas Clague	Henry Nelson
Lezayre:	Robert Crow	William Stevenson
	Nicholas Corlett	Ewan Curghey[229]
Bride:	Patrick Cowle	David Christian[230]
	John Cowle	
Andreas:	John Kee	John Lace
	William Brew, jr	
Michael:	Henry Woods	
Lupi [Malew]:	Henry Wainwright	Edward Shimin
Conchan:	Daniel Christian	
Jurby:	Dollin Clark	
Lonan:	Daniel Qualtrough	Philip Brew
	Thomas Quine	
Maughold:	Gilchrist Callow	Robert Kerruish
	John Kerruish	
Santan:	Nicholas Moore	Thomas Quay
	William Kissage	Christopher Kinnish
Braddan:	John Kewley	John Cannell
	Paul Gelling	
Runii [Marown]:	Nicholas Killey	William Cubbon
Arbory:	John Harrison	Henry Maddrell
	William Cubbon	

[227]Of the thirty-one absentees, the following were members of the sub-committee mentioned above: Richard Cowle (of Bride?); William Qualtrough (of Lonan?); William Teare (of Andreas?); William Caighan (of Michael?); and Finloe Kelly. The parishes of Ballaugh, German and Patrick were not represented at all.
[228]Captain of the parish.
[229]Captain of the parish.
[230]Captain of the parish.

Note: The reason why the full body of the twenty-four keys and the four men of each parish are not all inserted is because their meeting at Castle Rushen, the said thirtieth October [16]43 proved a very tempestuous day of rain and wind, they could not conveniently travel without hazard, etc., and therefore the names of them who happened to appear were only taken, as appears placed in the original of the aforesaid statutes.

THE INJUNCTION OF 1658[231]

To the ministers and churchwardens of each church and chapel within the isle.

That they shall not suffer or permit any minister of the isle, or stranger, to officiate within their several churches or chapels without the leave and express permission of such ministers first had and obtained under their hands in writing, neither shall they permit any person or persons whatsoever, not being in holy orders, to exercise or use preaching or any part of God's worship or service within the said churches or chapels upon any account or colour whatsoever;

And for better execution of this order the coroner,[232] lockman[233] and all substantial people of each parish are hereby required to be aiding and assisting when the minister or churchwardens shall call upon them in this behalf;

And it is further ordered and enjoined that no person or persons whatsoever shall be permitted to receive the Lord's Supper in any parish but that wherein they live without a certificate under the hand of the minister and churchwardens of such a parish, that such person or persons stands not presented for, nor lies not under any contumacy or disobedience for any scandalous sinful crime by them committed.

And lastly it is hereby ordered and enjoined that this act be fairly entered in the church register of every parish, and the same to be published openly in the congregation in every church and chapel upon receipt thereof, and also upon the first Sunday in Lent every year successively, the contrary hereof at your perils.

---

[231]Moore, *Sodor and Man*, pp. 149-50.
[232]There was a coroner for each of the six sheadings, chosen (it seems) by the governor. His responsibilities were considerably wider than those of a coroner today. See Dickinson, *Lordship of Man*, pp. 46-9.
[233]The coroner's deputy, whose name seems to derive from the word 'lock', a portion of grain due to him from every bag of meal sold in the parish. See *ibid.*, pp. 49-50.

THE INSTRUCTIONS OF BISHOP BARROW, 1663[234]

1. We order and decree that the archdeacon, officials or registrars shall have nothing to do with our fifteen episcopal causes above written, but only to act in such things as are proper and belonging to their jurisdiction for the half year, and keep records for them by themselves.

2. That our vicars-general shall have no power to make substitutes under them, but to act, and execute all things belonging to their place and office in their own persons, and to keep records of all their proceedings on their registry.

3. That our vicars-general shall not order, censure or decree any matter or cause ecclesiastical severally, but jointly and unanimously to keep sheading courts as formerly, and a monthly court for hearing and determining matters of difference and controversy in the convenients [sic] place that they shall think meet.

4. That our vicars-general shall not order or censure causes contrary to our statutes, and spiritual written laws, though there be some precedents otherwise, notwithstanding the statute[s] in such cases are to be observed until the ordinary's pleasure be further known touching the said statutes.

5. That all the ministers within this isle liable to our spiritual jurisdiction shall be careful and diligent in their places and callings, and be sober, and give good example in their lives and conversations, be obedient to observe all our directions formerly given touching the worship and service of God, obedience to the canons and laws of our church,[235] and if any offend herein he is immediately to be censured and punished according to the heinousness of the facts.

6. That no wills or decrees be proved or made but in a sheading court with inventories, and pledges written on whole sheets of paper, except it be in some cases of necessity and not otherwise.

7. That our registrar shall keep the court books in good order and give in all offenders' names presented to the court to be censured, to call in for certificate under every minister's hand touching the performance of their several censures into our records, that all fines may be given in to us to mitigate, and then return to the controllers to be recorded for the lord's prerogative.

8. And lastly, that our registrar shall take sufficient bonds for all children's goods under years for all fornicators, adulterers and all other crimes and offences as hath been usual and accustomed, and to give in bonds as formerly used not to relapse under penalty of forfeiting a fine to the lord of the soil. And further we order that all the licences, money for marriage and fees shall be equally divided betwixt

---

[234]Moore, *Sodor and Man*, pp. 166-8. Isaac Barrow was bishop of Sodor and Man from 5 July 1663 until October 1671. He was translated to St Asaph in March 1670.
[235]The 1603 (1604) canons applied to the Isle of Man.

our vicars-general, and that Sir Hugh Cannell[236] shall have power to grant licences in the archdeacon's half year only, not debarring the vicar-general notwithstanding of giving licences also, and receiving the fees, and also that all wills that are yet unproved that they be brought in and proved at the next sheading court, in penalty of three pounds *ad usum domini,* and in particular such wills and decrees to be made hath been lately complained of by creditors and legatories. Isaac, Sodor and Man.

---

[236]The senior vicar-general.

THE ACCUSTOMED UNWRITTEN ECCLESIASTICAL LAWS, 1667[237]

The accustomed unwritten laws until now practised continually by the church are as follows.

Rape

1. That such as are accused of rape be proceeded against in the spiritual court in manner and form as of sorcery, as is expressed in the fiftieth spiritual statute.[238]

Debts of the deceased

2. That when a debt appears to be due from a deceased to the lord, and the deceased's debts surmounting the inventory, the lord's debt is first to be paid; secondly, orphans' goods, and afterwards the claimer's penny pound like by the general sumner, if none else undertake to administer after the goods are sold at the market cross to their best value.

Excommunicates

3. That an excommunicate person persisting irregular is to be imprisoned and delivered over body and goods to the lord's mercy.
    4. That all fines imposed by the church are given in charge to the comptroller after that ordinary hath mitigated the same according to the spiritual statute.[239]

Inheritance by minors

5. That notwithstanding the eighth spiritual statute,[240] it hath been accustomed that if there hath been but one child betwixt man and wife and the man died intestate, the kindred of the father, by virtue of that statute, was to have the tuition of the said child and goods until he came to fourteen years of age, yet in regard by woeful experience, it was found that such orphans were very much neglected in their good usage, and the church conceiving it unfit to commit the tuition of a child to him or her that was to have his estate of lands and goods after his decease, ordered always as appears on record, and the mother, if she be alive, or if not, the next relation on

---

[237]Douglas, Manx National Heritage Library, MS M. M. 12C. According to this copy, made in 1738, the original was lost in 1714.
[238]1577/50. See above.
[239]1577/51-2. See above.
[240]1577/8. See above.

her side, should have the tuition of the said child, to whom none of the estate fell due by his death, and to be rewarded out of the profits of the said estate and goods, at the sight of four sworn men.

The same rule observed if the estate come by the mother, always provided that the court find such next relations capable of their charge. Otherwise they may decree as they think most fit for the child's safety and best usage. But all this in case there be not a will made, wherein the child and goods are otherwise disposed of.

Tithes

6. That if a farmer take in corn to thresh without notice given to the proctor, or taking of two neighbours according to the seventeenth spiritual statute,[241] the farmer shall swear what corn he so made use of that the proctor may have his due tithe, and the farmer be punished at the ordinary's discretion for his contempt.

7. That all farmers be sworn that will not bring into their folds all their sheep and lambs at such time as the proctor shall appoint, according to the twenty-third spiritual statute,[242] and for all other manner of tithe as occasion is given.

Probate of wills

8. That if any executor at lawful years do not demand a debt due from a creditor (except it be mentioned in the will) within a year and a day after the probate of the will, he nonsuits himself; but if any goods be concealed he is to look for relief, not in the spiritual but in the temporal court.

9. That all claimers that enter their claims and prove not the same in the spiritual court within a year and a day after the probate of the will are nonsuited, and such as have specialties or witnesses are to prove in court, and such who have none upon the graves, or to leave no further relief, and this because no perfect inventory can be brought in for orphan's goods, or pledges be procured to secure such goods and the office discharged.

10. That he that enters his claim within a year and a day after the probate of the will, and endeavouring to prove the same within the limited time without bill, bond or evidence, shall prove the same upon the grave of him or her from whom the debt was due, with lawful compurgators according to the ancient form, that is to say, lying on his back with the Bible on his breast, and his compurgators on either side one; and if he do not prove as well as enter within the year and a day, he is nonsuited in the spiritual court, and to have no hearing in the temporal when the orphans and relations are less able to answer or defend themselves.

11. That if a desperate debt be bequeathed unto any that cannot be recovered, the executor is not liable to make the same good to the legatory, but if the legatory find that this debt is lost through negligence of the executor for want of due

[241] 1577/17. See above.
[242] 1577/23. See above.

prosecution, and can justly prove the same, he is notwithstanding to be relieved, and the supervisors are concerned in this if the executor or legatory be under age.

12. That all legacies according to the statute be paid within fourteen days, yet when the executor or supervisor cannot within the said limitation possibly possess themselves of any of the goods answerable to those legacies, they being in the custody of others, the church in discretion may grant a longer time to the executor and that it be lawfully demanded.

13. That when a testator doth bequeath a legacy to any person, being in the hands of another man, and not the executors, and if that man and the legatory come to an agreement and pay any part of the legacy, the executor is free and not any more to be troubled.

14. That when a legacy is bequeathed to any man to whom also a debt is due from the testator, he may have both, unless the testator declared that the legacy is in consideration of the debt.

15. That when the goods do not extend to the payment of the debts no legacies are to be paid, but if the goods surmount the debts (and though the executor have but sixpence left when the legacies and debts are all defrayed) in such a case the legacies are to be paid; and if there be not so much as will pay all legacies (the debts being first paid) the legatories are to be paid penny pound like.

Defamation

16. That such as defame the dead are to make penance and to ask the kindred forgiveness, because it is done in disgrace of all his relations, and publication to be made that none revive the same in penalty of three pounds to the lord's use and forty days imprisonment.

17. That if any aspersion be cast on man or woman, the slanderer is to be punished if he cannot prove the same. And the like publication to be made for the living party as for the dead, as before next above mentioned.

Appeals

18. That when any appeal is made from the spiritual judge to the staff and the appellant not able to disprove the judication, that appellant to be returned to the church to be fined and punished for his unjust appeal.

Violence done to the clergy

19. That he that strikes a minister shall be excommunicated *ipso facto* and to do penance. And after satisfaction given to the law, to receive absolution and to be received at the church stile into the church by the minister reading before him the fifty-first psalm, and before the congregation to repeat his schedule after the minister.

Clerical discipline

20. That when a minister commits any heinous fault or crime very much unbeseeming his function, the ordinary may suspend him, and by the advice of the clergy may proceed further against him according to law and his desert.

21. That when a minister yields not canonical obedience to his ordinary or his chief officers, or commits any other fault deserving, the ordinary or his vicar-general shall suspend him *ab officio et beneficio* until he conform.

Slander

22. That he or she that calls a man a dog or a woman a bitch shall wear the bridle at the market cross or shall make seven Sundays' penance in several parish churches. And for every deposition in examination touching slander or difference to pay three pence.

Whoredom

23. That common whores be drawn after a boat in the sea, during the ordinary's appointment, and common whoremasters deeply fined and also severely punished at the ordinary's discretion.

Suicide

24. That he or she that strangles, drowns or spills themselves, receive not the Christian burial, besides the confiscation of their goods to the lord.

Intestates

25. That where no will is made, the church doth decree the brothers and sisters on the father's side administrators of the goods which came by the father, and the brothers and sisters on the mother's side administrators of the goods which came by the mother, married or unmarried (always provided there be no lawful issue) and afterward to descend to the next of kindred, whether by father or mother living.

Tithes

26. That if they pay their tithe in kind that break their prescription in not paying their money when, where and to whom it is due, viz., Easter Monday or Easter Tuesday at the parish church to the proctor if he be there; if not, that he make it appear by good witnesses that he himself was there and ready to tender the money.

27. That they shall pay tithe fish who pretend prescription by sea, for though they pretend prescription by land, yet cannot by sea, for that such prescriptions have not been allowed by the church, nor the pretended prescribers cannot defend it by virtue of any former statute.

28. That all lands under corn or kept for hay, bearing rent to the lord, are liable to pay tithe to the church or other agreement in lieu of tithe, excepting lime lands

according to a statute made lately, wherein for the term of three years it is tithe free, being lands broken up that never before were under corn.

29. That all boats at the herring fishing shall pay due tithe according to law, and that none of the said tithe be stopped, to pay any part of the castle mares.

Administration of the goods of the deceased

30. That when a man or woman dieth and the debts exceeding the goods and none of the kindred to take the administration, the general sumner is to administer, and publication publicly to be made in all the parish churches of the island, for claimers to come on a day appointed to prove their debts, their claims first being entered, that the general sumner may distribute the goods among them penny pound like, in case he can make no money of them, and to give an account thereof to the registrar for the discharge of the office. And such as will not come in on the said day shall be nonsuited, and the general sumner to be rewarded for his pains at the ordinary's discretion.

Holy communion

31. That there be a communion in every church at least three times in the year on the parish's account or cost, and for visitations to give the communion to such persons, but at Easter the proctor is to provide bread and wine on his own charges and to receive two pence from every communicant according to the forty-first statute. And all at fourteen years of age to receive, but first to be examined by the minister or be presented, unless a lawful cause appear.

32. That all persons make their wills before they receive the communion, and that the minister of the parish write all wills and inventories at large, setting the price of every particular goods on the head thereof, that orphans be not defrauded; and to receive twelve pence for every will and inventory except there be a legacy left by the deceased to the minister, to the value of twelve pence, and if the inventory be large, to have twelve pence for every day he is taking of it, but this in case another able clerk cannot be had.

Penance

33. Whosoever shall commit fornication shall make three Sundays' penance, and if they marry, that they go from the sheet to the ring.

34. That all offenders censured to penance are to perform their censures and satisfy the law before they be admitted to the holy communion, and to pay three pence to the minister for every Sunday's penance for writing certificates, and to the sumner two pence, and if the offender bring not wheat, he is to pay four pence to the sumner for furnishing him, and no appeal to be from the church censures for offenders to the staff, and none to be privileged from their censures.

35. That a woman that bears a bastard is to do penance and satisfy the law before she be churched.

36. That if a farmer's daughter be deflowered by a single man, he is to endow her or marry her, going from the sheet to the ring, and if he do marry her, his penance to be mitigated.

37. That if a cotter's son beget a farmer's or a cotter's daughter with child, the man and woman are to be at equal charges to bring up the child.

38. That if a woman claim a promise of marriage of a young man, her own oath is not authentic to prove the same without lawful witnesses. But for fathering the child the woman's oath is sufficient.

39. That whosoever accuseth man or woman of incontinency or any other slander, vilifying another person and cannot prove the same, shall be censured to penance, and to ask the party or parties forgiveness that are so slandered; and further as it is expressed in the seventeenth customary law.[243] But the minister, churchwardens and chapter-quest may present on common fame.[244]

Punishments

40. That when a minister makes a clandestine marriage, he that marries the couple and all present at the marriage shall be committed into St German's prison and excommunicated *ipso facto*.

41. That when a minister doth marry man or woman without licence or banns of marriage according to the rubric, he is to be suspended three years *ab officio et beneficio* according to the canons of the church,[245] unless the ordinary upon submission and bonds of reformation mitigate or remit the same.

42. A man convicted upon due proof by two juries for rape, one of which juries is panelled by the church and the other by the temporalty, and the grand jury clearing him for his life and forfeiting of goods to the lord, for want of due prosecution; that man committing adultery and incest (besides the rape) is to be returned back to the church to be fined and punished for the heinous fact, to pay the court fees and receive absolution from the church upon his remorse and true repentance.

First cousins

43. That cousin germans shall not marry or be witnesses to a will, the executor being so related for whose benefit they swear; yet the multiplicity of witnesses of this degree takes away the defect, at the ordinary's discretion.

Regulations concerning probate of wills and administration of intestates' goods

44. That there is no executor's crop to be decreed but in the same condition when the deceased dieth, whether in the ground, field, haggard or barn, the administrators

---

[243] 1577/17. See above.
[244] This is not stated in the English canons of 1603 (1604).
[245] 1603/62. See G. L. Bray ed., *The Anglican canons 1529-1947* (Woodbridge, 1998), pp. 352-3.

or executors are to enjoy it so and not otherwise, and the lord's rent to be paid by the executors or administrators proportionable to the corn he receives, and the rest by the heir and widow surviving as they are concerned in the crop.

45. That legatories be accounted lawful witnesses, their own legacies excepted, but the priest and clerk are competent for both.

46. That when a married man or wife happen to die intestate, the survivor is to have a legacy out of the deceased's goods, at the discretion of the ordinary.

47. That if any person presume to take away goods whatsoever belonging to the deceased before the will be proved or a decree made, he shall bring them back again to the place where they were. In case of refusal (being warned by the sumner) such refractory persons shall be committed. Yet in case of apparent danger of perishing, the executor or administrator, by the ordinary's consent, may have liberty (giving in bonds) to preserve them unto the court day, and if any take away goods wilfully and make use of them in this kind, and if the debts happen to exceed the inventory, he shall be liable to the administration and pay all debts whatsoever, though it were out of his own goods.

48. That if any person or persons do take upon them an administration in court, they shall not desert the same upon any pretence whatsoever, nor shall the church be troubled with the same any more in this respect.

49. That when there are two or three or more executors or administrators and a debt from the deceased due to any of them, the creditor shall lose but a proportion to his own part of the goods, and the other executors or administrators to make payment proportionably to their parts, as if it were to other claimers.

50. That when any administration is refused in court by the next relations, and that therefore the church is burdened; if the inventory shall happen to exceed the debts, the overplus shall be at the disposing of the ordinary, to be bestowed to pious uses.

51. That in a difference depending betwixt party and party, when one gives it to the other upon his oath absolutely, there shall be no further hearing of that matter in the spiritual court.

Marital and family matters

52. That when the husband and wife fall out and do not cohabit, the party guilty shall be committed, and before release to give bonds in a considerable fine to the lord, to cohabit with and use the other as he cometh.

53. That when the goods of children under age are put into the custody of supervisors or any other, such supervisors (or others who have the goods) shall pay the estimation in money to the children and no goods, unless the parties concerned do otherwise agree, with the children being at age and the trustees.

54. That if a young woman shall happen to have a child, having therefore satisfied the law, and afterwards do marry, if any do upbraid her therewith to the vexation of her husband, such are to be punished at the ordinary's discretion.

55. That the pledges taken in the spiritual court are not bound but until the executors do come to fourteen years of age, and then the executors are to come in with a copy of the inventory of record to the deemster and crave power to demand and take upon their own goods and release the bonds, for the church is no longer

concerned. The pledges if they be alive are to discharge themselves by seeing the goods paid as they come to age, but if the pledges be dead, their executors, if they be under age, are not concerned.

Causes reserved to the bishop

56. That the fifteen episcopal causes, viz.:

1. The clergy.
2. Excommunication.
3. Decrees.
4. Mitigation of fines.
5. Marriages and licences for marriage.
6. Divorcement.
7. Adultery.
8. Incest.
9. Witchcraft.
10. The calling of a woman a bitch and a man a dog.
11. The censuring of fornication upon relapse and other offenders the second or third time.
12. Effusion or spilling of blood in the churchyard.
13. Profaning the Sunday and other holy days.
14. Persons that refuse the communion in contempt of their own parish church.
15. The committing of offenders into St German's prison, which is the bishop's prison shall always belong to the ordinary's jurisdiction and censuring.

Sexual crimes

57. That if a young woman be forced by rape she is to discover the same immediately with signs and tokens of violence, and a married wife in the like manner; otherwise neither of them to be esteemed ravished.

58. That whosoever shall be found guilty of bigamy shall be tried according to the law already provided.

Court procedure

59. That merchants who pretend a debt due to them from the executor of any decedent shall swear to their books upon the grave in form as before mentioned in the tenth customary law,[246] and the proctors to their books before the court, and if the merchants or proctors be dead, the supposed debtors if they be living shall clear themselves upon the grave as aforesaid.

60. That when an inventory is brought in upon record with pledges, and continuing entire for a year and a day, no part thereof can be adempted upon any pretence, but added there may at any time as goods come to be discovered.

[246]See above, no. 10.

61. That when a difference in matter of scandal shall happen betwixt a minister and layman, and that the same shall need determination by a jury, the one half shall be ministers and the other laymen.

62. That when any laws touching spiritual causes are to be enacted, the bishop, archdeacon and whole clergy shall be made privy thereto, and join with the temporal officers and have their consent with them, before the same be established.

63. That where a decree hath been made in open court and so continuing for a year and a day, no pretended will shall be admitted of, upon any pretence whatsoever afterwards.

64. That after the witnesses are sworn to a will, they shall not upon any pretence of explanation or otherwise, adempt or add any more afterwards.

Miscellaneous provisions

65. That none shall sit or bury in the chancel of any church unless first he agree with the minister or whosoever is proctor.

66. Fornicators or lapsing shall pay three pounds fine to the lord (if they be able) with other punishment at the ordinary's discretion. If they be not able, they shall make seven Sunday penance each of them, and sit two whole hours in the stocks.

67. Transmarians have the liberty of three years to enter and prove their debts due unto them from a decedent, and no longer, viz., three years after the probate of the will.

68. Adulterers shall make seven days' penance in several parishes, and for relapse fourteen, and adding always the number of seven, as often as they transgress, besides a fine to the lord with imprisonment.

69. That no contract by using their words of matrimony or any part thereof shall be used before the solemnizing of matrimony publicly, because of the great abuses committed thereupon, to the dishonour of God and scandal of the Christian faith, in penalty of excommunication and further punishment at the ordinary's discretion.

Oaths

70. That whosoever shall curse an officer either temporal or spiritual, shall be committed immediately into St German's prison, and not released until first he give in good bonds to perform his censure, which is to wear the bridle four several market days at the several market towns, for the space of one hour, in the height of the market.

71. That whosoever shall swear an oath by taking the name of God in vain, shall for the first time pay twelve pence and sit an hour in the stocks, and for the second time two shillings, and so double for every such offence, to be levied by the churchwardens, afterward disposed of by the ordinary to pious uses.

72. That pledges, finding those for whom they are bound for children's goods, to imbevil and consume the same, whereby they (in respect of their obligation) may come to be damnified, shall have authority to possess themselves of all such goods, or cause the other for whom they are bound to give counter security. If they do not comply in doing the one or the other, they shall be committed until they submit.

And if such pledges shall thus come to possess these goods they shall also put in bonds themselves for the forthcoming of them.

Church cess and tithes

73. If any person living upon an intack have also a quarter or part of a quarter of land, he shall as well pay his assessment to the church out of the intack as out of the quarter land; out of the intack according to his ability, and out of the quarter land as other quarters in the parish are cessed.

74. That all cottiers living upon the quarter land shall pay their cessment to the church unless the farmers give them liberty to sit in their own pews.

75. That all boats fishing in another parish and not where the owners live shall pay the one half of their tithe in that parish and the other half to the proctors where the owners live, and the tithe wholly when they do land there, though the men belonging to the boat be of the other parish, provided the boat be not given out upon hire for term of years.

Probate of wills, etc.

76. That no security be liable to the payment of children's goods whilst the person or persons into whose hands they were deposited are able to make good payment out of their own goods, and the pledges not to be molested at law, but the persons in whose hands the goods were, that is to say, if they be able as aforesaid; if not, then the pledges, provided they demand it in due time.

77. That when a will or testament is made and an executor ordained, if this executor die before the will come to be proved, yet the executor of the said executor or administrator shall be capable of the benefit of the said will first made, and none else.

78. That when sufficient men are sworn to prize children's goods, the said goods shall not be forced on them under pretence of overrating them, for men must discharge their consciences, but the executors or overseers (if the executors be not capable) must take all things according to the prizement.

79. That when an executor is by the father's or mother's obligation, or both, concerned, being nominated in any specialty, the said executor, if he take upon him the executorship, shall be made liable to the parents' obligation.

Church administration

80. That the churchways for burial, christenings, marriages and for the minister to go on visitation may not be made up, but always passable on those occasions at all seasons of the year.

81. If the clerk neglect to do his duty after the first or second admonition, and therefore presentment made by the minister, churchwardens and chapter-quest, he shall not only lose his duty according to the statute, but the ordinary may put him out and another by the minister's and parishioners' election shall be installed by the bishop's approbation.

82. That though the sumner should have by the statute but a band of three lengths of three principal corns, portion like paid of every husbandman, yet it was always accustomed that he was to have half a stock of twelve sheaves of high corn from every farmer that hath a quarter land, or if more, to be paid according to the quarter land, and if less, after the same manner, and none to be privileged from the payment thereof to the sumner upon any score.

83. That the executors or administrators of all decedents be sworn to bring into our records a perfect inventory of all gold, silver, corn, cattle and goods, as soon as the court in discretion shall think fit, or be fined and punished. And if any of the aforesaid goods be concealed or left uninventoried, the court is to proceed against them for perjury.

84. That all offenders and disobedient persons ordered to be committed shall pay sixpence before their releasement, to the court.

85. That whosoever shall falsely accuse, scandalize or any way abuse the ordinary, vicars-general, official, or any ministers in bad words or deeds, shall be severely punished by the ecclesiastical court and proceeded against by suspension, excommunication, penance and fine, as the fault demerits.

86. That any who is indebted to any deceased and so left in his will, or any suspected by the executors to be indebted, shall clear themselves by oath within a year and a day after the probate of the will, in court. But all claimers are to go to the grave, as already mentioned in the ninth customary law.[247]

Robert Parr, John Harrison, vicars-general.

---

[247]See no. 9 above.

THE CONVOCATIONS OF 1680[248]

Wednesday 7 January 1680[249]

Sir, having received commission and special injunction from our reverend ordinary to call a convocation of the clergy of the isle, with all convenient expedition, you are therefore hereby desired to give personal summons to the whole clergy of this island particularly to make their personal appearance at Kirk Michael church, upon Wednesday next, being the seventh instant, to consult matters of great importance, which then and there shall be imparted unto them, and if any of them fail to answer this summons (which you are to give in his lordship's name, and by virtue of his authority) they must expect to be severely proceeded against for such their contumacy, as his lordship shall find just cause. Your own effectual execution hereof, and your appearance the same day with certificate of the discharge of your office herein, and the return of this our order, is also desired and expected, that the same may be recorded for our discharge in this behalf. Dated the second of January 1679/80.

John Harrison and Charles Parr, vicars-general.

To Mr Ewan Christian, general sumner; these to be speedily executed.

Thursday 21 October 1680

At a convocation of the clergy at Bishopscourt, the 21st day of October 1680, there appeared:

Charles Parr.
Thomas Allen.
William Crowe.
Thomas Thwaites.
Thomas Robinson.
Patrick Thompson.
Robert Fletcher.

Hugh Cosnahan.
Samuel Robinson.
Richard Thompson.
Samuel Wattleworth.
John Woods.
Edward Nelson.

---

[248]*Liber causarum.* See *Journal of the Manx Museum* II (1930), 201.
[249]Douglas, Manx Heritage Library, MS 9782, vicar-general's exhibits, no. 16.

Memorandum.

This twenty-first day of October 1680, the clergy of the Isle of Man were convened by Henry, lord bishop of Man, to consult with the said bishop about the discovery and distribution of the king's augmentation and the monies due out of the impropriations, ever since the first purchase of them in 1664, and because Mr Samuel Wattleworth and Mr Thomas Robinson are pretty well acquainted with the concerns thereof, and are not far distant from the officers with whom they are to negotiate this affair, therefore the said clergy, with the consent of the said bishop, have unanimously elected them two to solicit this business and to report their proceedings every twenty-first day of the month till this affair be brought to a good conclusion, and for their pains have agreed they shall be recompensed at the discretion of the said bishop out of the said monies, when it is received. As witness our hands hereunto subscribed, the day and year above written.

Henricus Sodorensis.

It is also jointly assented and consented unto by the bishop and all the clergy hereunto subscribed, that since the doctrine and rights of the church cannot be preserved without the due exercise of discipline, nor that be commodiously dispensed in this isle without keeping courts in several towns, churches and places thereof, which must necessarily occasion expense, that the vicars-general for the time being shall be allowed three pounds apiece yearly and every year out of the impropriation money during their officiating, and their successors likewise, as witness our subscriptions.

Henricus Sodorensis.	Thomas Thwaites.
Charles Parr.	Hugh Cosnahan.
Thomas Robinson.	John Woods.
Patrick Thompson.	William Crowe.
Samuel Robinson.	Edward Nelson.
Samuel Wattleworth.	Richard Thompson.
Thomas Allen.	Robert Fletcher.

THE CONVOCATION OF 26 JULY 1683[250]

At a convocation of the clergy of this isle before the reverend father in God John, by divine permission lord bishop of Sodor and Man,[251] in Kirk Michael church the twenty-sixth day of July in the year of our Lord God 1683 and in the first year of his consecration, it is ordered, ordained and decreed as followeth:

1. First, whereas general complaint is made by the whole clergy that most of their respective parishioners are very remiss and backward in attending divine service upon Sundays in the afternoon, as also upon holy days and such other days as are set apart for the service of God by the rubric of our church, which thing (if not seasonably reclaimed) may redound to the great decay of Christian piety amongst us, and to the end that such neglect may be redressed for the future and God the better glorified and honoured in his holy worship and religion the better propagated and established amongst us, it is therefore ordered, ordained and decreed that publication be made in the several parish churches throughout this isle, that all and singular the respective inhabitants and parishioners thereof (or one person out of each family at least) shall for the future repair to their parish churches to hear divine service every Sunday in the afternoon, as well as the forenoon, and upon all holy days and other days of prayer, duly and frequently under the penalty of forfeiting four pence from every person that shall neglect his duty in this nature, which the churchwardens are hereby ordered to levy and collect from time to time, as the same shall fall out to be distributed to some pious use, according to the ordinary's pleasure and appointment. And that this course may be better observed, the churchwardens of the respective parishes are likewise ordered to attend personally every Sunday and other days of public service as aforesaid, to take notice of such person or persons as shall neglect their duty in the premises, and to make presentment of their names once every month into the bishop's registry, that their fines may be ordered to be weighed and disposed of as aforesaid, wherein if the said churchwardens do fail or shall be found negligent in the punctual performance of their office in this behalf, and lawful conviction made thereof by their minister, they and every of them shall be severely proceeded against according to the utmost rigour that the law provides against such contempts.

2. And further it is ordered and decreed that all parents and masters or mistresses of families within this isle shall also for the future cause their children and servants to come duly upon every Sunday in the afternoon to be taught and instructed by the parson, vicar or curate of their parish in the Lord's Prayer, the

---

[250]Douglas, Manx National Heritage Library, M 9756, Diocesan Presentments, 1683.
[251]John Lake was bishop of Sodor and Man from 7 January 1683 until his translation to Bristol on 12 August 1684.

belief, ten commandments and the catechism set forth by the church, in such tongue as they are capable to learn the same, whereby they may be the better grounded in the principles of their faith and be the sooner filled and prepared for the receiving of the holy sacrament, and if any such parents, masters or mistresses be negligent or obstinate therein, and complaint or presentment made thereof either by the parson, vicar or curate, or the churchwardens (who are to take special notice of such contempts) such person or persons so offending shall be proceeded against by imprisonment and other punishments as the law provides.

3. And also whereas it is observed that there is a great undecency and disorder in all or most of the parish churches of this isle, that there are not sufficient and commendable seats and pews provided and set up in the said churches as is becoming the house of God, it is therefore also ordered and decreed that all and every the farmers and such other person or persons throughout the isle as have either a sitting or a burying place in any part of their parish church, that they and every of them shall take speedy counsel [for] the repairing and making up of their respective seats [or] pews in some handsome and orderly manner, according to their several abilities, at or before Easter Day next ensuing the date hereof, and if any of them be refractory therein or refuse to do the same at or before the time above limited, and due presentment made thereof by the churchwardens, such person or persons so offending shall be proceeded against by fine or punishment according as the nature of their contempt shall demand.

4. And whereas it is further observed that there hath been great neglect heretofore used in the keeping of a registry book in the several parish churches of this isle for christenings, marriages and burials, and that great inconveniences doth ensue thereby, it is therefore likewise ordered and decreed that every parson, vicar or curate within this isle shall for the future take special care either by themselves or their parish clerks to keep a true and perfect registry of all christenings, marriages and burials in their respective parishes, which to be written fair in a book to be provided at the charges of the parish for that purpose, wherein if any of them do fail or be found negligent, they are to be proceed[ed] against by suspension or such other punishment as the ordinary shall think fit to inflict. And it is also ordered and decreed that if there be any registry books in any parish church of this isle that are decayed or lacerated, that the parson, vicar or curate of that parish do forthwith take speedy course to have the same (or as much thereof as is legible and can be made use of) fairly transcribed into a new book, at the cost and charges of the parish, and the same so done, to be lodged up in the church, to be kept and preserved there for such use and purposes as the same is designated unto, according to the injunctions of the church for the same. And it is also ordered that copies of all register books in this isle be brought in once every year to be entered in the bishop's registry pro futuro, sub poena iuris. Johannes Parr, registrarius.

THE CONVOCATION OF 17 AUGUST 1685[252]

In capella sive ecclesia Sanctae Mariae apud Douglas decimo septimo die mensis Augusti anno Domini 1685.

Convocatio habita eodem die et loco presbyterorum et curatorum coram reverendo in Christo patre Domino Baptista providentia divina episcopo Sodorensi et Monensi.[253] Ita decretum est:

1. That every minister in his particular church do every Sunday catechize the children and youth of his parish in the church according to the catechism provided for that purpose in the service book or Book of Common Prayer of the Church of England, and this to be done in the afternoon service. Provided that some parts of the parish be catechized one day and some another according to the appointment of the minister, till the whole be sufficiently instructed, and then to begin again in the same method. And hereby parents are required to send their children, masters and housekeepers their servants, to the minister to be catechized, in which duty if any shall fail, the minister is to give in the name or names of such offenders to the bishop or in his absence to one of the vicars-general, that they may be punished according to their demerit.

2. That all parsons and vicars licensed do at least once every month preach to their congregations in their several churches, unless they shall be hindered by sickness or other impediment by us to be approved of; that on other Sundays in the morning according as appointed by the canons of the church, read to the people distinctly and with an audible voice one of the homilies licensed by authority.

3. That there be a register book kept by every minister within his respective charge, of the several christenings, burials and marriages that happen therein, and that none be churched in houses, nor infants baptized in houses, but in cases of necessity or upon some special licence obtained from the ordinary; otherwise both these duties shall be performed in the church, and that on such times as the rubric hath appointed, viz., baptism upon Sundays or holy days only, except as afforded upon case of necessity, and then if an infant through weakness hath received private baptism, yet as soon as the child's strength shall permit, it shall be brought into the church upon some Lord's Day, that the minister may certify the congregation of the lawfulness of that child's baptism according to the form in such cases provided in the Book of Common Prayer.

---

[252]Douglas, Manx National Heritage Library, MS 9756, Diocesan presentments (including causes), 1685.
[253]Baptist Levinz was bishop of Sodor and Man from 15 March 1685 until his death on 31 January 1693. There was then an interregnum for five years.

4. That reparations be lawfully made of the chancels and mansion houses belonging to the ministers themselves if they be faulty; also that they the said ministers take care to admonish the churchwardens to keep up the body of the church in due repair on the outside, and to furnish it with decent seats or forms within, such as become the house of God and may testify the respect the people bear to his service. In which duty, if the churchwardens prove remiss, let the minister give their names to the vicar-general, that they may be proceeded against according to law.

5. That the ministers in reading the service of the church observe the method prescribed in the rubric, reading each prayer in the same order as is there appointed, neither curtalizing the whole service nor reading any particular prayer out of its proper course, as there set down.

6. That the ministers be careful and diligent in the visiting their sick, and that they give them (if they are required and find it expedient for the comfort of the sick) the communion to them, but that they presume not to give it, but to such as they find penitent, and then that they communicate themselves with the sick, and after get the clerk or some one other fit person at least to communicate at the same time.

7. That the ministers call in their churchwardens and chapter-quest once every month to make and give their presentments of all crimes and misdemeanours in their respective parishes, that so all sins may be timely punished, and if possible, presented for the future, and if any churchwardens or chapter-quest fails, let him or their names be given in to the vicars-general, who are hereby enjoined to proceed against them with the utmost severity of law.

8. That the ministers and churchwardens take notice of all them that do not duly frequent the divine service, and that such person or persons as shall be absent from church more than one Sunday without lawful cause shall forfeit sixpence, which sixpence of every person so offending the churchwardens are to levy once every quarter of a year, to be disposed by the ordinary's discretion or by the vicars-general in his absence. In which duty, if the churchwardens are deficient, the ministers are required under pain of suspension to give in their names to the ordinary, or in his absence to one of the vicars-general.

9. That every minister that receives augmentation, either from his majesty's benefaction or the impropriation money, be obliged to teach an English school constantly in his respective parish, under the penalty of forfeiting his said augmentation, nor shall such minister be capacitated to receive such augmentation or augmentations, unless he or they bring a certificate from the churchwardens and parishioners of his or their due performance of this injunction. Moreover, because the ministers complain that they are discouraged from teaching school because the parishioners send not their children to them, they are hereby enjoined to present the parents of such children that are fit for the school and not sent thither, as oft as there is occasion in the bishop's court that such parents may be proceeded against according to the strictest severity of the law.

10. Lastly, let all these orders be forthwith put in execution under pain of suspension or sequestration, except the ordinary see just cause to dispense. Baptista Sodorensis.

THE CONVOCATION OF 23 AUGUST 1686[254]

N. B.: That on the twenty-third of August 1686 Baptist, lord bishop of this isle, held a court in Castletown where an order was made (and the above[255] certificate recited in it) concerning the seat and burial place of the family of Ballalough, which order is signed and sealed by his lordship. And another order against one Mr Roger Handley for scandalizing Mrs Mary Breteton, is signed by his lordship and his two vicars-general, at the said court held in Castle Rushen, the twenty-third day of August 1686.

Being called to certify a truth (according to my remembrance and knowledge) touching the seat and burial place of Ballalough in the church of Kirk Malew, belonging to the Calcotts, do say as follows:

That being curate under my brother, Parson Robert Parr, in that church in anno 1636, there was a loft over the reading place, down from the wall betwixt the chancel and church, and under the loft and below the reading-place, two quires (as they then termed them), one on the north side of the aisle (the passage up the church) and the other on the south side of the aisle opposite to the other, where I ever, in my time, saw the Calcotts of Ballalough sit in time of divine service, and buried there. When the quires were up, I saw others sit in that quire, but cannot remember their names, but one Kewley who sat upon a chest near the reading-place to answer the psalms. A year or two after (or thereabouts) orders came from his grace of York to the lord bishop of the isle (Dr Richard Parr) to uniform the churches here; his lordship caused the said quires to be taken away and the loft to be removed to the very bottom of the church, and seats to be made instead of those quires, and so the church was seated to the lower doors. In all which time, I do not remember any to bury in the said place or quire, but the Calcotts of Ballalough, myself being vicar of the parish at Easter 1641 (as I am yet) buried several of the children and grandchildren of Mr Henry Calcott, his brother Mr Robert Calcott, constable of Castle Rushen, himself and wife, and none else do I remember was buried there, till John Quayle of Ballasalley [Ballasalla] in November 1654 was buried at the very lower end of the quire, but how or by what interest or means he was buried there, I cannot tell, for Mr Henry Calcott died before that, in July 1650, and Captain Robert Calcott and his mother had the management of that estate when John Quayle was buried with his wife and daughter at after, and saw Mr William Stanley, Mary Lucas his wife, her son and sister sit in the said seat, but cannot tell by what right. Thomas Parr.

---

[254]*Liber causarum*, 1686. Copy in the Castle Rushen papers, Douglas, Manx Heritage Library, MS 9782, ecclesiastical courts, item 11.
[255]This note appears at the end of the document.

THE PROCLAMATION OF BISHOP LEVINZ, 1690[256]

Whereas... the Lord's Day is very much profaned and neglected to the great scandal and dishonour of our holy profession, and decay of Christian piety... we do order and require that no person within this our diocese do presume to do any servile work on that day, especially that no fisherman do offer to go to sea from Saturday at night till Monday morning, and that no miller do suffer his mill to grind from twelve of the clock on Saturday at night till nightfall on Sunday on a penalty of fourteen days' imprisonment in St German's prison, and penance in every church of the island for the first offence, and for every relapse double punishment and four pounds fine to the lord's use without mitigation.

[256]Moore, *Sodor and Man*, pp. 171-2.

THE ACT AGAINST NON-RESIDENCE, 1696[257]

Whereas it is observed that several great inconveniencies have attended this isle by reason of the bishop, archdeacon, clergy, temporal officers, soldiers and others, often withdrawing themselves from their respective duties within the same; for prevention whereof for the future, be it enacted by the governor, officers, deemsters and twenty-four keys aforesaid, that every bishop, archdeacon, parson, vicar, curate or others who now hold and enjoy the bishopric, archdeaconry or any parsonage, vicarage, curacy or such like ecclesiastical promotion within the isle, to the value of ten pounds per annum or upwards, as also every temporal officer, soldier or other person or persons having and enjoying any office, place or other employment from and under the right honourable lord of this isle, to the value of three pounds per annum or upwards, shall, from and after the first day of May next ensuing the date hereof [1 May 1697], inhabit and personally reside within this isle in and upon their respective livings, promotions, benefices, offices, places or other employments, and if they or any of them shall at any time after the said first day of May be non-resident, or not inhabit within the isle, in and upon their said respective livings, promotions, benefices, offices, places or other employments, but shall be found wilfully to absent him or themselves from his or their duties in the same (wind, weather, health and convenient shipping permitting) above the space of four months (to be accounted at several times) in any one year, commencing always upon the said first day of May in every year, such person or persons so offending shall (for the first offence) forfeit and lose the full value of one half year's profit, benefit and advantage of his or their said livings, promotions, benefices, offices, places or other employments, to be levied, collected and disposed of in manner and form as in any by this act is hereafter mentioned and expressed; and if any person or persons before mentioned be found to offend in the like nature as above declared and expressed at any time afterwards, he or they so offending shall for every such second offence, and for every other offence of that nature which he or they shall commit afterwards, forfeit and lose the full value of one whole year's profit, benefit and advantage of his or their said livings, promotions, benefices, offices, places and other employments aforesaid, and be declared and made incapable of receiving any further benefit or advantage thereof, until such time as he or they so offending shall return to his or their said respective duties as aforesaid.

And be it further enacted and declared by the authority aforesaid, that all such forfeitures are from time to time as they shall accrue or happen to be levied, taken, collected and received by order of the governor, deputy governor and the lord's council for the time being, directed to the coroner or coroners of the sheading or

---

[257]Mills, *Ancient ordinances*, pp. 154-5; Gill, *Statutes*, I, 152-3. Passed by Tynwald on 7 December 1696.

sheadings where such forfeitures shall happen to accrue, and the same when so levied, collected and received as aforesaid, to be employed and disposed of for such pious, charitable and public uses within this isle as the said governor, deputy governor and council shall have directions from the lord of this isle, for or concerning the same.

This is followed by an act for repealing the laws made against aliens, which was passed at the same session of Tynwald. Both acts are then signed as follows:

John Parr.[258]
Daniel Mylrea.[259]
Nicholas Sankey.[260]
John Rowe.[261]
Richard Stevenson.[262]
Thomas Huddleston.[263]

Charles Christian	John Kaighin
Nicholas Christian	Caesar Wattleworth
John Wattleworth	John Oates
Charles Moore	Patrick Christian
David Murray	James Banks
Nicholas Thompson	James Christian
Silvester Radcliffe	Robert Christian
John Bridson	James Oates
Thomas Christian	Robert Curghey
William Christian	Thomas Woods
John Corlett	

I am well-pleased with these several acts and do confirm the same, and will that they be published in due form upon the Tynwald Hill.

Derby.

---

[258]Deemster from 1693 until about 1724.
[259]Deemster from 1696 until about 1734.
[260]Governor from 1695 to about 1701.
[261]Comptroller from 1687 until after 1720.
[262]Receiver of the Isle of Man (1661-82) and then one of the commissioners for the revenue until 1701.
[263]Water bailiff and lord's attorney (1697-1701).

THE CONVOCATION OF 3 FEBRUARY 1704[264]

The constitution of the convocation[265]

[1] In the name of our great Lord and Master, the Lord Jesus Christ, and to the glory and increase of his kingdom amongst men.

We, the bishop, archdeacon, vicars-general and clergy of this isle, who do subscribe these articles, that we may not stand charged with the scandals which wicked men bring upon religion while they are admitted to and reputed members of Christ['s] church, and that we may by all laudable means promote the conversion of sinners, and oblige men to submit to the discipline of the Gospel, and lastly, that we may provide for the instruction of the growing age in Christian learning and good manners, we have formed these following constitutions, which we oblige ourselves (by God's help) to observe, and to endeavour that all others within our several cures shall comply with the same:

1. First, that when a rector, vicar or curate shall have any number of persons under twenty of his parish desirous and fit to be confirmed, he shall give the lord bishop notice thereof, and a list of their names, and shall suffer none to offer themselves to be confirmed but such he has before instructed to answer in the necessary parts of Christian knowledge, and who, besides their church catechism, have learned such short prayers for morning and evening as shall be immediately provided for that purpose.

2. That no person be admitted to the holy sacrament till he has first been confirmed by the bishop (or in case of his lordship's absence or indisposition) to bring a certificate from the archdeacon or vicars-general that he is duly qualified for confirmation.

[2] 3. That no person admitted to stand as godfather or godmother, nor to enter into the holy state of matrimony, till they have received the holy sacrament of the Lord's Supper, unless being an orphan, there be a necessity for his speedy marriage; and this to be approved of and dispensed with by the ordinary for a limited time to fit himself for the sacrament; and where any of them are of another parish, they are to bring a certificate from their proper pastor.

4. That all children and servants unconfirmed of such a division of the parish as the minister shall appoint (which shall be at least one-fourth part thereof) shall constantly come to evening prayers to be instructed in the principles of the Christian religion, at which time every rector, vicar or curate shall employ at least half an

---

[264]Douglas, Manx National Heritage Library, MS 802C.
[265]Sections 1-13 of this constitution were repealed by the pre-revestment written laws (ascertainment) act, 1978.

hour in their examination, and explaining some part of the Church catechism; and that all parents and masters which shall be observed by their children's and servants' ignorance to be grossly wanting in their duty in not teaching them this catechism, shall be presented for every such neglect, and severely punished; and to the end that this so necessary an institution may be religiously observed, every minister shall always (by the assistance of the churchwardens) keep a catalogue of such persons as are not confirmed, and is thereby required to present those that are absent without urgent cause, who shall be fined two pence the first Sunday they omit to come, four pence the second, and six pence the third; in which case the parents are to be answerable for their children, and masters for their servants, unless where it appears that the servants themselves are in fault.

5. For the more effectual discouragement of vice, if any person shall incur the censures of the church, and having done penance, shall afterwards incur the same censures, he shall not be admitted to do penance again (as has been formerly accustomed) until the church be fully satisfied [3] of his sincere repentance; during which time he shall not presume to come within the church, but be obliged to stand in a decent manner at the church door every Sunday and holy day the whole time of morning and evening service, until by his penitent behaviour and other instances of sober living, he deserve and procure a certificate from the minister, churchwardens and some of the soberest men of the parish, to the satisfaction of the ordinary; which if he do not so deserve and procure within three months, the church shall proceed to excommunication; and that during these proceedings, the governor shall be applied to not to permit him to leave the island; and this being a matter of very great importance, the minister and churchwardens shall see it duly performed under penalty of the severest ecclesiastical censures; and wherever any daring offender shall be and continue so obstinate as to incur excommunication, the pastor shall affectionately exhort his parishioners not to converse with him, upon peril of being partaker with him in his sin and punishment.

6. That the rubric before the communion, concerning unworthy receivers thereof, may be religiously observed, every rector, vicar or curate shall first privately and then publicly admonish such persons as he shall observe to be disorderly livers, that such as will not by this means be reclaimed may be hindered from coming to the Lord's table, and being presented, may be excommunicated; and if any minister knowingly admit such persons to the holy sacrament, whose lives are blemished with the vices of drunkenness, tippling, swearing, profaning the Lord's Day, quarrelling, fornication or any other crime by which the Christian religion is dishonoured, before such persons have publicly acknowledged their faults and solemnly promised amendment, the minister so offending shall be liable to severe ecclesiastical censure.

7. If any moar, serjeant, proctor or any other person shall presume on the Lord's Day to receive any rent or sums of money they shall be liable to ecclesiastical [4] censure, and shall always be presented for the same.

8. That the practice of commutation as has been formerly accustomed, namely of exempting persons obnoxious to the censures of the church from penance and other punishment appointed by law, on account of paying a sum of money or doing some charitable work, shall for the future cease.

9. For the promoting of religion, learning and good manners, all persons shall be obliged to send their children as soon as they are capable of receiving instruction to some petty school, and to continue them there until the said children can read English distinctly, unless the parents give a just cause to excuse themselves, approved of by the ordinary in open court; and that such persons who shall neglect sending their children to be so taught shall (upon a presentment made thereof by the minister, churchwardens or chapter-quest) be fined in one shilling per quarter to the use of the schoolmaster, who may refuse to teach those children who do not come constantly to school (unless for such causes as shall be approved of by the minister of the parish), and their parents shall be fined as if they did altogether refuse to send them to school.

10. And for the further encouragement of the schoolmasters, they shall respectively receive, over and above the salaries already allowed them, sixpence quarterly from the parents of every child that shall be taught by them to read English, and nine pence quarterly from such as shall be taught to write; which sums being refused, the sumner shall be ordered to require punctual payment within fourteen days, and upon default hereof they are to be committed till they submit to law.

11. Notwithstanding, where the parents or relations are poor, and not able to pay as aforesaid, and this be certified by the minister and churchwardens of the parish or the ordinary, such children are to be taught gratis.

12. And whereas some of the poorer sort may have just cause, and their necessities require it, to keep their [5] children at home for several weeks in the summer and harvest, such persons shall not be liable to the penalties aforesaid, provided they do (and are hereby strictly required to) send such children during such absence from school every third Sunday to the parish church at least one hour before the evening service, there to be taught by the schoolmaster to prevent losing their learning, and if any schoolmaster shall neglect his duty, and complaint be made and proved, he shall be discharged, and another placed in his stead, at the discretion of the ordinary; and every rector, vicar or curate shall, the first week of every quarter, visit the petty school and take account in a book of the improvement of every child, to be produced as often as the ordinary shall call for it.

13. For the more effectual suppression of vice, etc., the minister and churchwardens and chapter-quest shall, the last Sunday of every month, after evening prayers, set down in writing the names of all such persons as without just cause absent themselves from church; of parents, masters and mistresses, who neglect to send their children to be catechized; of parents and guardians who send not their children to school; and all other matters they are bound by their oaths to present; and that they may conscientiously discharge their duty, the articles of visitation are to be read to them at every such meeting, and this to be done under pain of the severest ecclesiastical censures.

[6] 14.[266] **Now forasmuch as some of the orders and constitutions in this synod agreed unto are such as do require the authority of the civil power to make them effectual to the ends they are designed, the bishop and archdeacon**

---

[266]The words in bold type are still in force (2005).

are earnestly desired to procure confirmation from the lord, his council and the twenty-four keys, to the glory of God and welfare of this church, and for the better government of the church of Christ, for the making of such orders and constitutions as shall from time to time be found wanting; and that better inquiry may be made into the execution of those that are in force, there shall be (God willing) a convocation of the whole clergy of the diocese on Thursday in Whitsun week[267] every year after this, at the bishop's chapel,[268] if his lordship be within this isle, or as soon as conveniently after his return, and that by these constitutions we may more effectually oblige ourselves and others, we do each of us subscribe our names this third of February 1703 [1704].

Thomas Sodor and Man.[269]
Samuel Wattleworth, archdeacon.
Robert Parr,
John Curghey, vicars-general.
Henry Norris.
Ewan Gill.
William Walker.
John Parr.
John Cosnahan.

John Woods.
William Gell.
Matthias Curghey.
Thomas Allen.
Samuel Robinson.
Robert Fletcher.
John Taubman.
John Christian.
Thomas Christian.

[7] *At a Tynwald court at St John's chapel the fourth day of February 1703/4.*

The before constitutions being this day offered by the lord bishop and archdeacon of this isle unto us the governor, officers and twenty-four keys, for our approbation, and having perused the same, do find them very reasonable, just and necessary, and do therefore approve of and consent to them as far as concerns the civil power.

John Parr.
Daniel Mylrea.
Robert Mawdesley.[270]
Christopher Parker.[271]
John Rowe.
William Ross.[272]
John Bridson.[273]
Thomas Stevenson.

Silvester Radcliffe.
John Bridson.
James Banks.
Robert Christian.
James Christian.
John Oates.
John Harrison.
Thomas Corlett.

[267]This can be any date from 14 May to 17 June inclusive. The convocation still meets on this day, even after 300 years.
[268]This phrase was altered by the statute law revision act, 1986 to read: 'at such place within this isle as the bishop may direct'.
[269]Thomas Wilson was bishop of Sodor and Man from 16 January 1698 until his death on 7 March 1755.
[270]Deputy governor from 1703 and then governor from 1704 to 1713.
[271]Receiver from 1701 until after 1709.
[272]Water bailiff from 1702 until after 1704.
[273]Lord's attorney from 1701 until after 1704.

Charles Moore.
Ewan Christian.
Thomas Christian.
John Wattleworth.
William Christian.

James Oates.
Robert Curghey.
Nicholas Christian.
Daniel Lace.
Robert Moore.

[8] I am well pleased with the before constitutions and do confirm the same, and require that they be published at the next Tynwald court in usual manner. Derby.

[*At a Tynwald court held at St John's chapel the sixth day of June anno Domini 1704.*[274]

The beforegoing constitutions were this day publicly proclaimed upon the Tynwald hill according to ancient form and custom. As witness our hands this day and year above written.

Thomas Sodor and Man.
John Parr, deemster.
Daniel Mylrea, deemster.
Robert Mawdesley.
Christopher Parker.
John Rowe.
William Ross.
John Bridson.
John Stevenson.
Ewan Christian.
William Christian.
Charles Moore.
Thomas Stevenson.
James Christian.

John Bridson.
John Wattleworth.
Robert Christian.
Thomas Christian.
James Oates.
Robert Curghey.
John Curghey.
John Oates.
Daniel Lace.
James Banks.
John Harrison.
Thomas Corlett.
John Wattleworth.]

---

[274]In Gill, *Statutes*, I, 160-1, but not in the convocation book.

THE CONVOCATIONS OF BISHOP THOMAS WILSON, 1704-54

Wednesday 23 August 1704[275]

Thanks sent to Dr Thomas Bray

At a convocation of the clergy at Douglas, August 23, 1704.

We the archdeacon, vicars-general and clergy of the diocese of Man, having had repeated instances of the great charity and pious industry of the very reverend Dr Thomas Bray,[276] who by his interest and proper bounty had laid the foundation of parochial libraries in all the churches of this land, and does still continue to augment them,

In a just sense of this great mercy, we do most heartily thank Almighty God for raising us up such friends, and do desire that our humble thanks may be rendered to, and accepted by the said Dr Bray, entreating him likewise that he would be pleased to signify our sense of this labour to all those good men whom he has engaged in our interest, assuring them that as we do daily feel the advantage of this uncommon benefit, so we shall be sure to transmit a grateful remembrance of it to posterity, not only by this solemn act of ours, but by a more acceptable service, hoping by the blessing of God to breed up the growing age in Christian knowledge and good manners in some measure answerable to these great advantages.

Samuel Wattleworth, archdeacon.	Henry Norris.
Robert Parr,	Ewan Gill.
John Curghey, vicars-general.	Joseph Cosnahan.
John Parr.	Matthias Curghey.
William Walker.	John Taubman.
Samuel Robinson.	John Christian.
John Woods.	William Gell.
Thomas Allen.	Thomas Christian.

4 September 1704. Examined per me John Woods, registrarium episcopi.

[275]Douglas, Manx National Heritage Library, MS 799C, fo. 26r.
[276](1656-1730). Rector of Sheldon (1690-5), founder of the Society for Promoting Christian Knowledge (1699) and of the Society for Propagating the Gospel (1701). Rector of St Botolph, Aldgate (1706-30).

Thursday 16 May 1706[277]

Captain John Wattleworth of Ramsey[278] was sentenced to three Sundays' penance in penitential habit for fornication, twice at Kirk Maughold and once at Lezaire, the other offender being the first to undergo the same.

Bishop Wilson proposed his form of receiving penitents, 'to be duly and devoutly observed in all churches and chapels within the diocese of Man.'

A form of receiving penitents

A form of receiving penitents to be duly and devoutly observed in all churches and chapels within the diocese of Man.
   After morning prayers, the person who is censured to penance, standing in the accustomed place and habit, the minister shall exhort him as follows:
   Brother, the church being a society of persons professing to live in the fear of God, and expecting the judgments of God to fall upon them if his laws are broken without calling the offenders to account; it is reasonable that every member of his society who has been guilty of any scandalous offence should either openly confess his sins and promise reformation for the time to come; or else be cut off from the body of Christ, which is the church.
   Now, to awaken you to a true sense of your condition, I will set before you the Word of God, that you may certainly know what will be the end of a wicked life, and that knowing the terror of the Lord, you may speedily turn unto him and make your peace.
   Hear then what the apostle St Paul saith of great offenders: 'Be not deceived; neither fornicators, nor adulterers, nor effeminate, nor thieves, nor covetous, nor drunkards, nor revilers, nor extortioners, shall inherit the kingdom of God.'[279] Hear also what the same apostle says: 'Now the works of the flesh are these, adultery, fornication, uncleanness, lasciviousness, witchcraft, hatred, variance, emulations, wrath, strife, seditions, heresies, envyings, murders, drunkenness, revellings and such like; of the which I tell you before, as I have told you in time past, that they which do such things shall not inherit the kingdom of God.'[280] 'It is a fearful thing to fall into the hands of the living God, who can destroy both body and soul in hell; where the worm dieth not and the fire is not quenched.'[281]
   These being the very words of God, you will do well to consider into what a condition you have brought yourself. And indeed the only comfort you have is this,

---

[277]This convocation is not in MS 802C. The account printed here is taken from J. Keble, *The life of the right reverend father in God Thomas Wilson, D. D.* (2 vols., Oxford, 1863), I, 237-40 and the text is reprinted from *The works of the right reverend father in God, Thomas Wilson, D. D.* (7 vols., Oxford, 1866), VII, 128-34.
[278]Probably a relative of the archdeacon's. He was 'captain' of Ramsey, one of the island's four towns, acting as a glorified constable. See Dickinson, *Lordship of Man*, pp. 52-3.
[279]1 Co. vi. 9.
[280]Ga. v. 19.
[281]He. x. 31.

that you are yet alive, and that the day of grace and repentance is yet afforded you. Which that you may make use of, I must also let you know what God has declared concerning such as repent and turn unto God, and bring forth fruits meet for repentance.

'To the Lord our God belong mercies and forgivenesses, though we have rebelled against him.'[282] 'If we confess our sins, God is faithful and just to forgive us our sins.'[283]

And our blessed Saviour, to show us what great compassion God has for him that has gone astray and returns to his duty, he represents him as a man who having found his lost sheep takes it upon his shoulders, rejoicing.[284] And in another parable, to make us understand the love of God for penitent sinners, he shows us how we may hope to be received, even as a compassionate father received his prodigal son, when once he became humble and sensible of his faults; he embraced him, he clothed him, he rejoiced with his whole family. And such joy is there amongst the angels of God when a sinner repenteth.[285]

Such great encouragement you have to return to God. But then you must do it sincerely; you must not only appear outwardly a penitent, but with a true penitent heart come before God and his church. Which if you do, you will not look upon this as a punishment inflicted upon you by the church, but as a wholesome medicine administered for the good of your precious soul. Without which you might have gone on adding sin to sin, until there had been no more space for repentance.

You will suffer yourself to be admonished; acknowledge your offence and give glory to God, in owning his power to punish you in the next life, though you should escape in this.

You will testify to others that it is indeed an evil thing and bitter to forsake the Lord. And owning this so publicly, you will be ashamed to return to your sins you have repented of.

Then we shall all pray to God that he would for Christ's sake accept of your repentance, that he would enable you to live for the time to come in obedience to the laws of Jesus Christ, that your soul may be saved at the day of judgment.

These are the wholesome ends the church proposes in her censures; following herein the apostle's directions: 'in meekness instructing those that oppose themselves, that they may recover themselves out of the snare of the devil, who are taken captive by him at his will'.[286]

Therefore, dear brother, consider that you are in the presence of God, the searcher of hearts. You may indeed deceive this congregation with a feigned repentance, but you cannot deceive him that made you; who, if you dissemble in this matter, will shut you out of heaven, though you continue a visible member of his church here.

---

[282]Da. ix. 9. This is one of the Scripture sentences used at the beginning of morning and evening prayer in the 1662 Prayer Book.
[283]1 Jn. i. 9. Also used as the preceding in the 1662 Prayer Book.
[284]Cf. Lk. xv. 1-6.
[285]Lk. xv. 11-32; Lk. xv. 7.
[286]2 Ti. ii. 25.

But that we may take all due caution, I must in the name of this congregation ask you these questions:

Are you from the heart sorry for the sin you have committed? *I am.*

Will you be more careful for the time to come, and by God's help avoid all temptations to it? *I will.*

Will you constantly pray to God to assist you to do so? *I will.*

Do you desire the forgiveness of all good Christians whom you may have offended? *I do.*

And do you desire that others, seeing your sorrow, may beware of falling into any grievous sin? *I do desire it.*

Will you take patiently the admonition of such as after a Christian manner shall advise you, if they shall see you forget yourself, and the promises you have now made? *I will.*

Then shall the minister say: May the gracious God give you repentance to life eternal; receive you into his favour; continue you a true member of the church of Christ; and bring you unto his everlasting kingdom, through the same Jesus Christ our Lord. Amen.

After which he shall speak to the congregation as follows:

Seeing now, dearly beloved brethren, that this person is moved by the good Spirit of God to confess his sins and to be afflicted for them, let us, that we may mourn with him as becomes good Christians, consider that we are all subject to sin and to death eternal, that there is nothing so vile and wicked which we should not run into, did not the grace of God prevent us, that therefore we have nothing to value ourselves for above others, but what the good Spirit of God has given us. 'Let him then,' as the apostle advises, 'that thinketh he standeth, take heed lest he fall.'[287] Let us ever remember the words of Christ: 'Watch and pray, that ye enter not into temptation'[288] because our adversary the devil, as a roaring lion, walketh continually about, seeking whom he may devour. Let us learn never to be ashamed to acknowledge our sins, but let us confess and forsake them, that we may find mercy. For it is far better to suffer shame here than the wrath of God hereafter. In a word, let us all with penitent hearts call our sins to remembrance and judge ourselves, though we are not censured by the church. Let us confess our sins unto God, who is most willing to pardon us if we turn unto him with all our hearts, steadfastly purposing to lead a new life. Which God grant we may all do, for Jesus Christ his sake. Amen.

Then shall be said distinctly the fifty-first psalm, together with the prayers appointed (in the communion office) for Ash Wednesday.

[287] 1 Co. x. 12.
[288] Mt. xxvi. 41; Mk. xiv. 38.

Supplementary provisions

My brethren, In the form for receiving penitents there ought to have been a prayer for persons performing penance, who are not yet to be received into the peace of the church. I mean where people do penance for the great crimes of adultery, fornication, perjury or incest. For lesser faults I think it may be omitted. I make no doubt but so edifying a practice, so very agreeable to the way of the primitive church, and so reasonable in itself, will be approved by you all, and conscientiously complied with. I am your affectionate friend and brother, Thomas Sodor and Man.

When penitents are to be received into the peace of the church, you are to use the form already in your hands; and at other times, this following prayer only, with proper exhortations.

Let the penitent be made sensible of the crimes for which he is censured, exhorted to humble himself before God and the church, and especially to manifest the sincerity of his sorrow by bringing forth fruits meet for repentance. After which, all kneeling shall devoutly pray as followeth:

The prayer

O God the fountain of mercy, who didst send thy Son into the world to call sinners to repentance, and who hast assured us that there is joy in heaven over one sinner that repenteth, look down with an eye of pity upon thy servant who has gone astray from thy commandments. Give him a clear sight of his sin and a deep sense of thy wrath against impenitent sinners, that seeing his danger, he may patiently submit to godly discipline and to all the difficulties of true repentance. And grant, O God, that he may not deceive himself by a counterfeit repentance, but that this public confession may produce a real change of heart and amendment of life, that he may utterly renounce and forsake all evil ways, break off all evil habits, and being ever mindful of his infirmities, he may be more careful of himself, and more earnest for grace for the time to come; working out his salvation with fear and trembling, that the church on earth and the angels in heaven may rejoice in his conversion.

Bless, O Lord, the discipline of this church, and make it effectual for the conviction of wicked men and gainsayers. Vouchsafe unto all penitents a true sense of their crimes, true repentance for them, and thy gracious pardon. Be merciful unto us all, and keep it ever in the hearts of thy servants that it is an evil thing and bitter to forsake the Lord. Keep us from presumptuous sins; in all temptations succour us, that no wickedness may get the dominion over us; but that continuing in the peace and unity of the church unto our lives' end, we may be made partakers of everlasting happiness with thy saints in heaven, through Jesus Christ our Lord and Saviour. Amen.

Then shall the minister say: May the gracious God give you repentance unto life, etc.

That the discipline of this church may not degenerate or fall into contempt, it is thought meet by this convocation that the form above mentioned be religiously observed (in the mother tongue) in all churches and chapels of this diocese, and that none omit it under penalty of the severest ecclesiastical censures.

That the minister and churchwardens, with some of the gravest of the parishioners, shall *bona fide* certify unto the bishop that all this was performed after a decent and Christian manner, which certificate, the person who has performed this censure shall be directed by his pastor to bring himself within seven days (and not to send it by any other person) that he may receive the bishop's blessing and such spiritual counsel and advice as may tend to the good of his soul.

Thomas Sodor and Man.	John Cosnahan.
Samuel Wattleworth, archdeacon.	Matthias Curghey.
Robert Parr.	John Woods.
John Curghey.	Ewan Gill.
Thomas Allen.	Thomas Christian.
John Parr.	William Gell.
Henry Norris.	

Form of excommunication[289]

My brethren, and all good Christians here met together, we are met upon a very unusual and mournful occasion. We have hitherto, blessed be God, preserved in some good measure the ancient discipline of the church, and notorious sinners have been prevailed upon to take shame to themselves in a public confession of their offences, and to desire the prayers of the church for the grace that is necessary for a true conversion.

I am sorry to tell you that there is a person now under the censures of the church who utterly refuseth to submit to this wholesome discipline, being more concerned for the shame that attends its censures than he is for his salvation.

We have laid before you his crimes, and the Christian methods which have been made use of to bring him to a sense of his guilt and danger, and to oblige him to make what satisfaction he can for the scandal he hath given.

You will see how very long we have waited in hopes of bringing him to submit to the discipline of the church, until at last our discipline begins to be slighted, as too weak for such offenders.

However, it ought not to repent us that we have waited with patience, when we consider with what mighty patience God himself waiteth to be gracious, and that the sentence of excommunication was never, in the primitive church, executed hastily, nor until all other probable ways had been made use of without effect.

Now, this being the last remedy which the church can make use of for awakening obstinate offenders, the whole church ought to be satisfied upon what grounds, and by what authority, we pronounce this sentence; and what will be the effects of such a sentence, when passed according to the will and appointment of Jesus Christ.

[289]*Works of Thomas Wilson*, VII, 121-7. This is not dated, but must come from about this time.

The Holy Scriptures tell us that our Lord Jesus Christ, who came to seek and to save his lost creatures, has appointed divers ordinances for the conversion and salvation of men. For instance, he has appointed preaching, to draw men to him; he has appointed the sacrament of baptism, by which we are admitted into his household the church, and that of the Lord's Supper, as a pledge of his love and of our communion with him. And lastly, he hath ordained godly discipline, that such as who do not live as becomes their Christian profession may be reproved, corrected and amended, or else cast out of his church.

And all these ordinances are committed unto his ministers who are also called his stewards, because to them he has committed the keys of his house and kingdom, that is, the church; that they may admit such as are worthy, and that they may shut out such as behave themselves disorderly in his family.

Jesus Christ, I say, committed this power to his apostles, and they to their successors, with this assurance from his own mouth: 'He that heareth you, heareth me, and he that despiseth you, despiseth me, and him that sent me.'[290]

So that you see, whoever makes a jest of church discipline makes a jest of an ordinance of God, and a man may as well despise the whole Christian religion as this power, which is as much the ordinance of Jesus Christ as preaching or the use of the sacraments.

The most unlearned Christian will understand this; when he is asked for what end he was baptized, he will answer, that he might thereby be made a 'member of Christ, a child of God, and an inheritor of the kingdom of heaven'.[291]

But why does he believe that baptism does give him a right to these blessings? Why, because Jesus Christ gave power to his ministers to baptize all nations, that such as are baptized into Christ have put on Christ, that is, are members of Christ's body, which is his church.

Now, will not our Lord Christ, who has promised to own you for his children when his ministers have admitted you into his church by baptism, will he not also disown you when the same ministers, acting in his name, shall, by the same power of the keys, shut you out of his church?[292]

For if you believe that they receive you into Christ's church by baptism, you must believe that they shut you out as effectually by excommunication.

In short, every Christian when he is baptized, is admitted into the church upon a most solemn promise to live as a Christian ought to do; if he does not do so, those very ministers who admitted him are bound to exhort, to rebuke, and to censure him; and if these methods will not do, to excommunicate him, that is, to cut him off from the body of Christ and from God's favour and mercy. Not that he may be lost for ever, but that he may see his sad condition and repent, and be saved.

The form of excommunication made use of by the apostles of our Lord was by delivering offenders to Satan. Now, because this is laughed at by profane people who do not know the Scriptures, I will show you what that means. The Spirit and Word of God has told us that the devil has a kingdom and subjects over whom he

---

[290]Lk. x. 16.
[291]From the Prayer Book catechism.
[292]The allusion is to Mt. xvi. 19.

reigns, that is, over the children of disobedience; that Jesus Christ has also his kingdom and subjects, and when the apostles gained over any of the subjects of Satan unto Christ, they are said to 'turn them from darkness to light, and from the power of Satan unto God'.[293]

Now, when any of Christ's subjects become rebellious and refuse to be governed by the laws of the gospel, his ministers are bound to admonish them of their sin and of their danger; and if they refuse to obey their godly admonitions, then to turn them out of that society of which Christ is the head, and consequently, such persons fall under the power of Satan again, who useth his subjects like slaves. And God permits him to do so, that sinners, if they are not utterly lost, may with the prodigal, when he was forced to herd with swine, see the state they are fallen from and repent, and desire to get out of the snare and power of the devil, and be restored to the favour of God.

So that excommunication is made use of, not as a punishment only, but as a remedy, that sinners seeing the evil state they are in, being deprived of all hopes of salvation while they are out of the church, may desire to be restored to God's grace from which they are fallen, that they may work out their own salvation with more fear for the time to come.

But here I must take notice of one thing which often hinders the discipline of the church from having this good effect upon sinners. They are apt to say: 'If I am shut out of this church, I can go to another.' Why, has Christ more churches than one? 'Is Christ divided?' saith the apostle.[294] Do not all Christians profess to believe one holy, apostolic church? And is not this church a member of that holy church? And have not the ministers of Christ here the same authority from their Lord and Prince as any other Christian bishop, namely, the authority of binding and loosing? And will not our sentence, when we proceed according to the rules which Christ hath given us, be confirmed in heaven? If so, what advantage will a sinner get by going to another society, if after all Jesus Christ shall confirm the sentence of his former pastor? And for want of being reconciled by him, shall shut him out of heaven?

It is true our Lord hath not given us any power to compel men by outward force either to come into or to continue in his church, but will people for this reason despise the power which Christ has given us? They will hardly do so if they know what St Paul hath said upon this: 'The weapons we use,' saith he, 'are not carnal, but mighty through God',[295] that is, God can humble the stoutest sinner and make the power of his ministers effectual when they use their power for his glory and according to his will.

You see, good Christians, that we take upon us no authority but what Christ has given us, what his apostles exercised and what we are bound by his most solemn vows to exercise.

Every bishop, for instance, at his consecration solemnly promises that he will correct and punish disobedient and criminous persons within his diocese, according

[293] Ac. xxvi. 18.
[294] 1 Co. i. 13.
[295] 2 Co. iv. 4.

to such authority as he has by God's Word. What authority he has by God's Word you have already heard. And all serious Christians must acknowledge that we should become adversaries to ourselves, to our church and to our country, if we should suffer church discipline to fall into decay while we are warranted and bound, both by the law of God and of this land, to exercise it; especially when vices of this kind begin to grow upon us.

Only let us take care that we use this authority as the apostle directs, for edification and not for destruction.[296] And if we must be forced to shut this unhappy person out of the church, let it be with the same compassion and reluctancy that a father turns his rebellious child out of his house, not with a desire that he should starve and be lost for ever, but that being made sensible of the misery of being out of his father's house, he may more earnestly desire to return and be received into favour, and become a more dutiful child for the time to come.

God has infinite expedients to bring back sinners that are gone away from him. We know how the prodigal son was brought to a sense of his condition by the miseries he met with when he was from under his father's care, how David's eyes were opened by a parable,[297] how Manasseh became an instance of repentance when in bonds,[298] and we should not despair, but be confident rather, that God will bless his own institutions in the hands of us his ministers, for the good of all such persons as draw these censures upon themselves. And it will be far from being severity to them, if by these means they be brought to a sense of their evil condition, and their souls be saved in the day of the Lord Jesus.[299]

This is the design of church censures, and that they may have this good effect, the apostle has given directions to all Christians not to accompany with such, that they may be ashamed.[300] And our holy church in her articles, as you will find it in the thirty-third article of the Church of England, has declared in these words: 'That person which by open denunciation of the church is rightly cut off from the unity of the church and excommunicated, ought to be taken of the whole multitude of the faithful as an heathen and publican, until he be openly reconciled by penance and received into the church by a judge that hath authority thereunto.'

Pursuant to which article the church in the eighty-fifth canon appoints that 'all persons excommunicated and so denounced, be kept out of the church by the churchwardens'.[301] And in the sixty-fifth canon directs: 'That all such as stand lawfully excommunicated, shall every six months be openly denounced and declared excommunicate, that others may be thereby admonished to refrain their company and society.'[302]

As for any temporal penalties or incapacities which an excommunicate person may be exposed to, these do not properly belong to the church; they are no part of

---

[296]Cf. 2 Co. x. 8.
[297]Cf. 2 Sa. xii. 1-10.
[298]Cf. 2 Ch. xxxiii. 10-13.
[299]Cf. 1 Co. v. 5.
[300]Cf. 2 Th. iii. 14.
[301]1603/85. See Bray, *Anglican canons*, pp. 378-81.
[302]1603/65. *Ibid.*, pp. 354-7.

our sentence, they are altogether in the hand of the civil magistrate. Our sentence is purely spiritual; it is the sentence of Jesus Christ and only concerns the good of the souls of those he has committed to our care. It is part of that ministry which we received by the imposition of hands, and which we most humbly pray God to enable us to exercise to his glory, to the putting a stop to the growing vices of the age, and to the edification of the church of Christ, which he hath purchased with his blood. Amen.

The sentence

It is with great reluctancy, God is witness, and after many prayers to God for their conversion, that we proceed to this last remedy which Christ has appointed for the conversion of sinners.

But we hope you are not shut out, that you may ever remain out of the church, but that you may become sensible of your errors, and return with more zeal to your heavenly Father.

In the meantime we must do our duty and leave the event to God.

In the name of Jesus Christ and by the authority which we have received from him, we separate you from the communion of the church which he has purchased with his blood and which is the society of all faithful people; and you are no longer a member of his body or of his kingdom, until you be openly reconciled by penance, and received into the church by a judge that hath authority so to do.

When persons excommunicated are received back into the church

I, an unworthy minister of Jesus Christ, by the same authority and power, even that of our Lord Jesus Christ, by which for thy obstinacy and other crimes thou hast been excluded from the communion of Christ's holy church; by the same power, I do now release thee from that bond of excommunication, according to the confession now made by thee before God and this church, and do restore thee again unto the communion of the church of Christ, beseeching the Almighty to give thee his grace, that thou mayest continue a lively member of the same unto thy life's end, through Jesus Christ our Lord. Amen.

Thursday 8 July 1708[303]

[9] At a convocation of the clergy at the parish church of Kirk Michael, Thursday the eighth day of July, anno Domini 1708.

Clergy present:

Samuel Wattleworth, archdeacon.   Matthias Curghey.
Robert Parr,   Ewan Gill.
John Curghey, vicars-general.   James Makon.

[303]Douglas, Manx National Heritage Library, MS 802C.

William Walker.	William Ross.
Thomas Allen.	Henry Allen.
Henry Norris.	John Woods.

Eodem die. Mr Thomas Christian and Mr Ewan Gill have obliged themselves *sub poena trium librarum ad usum domini* that they will within twenty-one days at mutual expenses bring to Kirk Marown the grand inquests (both the lord Derby's and the lord bishop's) to determine a controversy concerning a parcel of land near the churchyard of the aforesaid parish.

Mr [Samuel] Robinson vicar of Kirk Arbory having married one Thomas Steich (who is supposed to have a wife in south Wales) to one Sarah Rose, and this at uncanonical hours, and having been lately disordered in drink, as is proved by some of the parishioners, notwithstanding several admonitions heretofore given him by his diocesan, and that he has arbitrarily repelled one of his parishioners from the sacrament without giving notice to the ordinary within fourteen days after, according to the rubric before the communion, with other irregularities and omissions of his duty, to the great dishonour of the sacred function and scandal of religion. He is therefore now [10] suspended by the right reverend the lord bishop *ab officio et beneficio in triennium*, and in the meantime, the neighbouring clergy are to supply the cure by turns, for which they are to be satisfied out of the profits of the vicarage, which are to be forthwith sequestered by the churchwardens of the said parish.

Mr Thomas Christian the present incumbent of Kirk Christ Rushen having been two years ago required to reside in the said parish and since admonished by the right reverend the lord bishop to remove there with his family to avoid scandal, and to be in better capacity of discharging his duty in the same cure. He is now enjoined to go thither and reside there within twenty-one days under pain of suspension *ab officio et beneficio* (upon continuance in further disobedience and contumacy) deprivation of the said vicarage for ever. And if his wife do not, within forty days after, remove and cohabit with him, she is to be committed to St German's prison, there to remain till she give security to submit to this injunction, and the laws of this island.

Eodem die. John Robinson censured to three Sundays' penance for falsely and audaciously saying that Mr deemster Parr was a church robber.

Item, Thomas Steich ordered to St German's prison till he give security not to cohabit with Sarah Rose having (as is upon good grounds presumed) another wife in south Wales.

Item, an order for the religious observation of holy days.

Thursday 16 June 1709

[11] At our annual convocation on Thursday in Whitsun week, June 16, anno Domini 1709...

Thursday 1 June 1710

Bishop's charge against clandestine marriages

[12] My brethren, The acts of convocation lately passed to prevent clandestine marriages, as well as the marriages of such persons as have not been instructed in the principles of Christianity in order to fit them for confirmation and the Lord's Supper, being of great consequence to the honour of God and the good of souls to be most exactly observed, I find myself obliged to declare that if any person shall thereafter wilfully neglect or break these constitutions by marrying any couple without licence first published some Sunday before the said marriage shall be solemnized, or without banns called according to the rubric, or if any person shall grant a licence without a certificate from the rector or vicar of the parish where the persons inhabit, importing that such persons intending to intermarry have been confirmed and received the sacrament of the Lord's Supper (according to the true intent of the aforesaid acts) or if any person shall presume to marry those of another parish without his brother's knowledge and leave, that the person so offending shall be suspended *ab officio et beneficio* for one whole year, without any respect to any person under my jurisdiction. Thomas Sodor and Man.

Presentments for drunkenness and swearing

[13] Whereas it is observed and lamented by sober persons that the sins of drunkenness, swearing and cursing have of late much prevailed in the market towns of this island, to the great scandal of Christianity, it is therefore decreed that the churchwardens and chapter-quest shall take particular notice of those who are guilty of these sins and shall present their names to the court, whether they be strangers or inhabitants of the place, that such may be censured and reclaimed, if possible; at least, that their ill example may not infect the neighbourhood. And this to be published in the church or chapel of each town the next Lord's Day after this comes to the vicar's or chaplain's hands.

Thomas Sodor and Man.	Matthias Curghey.
Samuel Wattleworth, archdeacon.	William Gell.
Robert Parr,	Thomas Allen.
John Curghey, vicars-general.	John Christian.
John Parr.	William Walker.
Samuel Robinson.	John Woods.
Henry Norris.	

On 16 November 1710 Archdeacon Samuel Wattleworth named Henry Finch, dean of York, as his proctor in the York convocation, and Edward Finch as proctor for the clergy of Sodor and Man.[304]

[304]Original document preserved in the Manx National Heritage Library.

On 3 January 1711 the convocation assembled in order to elect William Walker, rector of Ballaugh, as its proctor in the York convocation. The proxy is signed by all the above (except the bishop, the archdeacon and William Walker himself) and in addition by Ewan Gill of Kirk Marown, Thomas Christian of Holy Trinity Rushen, John Taubman of Kirk Lonan, and John Cosnahan of Kirk Santan. The following day, Walker nominated Edward Finch, rector of Wigan in the diocese of Chester, as his proctor.[305]

Thursday 12 June 1712

Tenants on the abbey lands who refuse to pay their tithes

[14] The right reverend the lord bishop having this day signified to the clergy that some of the tenants of the abbey demesnes in the parish of Kirk Malew have petitioned his lordship for a confirmation of a favour formerly desired by them, with relation to the payment of their tithes, which favour some of them have so far despised as not to enjoy the benefit of it without putting the clergy to the trouble of a lawsuit, and which most of them desire may be void and null unless it be for ever continued to them and their posterity, the clergy do therefore look upon this their conduct to be highly ungrateful and their request unreasonable, and do therefore unanimously declare that they cannot at all comply with it, but expect that all and every of the said tenants shall for the future punctually pay the tithes of the said demesne lands in kind, or agree yearly for the same, as other tenants are accustomed and obliged to do.

Matthias Curghey.	Thomas Allen.
John Christian.	John Parr.
William Ross.	Henry Norris.
Henry Allen.	John Taubman.
Samuel Wattleworth, archdeacon.	John Woods.
Robert Parr.	John Cosnahan.
John Curghey.	William Gell.

[15] I do desire that the ecclesiastical court proceed according to this resolution and the act of settlement made in this behalf, for that the favour promised them by me was only conditional, the condition being that it should be acknowledged that they will all unanimously and thankfully embrace it, which most of them have refused. Thomas Sodor and Man.

The payment of corbs

[16] Whereas it appears that the corbs due to spiritual men have not been paid according as the law provides, some having received but part and others none at all for some generations past, in regard that they were not to be had, either through

---

[305]Douglas, Manx Heritage Library, MS 9782, ecclesiastical courts, item 19.

neglect or poverty, which now hath occasioned some disputes and difference betwixt the widows and executors of the late incumbents and their successors, which being taken into consideration by the whole clergy of the isle this day, they think it fit and reasonable and do unanimously consent unto, that the personal widows and executors of the late incumbents, viz., of Mr Robinson, late vicar of Kirk Arbory, of Mr Ewan Gill, late vicar of Kirk Marown, shall pay each of them ten shillings unto their successors in full of whatsoever corbs are payable from them by law, which ten shillings is to be laid out to buy a book or books at the discretion of the ordinary for the use of the successors for ever. And the same to be observed from time to time hereafter among such clergy as are by law obliged to pay corbs.

Thomas Sodor and Man.	John Taubman.
Samuel Wattleworth, archdeacon.	John Cosnahan.
Robert Parr.	John Christian.
John Curghey.	Matthias Curghey.
Thomas Allen.	John Parr.
Henry Norris.	William Gell.

Complaint against frivolous appeals from the spiritual to the temporal court

[17] We the bishop, the archdeacon, vicars-general and the rest of the clergy of this isle, being this day assembled in convocation and taking into consideration the manner of appeals from the ecclesiastical court to the staff of government, do find ourselves under a necessity of complaining that the liberty allowed by the laws in that behalf is now so greatly abused that within the course of a few years multitudes of appeals have been preferred, sometimes upon very frivolous occasions, to the great trouble, vexation and expense of the ecclesiastical court, and yet no one sentence given there for some years past has been found to deviate from the rules of law and justice, so as that the same has been thought fit to be reversed. We therefore humbly desire the honourable government to consider of such methods as may discourage unnecessary appeals pursuant to former orders of the lords of the land, and the practice in like cases, as appears in statute book, p. 99 and exchequer book 1632. And that redress to be made to the spiritual court for the unnecessary trouble of attending upon such occasions, when it appears that the judgments given in the said court are according to the laws and customs of this island.

Thomas Sodor and Man.	Matthias Curghey.
Samuel Wattleworth, archdeacon.	John Cosnahan.
Robert Parr.	John Taubman.
John Curghey.	William Gell.
Thomas Allen.	John Woods.
Henry Norris.	John Christian.

[18] *Memorandum.* I presented a copy of this representation to the honourable Robert Mawdesley esquire, governor of this island, June 16, 1712. John Woods, registrarius episcopi.

Settlement of the rents of the staffland of Kirk Maughold[306]

[19] The tenants of the staffland in Kirk Maughold hereafter named being this day called before the lord bishop and clergy, to agree for their several parcels of the said glebe, belonging to the impropriation third of the said parish, the clergy have consented and do hereby oblige themselves and their successors to give and set to them the said tenants, and their executors or assignees, the respective parcels hereunder named, paying to the clergy over and above the yearly rents, one year's rent as a fine payable at or upon Monday after the first of January next, for which said fine and rents we have given them the term of thirty years, commencing from Michaelmas last, which they have accepted of.

	Yearly rent	Fine
Daniel Cowle	0/11/0	0/11/0
Robert Callow	0/4/0	0/4/0
William Looney	0/9/0	0/9/0
Ewan Corkill	0/15/6	0/15/6
John Kermode	0/7/6	0/7/6
William Corkill	0/3/6	0/3/6
Robert Christian	1/10/0	4/0/0

Of which fine, Robert Christian is to pay 40s. as above and the other 40s. at Christmas 1713.

It is also conditioned that if any of the abovesaid tenants do dispose of the benefit of this lease before the expiration of it, the clergy are to have first proffer and preference of it, paying what any other person will *bona fide* give for the s[ame].

[20] Thomas Sodor and Man.   John Parr.
Samuel Wattleworth, archdeacon.   John Cosnahan.
Robert Parr.   John Taubman.
John Curghey.   Matthias Curghey.
Thomas Allen.   William Gell.
Henry Norris.   John Christian.

Memorandum: That Robert Christian in respect of his holding the most valuable part of the said staffland agreed to pay more than one year's rent, viz., four pounds, as within mentioned, for his time.

[306]See also Douglas, Manx National Heritage Library, MS 9756, which contains a looseleaf copy of this agreement.

Demand for a potato tithe[307]

[22][308] Whereas it is observed that the farmers and other tenants within this island have for five or six years past turned the tillage of very profitable parts of their respective holdings into planting of potatoes, upon which a great part of their manure is expended, which in time may be of pernicious consequence to the rights of the church. It is therefore ordered that all persons shall give a just account and proportion of their potatoes unto the rector, vicar or proctor of their respective parish, as of any other tithe growing or produced off and from the earth, which if any person refuse to do, they are by the sumner or in case of further disobedience, by a soldier to be committed. And all rectors, and vicars and other proctors are likewise to take care that no prejudice do accrue to the church by their neglect in this matter.

Thomas Sodor and Man.   Robert Parr.
Samuel Wattleworth, archdeacon.   John Curghey.

Thursday 20 May 1714

[23] *Memorandum*

1. James Read of Douglas having married one Catherine Le Mesurier (in Guernsey) who is yet living and yet was twice married to one Alice Corrin, it is the clergy's opinion that he and the said Alice Corrin be proceeded against at the next court, according to the law. And in the meantime that the said James Read be confined to St German's till he give good security to appear at the next court and not to cohabit with her till the truth be throughly discovered.
    2. That William Christian of Jurby who was lately excommunicated shall be permitted to undergo a voluntary penance in such churches as the lord bishop shall appoint, in order to be restored to the peace of the church, and in the meantime, that the child which Catherine Kermod bore to him be maintained by him, as long as she has nursed it.
    3. That the word 'drunkenness' be inserted in the churchwardens' charge, in the fourth article, immediately before the words 'curing and swearing'.
    4. The old law concerning the corbs of the clergy is to stand in force,[309] notwithstanding the act of convocation 12 June 1712, touching Kirk Marown and Kirk Arbory corbs.

---

[307]Though formally adopted, the potato tithe was never collected until an attempt was made to do so in the 1820s, causing such a scandal that the entire tithe regime came into question and was eventually abolished.
[308]P. 21 is out of chronological sequence; see below.
[309]1598/7. See above.

5. My lord bishop has given each of the clergy Dr Sherlock's *Practical Christian*, octavo.[310]

6. His lordship requires the vicars-general to receive from offenders the usual fees mentioned in the eighty-fourth customary law, and also the other clergy their fees for certificates given to offenders after the performance of their censures.

7. The clergy have unanimously elected the reverend Mr Walker, rector of Ballaugh and one of the vicars-general, to represent them in the convocation at York.

[24] 8. Forasmuch as a late indulgence with relation to holidays has been shamefully abused, it is ordered that for the future all the festivals and solemn fasts of the church shall be religiously and strictly observed by all persons within this diocese according to the ancient and laudable custom of this church, by attending God's public worship and abstaining from work on those days. And the clergy are to exhort their several congregations to a due observation of these seasons designed for their edification and so conducive to that end.

9. The right reverend the lord bishop has required the clergy to consider the first rubric before public baptism, and to admonish their congregations as they are there directed, and to take such other methods as may be most proper to promote the baptism of infants on Sundays and holidays.

10. If Mr Taubman and Mr Bridson do not, in their proper persons, before the next Lord's Day, give an account of their absence this day, the lord bishop will proceed to suspension.

11. His lordship designs to prepare shortly a form of prayer for the clergy who attend the boats at the herring fishing.

[12.] Lastly, it is the opinion of this convocation that the publication of marriage licences required in the convocation held May 27, 1708 may be dispensed with by the lord bishop as it is there declared, and that his lordship may empower the vicars-general and episcopal registrars to grant licences without an injunction for the publication of them, till some inconvenience be observed by his lordship for restraining this liberty, and his lordship will shortly provide seals for that purpose. John Woods, registrarius episcopi.

Clergy petition against alehouses

[25] To the right reverend father in God Thomas, lord bishop of Sodor and Man.

May it please your lordship, We the vicars-general and the rest of the clergy of your lordship's diocese of Man in convocation assembled do with deep concern presume to lay before your lordship the inconveniences and fatal consequences which attend the unlimited number of alehouses in all parts of this island, whereby many of the people are of late become not only tipplers but also infamous for sottishness and drunkenness, which are sins never to be too much lamented or restrained. It is to

---

[310]Richard Sherlock first published this at London in 1673. It appeared in octavo format from 1682 onwards. This was the sixth edition (London, 1713), which contains a biography of the author by Bishop Wilson.

this we have great reason to impute the growth of reported lewdness and the other odious sins of cursing, swearing, pilfering and some instances of incest, seldom heard of among our people. Moreover, it is evident that several young persons and servants, with others, whose circumstances will not allow them to misspend their money and time this way and who would scarcely have the confidence to be seen (neither would be harboured) in a regular and creditable public house, are encouraged and entertained in blind alehouses, whereby the youth in their immature unthinking years contract such corrupt habits as even age and experience will hardly be able to eradicate.

That therefore a timely stop may be put to these evils and disorders, that the present and succeeding generations may not be involved in these sins and the consequences of them, and that our exhortations to sobriety and temperance may not be as ineffectual and [26] fruitless as hitherto they have been, we humbly desire your lordship to represent this matter to the honourable governor, that he may confine the privilege of licences for selling ale to a select number of persons and that those few may be such as are known to be people of probity and prudence who will keep good order in their houses and who will not entertain drunkards, nor seduce youth, not only for fear of the laws, but also out of a principle of conscience.

We likewise desire your lordship to lay before the governor our honourable lord's order concerning reformation of manners. At Bishopscourt, May 20, 1714.

John Curghey,	William Ross.	William Gell.
William Walker, vicars-general.	John Parr.	John Quayle.
Thomas Allen.	John Cosnahan.	Henry Allen.
Henry Norris.	Charles Wattleworth.	Peter Lancaster.
Matthias Curghey.	John Christian.	Robert Parr.
John Woods.		

Thursday 9 June 1715

[27] Clergy present:

Samuel Wattleworth, archdeacon.	John Woods.
John Curghey,	John Cosnahan.
William Walker, vicars-general.	William Bridson.
Thomas Allen.	William Ross.
Henry Allen.	James Makon.
John Christian.	Peter Lancaster.
Henry Norris.	Charles Wattleworth.
Matthias Curghey.	John Quayle.
Robert Parr.	

Note: That Mr John Parr, rector of Kirk Bride and Mr John Taubman vicar of Kirk Lonan have not attended here, being both sick, and so is Mr William Gell, vicar of Kirk Conchan.

1. Whereas there has been an instance or two of persons who lately laid violent hands on themselves that were (notwithstanding the rubric before the office for the burial of the dead) solemnly buried according to the prescribed office, it is now decreed that for the future, that office shall not be used for any persons to whom the rubric prohibits Christian burial, and that no regard shall be had to the verdict of a jury in such cases, which cannot be a rule to the clergy, contrary [28] to the words of the rubric. And it is further declared and decreed that this prohibition shall extend to and be interpreted to comprehend any person or persons killed in a duel. And that such and all *felones de se*,[311] as also excommunicate persons, shall moreover not be permitted to be interred in the chancel, church or churchyard, even without the office aforesaid. And if any of the clergy shall transgress this decree, he shall be suspended for three years, without the least mitigation.

2. Whereas some of the laity pretend a right to bury in the chancel upon paying 3s. 4d. to the rector or proctor for breaking ground there, whereas the sole right and property of the chancel is invested in the rector or the lord bishop as guardian of the clergy's rights and impropriations, as well as his lordship's own chancels of the cathedral at Peel, Kirk Braddan and Jurby, it is now declared and decreed that no corpse shall hereafter be permitted to be interred in any of the chancels of this diocese without leave first obtained under the hand of the lord bishop, or the rector of the parish. And if any person shall presume forcibly to break the ground in a chancel without leave as aforesaid, that person shall be excommunicated, provided he be first advertised of this decree by the pastor of the parish. And if the lord bishop be out of the island, then application shall be made to the ordinary.

3. The clergy have unanimously elected the reverend Mr Walker, rector of Ballaugh and one of the vicars-general, to represent them in convocation at York, according to the archbishop's mandate dated at York, the seventh of February last.

4. The lord bishop having out of his lordship's great kindness to the clergy, advanced two years' augmentation out of his own pocket, and the same [29] not yet being paid to his lordship's agent at London, the clergy have engaged to indemnify his lordship if there shall be any miscarriage by a non-payment of that royal bounty.

5. The clergy are enjoined to pray before their sermons according to the fifty-fifth canon, varying the names according to the present occasion, and as they shall receive directions from the bishop.

6. The lord bishop has recommended to the clergy an exhortation to every adult member of their respective congregations for family prayers, and that they the said clergy would each keep a book containing the state of their parishes, commonly called *Parochialia*, and enjoins them to take care that their churches and rectory or vicarage houses be in good repair, and the register books and books for the use of the clergy be in good order, which his lordship designs to see sometime this summer.

7. Mr Henry Allen, vicar of Lezayre, having petitioned for four tithes (as he is vicar of pension) according to the statute, in lieu of four nobles of his stipend, it appears that there was an allowance for that privilege made to the vicar of that parish in the augmentation and impropriations, to supply that defect.

---

[311]Suicides.

The royal bounty for establishing petty schools, etc., 15 February 1676

[28A] King Charles the second out of his royal bounty did confer one hundred pounds on the clergy of the Isle of Man, which his majesty with his council at law proportioned and ordered to be observed for the future as follows, which appears by an instrument made in that behalf, February 15th, 1675/6.

First, for the teaching of six petty schools in the island, £18, viz.

To a petty school at Castletown, Douglas, Ramsey, Kirk Andreas, Kirk Bride and Ballaugh, £3 [each].

Secondly, for the augmenting of poor vicarages in the island, £82.

German	8/0/0	Conchan	9/0/0
Patrick	—	Braddan	9/0/0
Michael	—	Marown	7/0/0
Jurby	11/0/0	Santan	9/0/0
Lezayre	13/0/0	Malew	—
Maughold	1/0/0	Arbory	1/0/0
Lonan	5/0/0	Rushen	9/0/0

The clear of the impropriations per annum is £45 which may be distributed to the parishes for teaching schools there as follows:

Castletown	2/0/0	Maughold	2/0/0
Rushen	3/0/0	Lezayre	3/0/0
Arbory	4/0/0	Bride	—
Malew	—	Andreas	—
Santan	3/0/0	Jurby	2/0/0
Marown	4/0/0	Ballaugh	—
Braddan	4/0/0	Michael	5/0/0
Conchan	3/0/0	German	3/0/0
Lonan	3/0/0	Patrick	3/0/0

[29A]

Parishes	Lord's rent resolved	Proxy	Present value
Rushen	8/0/0		30/0/0
Arbory	3/0/0		9
Malew	12/0/0	2/0/0	8/0/0 (10/0/0, abbey demesnes)
Santan	5/0/0		Yet in lease
Marown	the rent in Lezayre rent		7/0/0
St Trinian's	ditto		2/18/6
Conchan	1/6/8		3/0/0

Lonan	6/0/0		4/0/0
Maughold	8/0/0	1/0/0	6/0/0
(and staffland)			
Lezayre	14/16/6	1/0/0	21/10/2[312]
Michael	8/0/0	1/0/0	7/10/0
Total:	66/3/2	5/0/0	108/18/8

The whole rectory of Kirk Malew being impropriations, the surplus, after paying the lord's rent and the clergy, is at present the vicar's salary.

Note: There will be an addition out of Kirk St Anne [Santan][313] when the lease is expired.

These impropriations, when purchased, were most of them in lease for three lives, and besides the above yearly sum of 66/3/2 lord's rent and the original purchase money, there is the sum of £130 to be paid every thirty years, which fine has been once already paid before half the old leases were expired.

Note: The clergy employ proctors to collect these tithes, who are answerable both for the lord's rent and for the sums payable to the clergy, whose salaries therefore are uncertain and are not here set down.

The petition of Reverend Henry Allen, 20 May 1714

[30] To the right reverend father in God Thomas, the lord bishop, the reverend archdeacon and vicars-general of this isle.

The humble petition of Henry Allen, vicar of Kirk Christ Lezayre, showing:

That since your petitioner became vicar of this parish (a vicarage of pension) he finds that by an ancient law there is three pounds and a noble stipend settled upon him as such, and not only so, but that by the same ancient law, he is privileged to have four nobles of his said stipend in tithes at the ancient rate, if he thought it conduced to his advantage. Which privilege, though for many years neglected to be made use of by your petitioner's predecessors, yet your petitioner humbly conceives that their indifference can be no bar to his or successors' right (if of any advantage, as your petitioner really supposes it must be to a vicar destitute of those useful privileges which a vicar of third has) since there is still an ancient standing law in his favour, never enervated by any subsequent act or deed.

Therefore your petitioner humbly craves the discontinuance of the use of the above privilege has necessitated him to take this method to come by what he is not yet persuaded of is his right, that you will be pleased to take it to consideration and to determine it so as may take away the occasion of any future dispute, and your petitioner shall ever pray, etc.

---

[312] A note adds 'communibus annis'.
[313] The designation 'St Anne' is frequently found in the documentation of this period because it was believed that 'Santan' was a corruption of it. It is now known however, that the church was named after the Irish St Sanctan.

[31] At Bishopscourt, May 20, 1714.

When the whole court shall meet, the archdeacon at present being not able to travel, this petition shall be considered of. Thomas Sodor and Man.

This petition is answered in the acts of convocation, June 9, 1715. John Woods, registrarius episcopi.

[21] The Reverend Mr Allen of Lezayre is empowered and desired to receive the within fines[314] amounting to 6/10/6 and to be accountable to the lord bishop by next Midsummer for the same. And if any of the tenants do refuse to pay their respective fines they are to be committed by the sumner or soldier into St German's prison, there to remain until they submit to law and pay all fees.

Thomas Sodor and Man.
Samuel Wattleworth,
John Curghey, William Walker, vicars-general.

Thursday 24 May 1716

[32] Clergy present:

[William] Walker,
[John] Curghey, vicars-general.
John Parr.
Henry Morris.
John Christian.
Henry Allen.
William Gell.
Matthias Curghey.

John Quayle.
Robert Parr.
Peter Lancaster.
William Ross.
James Makon.
John Woods.
Charles Wattleworth.
[John] Cosnahan.

The reverend Mr Archdeacon, Mr Thomas Allen, Mr John Taubman and Mr William Bridson have humbly desired to be excused for their absence this day.

1. It is this day ordered that all persons under the censures of the church shall be prohibited *ab ingressu ecclesiae* after publication of the censure, till that censure be undergone by the offender.

2. That there be particular care taken that the parishioners duly attend evening prayer, that being a duty too much neglected in some parishes of this diocese.

[33] 3. That those families and other persons who are notorious for absenting from divine service on the holy days and the solemn feasts of the church, be reproved by the rector or vicar, and if afterwards they continue obstinate, they are to be presented and censured.

---

[314]This refers to the fines imposed at the 1714 convocation (see above).

Thursday 13 June 1717

[35][315] Clergy present:

[John] Curghey,	John Woods.
[William] Walker, vicars-general.	[James] Makon.
Thomas Allen.	[Robert] Parr.
John Parr.	[John] Quayle.
Henry Allen.	Matthias Curghey.
[John] Taubman.	[Henry] Norris.
Anthony Halsall.	[John] Christian.
[William] Bridson.	[William] Gell.
[John] Cosnahan.	Charles Wattleworth.

1. Whereas there was an act of convocation in the year 1710 requiring the churchwardens and chapter-quest in the market towns of this island to make presentments of such persons (whether strangers or inhabitants) who were guilty of the sins of drunkenness, swearing and cursing, and the said act then published in the several churches and chapels, notwithstanding which, the above sins are still practised to the great scandal of Christianity, it is now decreed that a copy of that and this act be read in the chapels of the several towns and in the churches adjoining to them, the next Lord's Day, and that the churchwardens and chapter-quest shall immediately present the names of all those whom they observe, or by common fame are reported, to be [36] addicted to those sins, and that those presentments shall be forthwith sent to the lord bishop, to the end that the offenders may be called before the court, and then severely fined and censured, according to their demerits.

2. The lord bishop requires all the clergy to bring their church registers to the next sheading court, that his lordship may see in what order those books are, and that those who have not bound books for that use, may, at the charge of the parish, provide such immediately, there being a bookbinder lately come to the island.

3. The general sumner is to charge Edmund and Robert Christian of Kirk Maughold to appear at Lezayre next Thursday in order to answer the court whether they will make good and stand by the conditions of a lease of a parcel of the staffland granted at the convocation held June 12, 1712.

4. The vicars of Kirk Marown, Kirk Christ Rushen, Kirk St Anne and Kirk Michael were required by the lord bishop to reside at the vicarage house according to the usage of the church.

Thursday 20 June 1717

[37] At a convocation of the clergy at Kirk Christ Lezayre the twentieth day of June, 1717.

Robert Christian aforementioned appeared and utterly refused to stand by or perform the conditions of the lease given in the year 1712.

---

[315]P. 34 is out of chronological order; see below.

The trial of Robert Christian

[38] At a consistory court held in Lezayre church the twentieth of June 1717.

All the tenants of the staffland or impropriation glebe of Kirk Maughold excepting Robert Christian and Robert Callow having already paid to the trustee appointed the sums by them covenanted to be paid in way of fine for the several parcels (in their possession) of the said glebe, which sums were to be applied towards the discharge of the general fine of £130 payable every 30 years to the lord of this isle, and the court having in composition to the said Robert Christian and his family, born, for above four years past, not only with the non-payment of his fine of four pounds, but also with many provocations for the placing another tenant in his part of the said glebe, upon his refusal to comply with the favour done him, at his own request, and notwithstanding the said Robert Christian utterly refused this day in court ever to pay the fine aforesaid, the court being also informed that he is about to dispose of some part of the said land, contrary to a reformation in the lease aforementioned, it is still thought fit not to take advantage of his perverseness herein by ejecting him out of the said land, as might justly be done, but rather to oblige him to abide by the payment of the fine aforesaid. It is therefore hereby ordered that the trustee appointed for levying the said fines do immediately put in execution the power and authority granted him by an order dated the ninth of June 1715, according to the full purport and tenor thereof.

Thomas Sodor and Man.   William Walker.
John Curghey.   Samuel Wattleworth.

Financial provision for the vicars-general, 16 January 1718

[34] That my vicars-general may be better enabled to discharge their duty, and more especially that part which concerns the godly discipline of this church, that I may more effectually by their advice and assistance set forward, as much as in me lieth, quietness, love and peace among the men and such as be unquiet, disobedient and criminous within my diocese, correct and punish, according to such authority as we have by God's Word and the laws of this church, I do hereby assign them (besides the salaries and other perquisites which they have hitherto enjoyed) the proxies of Kirk Bride, Kirk Maughold, Kirk Christ Lezayre and Ballaugh, to be by them received yearly as they shall become due. And an attested copy of this shall be sufficient warrant for them to receive the same from any of the persons concerned in the payment thereof. Given under my hand and seal at Bishopscourt, this sixteenth of January 1717 [1718].

Thursday 5 June 1718

[39] In presence of:

[John] Curghey,   [John] Cosnahan.
[William] Walker, vicars-general.   John Woods.
[John] Parr.   [James] Makon.
Henry Allen.   [Robert] Parr.
[John] Taubman.   [John] Quayle.
[William] Gell.   [Matthias] Curghey.
[Anthony] Halsall.   [John] Christian.
[William] Bridson.   [Charles] Wattleworth.

1. Whereas it is found that persons under the censures of the church for the scandalous sins of adultery, repeated fornication, etc., are oftentimes very pressing to be restored, even before there be a moral assurance of their being throughly touched with the heinousness of their sins, it is now decreed that such offenders shall, from time to time, be privately admonished by their respective pastors and made sensible of the danger they incur by a feigned repentance, and that their solicitations for a mitigation of their censures be repelled for some months [40] or while there be just cause to hope that they are truly penitent and resolve to live more sober and regular lives for the future.

And the clergy are (among their other exhortations) to admonish such offenders to mortify themselves by fasting and by refraining public houses and diversions during the course of their penance.

2. When persons are presented for scandalous sins the rector or vicar or other incumbent shall, some time before the chapter court, privately advertise them of it and endeavour to prepare them for a meek and humble behaviour when they are reprimanded or admonished by the executive officers.

3. *Memorandum.* There is a year and a half of the royal bounty unpaid and due to the clergy at the last Lady Day, March 25, 1718, from the lord bishop, when received out of the treasury. And there was due out of the exchequer to his lordship Lady Day last, two years and a quarter bounty advanced by him to the clergy, whereof one hundred pounds was due in the late queen's time.

4. A resolution is taken that the governor be addressed to determine the matter of the staffland before the next Michaelmas sheading courts.

[41] 5. Antenuptial fornication is to be hereafter subject to ecclesiastical censures, and the offenders to wear the sheet as other fornicators.

Letter to the governor about impropriations

[42] To the honourable Alexander Horn esquire, governor of this isle.

The stafflands of Kirk Maughold be the glebe of the impropriation third of that parish purchased with the rest of the said impropriations by the late Bishop Barrow from the lord of this isle for the benefit of the church, and for which the clergy are obliged, besides a yearly rent of 66/3/2 to pay every thirty years a fine of £130 to the lord of this isle;

And whereas the said impropriation third and glebe of Kirk Maughold fell some years ago out of lease and into our possession, we called the tenants of the glebe, viz., the staffland holders before us, who all agreed to pay certain small sums in way of fine for the renewal of their term, the which was done by us, not only to preserve our own [rent] and that of our successors, but also to enable us to pay the fine of £130 aforesaid, which is very soon to come upon us. And the said sums so agreed upon having accordingly been paid by all the said tenants, excepting Robert Christian and William Callow, the former of whom refuses to pay the sum of four pounds consented to by himself, and also insists upon his having a right, independent of us, to the said land, and though we could very justly keep him to the terms of his agreement and to that end have already set forth orders to the trustee appointed in that behalf, yet we have hitherto suspended the execution of the said orders and do now unanimously in convocation humbly represent to your honour that as much as the said Robert Christian has attempted [not only to deprive us of][316] [43] our rights but also of the lord's prior right by which he conveyed the impropriations to us, and it being alleged that in this particular case we are both parties and judges, should it be determined by us, we have therefore ordered two of the clergy, viz., the vicars of Lezayre and Marown, to wait upon your honour to desire you would be pleased to take cognizance of this matter, which being concerning a glebe, is not subject to a trial at common law, for which reason and for peace sake, we pray there may be a speedy determination of this affair.

Thomas Sodor and Man.	John Woods.
John Curghey,	Matthias Curghey.
William Walker, vicars-general.	William Gell.
Charles Wattleworth, official.	John Christian.
John Parr.	John Quayle.
John Taubman.	Robert Parr.
John Cosnahan.	James Makon.
	Anthony Halsall.

Petition of Reverend Thomas Allen

[44] To the reverend archdeacon and vicars-general of this isle, the humble petition of Thomas Allen, vicar of Kirk Maughold, showing:

How that one Robert Christian, William Corkill, John Kermode, Ewan Corkill, Robert Callow, Daniel Kneale, John Lowey and his mother, all these occupants of a certain glebe which time beyond man's memory paid their yearly rent to the propriator of the impropriations in the Kirk Maughold parish, which parcel was distinguished from other holdings by the denomination of 'staffland', the aforesaid persons have, by the instigation of some pragmatical persons, peremptorily refused

---

[316]The line at the bottom of the page of the MS has disappeared through wear and tear.

to pay their usual rent for two years by past, and persist in this contumacy, notwithstanding they have been by the sumner charged several times to answer their wonted rent.

It is therefore humbly requested that the reverend court may vouchsafe to call the said persons to an account for this their refractoriness and to show reason for this their disobedience such as never was attempted by any their predecessors time out of mind. So shall your orator humbly pray, etc.

A statement about impropriations from the bishop, 16 April 1719

[54][317] Whereas by the late act of settlement the tenants of the abbey demesnes were obliged to pay tithes as all other the farmers of this land were by law bound to do, and it being afterwards represented unto us that the said tenants, having for some time been freed from paying of tithes, had therefore proportionably greater rents and customs than any other farmers, the bishop, archdeacon and clergy then present, moved by this representation, did consent to take in lieu of the tithes, half the lord's rent of every holding yearly, provided that the said tenants did unanimously and without any further trouble, agree to the said concession.

Notwithstanding which, most of the said tenants have not to this day subscribed to the said agreement, some of them having put the clergy to defiance, and have been compelled to pay their full tithes in kind, and others have voluntarily chosen to pay their tithes rather than the said half rent, the bishop therefore has reason to hope that posterity will not oblige the church to stand to the said agreement (though for the present it may be no great loss to those that enjoy the said tithes) especially so far as concerns such as have not subscribed unto it.

The bishop, for his part, acknowledging that the said concession was rash and unadvised, both as contrary to the act of settlement and as presuming to change the method which God, from the beginning, had established for the maintenance of his service. For which reason the said bishop resolves to make amends to the church forasmuch as he supposeth she may suffer by this act of his, and the clergy, hoping that his successor may be able to rectify this mistake of his, which for the reasons above set down he supposes he may righteously do, this being a true state[ment] of the case and the motives which induced him to do what he now repents of. Thomas Sodor and Man. April 16, 1719.

A court held at Kirk Christ, Lezayre, 27 October 1719

[46][318] The tenants of the staffland in Kirk Maughold, appearing this day and having nothing to object against the payment of the annual sums payable out of their respective holdings, but that there is controversy now depending before the governor concerning the fines which they covenanted to pay out of their said holdings, which having no relation to the said annual sums always heretofore paid by them and their predecessors, they are therefore ordered to make immediate

---

[317]Out of chronological order.
[318]P. 45 is crossed out.

payment of the arrears of the said annual sums, otherwise to be committed to St German's prison, there to remain until they give sufficient security to submit to law and pay all fees. Robert Horrobin. William Walker. John Curghey.

To the sumner of Kirk Maughold who, if disobeyed, is to call for soldiers from the constable.

Thursday 9 June 1720

[49][319] Clergy present:

William Walker,	Matthias Curghey.
John Curghey, vicars-general.	John Woods, jr.
John Parr.	John Christian.
Henry Allen.	William Ross.
William Gell.	James Makon.
William Bridson.	Anthony Halsall.
John Woods.	Charles Wattleworth.
John Quayle.	John Cosnahan, jr., assistant to his father.

Memorandum: That Mr Allen of Kirk Maughold, Mr Taubman of Kirk Lonan, Mr Cosnahan of Kirk Santan and Mr Parr of Kirk Arbory are sick and desire to be excused.

Letters of thanks to the archbishop of York and others

[50] To the most reverend father in God William, by divine providence lord archbishop of York and our metropolitan.[320]

We the clergy of the diocese of Man in convocation assembled do find ourselves in duty bound to render your grace our most humble and unfeigned thanks for your grace's zealous concern in behalf of this church and its discipline, and for countenancing and supporting our excellent bishop in the regular government of the one and due execution of the other. And as we have great reason to pray for your grace's long continuing our pious and vigilant patron, so we do, with all submission, desire your grace to accept this public testimony of our gratitude.

[51] The right reverend the lord bishop of this diocese of Man having intimated to us the clergy the pious and generous donation of the right reverend father in God Charles, lord bishop of Cloyne[321] in the Kingdom of Ireland to the present and succeeding vicars of Kirk Christ Lezayre, which will very much contribute to the said vicar's comfortable living there, we do now unanimously declare our just sense of his lordship's great and reasonable bounty to that church and its pastors, and

---

[319]Pp. 47-8 are out of chronological order; see below.
[320]William Dawes was archbishop of York from 20 February 1714 until 30 April 1724.
[321]Charles Crow, a Manxman, was bishop of Cloyne from 18 October 1702 until his death on 26 June 1726. (See p. 11 above.)

return our most humble thanks for the same, and do also earnestly desire that this our grateful acknowledgment may be transmitted to his lordship with all convenient speed.

[52] We the clergy of the diocese of Man in convocation assembled do render our humble thanks to the Reverend and Honourable Dr Finch, dean of York,[322] for his seasonable charity to the petty schoolmasters and the poor children who shall be by them instructed in learning and good manners, and as this will be a relief to their present necessity, so we do heartily desire to testify our gratitude to the pious donor.

[53] We the clergy of the diocese of Man in convocation assembled are very sensible of the Reverend Dr Maxwell's[323] zeal and care in making application to the right reverend the lord bishop of Cloyne for the bounty which his lordship has lately conferred on the vicars of Kirk Christ Lezayre, as also for the said Dr Maxwell's peculiar charity to the school of Douglas, and we humbly entreat him to accept this testimony of our gratitude for his hearty concern for the good of this church.

The appeal of Robert Christian and others, 20 February 1721

[47] To the reverend Mr Archdeacon Horrobin, Mr Curghey and Mr Walker, vicars-general in this isle. The humble appeal of Robert Christian and the rest of the occupants of that part of the crown land termed and known by the name of staffland in the parish of Kirk Maughold, humbly showing:

That your appellants for some years by past have laboured under unparalleled sufferings and hardships of several orders and judgments from the spiritual court relating the property, annual sums and tithe of the foresaid staffland by which they hold and find themselves very much aggrieved and do therefore hereby appeal from the foresaid reverend courts several and respective orders and defective proceedings relating the same unto the honourable staff of government in this isle, praying your acceptance hereof, which will oblige your appellants as bound to pray. February 20, 1720 [1721].

The reply of the vicars-general

Ascribing the presumption of the new and unheard of style which is here assumed of crown land tenants, to the insolence of these poor deluded people's instigators, we say that the controversies which have depended before us, touching the impropriation glebe of Kirk Maughold, called the staffland, have been, first:

Concerning the sums which in way [48] of time the several tenants obliged themselves to pay the clergy towards the discharging the great fine of £130 payable every thirty years to the right honourable lord of this isle, and secondly, concerning the rents or yearly sums payable by them to the proctors at Easter.

As to the first of these, though the clergy could, without all peradventure, have bound the tenants to abide by their own obligations, yet to leave them without

---

[322](1702-28).
[323]Robert Maxwell was prebendary of Tynan (Armagh) from 1709 to 1737.

excuse, the whole debate has been referred to the honourable governor and he has already taken a hearing of it, and it still lies before his honour.

And as to the second controversy, an order has been granted therein, and the tenants have been imprisoned, and have given security for the payment of their respective arrears, so that we see no room for the acceptance of an appeal, where the course of law has been gone through, and bonds of submission have been already given, as aforesaid. John Curghey. William Walker.

Thursday 1 June 1721

[55][324] Clergy present:

Robert Horrobin, archdeacon.	John Cosnahan, jr.
William Walker,	William Gell.
John Curghey, vicars-general.	Anthony Halsall.
Matthias Curghey.	William Bridson.
John Parr.	John Woods, sr.
Henry Allen.	William Ross.
John Christian.	Robert Parr.
Charles Wattleworth.	

Memorandum: Mr Thomas Allen, vicar of Kirk Maughold, Mr John Cosnahan sr, vicar of Kirk Santan, Mr John Quayle, vicar of Kirk Christ Rushen being sick, desire to be excused.

[56] This day the right reverend the lord bishop of this diocese was pleased to read to the clergy a part of his grace the lord archbishop of York his letter wherein his grace expresses his sense of the thanks of the clergy of this isle sent at the last convocation and his gracious promise to do all the favours in his power for this church and clergy.

The right reverend lord bishop now represents to the clergy that there are three years in arrear of the royal bounty, viz., one year in her late majesty's time and two since.

Likewise that there is deposited in his lordship's hand sixty-six pounds, eight shillings and eleven pence halfpenny towards paying the great fine for the impropriations.

The vicars general are to inquire at the next circuit whether catechizing is regularly observed in every parish, and whether any persons not confirmed are permitted to enter into the holy state of matrimony.

[324]P. 54 is out of chronological order; see above.

Thursday 22 May 1722

[57] Clergy present:

Robert Horrobin, archdeacon.	William Bridson.
William Walker,	John Cosnahan, sr.
John Curghey, vicars-general.	John Woods.
John Parr.	William Ross.
John Christian.	James Makon.
Charles Wattleworth.	Robert Parr.
John Cosnahan.	John Quayle.
William Gell.	Matthias Curghey.
Anthony Halsall.	Edward Moore, deacon.

[58] The Reverend Mr Henry Allen, vicar of Kirk Christ Lezayre with Mr John Woods jr., curate of Kirk Michael, [absent]. Mr Thomas Allen vicar of Kirk Maughold being very aged and infirm has desired to be excused.

Conflict between the bishop and the governor

This day the clergy present, being asked by the lord bishop after what manner briefs have been recommended in their time, have answered that whenever the lord bishop of this diocese was within the island, the governor under his hand desired his lordship to recommend the same to the clergy, excepting within these two years or thereabouts. And Mr Curghey, vicar-general, who has been in holy orders about forty-two years, declares further that the late Bishop Bridgman[325] did (in his time) by his own authority grant briefs in all parts of this diocese.

Mr archdeacon, who has lived here but about two years was not asked the question. Mr Henry Allen declares as the rest of the clergy, and that his uncle Mr Thomas Allen averred to him [59] some time ago (being fifty-five years vicar of Kirk Maughold) that the late governors Heywood[326] and Kenyon,[327] in their time, desired the lord bishop to recommend briefs to the clergy.

This day the lord bishop taking notice of a scandalous libel exhibited by the attorney-general[328] in the temporal court against his lordship and the vicars-general the ninth of February last, one article whereof was an arraignment of their proceedings in the case of Mr Bridson's suspension, the said Mr Bridson solemnly affirmed and offered to make oath that he was no way concerned in that accusation, and that he never made any complaint to occasion the same.

[325]Henry Bridgman was bishop of Sodor and Man from 1 October 1671 until his death on 15 May 1682.
[326]Robert Heywood was governor from 1678 to 1691.
[327]Roger Kenyon was governor from 1691 to 1693.
[328]Thomas Corlett held this office from 1712 to 1727. He was suspended by Tynwald in 1727 and replaced by a candidate of the lord's choosing.

Die et anno praedictis. Memorandum. The proceedings concerning Mr archdeacon Horrobin and his suspension *ab officio et beneficio* for his several crimes and misdemeanours there mentioned are registered in a particular book to be annexed to the book of causes for 1722.

Tuesday 24 November 1724

[60] Clergy present:

John Curghey,
William Walker, vicars-general.
Robert Parr.
Henry Allen.
John Cosnahan.
William Gell.
William Bridson.
[John] Woods.

Edward Moore.
John Quayle.
Matthias Curghey.
John Woods, jr.
[61] John Christian.
William Ross.
Anthony Halsall.

1. The depositions concerning the incestuous marriage betwixt Thomas Cown and Eleanor Martin of Kirk Bride being read, it is concluded that all persons therein concerned be summoned to Kirk Michael the next Tuesday in order to be censured.

2. For the more effectual suppression of wickedness, that the churchwardens and chapter-quest be often admonished to make diligent inquiry and constant presentments of all those (either strangers or natives) who [62] propagate impious principles, or are guilty of wicked practices.

3. That the constitution for monthly presentments be not neglected for the future.

4. That Captain Wattleworth's censure be put in execution.

5. That Robert Wainwright, soldier, be admonished by his pastor to appear at Kirk Michael on next Tuesday and due return made by both.

6. That Francis Davenport being presented for drinking the devil's health and other flagrant impieties, notice be sent to all churches that none presume to conceal him or clandestinely entertain him, *sub poena trium librarum ad usum domini.*

7. That John Norman be cited to appear next Tuesday to [63] answer two presentments, the latter whereof is of a very heinous and unheard of nature. And that the evidence against him be summoned.

8. That the clergy's humble thanks be sent to the Reverend Dr Bray for his bounty in sending many useful books for the parochial libraries.

Thursday 20 May 1725

[64] Clergy present:

[William] Walker,
John Curghey, vicars-general.

John Quayle.
Matthias Curghey.

Robert Parr.

Henry Allen.

William Gell.

William Bridson.

John Woods.

Edward Moore.

John Woods, jr.

[65] John Christian.

Charles Wattleworth.

William Ross.

James Makon.

Anthony Halsall.

Mr Horrobin, archdeacon, has humbly desired the lord bishop to dispense with his absence this day as being necessarily hindered by removing his family and goods from Castletown to Kirk Andreas.

Mr Thomas Allen, vicar of Kirk Maughold, is through age unable to attend.

Mr Matthias Curghey jr, curate of Kirk Lonan, is at present in Ireland.

Books given to the parochial libraries

[66] A catalogue of books for the parochial libraries of this island.

1699

1. *A course of lectures upon the church catechism*, vol. 1, folio.[329] Given by Dr Bray.

2. *The measures of Christian obedience [for the promotion of piety and the peace of troubled consiences.]*[330] By him.

3. *The practical believer.*[331] By him.

4. *The Christian sacrifice.*[332] By him.

5. *[Discourse of] the pastoral care.* By the author.[333]

6. *The life of Sir Henry Wotton, Dr Donne, etc.*[334]

7. *A practical discourse concerning swearing.* By the author.[335]

8. *The Christian Monitor, etc.*[336]

9. *The poor man's help [and young man's guide.]*[337]

10. *A brief exposition of the church catechism by the bishop of Chichester.* By the author.[338]

---

[329]Thomas Bray was the author of this work, originally projected as four volumes, but only the first of them was published (Oxford, 1696).

[330]By J. Kettlewell (London, 1683).

[331]By J. Kettlewell (London, 1689).

[332]By Bishop Simon Patrick (London, 1671).

[333]Bishop Gilbert Burnet (London, 1692).

[334]By Izaak Walton (London, 1670).

[335]By Archbishop William Wake (London, 1696).

[336]By J. Rawlet (London, 1686).

[337]By W. Burkitt (London, 1694).

[338]Bishop John Williams (London, 1689).

1703

11. *The account of the societies for reformation of manners in England and Ireland.*[339] By the society.

1704

12. *[A priest to the temple, or the character of] the country parson*, by Mr Herbert.[340] Given by Mr William Patten of London.
13. *Two select discourses of faith*, by William Allen[341]
14. *The practical believer*, by Mr Kettlewell, folio.[342] By Dr Bray.
15. *Catechetical lectures*, etc. edition 3. Folio, stitched.[343] By him.

1705

16. Mr Bonnell's life.[344] By his pious relict.
17. Mr Cradock's *Knowledge and practice.*[345]
[67] 18. Bishop Hopkins' *Works*,[346] by Mr Hoare.
19. Bishop Pearson *On the creed.*[347] By him.

1707, November 6th.

20. *The Manx catechism.* By the author.[348]
21. Mr Nelson's *Feasts and fasts.* By the author.[349]
22. Mr Camfield, [*A theological discourse*] *of angels.*[350]
23. *A catalogue of books*, stitched in blue paper.[351]
24. A collection of Psalms out of the new version.[352] By Dr Bray.

25. [*A discourse of the nature, ends and differences*] *of the two covenants*, stitched,

---

[339]By Josiah Woodward (London, 1699).
[340]George Herbert (1593-1632). The book was first published at London in 1652.
[341](London, 1703).
[342]See no. 3 above.
[343]See no. 1 above.
[344](London, 1705). This was James Bonnel (1653-99).
[345]Samuel Cradock. Published at London in 1659.
[346]Ezekiel Hopkins, bishop of Derry. Published at London, 1701.
[347]First published at London in 1659 and frequently reprinted.
[348]Bishop Thomas Wilson, *Principles and duties of Christianity... in English and Manks...* (London, 1707). This was the first book ever printed in the Manx language.
[349]Robert Nelson. The full title is *A companion for the festivals and fasts of the Church of England* (London, 1704).
[350]Benjamin Camfield. Published at London in 1678.
[351]*Bibliotheca parochialis*, compiled by Dr Thomas Bray (London 1707).
[352]*Collection of some verses out of the psalms of David, suited to several occasions* (London, 1698).

by William Allen.[353] By Dr Bray.
26. *A help to a national reformation*, octavo stitched in marble paper.[354]
27. *The baptismal covenant* abridged, octavo, edition 3, by Dr Bray.[355]

1714, Whitsun Thursday [20 May]

28. Dr Sherlock's *Practical Christian*, ed. 6, octavo, by the right reverend the lord bishop of this isle.[356]

John Woods, registrarius episcopi. 19 May 1725.

[68] Thursday in Whitsun week, May 20th, 1725.

Added to the parochial libraries by Dr Bray:

29. A set of Mr Blair's sermons in five volumes,[357] for every parish church in the island and for the libraries of Castletown and Douglas.
30. A set or collection of tracts against popery, as abovesaid.[358]
31. *Papal tyranny*, without the Latin letters, as abovesaid.[359]
32. Two of *Bibliotheca Parochialis*,[360] for the two libraries.
33. Dr Henry Moore's English works, folio,[361] for the libraries. Two copies.
34. *Papal tyranny*, with the Latin letters.[362] Two copies for the libraries.

N.B. Allen's *Discourse on faith* we had before. *Enchiridion precum*[363] and Arndthius, *De vero Christianismo*,[364] are not yet come to here.

Letter of thanks to Dr Bray

[69] We the bishop, vicars-general and the rest of the clergy of the diocese of Man in convocation assembled, having a grateful sense of the pious and charitable endeavours of the Reverend Dr Thomas Bray, vicar of St Botolph's, Aldgate,

---

[353](London, 1678).
[354]No author (London, 1700).
[355]*Short discourse on the doctrine of our baptismal covenant*, third edition (London, 1699).
[356]See above under the relevant convocation.
[357]James Blair, *Our Saviour's divine sermon on the mount... explained and the practice of it recommended in divers sermons and discourses* (London, 1722).
[358]No. 26 above?
[359]By Peter Du Moulin (London, 1674).
[360]No. 23 above.
[361]*An account of virtue, or Dr Henry More's abridgment of morals, put into English* (London, 1690). The original Latin title was *Enchiridion ethicum*.
[362]See no. 31 immediately above.
[363]By A. W. Boehme (London, 1715).
[364]Johannes Arndt published this at Jena in 1605 and it was reissued at London, in four volumes, in 1708.

London, hold ourselves obliged to tender him our most humble thanks for his having so much at heart the good of this church and nation in general, as well as of us the holy office in particular, as to have not only found and promoted the desire, but likewise contributed so largely himself towards the expense of erecting parochial libraries within this diocese, and with a truly Christian zeal disposed others to join in so very laudable and beneficial an undertaking.

To commemorate this benefaction, it is this day ordered that a fair catalogue of the books given, with the names of the pious donors of them, be preserved in the episcopal registry of this isle. And it is our humble request that when a duplicate hereof shall come to the hands of the learned and reverend gentleman before mentioned, he may be pleased in our behalf to assure the rest of the benefactors that the good effect of their bounty which is reaped by the present will extend to future ages, is accepted with the most becoming gratitude, and will always engage our prayers for their everlasting happiness.

Tuesday 7 September 1725

Letter of thanks to the earl of Derby, lord of Man

[70] At a convocation of the clergy of the diocese of Man in St John's chapel, the seventh day of September anno Domini 1725.

To the right honourable James, earl of Derby, lord of Man and of the Isles. We the bishop and clergy of your lordship's island of Man in convocation assembled beg leave to render your lordship our most humble and hearty thanks for the late most gracious intimations of your lordship's favour and countenance signified to us by Edward Stanley and Josiah Poole, esquires.

It has been our unhappiness to labour for some time past under the unpleasing effects of the ill offices done us with your lordship by the disturbers of our peace who have deservedly fallen under your lordship's displeasure and been divested of the authority they so much abused, whilst our conduct, we doubt not, will every day more and more commend itself to your lordship's approbation, and dissipate all jealousies and misunderstandings touching the exercise of the spiritual jurisdiction within this diocese.

Your lordship's faithful clergy have now encouragement to hope that your lordship's pious injunctions for the suppression of vice and immorality, lately published in our churches, will have a due influence on the lives and manners of the dissolute and profane among us, when they see your lordship so zealous for the promoting of virtue and piety in all your people, and particularly in such as have any employments of profit or trust under your lordship.

We likewise acknowledge with all due thankfulness your lordship's justice and goodness as well in ordering the fine imposed without any just cause on the vicar of Kirk Malew to be repaid him, as also in the directions given for the opening the chapel of Castletown, whereby the [71] worship of God so long obstructed in that place is now restored and established, to the great comfort of us of the holy function and the inexpressible joy of all the inhabitants.

The just and grateful sense of these high obligations to your lordship will constantly excite us to discharge with the utmost zeal and fidelity the duties of our several stations, in promoting your lordship's honour and interest, as well as the peace and happiness of your people, and in offering up (as it is our daily practice and as we are moved both by duty and inclination) our most unfeigned prayers to God, for your lordship's both present and eternal felicity. September 7, 1725.

Thomas Sodor and Man.	Henry Allen.
William Walker.	John Quayle.
John Curghey.	John Woods [jr].
Robert Parr.	John Cosnahan [jr].
William Ross.	Edward Moore.
Matthias Curghey.	Anthony Halsall.
John Woods [sr].	Matthias Curghey [jr].
William Gell.	James Makon.
John Christian.	

Memorandum: Mr Charles Wattleworth, curate of Kirk Andreas, was absent and Mr Thomas Allen, vicar of Kirk Maughold, could not attend by reason of his great age and infirmities. *Copia vera*: John Woods, registrarius episcopalis.

Thursday 2 June 1726

[73]^[365] Clergy present:

William Walker,	Edward Moore.
John Curghey, vicars-general.	[74] John Quayle.
Robert Parr.	Matthias Curghey, sr.
Henry Allen.	John Woods, jr.
Matthias Curghey, jr.	John Christian.
William Gell.	James Makon.
William Bridson.	Anthony Halsall.
John Woods sr.	

Memorandum: Mr Robert Horrobin, archdeacon, is at present in England. Mr Thomas Allen, vicar of Kirk Maughold, is through age and infirmities unable to attend. Mr William Ross, academical professor, desires to be excused, and Mr Charles Wattleworth desires also to be excused.

[75] N.B. The clergy were now desired to declare whether they are satisfied with the setting of the impropriations hitherto, to which they answer that they are.

2. And also whether that may be set hereafter to any one man, viz., to Mr Charles Wattleworth, who proffers in a letter, for the next three years, five pounds more per annum. They answer that they had rather let them be as they are, when the advance be very considerable and good security be given for the same.

And the whole clergy do with the utmost humility and gratitude acknowledge

---

[365]P. 72 is out of chronological order; see below.

the right reverend his lordship's great care, fidelity and trouble in setting the impropriations and receiving them for the time past.

Letter of thanks to the bishop for his action regarding the impropriations

[76] We the clergy of the diocese of Man in convocation assembled, being very sensible of the great care, trouble and fidelity of our right reverend diocesan the lord bishop in setting the impropriations and receiving the money due for the same and paying it to us, do with the utmost humility and gratitude acknowledge this favour and do also submissively beseech his lordship to accept this our sincere and public acknowledgment of his lordship's management of an affair so conducive to our subsistence.

William Walker.	Henry Allen.
John Curghey.	William Bridson.
Robert Parr.	John Quayle.
Matthias Curghey.	John Woods [jr].
John Woods.	John Cosnahan.
William Gell.	Edward Moore.
John Christian.	Matthias Curghey [jr].

The clergy proportions of the impropriation paid in 1726

[77] Clergy's proportion of the impropriation paid as followeth by the proctor of:

Kirk Arbory	2/0/0	and	
Lezayre	1/0/0		3/0/0 in all to Rushen.
Kirk Arbory	5/0/0		to Arbory.
Santan	2/5/0	and	
Kirk Malew	2/0/0		4/5/0 in all to Santan.
Paid by the proctor...	5/0/0		to Marown.
Kirk Marown	4/18/6;		
Kirk Malew	0/10/0	and	
Kirk Christ Lezayre	4/10/0		5/13/4 in all to Braddan.
Onchan	3/0/0	and	
Kirk Michael	2/0/0		5/0/0 in all to Onchan.
Kirk Lonan	4/0/0		to Lonan.
Kirk Maughold	4/0/0		to Maughold.
Lezayre	4/0/0		to Lezayre.
Kirk Malew	3/0/0		to Jurby.
Kirk Michael	5/0/0		to Michael.
Kirk Christ Lezayre	6/0/0		to Patrick and German.
Kirk Malew	3/0/0		to Vicar-general Curghey.
Kirk Malew	3/0/0		to Vicar-general Walker.
Kirk Arbory	2/0/0		to the petty school.

Kirk Malew	1/10/0	to Ballasalla school.
Kirk Christ Lezayre	1/0/0	to the archdeacon's registrar.
Kirk Malew	2/0/0	to the episcopal registrar.
Kirk Christ Rushen	30/0/0	to Castletown free school.

| [Total] | 96/8/4. |

[78] An account of the impropriations since the year 1715 when the clergy in convocation desired me to set them to their best advantage, and for the raising the sum of £130 payable to the lord of this isle every thirty years, due A. D. 1726.

Impropriations now set, to whom and how distributed:

1. What set for and to whom.
2. Lord's rent.
3. Proxy and stipend.
4. Clear to the clergy *communibus annis*.
5. Paid as followeth.
6. Remains towards the great fine.

Kirk Michael

1. To the curate formerly set for 16/10/0. Now:
      1723:   for 18/0/0.
      1724:   for 17/0/0.
      1725:   for 18/0/0.
2. 8/0/0.
3. 1/0/0.
4. 8/13/4.
5. To the schoolmaster   2/0/0.
      Vicar of Onchan   2/0/0.
      Vicar of Michael   3/0/0.
      Towards the great fine *communibus annis* 1/13/4.
6. As now set   1/13/4.

Lezayre

1. To the vicar and Mr Curghey
      1723:   for 32/0/0.
      1724:   for 40/0/0.
      1725:   for 40/0/0.
2.   14/16/6.
3.   Stipend: 3/6/8; proxy 1/0/0.
4.   1723:   12/16/10.
      1724:   20/16/10.
      1725:   20/16/10.

5. To the vicar: 4/0/0.
    To the vicar of Rushen: 1/0/0.
    To the vicar of Patrick and German: 6/0/0.
    To the archdeacon's registrar: 1/0/0.
    To the vicar of Kirk Braddan: 0/4/10.
    In all: 12/4/10.
6. 1723:   0/12/0.
    1724:   8/12/0.
    1725:   8/12/0.

Maughold

1. To the vicar for 15/0/0.
2. 8/0/0.
3. Proxy: 1/0/0.
4. 6/0/0.

5. To the vicar: 4/0/0.
6. 2/0/0.

Lonan

1. To the curate and vicar of Onchan: for 10/0/0.
2. 6/0/0.
3. −
4. 4/0/0.
5. To the vicar: 7/0/0.
6. −

Onchan

1. To the vicar for 4/6/8.
2. 1/6/8.
3. −
4. 3/0/0.
5. To the vicar: 3/0/0.
6. −

Marown

1. To the vicar and Mr Curghey for 9/18/6.
2. Included in the rent of Lezayre.
3. −
4. 9/18/6.
5. To the vicar: 5/0/0; to the vicar of Braddan: 4/18/6.
6. −

Santan

1. To the curate now out of lease for 4/13/4.
2. 5/0/0.
3. –
4. 2/13/4.
5. To the vicar: 2/5/0.
6. –

Malew

1. One part in the vicar's hands for his own salary and the other set by Mr Walker who is accountable to the clergy, for 38/0/0.
2. 1/2/3.
3. Proxy: 2/0/0.
4. –
5. To the vicar of Santan   2/5/0

Kirk Braddan	0/10/0
Jurby	3/0/0
Vicar-general Curghey	3/0/0
Vicar-general Walker	3/0/0
Ballasalla school	1/10/0
Registrar's salary	2/0/0.

6. Elements at Easter surplusage to the general fine 1/5/0.

Arbory

1. To the curate: 12/0/0. NB: Mr Moore the curate to give 13/0/0.
2. 3/0/0.
3. –
4. 9/0/0 and 1/0/0.
5. To the vicar: 5/0/0

Castletown petty school:	2/0/0
Schoolmaster of Rushen:	2/0/0.

6. –

Rushen

1. To a proctor by an order of the then governor and bishop, who pay the master of Castletown, for 38/0/0.
2. 8/0/0.
3. –
4. –
5. To the master of the free school of Castletown [no sum indicated].
6. –

Total

2. 66/3/2.
3. 8/6/8.

[79] The clergy in convocation June 9, 1715 desired me to take the impropriations under my management in order to raise a fine of £130 payable by them anno Domini 1726. I have received and paid as followeth:

Received:

The surplusage of the impropriations for 1715		11/2/0
Six pence in the pound deducted for the years 1715-19		9/19/8
1716	Kirk Maughold 2/0/0; old proctors of Kirk Michael 0/10/0	2/10/0
	Arrears from Mr Woods of Kirk Malew	6/16/7
	Lezayre 8/16/0; 0/4/0 paid to vicar-general Curghey, remains	8/12/0
	Kirk Michael	0/10/0
1717	Lezayre 0/16/10. Paid to vicar-general Curghey 0/4/10	0/12/0
	Maughold 2/0/0; Kirk Malew, part of Mr Woods' arrears	6/18/0
	Vicar-general Curghey an arrear of the impropriation in his hands	3/0/0
1718	Kirk Maughold 2/0/0; Lezayre 8/12/0	10/12/0
	Vicar-general, the remainder of the above arrear	4/1/4
	Kirk Malew, the remainder of Mr Woods' arrear	6/15/3
	Kirk Michael	0/10/0
1719	Maughold 2/0/0; Michael 0/10/0	2/10/0
	Lezayre	8/12/0
1720	Maughold 2/0/0; Michael 0/10/0; Lezayre 0/12/0	3/2/0
1721	Maughold 2/0/0; Michael 0/10/0	2/10/0
	Lezayre	8/12/0
	Mr Walker, out of Kirk Malew impropriations (February 9, 1722)	5/0/0
1722	Kirk Maughold 2/0/0; Michael 2/0/0	4/0/0
	Mr Walker out of Malew impropriations	5/0/0
	Lezayre	8/12/0
1723	Mr Walker out of Kirk Malew abbey demesnes	5/0/0
	Lezayre 0/16/8; 0/4/10 paid to vicar-general Curghey	0/12/0
	Kirk Michael 0/10/0; Kirk Maughold, 2/0/0	2/10/0
1724	Maughold 2/0/0; Kirk Michael 1/0/0	3/0/0
	Vicar-general Walker out of Kirk Malew impropriations 3/0/0; out of abbey demesnes 5/0/0	8/0/0

	Lezayre	8/12/0
1725	Maughold 2/0/0; Michael 1/0/0	3/0/0
	Vicar-general Walker abbey demesnes 5/0/0;	
	impropriations 3/0/0	8/0/0

NB: Mr Allen of Lezayre and Mr Curghey are in arrears for the year ending Easter 1726 and Mr Cosnahan for Kirk Santan, that being now raised, being out of lease. Mr Makon his proportion towards the great fine, he has paid 2/0/0.

Total:	158/10/11
Minus:	20/16/8
Remainder:	137/14/3

NB: The 10s. in Michael for 1723 should have been in A. D. 1722.

[80] Disbursed:

To the repairs of the chancel of Kirk Maughold	0/12/6
To the chancel of Kirk Lonan being new built	9/19/2
1716 For collecting the tithes of Kirk Malew and	
Mr Woods' arrears for 1716-19	3/10/0
Towards rendering the chancel of Kirk Arbory	0/15/0
An arrear to Mr Charles Wattleworth, archdeacon's registrar	1/0/0
To Kirk Marown chancel as allowed Mr Bridson	1/0/0
The collecting the tithes of Malew 1720	0/10/0
The Kirk Santan chancel as allowed by the clergy	1/10/0
To Mr Woods in arrear of his salary as registrar	2/0/0

NB: That during the time Mr Woods' arrear was in paying and before for some years, I paid Mr Woods' salary as registrar to the value of near £30 out of my own pocket.

Total:	20/16/8

To the great fine:	130/0/0
Remains in my hands:	7/14/3

NB: Upon casting up the monies which I have always kept in one drawer, I find I have more than I accounted for: 1/15/5

To that, I have in my hands:	9/9/8
And from Mr Makon in proportion:	2/0/0

Total:	11/9/8

[81] The right reverend lord bishop produced these acts which were read to the clergy and professed to be perused by them, that they may see whether there be any error in the casting up, etc. John Woods, registrarius episcopi.

Receipt for the payment of the great fine, 26 September 1726

[72] Castle Rushen, September the 26th, 1726.

Whereas by an indenture bearing date the first of November 1666, the late honourable Charles, earl of Derby, passed over to the right reverend father in God Isaac, then lord bishop of this isle, and the Reverend Mr Jonathan Fletcher, then archdeacon, for the use of the clergy of this isle and for the maintenance of schools, etc., the tenancies in the said indenture mentioned, for and in consideration of the sum of one thousand pounds, then paid to the said earl, and likewise for the several sums yearly payable by way of reasoned rent, and also for the fine of £130 payable every thirtieth year at the feasts of Pentecost and St Michael the archangel.

Therefore I, James Horton, receiver-general under the present right honourable James, earl of Derby, lord of Man and the Isles, do hereby acknowledge to have received from the right reverend father in God Thomas, lord bishop of this isle, by the hands of Mr Thomas Corlett the sum of sixty-five pounds due at Pentecost last past, and also to have this day received the like sum of sixty-five pounds due at the feast of St Michael the archangel now next ensuing, which two sums complete the sum of one hundred and thirty pounds, being the fine payable by the clergy of this isle to our right honourable lord every thirty years out of the impropriations aforesaid, and for which the said clergy are hereby acquitted and discharged; I say received for the use of the right honourable the lord of this isle the sum of £130. By me, James Horton.

Thursday 25 May 1727

[82] Clergy present:

Robert Horrobin, archdeacon.	Henry Allen
John Curghey, one of the vicars-general.	William Ross, sr.
Robert Parr.	William Ross, jr.[366]
John Quayle.	Matthias Curghey, jr.
Matthias Curghey.	[83] William Gell.
John Woods jr.	William Bridson.
John Cosnahan.	John Cosnahan [jr].
Edward Moore.	John Woods, sr.

Memorandum: That the Reverend Mr William Walker, vicar-general and rector of Ballaugh and Mr Anthony Halsall, chaplain of Douglas, are now in England.

And Mr Charles Wattleworth, vicar of Kirk Arbory being disabled by a fall off his horse, could not attend.

The lord bishop enjoins the curates to lay out every year a reasonable sum towards the repair of their vicarage houses and other improvements.

---

[366]Curate of Kirk Maughold.

Thursday 13 June 1728

[84] Clergy present:

William Walker,
John Curghey, vicars-general.
John Quayle.
Matthias Curghey sr.
John Woods jr.
John Christian.
Edward Moore.
Robert Parr.

William Bridson.
Matthias Curghey, jr.
William Gell.
Robert Radcliffe.[367]
[85] John Cosnahan.
John Woods, sr.
James Makon.

Memorandum: Kirk Arbory is vacant by the decease of Mr Charles Wattleworth.

Mr Henry Allen, vicar of Kirk Maughold and Mr William Ross academical professor being sick, humbly desire to be excused.

Mr Anthony Halsall, chaplain of Douglas, is in England.

Ordered that all receipts for the courts, the registrars insert the names of the offenders, who are to have their names crossed.

Thursday 29 May 1729

[86] Clergy present:

John Kippax, archdeacon.
John Curghey, vicar-general.
Matthias Curghey jr.
John Woods sr.
John Quayle.
John Woods jr.
John Christian.
Edward Moore.

Philip Moore.[368]
William Bridson.[369]
[87] Henry Allen.
William Gell.
John Cosnahan.
Paul Crebbin.[370]
William Ross.
James Makon.

Note: That the Reverend Mr Walker, vicar-general and rector of Ballaugh, is sick, and Mr Robert Radcliffe, curate of Kirk Lonan. Mr Anthony Halsall, chaplain of Douglas, is in England. Mr Matthias Curghey sr, vicar of [88] Kirk Patrick and German, absent.

NB: My lord bishop has sent to each of the clergy for the parochial libraries an excellent book, Mr Law's *Christian perfection*.[371]

---

[367]Curate of Kirk Marown.
[368]Curate of Kirk Bride.
[369]Vicar of Lezayre and now rector of Kirk Bride.
[370]Curate of Kirk Christ, Rushen.
[371]William Law (1686-1761) published this at London in 1726.

We the clergy in convocation assembled do again repeat our most humble thanks to our right reverend lord bishop for his great care and fidelity in the management of the impropriations and on this day paying to us the surplusage, after the great fine was paid in the year 1726. And as we are very sensible of his lordship's singular care of this church and his providing for it in every respect, so we humbly desire his lordship will be pleased to tender our unfeigned thanks to our charitable benefactors who have had a tender regard for us and our successors in augmenting the parochial libraries of this diocese.

[89] We do also with the utmost gratitude acknowledge Mr William Patten's indefatigable care and industry in soliciting and transmitting to us the royal bounty for many years, which we humbly desire may be signified to him by the first convenient opportunity.

John Kippax, archdeacon.	Henry Allen.
John Curghey.	Paul Crebbin.
William Gell.	Philip Moore.
Edward Moore.	John Woods [sr].
John Quayle.	John Woods [jr].
William Bridson.	John Cosnahan.
Matthias Curghey.	John Christian.

The surplus from the payment of the impropriation in 1726[372]

The right reverend the lord bishop having at the clergy's request in convocation 1715 undertaken the management of the impropriations in order to raise a fine of £130 payable out of the said impropriations, which being paid anno 1726, there was a surplusage in his lordship's hands, of which, as also of the sums paid for the years 1725 and 1726, the account is as follows:

[90] In my lord bishop's hands; surplusage of the great fine	11/9/8
Received since by his lordship for the year **1725**:	
from Mr Allen and Mr Curghey, proctors of Lezayre	8/12/0
proctor of Kirk Malew the said year	15/0/0
In Mr Cosnahan's hands as proctor of Kirk Santan	0/8/4

1726

From proctor of Kirk Maughold	2/0/0
Lezayre	0/12/0
Kirk Malew	2/0/0
In Mr Cosnahan's hands [as above]	0/8/4
In Mr Woods' hands as proctor of Kirk Michael	1/0/0
In Mr Moore's hands as proctor of Kirk Arbory	1/0/0
Total:	32/10/4

[372]The MS contains the following note: 'See the whole among the acts of Convocation, 1726.'

Of which paid to Mr Corlett for going to Castletown with the great fine of 130/5/10.

To Dr Walker for collecting for several years the abbey demesnes, which was not in his bargain 1/4/6.

Total: 1/10/4.

Remains: 31/0/0.

[91] Payable out of the impropriations as follows to:

Kirk Michael	5/0/0
Lezayre	4/0/0
Kirk Maughold	4/0/0
Jurby	3/0/0
Kirk Lonan	4/0/0
Kirk Conchan	5/0/0
Kirk Marown	5/0/0
Kirk Braddan	5/13/4
Kirk Santan	4/5/0
Kirk Arbory	5/0/0
Kirk Christ Rushen	3/0/0
Kirk Patrick and German	6/0/0
Dr Walker as vicar-general	3/0/0
Mr vicar-general Curghey	3/0/0
Mr Woods, episcopal registrar	2/0/0
Mr Gell, archdeacon's registrar	1/0/0

So that the sums formerly paid as above come to 62/18/4.

There is in bank of the profits of 1725 and 1726 and surplusage of the great fine as on the other side 31/0/0.

Taken out of the profits of 1727 in my lord bishop's hands to make up half of the sums formerly paid: 0/9/2.

Total to be divided now: 31/9/2.

Each one's proportion of which paid in the next page.

[92] Received my proportion for: (each one signed by the incumbent):

Kirk Michael	2/10/0
Lezayre	2/0/0
Kirk Maughold	2/0/0 as executor to Mr Thomas Allen.
Jurby	1/10/0
Kirk Lonan	2/0/0
Kirk Conchan	2/10/0
Kirk Marown	2/10/0
Kirk Braddan	2/16/8
Kirk Santan	2/2/6
Kirk Arbory	2/10/0
Kirk Christ Rushen	1/10/0

Mr Curghey, vicar of Patrick	3/0/0	(John Woods jr)
Dr Walker	1/10/0	(John Curghey)
Episcopal registrar	1/0/0	
Archdeacon's registrar	0/10/0	
Total:	31/9/2.	

[93] *Memorandum*: Mr Curghey of Kirk Braddan has received his usual sum of 4s. 10d. of Lezayre this day for the year 1726. He also received this day the like sum for the year 1725, which having been paid him before, as appears by the lord bishop's account of Kirk Braddan tithes for that year, is to be refunded into the stock.

There being in his lordship's hands of the profits of **1727**:

Of Kirk Christ Lezayre	8/16/10
Kirk Maughold	2/0/0
Total:	10/16/10.

There was taken out as aforesaid to make up half the sums formerly paid: 0/9/2. Paid out to vicar-general Curghey through mistake, which is to be refunded as above: 0/4/10.

Total: 0/14/0.
For that there remains now in his lordship's hands: 10/2/10.

Meeting of the trustees of the impropriations, 9 April 1730

[94] At a meeting of the trustees of the impropriations this day, it is agreed upon by the consent of the clergy that the setting of each parish for three years to come shall stand as for the last three years, viz., the ministers for the time being are to have the power and benefit of the impropriations of their respective parishes to their best advantage according to their last setting, but Mr Bridson the late proctor of Kirk Malew having quitted the setting of that part of the impropriations, it is concluded upon that Mr archdeacon shall have the same upon the like terms. And out of the money advanced upon the impropriations since the last settlement and proportioning of the clear profits, it is this day resolved that the sum of 4/6/8 shall be laid up yearly towards the great fine and to be lodged in the lord bishop's hands for that purpose. And whereas it appears that there is in the hands of the clergy the sum of fifty-three pounds or thereabouts being the advance money of the three last years, so much of the said sum is to be divided among the clergy at the next convocation as will make up half the sum formerly paid according to their several proportions, viz. thirty-one pounds nine shillings two pence, and the remainder kept in bank after laying by out of the same 4/6/8 per annum for the last three years towards the great fine as within mentioned. In order to which all persons who are in arrears as aforesaid are hereby required to pay in their respective sum into the hands of the lord bishop forthwith, and as the sum advanced upon the

impropriations being about seventeen pounds sixteen [95] shillings *communibus annis*, the division of the same among the several parishes is to be considered at the next convocation.

Thomas Horton.

Thomas Sodor and Man.

James Horton.

John Kippax.

Copia vera, John Woods registrarius episcopi, 21 May 1730. The original is in the archdeacon's hands.

Thursday 21 May 1730

[96] Clergy present:

John Kippax, archdeacon.

John Curghey,

John Woods jr, vicars-general.

Thomas Wilson.[373]

John Quayle.

Paul Crebbin.

Robert Radcliffe

William Bridson.

John Christian.

Edward Moore.

Matthias Curghey.

Matthias Curghey, jr.

Henry Allen.

William Gell.

[97] [John] Cosnahan.

Philip Moore.

John Woods.

William Ross.

James Makon.

Memorandum: Mr Anthony Halsall, chaplain of Douglas, is in England.

[98] An account of the advance profits of the impropriations for the years 1727-9, paid in now and before to the lord bishop, viz.:

Kirk Michael 1/6/8 per annum per Mr Woods		4/0/0
Lezayre for:	1727 Mr Allen	8/12/0
	1728 Mr Bridson	8/12/0
	1729 Mr Bridson	0/12/0
Kirk Maughold for:	1727 Mr Ross	2/0/0
	1728 Mr Allen	2/0/0
	1729 Mr Allen	2/0/0
Kirk Santan for three years at 0/8/4 by Mr Cosnahan		1/5/0
Kirk Malew for three years at 6/16/0 by Mr Bridson		20/8/0

[373]The bishop's son, who was officiating chaplain of Douglas at this time.

Kirk Arbory for:	1727 Mr Wattleworth	1/0/0
	1728 Mr Wattleworth	1/0/0
	1729 Mr Quayle	1/0/0

Total: 52/9/0

Of which taken to make up the money divided at the last convocation May 29, 1729: 0/9/2.
Expended at a meeting of the trustees, April 9, 1730: 0/14/9.
Total: 1/3/11.
Rests: 51/5/1.
To which add an arrear of Kirk Malew 3/0/0.
Total: 54/5/1.

[99] Of which 54/5/1 there is now divided, viz., half the sums payable to the clergy: 31/9/2.

Kirk Michael	2/10/0
Lezayre	2/0/0
Kirk Maughold	2/0/0
Jurby	1/10/0
Kirk Lonan	2/0/0
Kirk Conchan	2/10/0
Kirk Marown	2/10/0
Kirk Braddan	2/16/8
Kirk Santan	2/2/6
Kirk Arbory	2/10/0
Kirk Christ Rushen	1/10/0
Kirk Patrick/German	3/0/0
Vicar-general's salary	3/0/0
Registrar's salary	1/0/0
Archdeacon's registrar's salary	0/10/0
Total:	31/9/2.

Laid up for the last three years 4/6/8 per annum towards the great fine: 13/0/0.
Total: 44/9/2.
In the bishop's hands remains: 9/15/11.

[100] It is this day resolved and concluded upon by the clergy in convocation that the parishes of Kirk Conchan, Kirk Braddan, Kirk Christ Rushen, Kirk German and Jurby shall be allowed the sum of one pound each per annum out of the advanced profits of the impropriations, and the remainder to be proportioned among the clergy according to the former settlement. John Woods, registrarius episcopi.

It is also agreed upon that the archdeacon's official shall be allowed the sum of thirty shillings per annum out of the said money.

Thursday 10 June 1731

[101] Clergy present:

John Kippax, archdeacon.	Mr [blank].
John Curghey,	Henry Allen.
John Woods, vicars-general.	John Allen.[374]
Thomas Wilson.	William Gell.
Paul Crebbin.	Philip Moore.
Robert Radcliffe.	John Cosnahan.
William Bridson.	John Woods, sr.
John Christian.	William Ross.
Edward Moore.	James Makon.
Matthias Curghey sr.	

Memorandum: Mr John Quayle, vicar of Kirk Arbory, is sick.

[102] We the clergy humbly desire the Reverend Mr Wilson to return Sir John Philips, baronet, our most humble thanks for his very generous benefaction to the widows and children of the present and succeeding clergy of this diocese, and we do at the same time gratefully acknowledge the said Mr Wilson's great zeal and goodness in procuring this and other benefactions for the purposes aforesaid.

John Kippax.	Robert Radcliffe.
John Curghey.	Paul Crebbin.
John Woods.	Philip Moore.
Matthias Curghey.	Matthias Curghey.
William Bridson.	John Allen.
Edward Moore.	Henry Allen.
William Gell.	John Woods.
John Christian.	John Cosnahan.

Memorandum: The clergy desire that according to the method for several years past, the impropriation money be lodged and secured in the lord bishop's hands, in order to be distributed as heretofore.

Letter of thanks to the widow of Bishop Levinz

[103] To Madam Levinz at Oxford.

Madam, We the bishop and clergy met at our annual convocation beg leave to return our most sincere thanks for your noble charity to our widows and children by the hands of the Reverend Mr Wilson.

---

[374]Curate of Kirk Lonan.

We doubt not but that your worthy husband our late right reverend prelate would have been a great benefactor to a design of this nature, but as God was pleased to deprive us of him, your ladyship has in some measure made up for that loss by a present which will endear both your memories to our latest posterity and oblige us all with grateful hearts to offer up our prayers to the throne of grace, that you may enjoy all the happiness the world affords and at last partake of the joys promised to those that do so much good in their generation.

We are, Madam, your most faithful and obliged humble servants:

Thomas Sodor and Man.	John Allen.
John Kippax, archdeacon.	John Woods.
John Curghey.	John Cosnahan.
John Woods.	Robert Radcliffe.
Matthias Curghey.	Edward Moore.
William Bridson.	William Gell.
Henry Allen.	John Christian.
Philip Moore.	Paul Crebbin.
Matthias Curghey.	

Letter of thanks to the widow of Bishop Crow of Cloyne

[104] To Madam Crow at the city of Cork.

Madam, We the bishop and clergy met at our annual convocation desire to return our most hearty thanks for your very generous and noble benefaction to our widows and children, now reported to us by the Reverend Mr Wilson.

We are also gratefully to acknowledge your kindness in joining so cheerfully with your worthy husband the late lord bishop of Cloyne in confirming his generous donation to this church.

For which repeated favours we beg of God to reward you with the blessings of this life and the next and are with the greatest reason and truth, madam, your most faithful and obliged humble servants.

Thomas Sodor and Man.	Matthias Curghey.
John Kippax, archdeacon.	John Woods.
John Curghey.	John Christian.
John Woods.	Robert Radcliffe.
Matthias Curghey.	Paul Crebbin.
John Cosnahan.	Henry Allen.
William Bridson.	Philip Moore.
Edward Moore.	John Allen.
William Gell.	

Enactment regarding dilapidation and rebuilding of clergy houses

[105] Forasmuch as several of the vicarages and one of the rectories of this isle have not for some ages past had any houses for the incumbents to reside in, and

some others are in a ruinous condition, that due encouragement may be given for the building such houses as are wanting, and keeping them in good repair, we the bishops and clergy of the said isle do humbly desire that it may be enacted:

That any rector or vicar who shall build, add to, or repair any house or outhouse upon the glebe of the respective churches to be fit, convenient and durable for himself and successors, he or his executors shall have and receive from his next and immediate successor or his executors two-thirds of the sum or sums really and truly expended by him upon such buildings, additions or repairs (necessary yearly reparations excepted) each said sum or sums shall be finally settled and adjusted by certificate under the hand and seal of the bishop or ordinary for the time being, whereof he is to be satisfied by a fair account upon oath of such expenses, or by a jury of four sufficient men to be appointed for that purpose. And such successor or his executors as aforesaid having paid the two-thirds of such sum or sums shall receive one moiety thereof, that is, one-third of the first disbursement from his next successor or his executors as aforesaid, which said sum or sums shall be paid by such succeeding rectors or vicars within two years, to be accounted from the Easter after the removal or death of such predecessor. And shall and may be received by the party who ought to receive the [106] same by sequestration of one moiety of the tenth and profits of such benefice by the bishop or ordinary for the time being, or by the common course of law against such successor or his executors in the ecclesiastical court.

And for preventing dilapidations, any person who shall suffer such buildings to go to decay or out of repair, that then his successor may recover such sum or sums in the ecclesiastical court as shall be judged equitable according to the practice in like cases, and such sum or sums to be laid out as the canon directs.

And whereas several well-disposed persons have given a considerable number of very useful and practical books to every parish of this isle, in order to preserve the same from embezzlement, and that all future benefactors may be satisfied that their pious intent shall not be frustrate, be it also enacted that every rector, vicar or curate or their executors shall be accountable for such books as are already, or shall hereafter be given, or the full value of the same as the ordinary shall direct. And every rector, vicar or curate shall immediately after his induction or licence, make a new catalogue of all the books belonging to their respective churches, and shall deliver the same to the ordinary to be registered.

And whereas the corbs due to the clergy from their predecessors or executors have not for some time been paid as the law directs, be it also enacted that the payment of such corbs shall, for the future cease, and that the present clergy who received any corbs [107] shall give an account thereof to the ordinary and the value of them to be applied towards the repairs or improvement of the respective houses after the passing hereof into a law, in order to which the reverend Mr archdeacon is desired to lay this our request before the honourable governor with all convenient speed.

Thomas Sodor and Man.	Henry Allen.
John Kippax, archdeacon.	John Cosnahan.
John Curghey.	Edward Moore.
John Woods.	Matthias Curghey [jr].

Matthias Curghey.
William Bridson.
John Woods.
William Gell.
John Christian.

Robert Radcliffe.
Paul Crebbin.
Philip Moore.
John Allen.

First donations for establishing the clergy widows' fund

[108] Having received from my son the sum of one hundred pounds Irish value sent unto him by the relict of the right reverend Dr Crow, late lord bishop of Cloyne, towards establishing a fund for the desolate widows and children of clergymen in this island, as also fifty pounds British value sent unto him by the widow of the late lord bishop Levinz for the same use, and thirty pounds from Sir John Philips, baronet, I do hereby make myself accountable for the said sums, as also my heirs, executors, administrators and assignees, until it can be laid out either upon lands or in some public fund for the perpetual uses above mentioned, as witness my hand the day and year above written. Thomas Sodor and Man.

Let this be lodged in my registry until this money and what more may be given can be laid out on lands or put into some of the public funds. Thomas Sodor and Man.

Meeting of the trustees for the impropriations, 8 May 1732

[109] At a meeting of the trustees for the impropriations May the eighth 1732, the clergy concerned present.

It is concluded and agreed upon that the distribution of the clear profits of the impropriations commencing anno 1730 shall be as of late years, and the sums advanced out of the following parishes to be forthwith paid into the lord bishop's hands, viz.

Out of Kirk Maughold	2/0/0
Kirk Santan	0/8/4
Kirk Malew	6/15/0
Kirk Arbory	1/0/0
Kirk Michael	1/6/8
In all	11/10/0

Out of which payable according to the resolution in convocation 1730:

To the minister of Rushen	1/0/0
Kirk German	1/0/0
Jurby	1/0/0
Conchan	1/0/0
Braddan	1/0/0
To the archdeacon's official as allowed this day	2/0/0
To the schoolmaster of Ballasalla, besides his usual salary	0/10/0

Total: 7/10/0.
Remainder: 4/0/0.

Which sum of four pounds is to be lodged in the lord bishop's hands for the clergy's use.

[110] And whereas the sums advanced out of Lezayre:

> for the year 1730 is 8/12/0
> for the year 1731 is 8/12/0 and
> for the year 1732 is 0/12/0.

> Total 17/16/0.

The same is also to be lodged in his lordship's hands and thereof the sum of 4/6/8 per annum to be laid up towards the great fine according to the resolution of the trustees, April 9, 1730, and the remainder reserved for the reparation of chancels or otherwise applied to the clergy's use, as shall be found necessary. Dated ut supra.

Thomas Sodor and Man.   Charles Moore.
John Kippax.   Nicholas Christian.

[111] In order to indemnify the clergy from the payment of 6/13/4 per annum, being a fee farm rent payable to the crown out of the rectories of St Michael and St Maughold, we beg leave to observe:
    1. That as the property of the abbey lands and tithes is in the right honourable the lord of this isle by grant from the crown under a fee farm rent, so are these rectories of St Michael and St Maughold under the rent now demanded, as appeared in the records of the rolls chapel.
    2. That as the lords of this isle by virtue of such grant did lease out the abbey lands, etc., so did they give leases of these two rectories to several persons, they themselves always paying this fee farm rent.
    3. That in anno 1666 the right honourable the lord of this isle gave a lease of these two rectories with several others in reversion as the old leases should expire to the bishop and archdeacon in trust, for the use of the clergy without any other charge or incumbrance than a reserved rent of sixteen pounds per annum (being the old rent paid by the former lessees) and a proportionable part of 130 pounds fine payable every thirty years for the whole.
    4. That the reserved rent of sixteen pounds per annum out of these two parishes being much greater in proportion than those of the other rectories, it may justly be presumed that this was on account of this fee farm rent now demanded.
    Forasmuch therefore as the lords of this isle did pay this demanded fee farm rent for these two parishes during the former leases granted to Cannell and Murray, so [112] they continued to pay the same for thirty years after the lease made to the clergy, as may appear by the records in the auditor's office, not only Earl Charles who gave the lease, but his successor Earl William, which we presume will

indemnify the clergy from such demands, there being not in their lease any mention of this rent demanded or any other charge than as above mentioned. Dated at Bishopscourt, November 23, 1731.

Thomas Sodor and Man.
John Kippax, archdeacon.

Thursday 1 June 1732

[116][375] Clergy present:

John Kippax, archdeacon.	Matthias Curghey, jr.
John Curghey,	Paul Crebbin.
John Woods, vicars-general.	Edward Moore.
Matthias Curghey.	John Allen.
William Ross.	James Makon.
John Christian.	Philip Moore.
William Gell.	Thomas Christian.[376]
Henry Allen.	John Woods.
John Quayle.	

And that the Reverend Mr Bridson, rector of Ballaugh, Mr Robert Radcliffe, vicar of Kirk Patrick, Mr John Cosnahan, curate of Rushen, and Mr Thomas Birkett chaplain of Douglas, are absent.

Mr Cosnahan having been detained has now attended at the convocation.

[117] *Memorandum*

1. At this convocation there was read to the clergy the archbishop of York's letter to our lord bishop, dated March 9, 1726 and here now recorded.

2. The lord bishop's injunctions for the keeping of regular church registers which are to be produced at the next chapter court and afterwards every year, in May or June visitations.

3. That the lord bishop is very ready to consent to the building a new church in the most convenient place of the parish of Kirk Lonan when the parishioners shall give sufficient security for the purchase of a new glebe, as also for the building of a new chancel and vicarage houses at least as good as those that are there at present. Provided also that there be an act of Tynwald and the consent of the patron to this purpose.

4. That Mr Witham's censure for a relapse into fornication be immediately sent forth and his fine returned.

---

[375]Pp. 113-14 are blank; p. 115 is missing.
[376]Curate of Kirk German.

5. An order that Mr Philip Moore, curate of Kirk Marown shall lay out the five pounds (paid by Mr Bridson sometime vicar there) with what other sums shall be appointed, towards the repairs of the vicarage house of that parish.

6. That due inquiry be made for the books a-wanting in the parochial library of Kirk Christ Rushen.

7. That the clergy take particular care to catechize all the young people of their respective parishes every Sunday at evening service.

[118] 8. That the parishioners of Kirk Patrick having a church of their own, necessary orders will be given for the regulating the seats in Kirk German church whenever the same shall be desired.

9. That the articles of the churchwardens charge be read in court by one of the vicars-general once every year.

10. That Mr Radcliffe, late curate of Kirk Lonan, do lay out the sum of the twenty shillings he has promised for the repair of the vicarage houses in that parish.

The statement of Dr Thomas Wilson jr regarding the clergy widows' fund

[119] Bishopscourt, Isle of Man, August 6, 1731.

Whereas my father was pleased to give one hundred pounds towards raising a fund for the perpetual use of desolate widows and children of the clergy of this isle, and being very desirous to forward so good a design, I applied to some of my friends and received the following sums, viz., from Madam Levinz, widow of the late lord bishop of this isle, fifty pounds. From Sir John Philips, baronet, thirty pounds, both British currency. As also from Madam Crow, relict of the right reverend the late lord bishop of Cloyne the sum of one hundred pounds Irish value, these sums being lodged in my hands for the abovementioned use, I do desire my father, the right reverend the lord bishop of this isle to lay out these and such other sums as may hereafter be given in some secure fund in England, and that he would also dispose of the interest arising from the same as it shall become due to such person or persons as he shall think the most proper objects of this charity. And I also beg that he would be pleased to nominate and appoint such trustees in whose hands he shall think this charity will be most securely lodged and faithfully distributed after his death. And I do by these presents as far as I am concerned, make over the entire and sole disposal of the above mentioned sums to my father, as also the power of nominating trustees for the same. As witness my hand the day and year above written. Thomas Wilson.

The indenture for the clergy widows' fund, 20 November 1731

[120] Whereas I, Thomas Wilson, A. M., student of Christ Church, Oxon am possessed of or otherways interested in and intituled unto the sum of two hundred pounds share or interest in the capital stock and funds of the governor and company of the Bank of England, and the said share or interest in the said capital stock and funds is transferred unto me, and doth now stand in my name, as by the books of the said governor and company relation being hereunto had may more fully and at large appear:

Now know all men by these presents that I the said Thomas Wilson of Christ Church, Oxon, A. M., do hereby acknowledge and declare that I am only nominated in the said transfer of the said two hundred pounds share or interest in the said capital stock and funds, by and on the behalf of the right reverend father in God Thomas Wilson, D. D., lord bishop of Sodor and Man trustee and the distressed widows and orphans of the clergy of the Isle of Man, and that I am intrusted only therein and thereby for them the said Thomas Wilson, D.D., lord bishop of Sodor and Man and the distressed widows and orphans of the clergy of the Isle of Man, their successors or assigns, disclaiming all right, title and interest in or unto the said two hundred pounds share or interest in the said capital stock and funds or any profits or advantage thereof or arising thereby, for or by any reason or means of the said transfer so made unto me as aforesaid, but only to and for the use, benefit and behoof of the said Thomas Wilson, D.D., lord bishop of Sodor and Man and the distressed widows and orphans of the clergy of the Isle of Man, their successors and assigns;

And I the said Thomas Wilson of Christ Church, Oxon, A. M., do hereby for me, my executors and administrators, covenant, promise and agree to and with all the said Thomas Wilson, D.D., lord bishop of Sodor and Man and the distressed widows and orphans of the clergy of the Isle of Man, their successors and assigns, that I the said Thomas Wilson of Christ Church, Oxon, A. M., my executors and administrators, shall and will from time to time and at all times hereafter, upon reasonable request, and at the proper costs and charges of the said Thomas Wilson D. D., lord bishop of Sodor and Man and the distressed widows and orphans of the clergy of the Isle of Man, their successors or assigns, retransfer and assure the said two hundred pounds share or interest in the said capital stock and funds unto the said Thomas Wilson D. D., lord bishop of Sodor and Man and the distressed widow and orphans of the clergy of the Isle of Man, their successors or assigns, or unto such other person or persons as they shall nominate, direct and appoint.

In witness whereof I have hereunto set my hand and seal this twentieth day of November in the fifth year of the reign of our sovereign lord George the second, King of Great Britain etc, and in the year of our Lord 1731. Thomas Wilson.

Sealed and delivered (the paper being first duly stamped) in the presence of us, David Selgros, Nathaniel Eeles.

First accounts for the clergy widows' fund

[123][377] Towards establishing a fund for the widows and orphans of the clergy of this diocese, the bishop, in order to prevail with some of his own, and his son's pious friends, first gave:

	Manx value	British value
	116/13/4	100/0/0

---

[377]Pages 121-2 are out of chronological order; see below.

The late lord bishop of Cloyne's widow, Irish value	100/0/0	92/6/8
Sir John Philips, upon my son's letter		30/0/0
The late lord bishop Levinz' lady and widow		50/0/0
Lady Elizabeth Hastings		25/6/8
Total		297/6/8

The two original stocks cost 296/0/0. Incident charges in returning the Irish and English monies and to brokers and instruments, etc. 3/0/0 but charged only 1/6/8. Total 297/6/8. Thomas Sodor and Man.

The clergy's response to the establishment of the clergy widows' fund

[125][378] The right reverend the lord bishop having this day communicated to us the annexed account and settlement of several sums of money given by his lordship and other charitable persons of quality towards a fund for the use and benefit of the desolate widows and orphans of the clergy of this diocese, we the clergy of the said diocese in this present convocation assembled, do with the utmost gratitude, acknowledge his lordship's pious zeal in laying the foundation of so good a work, as also the Reverend Mr Wilson's indefatigable care and voluntary solicitations for carrying on and perfecting the same, as it is now settled and secured in the Bank of England.

And we do humbly desire that the profits and interest of the two hundred pound share in the said bank may be disposed of during his lordship's life (which we pray may be long and happy) as his lordship in his wisdom shall think fit. And afterwards, in such manner and method as his lordship who is the sole trustee, shall please to order in his lordship's last will or otherwise.

John Kippax, archdeacon.	John Quayle.
John Curghey,	John Cosnahan.
John Woods, vicars-general.	Edward Moore.
Matthias Curghey.	Matthias Curghey [jr].
William Ross.	James Makon, A. M.
John Woods.	Philip Moore.
William Gell.	Paul Crebbin.
John Christian.	John Allen.
Henry Allen.	Thomas Christian.

Thanks to Lady Elizabeth Hastings

[126] We the clergy of the diocese of Man in this present convocation assembled do gratefully acknowledge the right honourable the Lady Elizabeth Hastings her generous benefaction towards the support of the widows and children of the clergy

---

[378]P. 124 says merely: 'Fund for clergymen's widows and orphans', referring to p. 123.

of this said diocese, and do humbly desire that this our public thanks may be acceptable to her ladyship so justly eminent for piety and works of charity.

John Kippax, archdeacon.
John Curghey,
John Woods vicars-general.
Matthias Curghey.
William Ross.
John Woods.
William Gell.
John Christian.
Henry Allen.

John Quayle.
John Cosnahan.
Edward Moore.
Matthias Curghey.
James Makon, A. M.
Philip Moore.
Paul Crebbin.
John Allen.
Thomas Christian.

Thursday 17 May 1733

[127] Clergy present:

John Kippax, archdeacon.
John Curghey,
John Woods, vicars-general.
William Ross.
William Bridson.
John Woods.
John Christian.
John Quayle.
William Gell.

Robert Radcliffe.
Edward Moore.
Matthias Curghey.
John Allen.
Philip Moore.
Henry Allen.
Thomas Christian.
Paul Crebbin.

Note: That Mr Matthias Curghey, rector of Kirk Bride, Mr John Cosnahan, curate of Kirk Christ Rushen, and Mr James Makon, master of the free school at Castletown, desire to be excused.
[128] Note also that Mr Thomas Birkett of Douglas is absent.
     Hora prima post meridiem Mr Thomas Birkett is come to the convocation.

It is this day agreed that the augmentation of twenty shillings per annum to each of the ministers of Kirk Christ Rushen, Kirk German, Jurby, Conchan and Braddan commencing from the year 1730 (according to the resolution of the clergy in convocation that year and the order of the trustees, May 3, 1732) as also the sum of 10s. to the schoolmaster of Ballasalla commencing in the year 1732 is to be paid out of the impropriations of Kirk Malew.

On 30 May 1734 Dr Thomas Wilson, the bishop's son, was chosen to be proctor for the clergy of Sodor and Man in the York convocation.[379]

---

[379]Original document in the Manx National Heritage Library.

Thursday 6 June 1734

[129] Clergy present:

John Kippax archdeacon.	John Quayle.
John Woods,	Edward Moore.
John Cosnahan, vicars-general.	Matthias Curghey.
William Ross.	Robert Radcliffe.
Matthias Curghey.	Paul Crebbin.
William Bridson.	John Allen.
John Woods.	James Makon.
William Gell.	Philip Moore.
John Christian.	Thomas Christian.
Henry Allen.	Nicholas Christian.[380]

The right reverend the lord bishop has now given to each of the clergy an excellent book intitled *A short plain instruction for the better understanding of the Lord's Supper*, etc.,[381] for which they return his lordship their humble thanks.

[130] The clergy humbly desire to repeat their unfeigned thanks to the reverend Mr Wilson for his very laudable zeal and indefatigable care in soliciting the benefactions of charitable and well-disposed persons towards the support and comfortable subsistence of the widows and orphans of the clergy of this island, his native country.

Mrs Edmonds of Kirk Conchan in her last will bequeathed the remainder of her effects to pious uses at the discretion of the lord bishop and clergy. It was this day resolved upon that the same be applied towards the purchasing of a convenient place and the building of a schoolhouse thereupon in the said parish, if the parishioners will put to their helping hand so as that the said intended work may be perfected and kept in repair, which proposal the reverend Mr Gell of the said parish is to signify to them the next holy day.

[Thursday 29 May 1735]

[131] *Memorandum*. No convocation in the year 1735, the lord bishop being then in England.

A further indenture for the clergy widows' fund, 4 July 1735

[121] Whereas one hundred pounds share or interest in the new joint stock of South Sea annuities hath been transferred into and doth now stand in the name of Thomas

---

[380]Curate of Trinity, Rushen.
[381]Written by the bishop and published at London, 1733.

Wilson M. A., of Stoke Newington in the county of Middlesex,[382] now know all men by these presents that I the said Thomas Wilson do hereby acknowledge and declare that the said one hundred pounds is the property of and held by me in trust for the right reverend father in God Thomas Wilson D. D., lord bishop of Sodor and Man and I do hereby for myself, my heirs, executors and administrators disclaim all right, title, interest and property of, into or out of the said one hundred pounds New South Sea annuity stock, or any profit or advantage that shall, may or can be had or made of or from the same, but only to and for the use, benefit and behoof of the said lord bishop of Sodor and Man. And I do for myself, my heirs, executors and administrators hereby covenant, promise and agree at any time or times hereafter to retransfer and assign the said stock to the said lord bishop or to any such person or persons as he by writing shall nominate, direct or appoint. In witness whereof I have hereunto set my hand and seal this fourth day of July in the year of our Lord one thousand seven hundred and thirty-five [4 July 1735]. Thomas Wilson.

[122] Dividend paid for Midsummer 1735, four per cent.

Letter of thanks from the clergy to the bishop, 3 November 1735

[132] To the right reverend father in God Thomas lord bishop of Sodor and Man.

We the archdeacon, vicars-general, rectors, vicars and curates of the diocese of Man do desire your lordship to return our most humble thanks to Joseph Hayward of Stoke Newington, gentleman and merchant, for his most generous present of Mr Fox's New Testament with references, etc., to each of our parochial libraries, assuring him for ourselves, as we hope for our successors, that his most valuable benefaction shall neither be forgotten nor lost upon his most grateful humble servants. Your lordship's most dutiful sons and clergy, November the third, 1735.

John Kippax, archdeacon.
John Woods, vicar-general.
John Cosnahan, vicar-general.
Edward Moore, official.
[133] John Woods.
Matthias Curghey.
William Bridson.
John Christian.
William Gell.

Henry Allen.
John Quayle.
Matthias Curghey [jr].
Robert Radcliffe.
Paul Crebbin.
Thomas Christian.
Nicholas Christian.
Nathaniel Curghey.[383]

---

[382](1703-84). He was the son of Bishop Wilson, a student of Christ Church, Oxford, from 1724 and rector of St Stephen's, Walbrook (1737-84). In 1743 he became a canon of Westminster. He remained very closely attached to the Manx church all his life.
[383]Curate of Kirk Lonan.

Thursday 17 June 1736

[134] Clergy present:

John Kippax.	John Quayle.
John Woods.	Edward Moore.
John Cosnahan.	Matthias Curghey.
William Ross.	Robert Radcliffe.
Matthias Curghey.	Paul Crebbin.
William Bridson.	Nathaniel Curghey.
John Woods.	Thomas Christian.
John Christian.	Nicholas Christian.
William Gell.	Philip Moore.
Henry Allen.	

James Makon, A. B., schoolmaster of the grammar school at Castletown, humbly desires to be excused.

[135] Mr Thomas Allen being to receive deacon's orders the next Lord's Day, the clergy are desired by the lord bishop to declare whether they have any objection to it, and there was not any objection made.

It having been resolved upon in convocation anno 1734 that the legacy left for pious uses by Mrs Edmonds of Kirk Conchan should be applied towards the building of a schoolhouse in that parish. The same is now finished as represented unto us by the vicar.

Letter of thanks to Mr Edward Harley

[136] To the honourable Edward Harley,[384] esquire.

Our right reverend diocesan having acquainted us with the several favours of the pious and honourable Mr auditor Harley your father and particularly with his last noble benefaction of the two volumes of his own composing upon the Holy Scriptures[385] for each of our parochial libraries, as also several Bibles and other books proper to preserve and increase the fear of God and a sense of religion amongst us, and it having pleased God to take him unto himself, before we could give him thanks in such a solemn manner as his favours required, we beg you will accept of our most grateful acknowledgment, assuring you that his memory will ever be sacred unto us and to our successors, as long as our records and a sense of piety shall last. In the meantime, we subscribe ourselves as bound in gratitude, your honour's most obliged humble servants

---

[384]Third earl of Oxford (1741-55).
[385]Edward Harley (1664-1735) was auditor of the imprest from 1702 to 1735. The books in question were *A harmony between the psalms and other parts of Scripture* (London, 1724) and *An abstract of the historical part of the Old Testament* (London, 1730).

John Kippax.

John Woods.

John Cosnahan.

Edward Moore, official.

[137] Matthias Curghey.

William Bridson.

John Woods.

William Gell.

John Christian.

Henry Allen.

John Quayle.

Matthias Curghey [jr].

Robert Radcliffe.

Paul Crebbin.

Philip Moore.

Thomas Christian.

Nicholas Christian.

Nathaniel Curghey.

Thanks to Sir John Cheshire

[138] The right reverend the lord bishop having signified unto us that Sir John Cheshire, his majesty's serjeant at law,[386] has lodged in his lordship's hands the sum of twenty pounds towards the building of two vicarage houses within this diocese, we do gratefully acknowledge the favour and desire that his lordship will please to return our humble thanks for this his generous benefaction, being well assured that the same will be applied so as to be a lasting monument to his charity.

John Kippax.

John Woods.

John Cosnahan.

Edward Moore.

Matthias Curghey.

William Bridson.

John Woods.

William Gell.

John Christian.

Henry Allen.

John Quayle.

Matthias Curghey [jr].

Robert Radcliffe.

Paul Crebbin.

Philip Moore.

Thomas Christian.

Nicholas Christian.

Nathaniel Curghey.

Receipt of the royal bounty for schools

[139] Whereas his majesty King Charles the second of his princely goodness did by his letters patents grant unto the right honourable George Richard, earl of Derby, Thomas Cholmondeley of Vale Royal in the county of Chester esquire and William Bankes of Winstanley in the county of Lancaster esquire and their heirs as trustees for the ministers of this isle the sum of one hundred pounds per annum and the trustees having in anno 1701 nominated and empowered our right reverend lord bishop their assignee or attorney with full power of appointing a lawful agent for the receipt and payment of the said sum of 100 pounds yearly, we the clergy of the diocese of Man in this convocation assembled do with a due sense of gratitude acknowledge and hereby declare and certify all whom it may concern that the said sum hath been duly paid until Christmas last according to the settlement of his said majesty since his lordship was concerned therein as appears this day by the several

---

[386]Appointed a serjeant-at-law on 8 June 1705 and queen's serjeant in 1711 (king's serjeant from 1714).

receipts of us and our predecessors, and also of the several schoolmasters concerned, excepting one half year not yet received by his lordship being unpaid upon the death of Queen Anne and from the twenty-fifth of March 1728 until the eleventh of June following upon the decease of his late majesty King George. Witness our hands this seventeenth day of June 1736.

John Kippax.	Henry Allen.
John Woods.	John Quayle.
John Cosnahan.	Matthias Curghey [jr].
Edward Moore.	Robert Radcliffe.
Matthias Curghey.	Paul Crebbin.
William Bridson.	Philip Moore.
John Woods.	Thomas Christian.
William Gell.	Nicholas Christian.
John Christian.	Nathaniel Curghey.

Payments made with respect to the impropriations

[140] The remainder of the advanced profits of the impropriations in his lord's hands, May 21, 1730: 9/15/11.

Payable since then out of:

Kirk Michael	1730-4 Mr Woods at 1/6/8 per annum	6/13/4
	1735 Mr Allen	1/6/8
Lezayre	for the above six years	35/14/0
Kirk Maughold	for the above six years at 2/0/0 per annum	12/0/0
Kirk Santan	Mr Cosnahan for 1730-1 at 0/8/4	0/16/8
	Mr Crebbin for 1732-5 at 0/8/4	1/13/4
Kirk Arbory	for the above six years at 1/0/0	6/0/0
Total:		73/17/11.

[141] Paid out of the within sums by his lordship at a meeting of the trustees at St John's chapel, May 3, 1732.

To Mr Philip Moore for repairs of the chancel of Marown:	0/11/6
To Mr Crebbin for repairs of Kirk Santan chancel:	1/1/1
To Mr Curghey Lezayre for the repairs of that chancel:	0/9/4
To the archdeacon for the repairs of Kirk Malew chancel:	2/9/0
Laid by towards the great fine for the years 1730-2 at 4/6/8 per annum:	13/0/0
Total:	21/10/6

Divided this day in convocation among the clergy concerned: 34/19/2

To Mr Cosnahan in consideration of his voyage and journey
to Cloyne, in order to get the settlement of the new glebe of
Lezayre from Bishop Crow: 1/16/9
Total: 58/6/4.

[142] Disbursement brought over: 58/6/4
Towards the great fine for the years 1733-5   13/0/0
Total: 71/6/4.

The stock being 73/17/11, there remains after the above and
within disbursements: 2/11/7

Memorandum: The £13 above mentioned for the great fine for the years 1733-5 is
not yet put into the stock bag for that purpose, in regard the chancels of Michael and
Santan want considerable repairs.

[143] Half the sums payable to the clergy since the addition of one pound per
annum each to the parishes of Kirk German, Kirk Braddan, Kirk Conchan, Kirk
Christ Rushen and Jurby, and the officers' salary:

Kirk Michael	2/10/0
Lezayre	2/0/0
Kirk Maughold	2/0/0
Jurby	2/0/0
Kirk Lonan	2/0/0
Kirk Conchan	3/0/0
Kirk Marown	2/10/0
Kirk Braddan	3/6/8
Kirk Santan	2/2/6
Kirk Arbory	2/10/0
Kirk Christ Rushen	2/0/0
Kirk Patrick	1/10/0
Kirk German	2/0/0
Vicar-general's salary:	3/0/0
Official's salary:	1/0/0
Episcopal registrar's salary:	1/0/0
Archdeacon's registrar's salary:	0/10/0

Total: 34/19/2.

[144] Received as witness our subscriptions. [All signed. The vicars-general divided
the 3/0/0 as 1/10/0 each.]

Wednesday 4 August 1736

The clergy's protest about the impropriations

[145] At a meeting of the clergy at St John's chapel, the fourth August 1736.

To the honourable James Murray esquire, governor of this isle.

Whereas the clergy concerned in the impropriations of this isle have represented unto us that they have been served with a writing by Mr William Christian attorney-general[387] in the name and behalf of his grace the duke of Atholl, lord of Man and the isles, warning and requiring them not to pay the profits of the impropriated thirds of tithes to the clergy of the diocese or their trustees for the future, but that for the present current year and so always for every year afterwards as long as they are concerned that they are to be accountable and responsible for the amounts of the said thirds of tithes and their appurtenances unto the said lord of Man or his agent or receiver for his grace's use, and this at their peril.

We the bishop and archdeacon of this isle beg leave to acquaint your honour that the right honourable Charles, earl of Derby, by an indenture of lease anno 1666 to the then lord bishop and archdeacon and their successors as trustees for the clergy of the diocese of Sodor and Man, and for the maintenance of schoolmasters, did grant the second impropriations, rectories and tithes therein mentioned as by the said deed may more fully appear, in consideration of which the said right honourable Charles, earl of Derby, had paid unto him the sum of one thousand pounds, the receipt whereof appears in the comptroller's office, attested by the then officers both spiritual and temporal, besides which there is the sum of sixty-six pounds three shillings and two pence per annum reserved rent, and a hundred and thirty pounds fine every thirtieth year, for a continuation of the said [146] lease, the last of which was paid within these ten years. Notwithstanding that several of the said impropriations were in lease before for three lives and reverted to us as the others expired.

We do further desire to observe to your honour that several of our chancels have from time to time been rebuilt and repaired by us out of the said impropriations, that the maintenance of the clergy does in a great measure depend upon them, together with the free school in Castletown and thirteen petty schools in several parishes, which schools must entirely be laid down, there being no other provision for them. And that the clergy will suffer considerably and be reduced to very great difficulties, by being thus disherited in the possession of a lease enjoyed seventy years without interruption, out of which we do presume they are not to be ejected without legal trial. We do therefore desire that your honour will upon consideration of the premises be pleased to interpose so as the above requirement of the attorney-general may be countermanded, or otherwise that the matter may be heard and determined by law as usual in the like cases.

---

[387]He held this office from 1727 to 1748.

Memorandum: Besides the sums before mentioned, the clergy pay the further sum of five pounds per annum proxy to the bishop.

Thomas Sodor and Man.
John Kippax.

[147] It is thus agreed to by the clergy that the expenses necessary for defending their possession of the impropriations, etc. are to be allowed out [of] the money lodged in the lord bishop's hands towards the future payment of the great fine of 130 pounds, and that the reverend the archdeacon and vicar-general do attend when the deemsters and twenty-four keys take cognizance of the said impropriations. John Woods, registrarius episcopi.

Thursday 2 June 1737

[148] Clergy present:

John Kippax.	John Quayle.
John Woods,	Edward Moore.
John Cosnahan, vicars-general.	Matthias Curghey, jr.
William Ross.	Robert Radcliffe.
Matthias Curghey.	Paul Crebbin.
William Bridson.	Thomas Christian.
John Woods, sr.	Nathaniel Curghey.
John Christian.	Nicholas Christian.
William Gell.	Philip Moore.
Henry Allen.	Thomas Allen.

[149] The reverend Mr archdeacon, the vicars-general with Mr Bridson and Mr Edward Moore are elected and appointed to confer what shall be the proportion allotted to the widows and children of the clergy of this diocese according to their respective circumstances, with rules to be observed.

Mr Edward Harley's reply, 20 July 1736

[150] To the reverend the clergy of the diocese of Sodor and Man.

Gentlemen, I cannot be too early in returning my humble thanks for the notice you have been pleased to take in your convocation of my dear father's books. Could he have known of the approbation you intended, it would have given him the highest satisfaction, and he would have esteemed it a sufficient reward for the pains he took in the composition.

   The honour you have been pleased to pay to his memory demands from me the most grateful thanks, and a higher obligation than this you could not have laid upon me, except that of allowing me a share in your prayers, that I may in the course of my life imitate his example.

That it may please the Almighty to prosper and succeed the labours of your ministry, that you may long enjoy the blessing of the instructions [151] and example of your excellent bishop, that living pattern of primitive Christianity, that the same piety and orthodoxy for which you are so remarkable, may deeply flourish and be constantly preferred among you, is the most hearty prayer of your most obliged and most humble servant, Edward Harley. Eynwood in Hertfordshire, July 20, 1736.

Thursday 25 May 1738

[152] The right reverend the lord bishop does now require Mr Nathaniel Curghey, curate of Kirk Lonan, to reside in the vicarage house within thirty days, under penalty of suspension.

His lordship orders the Reverend John Cosnahan, vicar-general, and Edward Moore, official, to inspect the episcopal registry and to make a return within forty days, whether or no due care has been taken touching the probate of wills, of administering the goods of the dead, of justifying inventories and securing the effects of children, etc. by sufficient pledges.

Ordered also that the names of all persons confirmed shall for the future be recorded in the church registers.

Resolved and agreed upon by the consent of the clergy in convocation that for the future, deacons and curates of the vacant livings shall yearly pay to the officiating priest who assists them in the sacerdotal offices the sum of twenty shillings, and that forty shillings per annum shall be sequestered out of their livings to be laid out upon the repairs of their respective curacies by proper persons to be appointed by the ordinary to that purpose. And this pursuant to an order made and resolved upon in convocation, anno 1727.

[153] Resolved this day in convocation and agreed upon that of the money of the impropriations lodged in the hands of the right reverend the lord bishop the charge which has hitherto been expended for copies of the original deeds and the other necessary costs about that affair be refunded to his lordship, and that whatever sum of money appears to remain in his lordship's hands after the settlement of accounts this day stated and settled touching the impropriations shall be applied by his lordship towards the recovery of their collateral security, and in case the stock now in bank may not be sufficient and that it shall be found necessary to raise a greater sum for the carrying on of that work, the clergy are to contribute thereunto in proportion to the advance which has been made, and that they have paid out of their several impropriations.

John Woods,	Matthias Curghey.
John Cosnahan, vicars-general.	Robert Radcliffe.
Edward Moore, official.	John Woods, episcopal registrar.
William Ross.	Paul Crebbin.
William Gell.	Thomas Christian.
Henry Allen.	Nicholas Christian.
John Christian.	Nathaniel Curghey.
John Quayle.	

Memorandum: The several schoolmasters are to contribute to the above charge in proportion.

[154] Upon the settlement now examined and stated of the accounts of the impropriation money in the lord bishop's hands towards the payment of the great fine for the use of the clergy, it appears that there was in bank secured in his lordship's hands, June 17, 1736, the sum of 41/11/7. Out of which expended at a meeting of the clergy, August 4, 1736, 0/14/7.

Paid to the clerks of the rolls chapel for copies of the deeds, British		5/5/0.
Mr Wilson's expenses attending there		1/1/0.
Coach hire waiting twice on Lord Derby		0/6/0.
Expenses by Messrs Sanforth and Morstby to Vale Royal, British 6/18/0.	Manx:	8/1/0.
	Total:	8/15/7.

May 28, 1738. There remains now in the lord bishop's hands 32/16/0.

[155] By Dr Wilson's account in his letter to the right reverend the lord bishop dated 24th December 1739, there appears to have been expended by him upon the affair of the impropriations:

1738

January 2	To two new copies of lease and release of the impropriations for the duke's lawyer from the rolls: 4/18/0.
April 12	To charges waiting upon the duke, Mr Melinoth and co. About the impropriations: 3/3/0.
May 3	To several letters to and from Mr Cloptyn, Bishop Barrow's relation: 0/12/8.
May 9	Mr Prime the attorney's bill, seeing Mr Melinoth, copies, etc., and drawing up the case: 8/14/6.
November	Waiting several times on the duke, Mr Sharp, etc., about the clergy's affair: 0/10/6.
Total:	17/18/8.

Memorandum: This 17/18/8 makes in Manx 20/18/4 and was paid to Dr Wilson this 28 February 1739 by the hands of the right reverend the lord bishop.
    Witness: Edward Moore. Acknowledged by me, Thomas Sodor and Man.

Thursday 14 June 1739

[157][388] Clergy present:

John Kippax, archdeacon.	John Quayle.
John Woods,	Matthias Curghey, jr.
John Cosnahan, vicars-general.	Robert Radcliffe.
William Ross.	Paul Crebbin.
Matthias Curghey.	Thomas Christian.
William Bridson.	Nathaniel Curghey.
John Woods sr.	Nicholas Christian.
John Christian.	Philip Moore.
William Gell.	Thomas Allen.
Henry Allen.	John Craine, deacon.

Dilapidation and repairs

[158] Pursuant to the resolution taken and agreed upon at our last annual convocation that deacons being curates of vacant livings should pay yearly to the officiating priest who assists them in the sacerdotal offices the sum of twenty shillings for their trouble, and that forty shillings per annum should be sequestered out of their livings to be laid out upon necessary repairs or buildings in their respective curacies by persons to be appointed by the ordinary for that purpose, it is now ordered and agreed upon that twenty shillings be paid unto the Reverend Mr Gell for his trouble in the last year upon visitations and other priestly offices in the parish of Kirk Lonan and that the further sum of forty shillings per annum be taken out of the profits of that curacy towards such necessary buildings upon the new glebe as shall be appointed by the ordinary, all which amounting to three pounds per annum is to be paid out of the augmentation money payable to the vicars of Lonan.

In like manner that twenty shillings be paid unto the Reverend Mr Quayle for his trouble yearly in the parish of Trinity Rushen and that forty shillings per annum be laid out of the profits of that living upon repairs, buildings or such necessary works upon that vicarage as shall be appointed by the ordinary. And this also is to be deducted out of the augmentation payable to the incumbents of Trinity Rushen.

[159] At the convocation the right reverend the lord bishop orders that the curates of vacant livings being deacons shall for the future, on the Lord's Day at morning service, plainly, distinctly and audibly read one of the homilies of the church, standing in the reading desk, and this to be continued two Sundays in every month.

Complaint being made by the Reverend Mr Cosnahan, vicar-general, that inventories, deductions of debts and other papers are and have been recorded in the episcopal registry without his knowledge and consent, whereby orphans and creditors are injured in their just rights, the right reverend the lord bishop orders

---

[388]P. 156 is chronologically out of order; see below.

that for the future no paper shall be registered whereby orphans or creditors may suffer, but by the allowance and directions of the vicar-general or other competent judge.

The right reverend the lord bishop orders that pursuant to the law and constitution in 1703, the several rectors and vicars do for the future frequently visit the schools in their respective parishes and that they do twice every year return an account to his lordship, viz., within one month after Michaelmas and within a month after Lady Day what number of scholars there are, what books they read, and what proficiency they make in their learning, and that due care may be taken about the return of such a certificate. The incumbents are to take along with them when they visit the schools, one or two churchwardens with [... the rest of the sentence has worn away.]

[160] The right reverend the lord bishop does now signify to the clergy in convocation that the Reverend Mr Philip Moore, chaplain of Douglas, is desirous to enter into priest's orders, and that his lordship purposes to ordain him priest as soon as his lordship is in a condition to travel.

The Reverend Nathaniel Curghey, curate of Lonan, having not appeared this day in convocation, ordered that he appear at the chapter court to be held in Kirk Michael on Tuesday the 26th instant, and this in obedience to the right reverend the lord bishop, his express command.

All the beforegoing orders and directions are resolved, consented unto and agreed upon by the lord bishop and clergy in convocation. Edward Moore.

His lordship requires that the schoolmaster of Lonan shall bring the register book of that parish to the chapter court to be held at Douglas on Tuesday the 19th instant, to inspect whether or no due care has been taken to register baptisms, marriages and burials. Edward Moore.

Dr Wilson's letter to the bishop regarding the clergy widows' fund, 24 October 1739, and the bishop's response[389]

[27] I have the money from Mr Parr, the copy of the receipt is inclosed, and the copy of a paper which it is necessary for you and the government to sign and send him that so much money as is paid of by the government two years ago and which now lies without interest in the bank may be reinvested in the South Sea annuities again, this was Mrs H's case when I bought in again for her. It will cost some money to do this, but that he will repay himself out of the next receipts.

[28] We desire that the sum of twenty pounds and ten shillings, being 6/16/8 per cent received by the bank in part of the £300 South Sea annuity standing in your name may be invested in the purchase of South Sea annuities to be transferred to you in trust in the cause Buckby contra Stanlake, and this shall be your sufficient warrant. As witness our hands this ... day of November 1739. To the accountant general of the court of chancery. Thomas Sodor and Man.

---

[389]Douglas, Manx National Heritage Library, MS 803C.

Thursday 25 May 1738

[162]³⁹⁰ Clergy present:

John Kippax, archdeacon.	John Quayle.
John Woods,	Edward Moore.
John Cosnahan, vicars-general.	Matthias Curghey, jr.
William Ross.	Robert Radcliffe.
Matthias Curghey.	Paul Crebbin.
William Bridson.	Thomas Christian.
John Woods, sr.	Nathaniel Curghey.
John Christian.	Nicholas Christian.
William Gell.	Philip Moore.
Henry Allen.	Thomas Allen.

[163] 1. Mr Nathaniel Curghey, curate of Kirk Lonan, is now enjoined by the lord bishop to reside in the vicarage house within thirty days under pain of suspension.

2. The curates of vacant livings being deacons shall yearly pay the officiating priest twenty shillings for assisting them in those offices which are peculiar to the priesthood and to expend yearly 40s towards the repair of the vicarage houses.

3. The episcopal registry to be inspected by the Reverend Mr Cosnahan and Mr Edward Moore and a return to be made within forty days.

4. The names of confirmed persons are to be for the future inserted in the church's registries, or in a book to be made for that purpose.

Thanks of the clergy to Mr Thomas Wilson, jr.

[164] We the clergy of the diocese of Man in convocation assembled having a just sense of the great zeal of the Reverend Mr Wilson in many instances for our advantage, and particularly for his indefatigable care in finding out the original deeds of the impropriations, do hereby desire him to accept this our sincere acknowledgment of his signal favours so beneficial to us and our successors in all future ages.

John Kippax.	John Quayle.
John Woods.	Matthias Curghey.
John Cosnahan.	Robert Radcliffe.
William Ross.	Paul Crebbin.
Edward Moore.	Thomas Christian.
John Woods.	Nicholas Christian.
William Bridson.	Nathaniel Curghey.
John Christian.	Philip Moore.
William Gell.	Thomas Allen.
Henry Allen.	

---

³⁹⁰P. 161 is chronologically out of order; see below.

Thursday 29 May 1740

[1][391] Clergy present:

John Kippax.   Robert Radcliffe.
John Cosnahan, vicar-general.   Paul Crebbin.
Edward Moore, official.   Thomas Christian.
William Ross.   Philip Moore.
Matthias Curghey.   Nathaniel Curghey.
William Bridson.   Thomas Allen.
John Christian.   Nicholas Christian.
William Gell.   John Craine.[392]
John Quayle.   John Moore.
Matthias Curghey, jr.

Memorandum. The Reverend Mr Henry Allen, vicar of Kirk Maughold, being indisposed has by letter prayed to be excused.

[2] *Memorandum.* A transcript out of Lady Elizabeth Hastings[393] her will relating to her charitable benefaction settled upon the petty schools in this diocese is recorded in the lord bishop's registry *in libro tertio pro anno* 1739. Edward Moore, May 29th, 1740.

Rules for schoolmasters and schoolmistresses

[3] The right reverend the lord bishop does now signify to the clergy in convocation that the right honourable Lady Elizabeth Hastings has in her will left the sum of twenty pounds per annum towards the maintenance of petty schools within this diocese upon the following conditions.

First, that the masters of the said schools do constantly do their duty according to the purport of the licences granted by the bishop of Man or his substitutes, and that this may be known, every master or mistress shall yearly and every year apply to the vicar or incumbent of their respective parishes (who are by law obliged to visit their schools the first week in every quarter) for a certificate in these words, viz., that such vicars or incumbents have respectively visited the said schools in their respective parishes according to the laws and constitutions of 1703, and that the children have been carefully taught and do improve in learning and good manners, are taught to say their prayers and catechism, and do duly attend the public service of the church, which certificate is to be signed by such vicar or incumbent.

And if such masters or mistresses shall not desire and obtain and bring every year to the bishop or in his absence to his vicars-general such certificate, then the

---

[391]P. 165 is crossed out. A new book begins here, Manx National Heritage Library, MS 803C.
[392]Curate of Kirk German.
[393](1682-1739). She lived at Ledstone Park, near Pontefract (Yorkshire). Her charity still exists in the diocese.

part of this charity appointed for the master or mistress so neglecting to obtain or bring such certificate, shall be divided [4] amongst such masters and mistresses as shall bring the same.

Secondly, that this charity shall not upon any pretence whatsoever lessen the payment of forty shillings a year to the said schools out of the impropriations whensoever they or the value of them shall be recovered or restored to the church, nor shall this charity be understood to excuse such parents as are able from paying such sums quarterly as the law appoints or shall be agreed upon betwixt the masters or mistresses and parents of such children.

That these conditions may be strictly observed, his lordship does now further signify to the clergy and requires them to give particular notice of these rules (by reading the same) to their respective masters or mistresses and to observe the same themselves upon pain of ecclesiastical censure, and further to acquaint them that his lordship is fully resolved that no part of this charity nor of the royal bounty shall be given to any of such masters or mistresses but to such as shall obtain certificates quarterly according to the conditions within mentioned. A copy hereof is to be sent from the vicar of Kirk Michael to the rector of Ballaugh, and so on in course from one clergyman to another, who are to take copies till the same is brought to the episcopal register, and the several clergymen are to read these rules to their respective masters and mistresses, that the same may be duly observed.

The fund for purchasing arms and ammunition

[5] Half of the sum to be raised amongst the clergy towards purchasing arms and ammunition, amounting to 16/6/8, the same is by consent proportioned by the members as follows:

The right reverend the lord bishop	7/0/0
Archdeacon and curate	1/8/8
Ballaugh	0/14/4
Kirk Bride	0/14/4
Vicar-general Cosnahan	0/10/9
Kirk Michael, official	0/10/9
Academical professor	0/10/9
Chaplain of Douglas	0/10/9
Malew	0/7/2
Jurby	0/7/2
Lezayre	0/7/2
Maughold	0/7/2
Conchan	0/7/2
Marown	0/7/2
Santan	0/7/2
Lonan	0/7/2
Rushen	0/7/2
German	0/7/2

Arbory   0/7/2
Kirk Patrick   0/7/2
Total: 16/6/4.

Memorandum: Their proportions are not paid by my lord bishop, rector of Kirk Bride, vicar of Maughold, curates of Lonan and Rushen, there having been no necessity for arms.

[6] Resolved and agreed upon that the money to be raised among the clergy towards purchasing arms and ammunition for the service of the country be paid into the hands of the Reverend Mr Moore, official, within fourteen days after date, and this according to the several and respective sums proportioned among themselves.

Thursday 21 May 1741

[7] Clergy present:

John Kippax.	Robert Radcliffe.
John Cosnahan.	Paul Crebbin.
Edward Moore, vicar-general.	Philip Moore.
Matthias Curghey.	Thomas Allen.
William Bridson.	Thomas Christian.
John Christian.	Nathaniel Curghey.
William Gell.	Nicholas Christian.
John Quayle.	John Craine.
Matthias Curghey	John Moore.

1. The Reverend Henry Allen has sent a letter of excuse for his absence, which is not to be admitted for the future.

[8] 2. The Reverend Mr Curghey, rector of Kirk Bride, has also sent a letter of excuse, which is not to be regarded for the future.

3. The right reverend the lord bishop does now order the clergy to call together their wardens and chaplains once every month to be examined upon the articles of their charge, in order to make presentments, and that for the future they do signify the same in their petitions at our chapter courts.

4. His lordship requires the clergy that for the future they recommend none for confirmation but such as are at full years, and are also instructed and prepared for the holy communion.

5. His lordship requires vicar-general Cosnahan to lay out forty shillings per annum upon the vicarage of Kirk Lonan, the profits being at present sequestered into his hands, as also that the Reverend vicar-general Moore shall expend forty shillings yearly towards repairs upon the vicarage of Kirk Arbory, out of the vicar's third of that parish, which during the vacancy is sequestered into his hands.

6. His lordship desires the archdeacon that sometime this summer he will make a parochial visitation through the diocese in order to enquire into the state of the fabrics, the utensils and ornaments of the churches, and that a particular account thereof be returned.

Petition of the clergy and schoolmasters to the lord of the isle

[9] Douglas, May 27th, 1741.

Right honourable, We the clergy and schoolmasters of the diocese of Sodor and Man whose names are underwritten are constrained by hard necessity to become your lordship's most humble supplicants in behalf of ourselves, our children and our families, and to represent unto your lordship that the impropriate tithes of this isle, having been purchased by the charity of many of the nobility and bishops and of other well-disposed persons within the realm of England, have been the great support of most of the clergy and schoolmasters, our predecessors, for above seventy years, until his grace the duke of Atholl took possession of them as of right belonging to him, and although in great compassion to so many families he has been pleased to permit us to enjoy the profits of the same hitherto, upon our giving bonds to repay him when we shall receive the value of them, out of the estates settled for our security which are now in your lordship's possession, yet we are given to understand that this favour is not to be continued to us much longer.

We do therefore most humbly beseech your lordship to consider our case and to give relief to so great a number of otherwise miserable families.

[Crossed out] *we have applied to our right reverend the bishop and the reverend the archdeacon the trustees appointed in the deeds of settlement which we presume your lordship* [10] *and council have by Dr Wilson been made acquainted with, and they assure us that they have made application to your lordship and sent a true state of our case (a copy of which we have presumed to inclose) and that they have desired Dr Wilson to represent unto your lordship the great difficulties we labour under.*

This is all that our distant situation and mean circumstances will permit us to do, and in order to obtain your honour's favour and speedy redress, we have presumed to inclose a true state of the case of your lordship's most humble and distressed petitioners.

John Cosnahan.	Henry Allen.
Edward Moore.	Thomas Christian.
William Gell.	Paul Crebbin.
John Christian.	Nicholas Christian.
John Quayle.	Nathaniel Curghey.
Robert Radcliffe.	John Craine.
Matthias Curghey.	John Moore.[394]

John Kewley, schoolmaster of Kirk Michael.
John Stole, schoolmaster of Kirk Braddan.
William Christian, schoolmaster of Kirk Conchan.
William Saul, schoolmaster of Patrick.
Rebecca Mordy, schoolmistress of Kirk Santan.

[394]Curate of Kirk Arbory.

Robert Rogers, schoolmaster of Lezayre.
John Killip, schoolmaster of Lonan.
James Clagg, schoolmaster of Marown.
Robert Quayle, schoolmaster of Malew.
John Garrett, schoolmaster of Rushen.
Robert Allen, schoolmaster of Kirk Maughold.
William Kneale, schoolmaster of Arbory.
Matthew Crellin, schoolmaster of German.

To the right honourable Edward, earl of Derby.

The clergy's case for the impropriate tithes

[11] A state[ment] of the case of the impropriate tithes within the Isle of Man.

In the year 1666 the impropriate tithes within the Isle of Man being then in lease, many of them for three lives, the reversion of the said tithes was made over unto the then lord bishop and archdeacon of Man for the support of the poor clergy by the right honourable Charles, earl of Derby and lord of the said isle, and this by an indenture bearing date the first of November 1666, for the term of ten thousand years, in consideration of the sum of one thousand pounds paid in hand and of an hundred pounds paid afterwards (as appears by his lordship's receipt) as also of an annual rent of sixty-six pounds three shillings and two pence, and a fine of one hundred and thirty pounds to be paid every thirty years during the said term.

And the said earl in order to secure unto the clergy these impropriate tithes or the full value of them did by another instrument or indenture, bearing date the 29th January 1666 [1667] make over unto the said bishop and archdeacon and their heirs and assigns certain lands and tenements in the county palatine of Lancaster, called by the names of the manor of Bispham and Methop, as a further and collateral security for the full and peaceable enjoyment of the said impropriate tithes, against any person lawfully claiming the same. The said bishop and archdeacon permitting the said earl and his heirs to hold and enjoy the said lands and tenements until they or their successors shall be molested or interrupted in the peaceable possession of the aforesaid impropriate tithes, etc. and that in such case, they who are their heirs shall have power to re-enter into the said lands and to receive and hold the profits of the same until they shall have received such sums of money as shall be sufficient from time to time to satisfy all manner of losses, damages and expenses as may be sustained by reason of any such interruption or disturbance, the trust above limited in behalf of the said earl or his heirs notwithstanding.

Pursuant to these indentures, the originals of which were recorded [12] in chancery and are now in the chapel of the rolls, the clergy were put into possession of the said impropriate tithes as the leases became void, and held the same for seventy years, during which time they paid two fines of one hundred and thirty pounds each, the last fine being in the year 1726.

In the year 1736 his grace the duke of Atholl having taken possession of the Isle of Man, took possession also of the impropriate tithes as part of his inheritance and property, and ordered a particular account of their true value to be taken, and obliged the several clergy and their proctors to be accountable for the future to his grace's receiver general for the same, as they have been ever since.

Now that the right honourable Edward, earl of Derby (in whose possession the manors given in counter security as aforesaid are at present) may see how great sufferers the clergy and schoolmasters are by their being deprived of these tithes, here follows an account of the same as taken by order of the government at two several times, of the truth of which his lordship may satisfy himself by any way he may be pleased to require.

Kirk Michael *communibus annis*	22/6/0
Kirk Lezayre *communibus annis*	52/7/2
Maughold	21/0/0
Lonan	16/13/8
Onchan	8/19/4
Marown	17/13/6
Santan	13/0/0
Malew	81/0/0
Arbory	20/18/4
Rushen	54/6/7
The whole.	308/4/7.

To be deducted out of the impropriations:

The yearly reserved rent	66/3/2
Proxies to the bishop	5/0/0
The yearly interest of the great fine	4/6/8
Stipends to Lezayre, Malew, etc.	11/6/8
Allowance for collecting	30/0/0
Besides the yearly repairs of chancels.	

By the annexed account of the times when the reversion of the several leases fell into the hands of the purchasers and their [13] successors, it will appear that they had no favour shown them in the purchase.

The purchase made anno Domini	1666	
Kirk Christ Rushen became void	1667	
Kirk Lonan	1669	
Malew	1673	
Arbory	1672	
Onchan	1691	25 years after the purchase.
Lezayre and Marown	1697	31 years after the purchase.
Kirk Maughold and Michael	1704	viz., 38 years after the purchase.
Kirk Santan	1723	viz., 57 years after the purchase.

May 21, 1741.

Thursday 10 June 1742

[16][395] Clergy present:

John Kippax, archdeacon.	Matthias Curghey, jr.
John Cosnahan,	Robert Radcliffe.
Edward Moore, vicars-general.	Paul Crebbin[396]
William Ross, absent, infirm.	Thomas Christian.
Matthias Curghey.	Philip Moore.
William Bridson.	Nathaniel Curghey.
John Christian.	Thomas Allen.
William Gell.	Nicholas Christian.
John Quayle.	John Moore.
Matthias Curghey, jr.	

Kirk German vacant by the death of Mr John Craine, vicar.

Mr Henry Allen, vicar of Kirk Maughold, being unable to travel has prayed to be excused.

[17] The deed concerning the fund settled towards the maintenance of clergymen's widows of this diocese was now read in convocation. The right reverend our lord bishop, the Reverend Dr Thomas Wilson, rector of St Stephen's Walbrook, London, and Mr Stephen Hales, minister of Teddington,[397] are trustees for this charity. The fund at present is three hundred pounds secured and settled as more fully set forth in the deed dated the 26th day of February 1740.

The right reverend the lord bishop requires that the two clergy shall for the future recommend none for confirmation but such as are fifteen years of age complete and well instructed in the Christian religion as also fitted for the Lord's Supper.

His lordship signifies to the clergy that he purposes (God willing) to admit Mr Thomas Allen, curate of Kirk Andrews [sic], to the order of priesthood and to ordain Mr James Wilks deacon, against the ember season in September next or sooner if the necessity of the church should require it.

Some of the clergy having in the convocation held anno 1740 consented to raise some money towards purchasing arms for the defence of the country and there having been no necessity, at their request and by the approbation of our right reverend diocesan, their several sums are now returned to such persons as at that time contributed to that purpose, the same having until now been as resolved upon, lodged in the hands of Mr Moore, the then official.

---

[395]Pp. 14 and 15 are exact copies of pp. 9 and 10 respectively.
[396]Absent burying the dead.
[397]Perpetual curate of Teddington (1708-61).

Fund for purchasing arms and armaments

[18] Convocation 1740. The money paid towards purchasing arms, etc. by the persons following:

Archdeacon and curate	1/8/8
Rector of Ballaugh	0/14/4
Vicar-general Cosnahan	0/10/9
Kirk Michael, official.	0/10/9
Academical professor	0/10/9
Chaplain of Douglas.	0/10/9
Vicar of Malew	0/7/2
Jurby	0/7/2
Lezayre	0/7/2
Conchan	0/7/2
Marown	0/7/2
Santan	0/7/2
German	0/7/2
Curate of Arbory	0/7/2
Vicar of Kirk Patrick	0/7/2
Total:	7/10/6.

At convocation 1742 the money returned to the clergy and received by them as appears by their several rescripts above written. [All signed opposite their titles.]

Financing the lawsuit regarding the impropriations, 26 October 1742

[156][398] At Bishopscourt, October 26, 1742.

The court having allowed ten guineas for supplying the cure of Ballaugh during the absence of the Reverend Mr Bridson about six months in attending the administration and recovering the assets of his brother Mr Christopher Bridson, and the said Mr Bridson having for himself and co-administrators paid that value into the hands of the right reverend the lord bishop, who in the absence of the rector had the greatest trouble in performing the service of that church, his lordship, with the advice of his vicars-general, is pleased to apply the same towards the expenses of the clergy in carrying on the affair of the impropriations, which is accordingly put into the bag with the remainder of the money in stock for that purpose, so that the case stands at present as follows:

February 28, 1739: Remainder of the money in my lord bishop's hands after expenses paid: 11/17/8.

The above ten guineas added this 26th October 1742 makes in Manx money 12/5/0. There is now in stock 24/2/8. John Cosnahan. Edward Moore.

---

[398]Douglas, Manx National Heritage Library, MS 802C.

Thursday 26 May 1743

[19] Clergy present:

John Kippax, archdeacon.	Robert Radcliffe.
John Cosnahan,	Paul Crebbin, absent.
Edward Moore, vicars-general.	Philip Moore.
William Ross, absent.	Thomas Christian, absent.
Matthias Curghey sr, absent.	Philip Moore.
William Bridson.	Nathaniel Curghey, absent.
William Gell.	Thomas Allen.
Henry Allen, absent.	Nicholas Christian.
John Quayle, absent.	John Moore.
Matthias Curghey, jr.	John Wilks.[399]

Jurby vacant by the death of the Reverend John Christian, late vicar.

For the prevention of clandestine marriages

[20] For the more effectual preventing of clandestine marriages and the sad consequences of such irregular and unlawful contracts whereby the laws of God and of the church are broken and the honour and authority of parents and guardians violated, that no person whatever may be ignorant of the severe penalties which the law inflicts in such cases, nor be surprised to be present at such illegal meetings, it is resolved upon in convocation and accordingly ordered that the laws provided in that behalf be published in the several churches and chapels of this diocese upon the Lord's Day immediately after the Nicene Creed within one month after the date hereof, which are as follows:

Customary law 40.[400] That when a minister makes a clandestine marriage, he that married the couple and all present at the marriage shall be committed into St German's prison and excommunicated *ipso facto.*

Customary law 41. That when a minister doth marry man or woman without licence or banns of marriage according to the rubric he is to be suspended three years *ab officio et beneficio* according to the canons of the church, unless the ordinary upon submission of bonds of reformation mitigate or remit the same.

And that the wholesome discipline of the church in these respects may be duly observed, the ministers, churchwardens and chapter-quest [21] in their several parishes are hereby admonished and required to make presentment of all such offenders according to their oath and the articles of their charge.

Thomas Sodor and Man.
John Cosnahan, Edward Moore, vicars-general.

[399]Curate of Kirk German.
[400]These are the laws of 1667; see above.

[22] Resolved in convocation that for prevention of clandestine marriages the laws setting forth the penalties to be inflicted upon such are to be published upon the Lord's Day in the several churches of the diocese.

The right reverend my lord bishop recommends to the parochial clergy, and it is accordingly resolved upon, that the Psalms of David be read at least once a month in the churches both at morning and evening service in the Manx language, and that by the minister only.

The curate of Arbory having neglected to make a return of the parochial register for the years 1741 and 1742 is to be admonished to send a copy thereof to the episcopal registry within fourteen days *sub poena iuris*. Sent and registered.

Accounts for the repair of the vicarage of Rushen, 11 March 1742

[24][401] March 11, 1742. The within accounts expended upon the vicarage of Rushen by Mr Nicholas Christian, curate, were delivered by him to the reverend the archdeacon who transmitted the same to the right reverend the lord bishop. Edward Moore. Bishopscourt, April 25, 1743.

The grates, locks, dressers and the other goods mentioned in the within bill are to remain and so forthcoming upon the vicarage for the benefit of the future incumbents in the parish of Rushen, Mr Christian having laid out the within sums pursuant to the resolution in convocation at forty shillings per annum, the sum of 1/7/2½ being the surplusage at present, rests in my lord bishop's hands, which is to be laid out for the use of the vicarage as shall be agreed upon in convocation. Edward Moore.

Memorandum: The above 1/7/2½ has been paid to Mr Allen by my lord bishop.

1740 Disbursements on improvements and reparations upon the vicarage of Rushen *ut sequitur*.

1740 or thereabouts.

To a new leaf and door case to the garden	0/3/6
To John Nelson for taking the church road out of the glebe into his land	0/13/0
To four labourers unto the said Nelson upon the said account	0/1/8
To repairing the outhouses being very much abused by storm	0/6/8
To timber upon the said account	0/1/0
To repairing the kitchen chimney, which was blown down by storm and some of the house shaken thereby	0/2/1
To a new threshold and lintel for the barn door	0/0/7
To a threshold for the kitchen door	0/0/4
Total:	1/8/10

---

[401]Pp. 23 and 24 do not follow in the normal sequence, because of the way they were inserted into the MS.

[23] **1740** [carried over]	1/8/10

To the kitchen grate three crowns	0/17/6
To the parlour and room over the kitchen grate	0/4/8
To a lock for the barn door	0/2/10
To a lock for the cellar door	0/2/4
To a lock for the buffet in the parlour	0/1/2
To a lock for the room over the parlour	0/2/4
To a lock for the room over the kitchen	0/2/2
To a lock for the closet in the kitchen	0/1/2
To twelve dales for the dresser, etc.	0/14/0
To three carpenters two days making the dressers rack and chimney piece	0/6/0

1741

To new window cases and sash frames for the two rooms above stairs	0/11/8
To painting and glazing the said sashes	0/10/8
To half a barrel of lime	0/0/9
To a mason two days enlarging and making up the said windows	0/2/0
To a labourer two days	0/0/10
To three kishons of lime unslacked	0/0/3
To a workman mending the plaster and whitewashing the house	0/1/0
To drawing stones and sand from Port Erin	0/1/0
To half a barrel of lime	0/0/9
To a mason one day making a new hob in the kitchen setting the grate and preventing its smoking	0/1/0
To a labourer one day to serve the mason	0/0/5
To stones and putting a new large course on one end of the house	0/0/6
To a hearth stone from the kitchen	0/0/4
To roping the outhouses	0/1/6
To a man one day repairing the garden fence	0/0/5

Total:	1/13/1

1742

To fifty bundles of thatch for the outhouses at 1d per bundle	0/4/2
To ropes	0/0/10
To four labourers	0/1/4
To eight labourers building and repairing the glebe fence at 5d. per...	0/3/4
To building a new pigsty and henhouse	0/3/0
To six kishons of lime	0/0/4½
To repairing and plastering a part of the cellar	0/0/6
To six oak boards at 6d per...	0/2/0

To making a new leaf for the stable door of the said boards	0/0/8
To three-quarters of eight-penny nails	0/0/6
1742	0/16/8½
1741	1/13/1
Total:	6/12/9½.

Account of the repairs done to the vicarage of Kirk Arbory

[25] Account of the labours and works done towards the house belonging to the church of Kirk Arbory as follows:

Labourers – days work:	Thomas Clague	0/10/0
	Henry Corlett	0/9/0
	John Preston	0/4/0
	Philip Corrin	0/4/0
	John Maddrell	0/1/0
	William Quayle	0/6/0
Total:		0/15/0.

To quarrying in William Quayle's quarry:	John Harrison	0/2/0
	John Cornish	0/2/0
	William Quayle ·	0/2/0
Those six days at 7d. per day.	Total:	0/6/6.

Mr Bickerstaff's cart, eight days at four shillings British per day	1/17/4
Mr Moore's wheelbarrow and two horses six days at two English shillings per day	0/14/0
Agreed with William Quayle for the liberty of his quarry for 3s.	0/3/0

Mason work.

John Cubbon: three days and a half at 12d. per day	0/3/6
John Cregeen: three days and a half at the same wages	0/3/6
Henry Clague: three days and a half at 10d. per day	0/2/11
John Watherston: three days and a half at 10d. per day	0/2/11
Total:	4/11/11.

July 12, 1744. Received three pounds in part of the above from the Reverend Mr Moore of Kirk Michael by me, William Harrison.

[26] August 9, 1744. Then received from Mr Moore of Kirk Michael towards building the outhouse in Kirk Arbory the further sum of three pounds, which besides the three pounds paid before makes up six pounds, by me, William Harrison.

April 29, 1745. At Kirk Arbory. Then paid Mr William Harrison towards the building of the outhouse the further sum of twenty shillings, by me, Edward Moore.

The petition of Nicholas Christian, curate of Kirk Christ Rushen

[29][402] To the right reverend father in God the lord bishop of Sodor and Man.

The humble petition of Nicholas Christian, curate of Rushen, showeth,

That some years ago it was laid down as a rule and resolved upon in the annual convocation that every deacon curate residing upon any of the vicarages of this isle should have a deduction made from their respective annuities of forty shillings to be yearly expended for the benefit of the next vicar upon some necessary improvements. That the vicarage of Rushen, where your lordship's petitioner now resides, labours under many inconveniences well-known to some worthy gentlemen here present, and the living itself so small that with the most frugal management it will not afford bare necessaries of life even to a very small family, and is now become very uncomfortable by putting the said resolution of convocation in execution.

Your lordship's petitioner therefore humbly prays that your lordship would be graciously pleased to take into consideration the petitioner's present case and circumstances and grant him relief in this matter by revoking the said resolution and he as duty bound shall ever pray, etc.

Funds for purchasing arms and armaments

[30] Money paid by the clergy on the north side towards purchasing arms, etc.

The right reverend the lord bishop	7/0/5
Archdeacon	1/1/6
Kirk Bride	0/14/4
Ballaugh	0/14/4
Kirk Michael; vicar-general.	0/10/9
Lezayre	0/7/2
Kirk Maughold[403]	0/7/2
Kirk Patrick	0/7/2
Kirk German	0/7/2
Minister of Jurby	0/7/2
The first payment being one half:	11/16/9
The curate of Kirk Andrews	0/7/2
Total:	12/3/11.

April 30, 1744. This 12/3/11 sent in the care of Thomas Cannell of Churchtown to be delivered to the comptroller. Edward Moore.

---

[402]Pp. 27-8 are chronologically out of order; see above.
[403]This parish is on the south side.

Thursday 17 May 1744

[31] Clergy present:

John Kippax, archdeacon.	Paul Crebbin.
John Cosnahan,	Thomas Christian.
Edward Moore, vicars-general.	Philip Moore.
William Bridson.	Nathaniel Curghey.
John Quayle.	James Wilks.
Matthias Curghey, jr.	John Moore.[404]
Robert Radcliffe.	Nicholas Christian.[405]

Absent: Matthias Curghey, old and prays to be excused.
    Henry Allen, very infirm.
    William Gell, infirm and makes excuse.
    William Ross, academical professor, absent.

[32]1. At this convocation the lord bishop recommends to his clergy to have the sacrament of the Lord's Supper more frequently administered in the parish churches with the great blessings which may be expected from frequent communion.

2. He recommends also a religious observation of the fasting days appointed by the church as very necessary to be observed, at this time especially, when we are threatened with God's judgment by war.

3. His lordship especially requires that for the future the parochial clergy be very punctual in reading the Psalms of David once every month on the Lord's Day in the Manx language, and that by the minister only, in the following order, for three months on the first Sunday in the month, for three months on the second Sunday in the month, for three months on the third Sunday, and for three months on the fourth or last Sunday in the month, that the congregation may thus have the benefit of hearing that most edifying and excellent part of the church service in their own language.

4. The clergy are ordered to give notice to their schoolmasters and schoolmistresses who are intituled to Lady Betty Hastings' charity that for the future they are to wait on the lord bishop upon Thursday in Easter week with proper certificates to receive their stipends.

5. The deacons having hitherto had several admonitions both public and in private to qualify themselves for priests orders are now also admonished by his lordship to prepare themselves by a sober life and conversation to a diligent application to their studies, otherwise the younger deacons behaving themselves as becomes them are to be preferred before them.

6. Decency of habit is recommended to the clergy according to the canon and the usage of grave and sober clergymen.

---

[404]Curate of Kirk Arbory.
[405]Curate of Rushen.

Funds for repairing the school at Castletown

[33] Contributions towards repairs of the schoolhouse of Castletown, which is at present in ruinous condition.

The right reverend the lord bishop	1/0/0
Archdeacon	0/5/0
Vicar-general Cosnahan	0/5/0
Vicar-general Moore	0/5/0
Mr Ross	0/5/0
Mr Bridson	0/5/0
Mr Robert Radcliffe	0/5/0
Mr Quayle	0/5/0
Mr Crebbin	0/2/11
Mr Christian	0/2/11
Mr Curghey, Lezayre	0/5/0
Mr Allen, Maughold	0/5/0
Mr Allen, Kirk Andrews	0/5/0
Mr Philip Moore	0/2/11
Mr Wilks	0/2/11
Mr Moore, Arbory	0/2/11
Mr Curghey, Lonan	0/2/11
Mr Cubbon	0/2/11
Mr Curghey, Kirk Bride	0/3/0
Mr Gell	0/3/0
Mr Christian, Rushen	0/2/0
Mr Halsall, Crosby	–
Total	4/18/5
Mr Thomas Woods, schoolmaster of Ramsey	0/2/11

The reverend Mr archdeacon is pleased to collect and to receive the several subscriptions of well-disposed persons and the Reverend Mr Ross, academical master and master of the free school, together with the Reverend Mr Quayle, vicar of Malew, and the Reverend Mr Crebbin, vicar of Santan [34] .... take the care of finishing the... may be done firm, decent and substantial... [Mr Quayle] and Mr Cubbon engage to use their best endeavours... [compl]ete and perfect this good work, and the same is by [the] clergy in convocation prayed to be recommended to the Reverend Mr Ross.

[35] Received from Mr vicar-general Moore on account of the clergy's assess[ment] twelve pounds three shillings and eleven pence, this 2nd May 1744. John Quayle.

Another indenture for the clergy widows' fund, 19 March 1745

[37/38][406] Whereas the Reverend Thomas Wilson, master of arts, student of Christ Church, Oxford as appears by a deed signed and sealed by him the twentieth day of November one thousand seven hundred and thirty-one was intituled unto the sum of two hundred pounds share or interest in the capital stock or funds of the governor and company of the Bank of England, and that the said share in the capital stock was transferred unto him and stood in his name, and that the said Thomas Wilson acknowledgeth in the aforesaid deed that he was only nominated in the said transfer by and on behalf of the right reverend father in God Thomas Wilson, Doctor of Divinity, lord bishop of Sodor and Man their successors and assigns,

And whereas the further sum of one hundred pounds share in the true joint stock of South Sea annuities which stood in the names of the reverend Doctor Stephen Hales, minister of Teddington and of the said Thomas Wilson then of Stoke Newington in the county of Middlesex is also acknowledged by him the said Thomas Wilson to be the property of and held in trust by him the said Stephen Hales for the right reverend father in God Thomas Wilson, Doctor of Divinity, lord bishop of Sodor and Man as may more fully appear by a deed dated the fourth day of July one thousand seven hundred and thirty-five, they the said Thomas Wilson and Stephen Hales disclaiming all right, title and interest in and unto the said two hundred pounds share in the said capital stock, as also in and unto the one hundred pounds share in the new joint stock of South Sea annuities, but only to and for the use and behoof of the said Thomas Wilson, lord bishop of Sodor and Man and the distressed widows and orphans of the clergy of the Isle of Man,

Now know all men by these presents that we the aforesaid Thomas, lord bishop of Sodor and Man, Doctor Thomas Wilson, rector of St Stephen's Walbrook, and Doctor Stephen Hales, minister of Teddington in the county of Middlesex, who have been chiefly concerned in promoting this charity to the end that our pious intent and the pious design of those who have contributed towards [39] this charity may be the better answered, we have appointed these following rules to be observed for the better distributing of the yearly interest arising from this fund, provided always that it shall be lawful for the said right reverend the lord bishop of Sodor and Man to appoint a trustee or trustees in whose names the aforesaid two hundred pounds bank stock and the one hundred pounds new South Sea annuities shall be transferred in case the aforesaid Stephen Hales or Thomas Wilson or either of them shall depart this life during the life of the said lord bishop of Sodor and Man, and it is also further provided that in case either the said Doctor Stephen Hales, minister of Teddington, or the said Doctor Thomas Wilson, trustees for this fund shall depart this life and that there shall be remaining living only one of the trustees, that then it shall be lawful for such surviving trustee to assign the said trust to the use of himself and one other person as trustees to the intent that the said trust may always be full. Which said surviving trustee and the trustee so to be elected shall stand and be interested in the stocks and funds before mentioned to the ends and purposes in this deed mentioned and intended, and to no other ends or purposes whatsoever.

---

[406]P. 36 is chronologically out of order; see below.

First, that the two vicars-general of the diocese of Man for the time being shall be the standing stewards for the distribution of the charity under the direction of the aforesaid lord bishop of Sodor and Man, that they are empowered to ask and receive the yearly profits or interest thereof from the trustees and to give receipts for the same, and they are to produce their accounts in convocation, at which time they shall show the receipts and acquittances, that it may appear what has been expended and what remains in stock.

Secondly, that there shall always be in bank in the hands of the right reverend the present lord bishop of Sodor and Man for his life or of the stewards a stock of ten pounds at the least towards the securing of the principal, in case of any emergency that may happen.

Thirdly, that the widows of all instituted clergymen within this diocese, if approved of by the present lord bishop of Sodor and Man [40] and not otherwise, shall receive yearly at two payments out of this charity four pounds per annum towards their maintenance during the time of their widowhood and their living within the diocese.

Fourthly, that if there shall be a surplusage after the payment of five pounds per annum to each widow, the same or such part thereof as shall be judged proper shall be applied towards keeping the orphans of clergymen to school, or towards putting them to some honest employment as the present lord bishop of Sodor and Man shall appoint and direct.

Fifthly, that the widows who shall be entitled to this charity be women of grave and sober conversation, that they are industrious, ruling their children and their houses well, giving no offence, not noted for pride or extravagancy, but in all things demeaning themselves as becometh widows of the ministers of Christ.

Sixthly, we do direct and appoint that the stewards above mentioned shall do nothing in the affair without the express advice and approbation of the present lord bishop of Sodor and Man during his life.

In witness whereof we have hereunto set our hands and seals the nineteenth day of March in the year of our Lord one thousand and seven hundred and forty-four and in the eighteenth year of the reign of our sovereign lord George the second, King of Great Britain and so forth. Stephen Hales. Thomas Wilson.

Signed, sealed and delivered (being duly stamped) by the said reverend Stephen Hales and Thomas Wilson in the presence of Joseph Wallin, George Schutz, notaries public, 1744 [1745].

The form on [37] is dated 26 February 1740 [1741] in the fourteenth year of George II and was witnessed by Thomas Williams and Joseph Wallin. That the document is certified by John Perkins, notary public, and Abraham Ogier, notary public, further attests that Perkins is a bone fide notary public.

Thursday 6 June 1745

[41] Clergy present:

John Kippax.

John Cosnahan,[407]

Edward Moore, vicars-general.

William Bridson.

John Quayle.

Robert Radcliffe.

Thomas Allen.

Matthias Curghey, deacon.

Nicholas Christian, deacon.

Matthias Curghey.

William Crebbin, deacon.

Thomas Bacon, priest.

William Mylrea, deacon.

Samuel Gell, deacon.

Mr Henry Allen, vicar of Maughold, infirm and prays to be excused.

Mr Matthias Curghey, rector of Kirk Bride, infirm and prays to be excused.

Mr William Gell, vicar of Conchan, old and prays to be excused.

Memorandum: This was a very rainy day, which began about four o'clock and continued to rain heavily till about three in the afternoon.

Mr vicar-general Cosnahan came at one of the clock and Mr Thomas Christian, vicar of Marown.

Mr Philip Moore, chaplain of Douglas, and Mr Paul Crebbin are absent, this owing to the severity of the day.

Mr Wilks to sue for the maintenance of the academic lecturer

[42] Mr James Wilks, vicar of Kirk German, being commissioned by the trustees of the academic school to sue for the sum of £250, a part of the fund settled for the maintenance of the academic lecturer, and having sailed for Dublin for that purpose, the persons following are to supply that church in his absence:

June 9:   Mr Thomas Bacon.

June 16 and 23:   Mr William Mylrea.

June 30:   Samuel Gell.

Further contributions to the repair of the schoolhouse at Castletown

The contributions of the clergy and others towards repairing the old schoolhouse in Castletown the last year having fallen short and the work unfinished, the undertaker being also in arrear on that account, some further contributions are now made:

The right reverend the lord bishop	0/5/0
Vicar-general Cosnahan to give	0/2/11
Vicar-general Moore	0/2/11
Mr Bridson of Ballaugh	0/1/0

---

[407]Came about one of the clock.

Mr Curghey of Lezayre, vicar, has now paid to the archdeacon. He says he paid last year.

Second account of the building of the vicarage at Kirk Arbory

[43] Account of the building of the house belonging to the church of Kirk Arbory.

Labourers (days worked)

Thomas Clague	13	John Preston	9	
Henry Corlett	12	William Quayle	10	
Philip Corrin	4	John Maddrell	1	
Total:				1/3/9

Quarrying days at 7d. per day

John Harrison	3	
John Cornish	3	
William Quayle	3	
Total:		0/5/3

Mortgage to Mr Bickerstaff for his court, ten days at 4s. British per day: 2/6/8
Mr Moore and myself and a wheel cart, six days at 2s. British per day: 0/14/0

Masons.

John Cubbon:	six days at 12d. per day		
John Cregeen:	six days at 12d. per day	Total.	0/11/0
Henry Clague:	four days at 10d. per day		
John Watherston:	six days at 10d per day.	Total	0/7/11

John Harrison and William Quayle: eight horses and two men drawing stones from the quarry	0/3/0
To William Harrison for timber	0/6/2
To Mr Hewish for timber for door homes	0/1/10
To John Corrin for six deals	0/7/6
To William Quayle for the liberty of the quarry	0/3/0
To Mr Taubman for eight deals for the doors	0/3/3
William Quine and three horses drawing tiles for one day	0/1/6
John Harrison for liberty of the tiles	0/1/0
To John Cook for cutting the tiles	0/1/2
To horses for drawing the timber and deals from Derbyhaven and Castletown and Rushen	0/2/4
For the gudgins and hinges for the doors with smith work	0/2/0
To William McKenna for ten packs of ling and thirty fathom of gadd for the house	0/2/4
To Mr Taubman a hundred of 12d. nails	0/1/0

[44] To John Preston for making the roof, the doors and door hoses   0/3/4
To drink for he that was driving the cart and the quarrymen   0/2/6
Total: 7/10/6

[45] 1744: Now in Edward Moore, at three payments paid.

In my hands   8/0/0
For William Harrison   7/0/0
Remainder   1/0/0

Forty shillings for the year 1745 sequestration: 2/0/0
Ditto for 1746   2/0/0
To John Moore curate, lent for Curgheys   1/8/0
In my hands   3/12/0

Memorandum: The sequestration money, viz. 40s for 1744 was upon his petition returned to the curate by lord bishop's order and for the year 1747 remains in his own hands. Edward Moore.

Due to Mr Harrison:

His expense   0/10/6
Trouble   0/10/0
Total   1/0/6
Remains   2/11/6.

May 12, 1748. Then accounted with the reverend Mr Moore, vicar-general, for the sequestration money of Kirk Arbory to this day and allowed for eight pound and six pence for building outhouses on the vicarage and received the balance of the whole, viz., two pound eleven shillings and six pence, per me, John Moore.

[46] July 12, 1744. Then paid Mr William Harrison in part of a bill of particulars expended by him towards building the new barn and stable upon the vicarage of Kirk Arbory the sum of 3/0/0.

August 9, 1744. Then paid Mr Harrison the further sum on said account of 3/0/0.

April 23, 1745. At Balla Varcus in Kirk Arbory paid Mr Harrison the sum of 2/0/0.

January 17, 1748. Lent Mr William Harrison per John Hinkey the post 0/10/0.

The petition of John Moore, curate of Kirk Arbory and the bishop's response

[47] To the right reverend father in God Thomas lord bishop of Sodor and Man.

The humble petition of John Moore, curate of Kirk Arbory, showeth,

That the sum of forty shillings per annum having pursuant to the resolution in convocation been for five years past sequestered out of the profits of that vicarage to be applied towards the building of outhouses and other conveniences for the benefit of the incumbents, and the same having from year to year been lodged in the hands of the reverend vicar-general Moore, it appears by the accounts produced and computation made that eight pounds will be sufficient to finish the barn and stable lately built.

And as there are forty shillings for the year 1744 which are not yet laid out, your petitioner's humble request is that in consideration of the great scarcity with which it hath pleased God to visit our land at this season and other urgent occasions, your lordship will be pleased to allow the said 40s towards his subsistence and give Reverend Mr Moore, vicar-general, directions accordingly, and your petitioner shall ever pray, etc.

[48] At Bishopscourt, June 6, 1745.

Upon consideration of the reasons mentioned by the petitioner I do allow Mr vicar-general Moore to pay him the forty shillings which were sequestered into his hands for the year 1744, and for the future let the sequestration be continued as formerly and till a vicar shall be instituted. Thomas Sodor and Man.

Pursuant to the right reverend the lord bishop's reference to [the] within petition, I have received the above mentioned forty shillings, being the sequestration for the year 1744. As witness my hand the 6 of June 1745. John Moore.

Mr Wilks' expenses on his trip to Dublin

[48A] An account of the expenses that attended my going to Dublin concerning the academical money pursuant to a power of attorney dated 20 November 1744, given by peter Leigh of Lime and Charles Cholmondeley of Vale Royal, esquire, trustees for said money, to me, James Wilks. To:

Dec 10	Horse hire to Bishopscourt for my instructions, etc.	0/1/9
Dec 11	Horse hire to Derbyhaven in order to go to Dublin	0/2/0
	Expenses there and at Castletown	0/1/6
Dec 26	Horse hire to Derbyhaven and expenses there	0/2/6
	Sea shore, etc.	0/2/6
	My passage	0/5/10
Total	This is Manx	1/15/6

Dec 27	A boat for putting me ashore from Polebeg	0/1/1
	Supper lodging, etc. at Ringsend	0/1/7½
	A boy for carrying my portmanteau to Dublin	0/0/4½
	A chaise to Mr Keane's at Clontarf	0/0/6½
	Ale for the sailors	0/0/6
	A chaise to Clontarf for advice and waiting one hour	0/0/9
	A coach with Mr Keane to Mr Walker's	0/1/1
	Mr Keane's servant being sent home with one	0/0/6
	The ferry-boat four times	0/0/2
	A chaise to Mr Keane's for advice and waiting three hours	0/1/3

Paper, ink and pens	0/0/4
A chaise to Rathfarnham after Mr Walker	0/0/4
A returned chaise from Mr Keane's, having gone there in the morning with Mr Walker	0/0/4
A bottle of wine with Mr Meares, Dublin notary	0/1/8
A coach with Mr Keane to Mr Walker's	0/1/1
Expense extraordinary at the Black Lion, Fleet Street	0/2/0
Ditto at Lestrange's with Mr Moor, Dublin notary	0/1/8
A porter with a letter to Mr Walker	0/0/9
A chaise to Mr Keane's, etc. and waiting four hours	0/1/7½
Expense at the Black Bull with Mr Batters, the gentleman who has the L 250	0/3/0
A coach with Mr Keane to Mr Walker's	0/1/1
Coffee at Lucas's	0/0/3
Wine at the Black Bull after receiving the money from Mr Walker, with Mr Moor, Dublin notary, and others	0/6/8
Ditto, making acquaintance with Mr Dalton, Dublin notary, in order to get the money speedily laid out on good security	0/3/4
Ditto at the Globe coffee house, treating with the Reverend Mr Carr	0/1/8
Lunch for Mr Coultis, attorney and others at the Black Bull	0/2/0
Ale at the quay	0/0/8
Wine with Ben Johnson	0/1/8
A chaise to Mr Keane's with Mr Meares' proposals	0/1/0
Expenses at the Dog and Duck	0/0/10
Total	1/19/3

[48B]	Brought over	1/19/3
	Brought over also 15/6 Manx which makes 0/14/2½	
	Expenses with Mr Bush, treating about the L 250	0/1/8
	A porter with a litter to Mr Bush	0/0/2
	Ale, etc. at the quay	0/0/10
	A chaise to Mr Keane's with Mr Bush's proposal and waiting two hours	0/1/0
	Ditto with the Reverend Mr Carr's proposals	0/1/0
	Expenses at the Black Bull, receiving Mr Batter's proposals	0/1/8
	A chaise to Clontarf with ditto	0/0/10
	Porters with letters to Messrs Dalton, Johnson, Meares, etc.	0/0/5
	Expenses at the Black Bull with Mr Batters	0/1/6
	A chaise to Kilcock to see the concerns to be mortgaged	0/7/7
	Expenses on the quay, bespeaking my passage home	0/1/0
	A coach with Mr Keane to Mr Moor's to see the deeds perfected	0/1/0
	Expense at the Black Bull after supper with Messrs Batters, Ward, etc., after the deeds were perfected	0/3/4
	Porter with my portmanteau, etc., to Harrison's on the quay	0/0/10
	Breakfast at Ringsend	0/0/4

A chaise to Mr Keane's for letters and waiting four hours	0/1/7½
A room for seven weeks at 4s. per week	1/8/0
Hire and candle, etc. for seven weeks	0/7/4
Diet for seven weeks at 1/2 per week	2/9/0
Barber, shoeboy, etc.	0/6/9½
The servant where I lodged	0/1/1
My passage home	0/8/1½
A boat for putting me ashore, being a storm	0/1/1
Other incidental expenses, occasioned chiefly by Mr Walker's unnecessary and tedious delays in paying the money, as also since the money was settled, till I did get a passage home	2/1/6
Total	11/16/8

Bishopscourt, March 4th, 1745/6.

I have considered the above account of Mr Wilks, his expenses in recovering and securing 250 pounds of the academic monies, and upon discoursing with him upon the several particulars, I do find the account and demand to be very just and reasonable, and of which I shall give the honourable trustees an account. Thomas, Sodor and Man.

Thursday 22 May 1746

[49] Clergy present:

John Kippax, unwell.	Paul Crebbin.
John Cosnahan.	Philip Moore.
Edward Moore.	Nathaniel Curghey.
William Bridson.	Nicholas Christian.
Matthias Curghey, old and infirm.	John Moore.
Matthias Curghey.	James Wilks.
Thomas Allen.	William Crebbin.
William Gell, old and prays to be excused.	Samuel Gell.[408]
John Quayle.	William Mylrea.[409]
Robert Radcliffe.	

Memorandum: Mr William Ross, academical professor, old and very infirm, absent.
Present also: Mr Paul Crebbin, vicar of Santan.
                             Mr William Crebbin, curate of Jurby, deacon.

[50] My lord bishop acquaints the clergy in convocation that he has suspended Mr Thomas Christian, vicar of Kirk Marown, for rash and scandalous discourses uttered by him, tending to his affection to his sacred majesty King George, etc. The

---

[408]Of Kirk Lonan, assists his father.
[409]Curate of Kirk Andreas.

clergy are well pleased with his lordship's proceedings, expressing their loyalty and inviolable attachment to the person and government of his majesty King George, with their utter abhorrence of all popish doctrines and of a popish pretender.

The Reverend Dr Thomas Wilson's account of the royal bounty is now read and the same paid until Christmas 1743.

The petition of complaint of Isabel Corkish of Kirk Christ Rushen is read in behalf of her daughter Isabel Lowey orphan, representing that her said daughter was without her knowledge by wilful means married to William Cashin a minor, also married by Mr Nicholas Christian the curate. The matter is to be heard in consistory.

The clergy are required to be very careful in giving out certificates to obtain licences for marriage.

His lordship signifies to the clergy that he intends to admit Mr William Crebbin of Jurby and Mr William Mylrea, curate of Kirk Andrews, deacons, to the order of priesthood against the next ordination season. There does not appear to be any objection.

A case of defamation, 9 May 1747[410]

[161] May 9, 1747 at Kirk Michael.

Whereas some indiscreet persons who cannot be discovered have uttered unguarded expression tending to the defamation of Mr Goldsmith and Margaret the wife of Mr Quayle, whereby very great discomfort and uneasiness hath arisen in families, which is made matter of ridicule and laughter amongst the wicked and profane, but to them grief of all serious [?] will disposed them, having this day...

Thursday 11 June 1747

[51] Clergy present:

John Kippax, indisposed.
John Cosnahan, absent being indisposed.
Edward Moore.
Matthias Curghey, absent.[411]
William Bridson.
William Ross, absent, old and infirm.
William Gell.
John Quayle.
Matthias Curghey.
Robert Radcliffe.
Philip Moore.

Paul Crebbin.
Thomas Christian.
Thomas Allen.
James Wilks.
Samuel Gell.
William Mylrea.
Nicholas Christian, deacon.
John Moore, deacon.
Nathaniel Curghey, deacon.
Thomas Woods, deacon.

---

[410]Douglas, Manx National Heritage Library, MS 802C. Incomplete.
[411]Prayed to be excused.

The clergy's thanks to Dr Thomas Wilson jr for his work in establishing the clergy widows' fund

[52] To the Reverend Doctor Wilson now at Bishopscourt.

Reverend sir, We the clergy of this diocese assembled at our annual convocation, highly sensible of your pious zeal and indefatigable endeavours for promoting in many instances the prosperity of this church and nation, beg leave with the utmost gratitude to us and to our families and to our latest posterity, and in particular, for your laying a foundation and settling a fund for the support of the desolate widows and orphans of the clergy of this diocese, a most comfortable benefaction distributed with great fidelity and prudence by our right reverend and most worthy diocesan.

For your great concern for us and your unwearied application on our behalf in remitting the royal bounty.

And whereas we have for several years past been deprived of the benefit of the impropriations, a considerable branch of our livings, encumbered with a lawsuit now depending in the high court of chancery of England, we return you, kind sir, our most hearty thanks for the great pains you have taken and for your continual solicitations on our behalf, under difficulties which without the blessing of so very excellent a friend had been to us insupportable.

We further beg leave to make this public acknowledgment of your goodness to this church and nation by your purchasing a glebe for the vicar of Kirk Michael and his successors for ever.

And we praise God for prospering your labours in building the new chapel at Ramsey, now happily finished and consecrated to the service of Almighty God, beseeching him to reward your labour of love to us and to our families, to our successors and to this church and nation.

May God Almighty grant you all the happiness which this world affords, and after you have long and with great success laboured in his vineyard, make you partaker of the joys promised to [53] those happy souls who do so much good in their generation. Reverend Doctor, we are with the greatest sincerity and thankfulness, your most obliged and most humble servants and brethren.

Edward Moore.	Thomas Allen.
William Bridson.	James Wilks.
John Quayle.	Samuel Gell.
Matthias Curghey.	William Mylrea.
Robert Radcliffe.	Nathaniel Curghey.
Paul Crebbin.	Nicholas Christian.
Philip Moore.	John Moore.
Thomas Christian.	Thomas Woods.

Bishopscourt, June 11, 1747.

On 5 August 1747 Edward Moore, vicar-general and rector of Kirk Michael, was appointed clergy proctor for Sodor and Man in the York convocation.[412]

Thursday 2 June 1748

[54] Clergy present:

John Kippax, absent.	Paul Crebbin.
John Cosnahan, absent.	Thomas Christian.
Edward Moore.	Thomas Allen.
Matthias Curghey, absent.	James Wilks.
William Bridson.	Samuel Gell.
William Ross, absent.	Nicholas Christian.
Kirk Conchan.[413]	John Moore.
John Quayle.	Nathaniel Curghey.
Matthias Curghey.	William Mylrea.
Robert Radcliffe, official.	Thomas Woods.
Philip Moore.	Joseph Cosnahan, deacon.

Procedures for confirmation

[55] My lord bishop, after a very politic manner, recommends to the clergy the great necessity and benefits of catechizing the youths, in order to qualify them for the sacred ordinance of confirmation, and requires that for the future, certificates be returned in these words, viz.: 'I have instructed this person in the nature, the necessity and blessings of confirmation.' His lordship directs further that afterwards the persons confirmed be well instructed in the nature of the sacrament of the Lord's Supper, and that none be admitted but such as have been duly qualified by their pastors.

His lordship acquaints the clergy that there is to be a parochial visitation this summer, sometime in the month of July, and appoints Mr vicar-general Moore, Mr official Radcliffe and in case Mr vicar-general Cosnahan shall then be in a condition to travel, that he also shall visit the churches, church houses, schools, etc., and to represent unto his lordship the state and condition of the several particulars which are then to be inquired into. In case of Mr Cosnahan's inability to travel, the Reverend Mr Philip Moore is appointed by lord bishop to assist on the visitation.

It is also now ordered that the churchwarden's charge is to be read once a quarter on the Lord's Day after the Nicene Creed, viz., the first Sunday of each quarter, and the wardens and chapter-quest to be presented, unless after public notice, they attend to hear their charges then read.

---

[412]Original document in the Manx National Heritage Library.
[413]Vacant by the decease of Mr William Gell.

Request for confirmation, 11 March 1749

[57][414] Kirk Arbory, March 11, 1748 [1749].

May it please your lordship, Being informed of a confirmation to be held tomorrow at Kirk Michael, I have made bold to trouble your lordship with four catechumens prepared for confirmation, viz., a son and daughter of Mr Stanley's receiver-general, Mr Hamilton's servant and another grown up to man's estate. I hope your lordship will excuse my sending them without having notice as there is a necessity of some of them leaving the country before there may be another confirmation. I am, my lord, with all my best wishes for you lordship's long continuance in good health, your lordship's most obedient and faithful servant, John Moore.

Thursday 18 May 1749

[56] Clergy present:

John Kippax, unwell, absent.
John Cosnahan, unwell, absent.
Edward Moore.
Matthias Curghey.[415]
William Bridson.
William Ross.[416]
Robert Radcliffe.
John Quayle.
Matthias Curghey.
Paul Crebbin.
Philip Moore.

Thomas Christian.
Thomas Allen.
James Wilks.
John Moore.
Nicholas Christian.
Nathaniel Curghey.
William Mylrea.
Thomas Woods.
Samuel Gell.
William Crebbin, deacon.
Joseph Cosnahan, deacon.

[58] At the convocation, the right reverend my lord bishop ordered the parish clergy to be very serious and earnest in their public and private admonition of persons under excommunication, and having regard not only to the offence but also to frustrate others from falling into sin, and that the clergy take particular care not to grant certificates to any but them who have given very full testimony of their repentance.

His lordship orders also that the presentments of every church may be laid before him before the canons are sent out, that adultery and profaneness may be provided against by excommunication, etc., as the nature of their sins shall direct.

His lordship exhorts the clergy to close application in their study and that the younger clergy be not too forward to dispose of themselves in marriage, showing the great ill consequences arising from them.

---

[414]This page is chronologically out of order. For p. 56 see below.
[415]Old and prays to be excused.
[416]Old and unable to appear.

His lordship, in regard to his old age and infirmity proposes that some persons may be appointed to manage the affairs of the royal bounty and to receive and distribute Lady Elizabeth Hastings her annual charity to the schoolmasters.

His lordship having managed these convocations for several years to the satisfaction of the clergy, they with submission pray that his lordship may be pleased still to continue to negotiate those affairs and that they will give their full assistance to make it as easy to his lordship as possible, and that upon notice given, every parson in and for the future to attend upon a certain day to be appointed by his lordship to receive their respective proportions.

[59] To the right reverend father in God Thomas, lord bishop of Sodor and Man and to all and singular the clergy of this diocese in the present convocation assembled, May 18, 1749.

Philip Moore's proposal for establishing a clergy retirement fund

An inferior member of this assembly begs leave with all due submission to lay before your lordship and this house the following proposals:

1. First, that whereas your lordship and your son the Reverend Doctor Wilson, prebendary of St Peter's, Westminster, rector of St Stephen's Walbrook and chaplain in ordinary to his majesty have been chiefly instrumental, by the blessing of God, in settling a fund for the support of clergymen's widows in this diocese, it is hereby proposed that a fund be established on the same plan by and amongst the clergy of this diocese, the benefit and advantage of said fund to extend to the children of clergymen and such other purposes as shall hereafter be mentioned.

2. Secondly, that a sum not exceeding ... pounds, accruing from the profits and interest of the said intended fund, be granted and applied to enable clergymen or the widows of clergymen to educate their sons for the service of the church, or to put them out, each as they grow up, to some honest employment or occupation.

3. Thirdly, that a sum not exceeding the same value as above be granted and given as a compliment or present to the daughters of clergymen on their marriage with some honest landed man or other creditable tradesman, to help them to begin the world.

4. Fourthly, that such of the inferior clergy as through age or infirmity shall be rendered incapable of discharging the duties of their office be allowed a sum not exceeding ... pounds a year, the better to enable them to employ an assistant minister with the consent and approbation of the right reverend the lord bishop.

5. Fifthly, that in order to raise a competent fund for these good and necessary purposes, an act of convocation be passed, by and with the consent of this whole house, whereby every clergyman of this diocese, from the lord bishop inclusive, shall be bound and oblige himself to pay into the hands of the proper trustees, annually at convocation, [60] one shilling out of the pound or such other proportionate donation as shall be agreed on by your lordship and the majority of this house, and of the computed value of his living or benefice in the church.

6. Sixthly, that the right reverend father in God the lord bishop of this isle, the reverend Mr archdeacon, the vicar-generals and two rectors, all for the time being, be constituted and appointed trustees to receive the said annual contributions or

such other donations as lovers of the clergy for their work's sake amongst the laity, may think proper to bestow for the same good ends.

7. Lastly, that the aid trustees shall take such measures from time to time as they shall judge most advisable and expedient for laying out the annual contributions of the clergy to the best advantage and with all convenient speed, on some durable security, either to interest or on some good purchase of lands, and annually at convocation apply the issues and profits of the fund to the uses and purposes above recited.

And may Almighty God give his blessing to and prosper the design.[417]

Thursday 7 June 1750

[61] Clergy present:

John Kippax, absent, infirm.	Thomas Christian, absent, infirm.
Edward Moore,	John Moore.
Robert Radcliffe, vicars-general.	Nicholas Christian, absent.
Matthias Curghey, absent and infirm.	James Wilks.
William Bridson.	Nathaniel Curghey.
John Quayle.	William Mylrea.
Matthias Curghey.	William Crebbin.
Paul Crebbin.	Samuel Gell.
Philip Moore.	Thomas Woods.
Thomas Allen.	Joseph Cosnahan.

Regulations governing the clergy widows' fund

[62] Whereas by a deed bearing date the 19th of March 1744 for the settlement of a fund for the distressed widows and orphans of the clergy of this diocese it is provided that the widows of all instituted clergymen within this diocese of Sodor and Man shall receive yearly at two payments out of the charity founded in that deed four pounds British per annum towards their maintenance during the time of their widowhood and their living within the diocese, it is now resolved upon and agreed unto by our right reverend diocesan and the clergy in convocation assembled that the time of the commencement of such widows upon that stipend shall be from Easter Sunday next following the decease of said clergyman, the first payment of which to be at Michaelmas next following and the other payment at Lady Day next ensuing the date. And forasmuch as at present the yearly profits of that fund does not amount to the payment of four pounds British to each widow, it is resolved that for the future they are to be paid four pounds in Manx value till otherwise ordered, and that the surplusage, if any be, shall be added to the stock in my lord bishop's hands. And whereas his lordship has for many years managed the affair of the royal bounty to the great satisfaction of the clergy and all others concerned, his lordship proposes his being no longer concerned in that affair on account of his great age and

---

[417]Written by Philip Moore but not signed.

infirmity, [63] and that the clergy now present may nominate some persons to act in that concern, as also in this fund for the benefit of the clergymen's widows and orphans. His lordship with the clergy in convocation have thereupon nominated and appointed the Reverend Edward Moore and the Reverend Robert Radcliffe vicars general to negotiate the said funds to the purposes intended, who are to proceed upon those trusts when his lordship shall think proper.

Thomas Sodor and Man.

Edward Moore.

Robert Radcliffe.

William Bridson.

John Quayle.

Matthias Curghey.

Paul Crebbin.

Philip Moore.

Thomas Allen.

Samuel Gell.

John Moore.

Nicholas Christian.

James Wilks.

William Mylrea.

William Crebbin.

Thomas Woods.

Joseph Cosnahan.

Thursday 30 May 1751

[64] Clergy present:

John Kippax, infirm.

Robert Radcliffe.

Matthias Curghey.

Matthias Curghey, Kirk Bride, infirm.

Rectory of Ballaugh, vacant.

Edward Moore, infirm.

William Ross, infirm.

John Quayle.

Paul Crebbin.

Philip Moore.[418]

Thomas Christian, infirm.

Thomas Allen.

James Wilks, episcopal registrar.

John Moore.

Nicholas Christian, absent.

Joseph Cosnahan.

Samuel Gell.

Nathaniel Curghey.

Thomas Woods.

William Mylrea.

William Crebbin.

Robert Christian.

Thomas Quayle.

Philip Moore's apology for absence

[65] Douglas, May 29, 1751.

My lord, After attending your lordship at one and twenty convocations, it is with deep regret that I find myself under a necessity of absenting myself from the present assembly of my brethren beloved in Christ, the nature of my indisposition being such as will not permit me to ride a mile, and therefore hope your lordship will excuse and dispense with my attendance, assuring your lordship and my dear brethren the clergy that I am with you in heart and spirit, praying God to bless all

---

[418]Infirm, and by letter desires to be excused.

your consultations for the good and prosperity of his poor distressed church amongst us. With these sentiments I am with humble duty and respect your lordship's most obedient son and servant, Philip Moore.

[66] Our right reverend diocesan acquaints his clergy in convocation assembled that considering the necessities of this church and that there are not any youths intended for the service of the church at canonical years fit for ordination, that he wrote to his grace the archbishop of York, acquainting him with our present situation, upon which his grace thought proper to dispense with his lordship's ordaining any persons qualified for the ministry, provided they be 21 years of age, but not under.

His lordship also acquaints his clergy that he intends, God willing, to ordain Mr John Christian of Kirk Marown and Mr Clare Quayle of Castletown into the office of deacons, at farthest by Michaelmas ember season, and desires to know of his clergy whether there be any objection against said persons.

His lordship likewise pressingly enjoins his clergy to visit the petty schools of their respective parishes according to the constitutions of 1703.

Thursday 21 May 1752

[67] Clergy present:

John Kippax, infirm and absent.	James Wilks.
Robert Radcliffe.	Joseph Cosnahan.
Matthias Curghey, vicars-general.	Samuel Gell.
William Ross, infirm and absent.	Thomas Woods.
Matthias Curghey, infirm.	William Crebbin.
Philip Moore.	Nathaniel Curghey.
John Quayle.	William Mylrea.
Paul Crebbin.	Robert Christian, deacon.
Thomas Christian, infirm.	John Christian, deacon.
Thomas Allen.	John Gill, deacon.
Nicholas Christian.	Thomas Quayle, deacon.
John Moore.	

[68] His lordship having signified to his clergy that as far as the necessities of the church required it he intended to ordain Mr Robert Brew of Balla Quaggin into the sacred order of deacon, and requested that if any of his clergy had or knew of any objection why he should not be ordained, that they would signify the same to his lordship.

The Reverend Mr Philip Moore, rector of Ballaugh, was also appointed to preach at the Tynwald court. James Wilks, episcopal registrar.

Thursday 14 June 1753[419]

[69] Clergy present:

Robert Radcliffe.	Thomas Woods.
Matthias Curghey.	William Crebbin.
Philip Moore.	Robert Christian.
John Quayle.	John Christian.
Thomas Allen.	William Mylrea.
James Wilks.	Nathaniel Curghey.
John Moore.	John Gill at Ballaugh.
Nicholas Christian.	Thomas Quayle.[420]
Samuel Gell.	Robert Brew.[421]
Joseph Cosnahan.	

NB: The Reverend Mr John Kippax, archdeacon, the Reverend Mr William Ross, academical professor, being both old and infirm, cannot attend.

The Reverend Mr Matthias Curghey, rector of Bride, having lost his eyesight and the Reverend Mr Paul Crebbin of Santan being sick cannot likewise attend, Mr Crebbin having by letter signified the same.

[71][422] At this convocation our right reverend diocesan having signified to his there assembled clergy that he, with the assistance of his son the Reverend Dr Thomas Wilson, rector of St Stephen's, Walbrook, prebendary of Westminster, have for many years managed the affairs of the royal bounty and his lordship hopes to the satisfaction of all concerned, and having acquainted them that he lately received two-quarters of that bounty which is this day ready to be paid, and at the same time proposes his being no longer concerned in that affair on account of his great age and many infirmities, and desires that the clergy now present may nominate some persons to act in that concern in his lordship's behalf, as also in the fund for the benefit of clergymen's widows and orphans. Thereupon his lordship with the clergy now assembled in convocation have unanimously appointed the Reverend Robert Radcliffe and the Reverend Matthias Curghey vicars-general to negotiate and manage the said funds to the purposes intended, who by their own consent are forthwith to enter upon the said trusts, and to return an account of their proceedings herein annually at our convocation for the satisfaction of all concerned.

Thomas Sodor and Man.	John Christian.
Robert Radcliffe.	William Crebbin.
Matthias Curghey.	Joseph Cosnahan.
Philip Moore.	Nathaniel Curghey.

---

[419]N.B. The new calendar came fully into effect on 14 September 1752.
[420]Archdeacon's curate at Castletown.
[421]Deacon and curate of Bride.
[422]P. 70 is a fair copy of p. 69.

John Quayle.
Thomas Allen.
John Moore.
James Wilks
[72] Samuel Gell.
Nicholas Christian.

Robert Christian.
Thomas William Joseph Woods.
William Mylrea.
John Gill.
Thomas Quayle.
Robert Brew.

We the foresaid clergy in convocation assembled do beg leave to return your lordship our right reverend diocesan and son the reverend Dr Thomas Wilson our sincere and grateful thanks for your pious zeal in promoting our welfare and that of our families in many instances, but more especially for laying the foundation of and settling that comfortable fund appropriated for the support of the desolate widows and orphans of the clergy of this diocese, and to your lordship in particular for your great fidelity and prudence in distributing the same.

[73] We further beg your lordship and your most worthy son would accept our thanks for your great care in negotiating the royal bounty for the time past so very much to our satisfaction and humbly crave the continuance of the Reverend Dr Wilson's favour and interest in soliciting the payment of that bounty, without which, we are highly sensible of the many difficulties we should labour under.

Robert Radcliffe.
Matthias Curghey.
Philip Moore.
John Quayle.
Thomas Allen.
Nathaniel Curghey.
Thomas William Joseph Woods.
William Mylrea.

John Christian.
William Crebbin.
Joseph Cosnahan.
Samuel Gell.
John Gill.
Thomas Quayle.
Robert Brew.
James Wilks.

Memorandum: A copy hereof was given to Doctor Wilson, 20th July 1754. James Wilks.

Appointment of administrators for the royal bounty

[74] Whereas by an act of convocation dated at Bishopscourt on the fourteenth June last past our right reverend diocesan Thomas, lord bishop of this isle desired that, considering his great age and many infirmities, the clergy then in convocation assembled would nominate and empower some person or persons to negotiate and transact the funds of the royal bounty as well as that of the clergymen's widows, and that his lordship and the said clergy then appointed and empowered, the reverend professor Robert Radcliffe and Matthias Curghey vicars-general for the future to negotiate the said thanks and to apply the profits of the same to the uses intended, and likewise to receive from his lordship whatever arrears of said funds or either of them remained in his hands, and that the said vicars-general having this day met at Bishopscourt for the purposes aforesaid do find by receipts under the hands of the clergy and schoolmasters that the royal bounty has been paid them severally till Christmas 1751 inclusively, excepting eleven quarters of the salary due to the petty

school of Ramsey at 15s. per quarter amounting in the whole to 8/5/0 to be disposed of as we shall judge most advisable, and the receipt of which we do hereby acknowledge. And we also find by an account of the interest of the fund towards the support of clergymen's widows and orphans settled by his lordship anno 1748 that he then had a surplusage of 61/19/8 in his hands, as also that [75] his lordship has received the interest of said fund from Lady Day 1748 to Lady Day 1753 together with some interest from Captain Kaighin which amounts to the sum of 91/5/9, the whole amounting to 153/5/5. And likewise that his lordship has disbursed thereout to the said widows, etc. 61/5/5 and laid out in mortgage to Captain Kaighin 25/14/3½ also given in a bond of John Hughes for 42/0/0 and likewise given us in cash this day 24/9/9 amounting in the whole to British 153/9/5½.

And whereas I the Reverend Robert Radcliffe do choose to have management of the fund and interest for the use of the clergymen's widows rather than the other, I do hereby acknowledge to have received the same as the account is above and in my lordship's book this day stated, for the forthcoming whereof with the growing interest I own myself chargeable and accountable to all concerned therein, and I the Reverend Matthias Curghey do also acknowledge to have received the 8/5/0 Manx of the royal bounty within mentioned, for which until it is otherwise ordered to be disposed of I own myself chargeable and accountable, together with whatever payments shall be made me of said bounty to be disposed of according to his majesty's letters patent. In testimony whereof we have hereunto subscribed our names this 26 July 1752. Robert Radcliffe. Matthias Curghey.

Let this be annexed to the proceedings of last convocation. A copy was given to Dr Wilson, 6 July 1754.

On 30 May 1754 John Fountain, dean of York, was appointed proctor for the clergy of Sodor and Man in the York convocation.[423]

Thursday 6 June 1754

[76] Clergy present:

John Kippax, infirm.	Samuel Gell.
Robert Radcliffe.	Joseph Cosnahan.
Matthias Curghey.	Thomas Woods.
William Ross, infirm.	William Crebbin.
Philip Moore.	John Christian.
John Quayle.	Nathaniel Curghey.[424]
Paul Crebbin.	William Mylrea.
James Wilks.	John Gill.
John Moore.	Robert Brew.
Nicholas Christian.	Thomas Quayle.

---

[423]Original document in the Manx National Heritage Library.
[424]Alleged to be charged to the chancery court.

The rectory of Bride, the vicarage of Maughold and the vicarage of German vacant.

[77] The Reverend Robert Radcliffe vicar-general to the fund for the support of clergymen's widows and orphans.

1753　To the value of a bond of John Hughes, dated 6 June 1752. Received from said Hughes 42/0/0.

July 26　To cash received from the right reverend the lord bishop being surplusage of this fund remaining in his lordship's hands: 24/9/9

British:　　　　　　　　66/9/9
　　　　　　　　　　　　53/4/10
Balance in my hands:　13/4/4.

[78] **1753**

August 11	Paid Mrs Cosnahan widow four quarters ending Midsummer 1753, 4/0/0.
August 27	Paid Mrs Gell three quarters ending ditto 1753, 3/0/0.
November 8	Paid Mrs Woods 2/0/0 ditto ending Michaelmas 1753, 2/0/0.

1754

February 15	Paid Mrs Gell 2/0/0 ditto ending Christmas 1754, 2/0/0.
April 20	Paid Mrs Woods 2/00 ditto ending Lady Day 1754, 2/0/0.
Total :	13/0/0 Manx; British 11/2/10.

1753

October 29	Advanced to carry on the lawsuit touching the impropriations on account of our lordship's promise to contribute £50 British, 40/0/0.
	Advanced to Mr Stevenson on his going to London in order to solicit the foresaid cause: 2/2/0.
Total:	53/4/10.

Letter of thanks to Dr Thomas Wilson, jr, 1 July 1754

[79] To the Reverend Dr Thomas Wilson, rector of St Stephen's Walbrook and prebendary of Westminster.

We the clergy and schoolmasters of this isle who partake of his majesty's royal bounty being this day met pursuant to notice given us to receive three quarters thereof ending at Christmas 1753 do hereby severally acknowledge to be now and before fully paid and satisfied our respective proportions of the same to Christmas 1753 and being highly sensible of your kind and friendly solicitations in so seasonably procuring us his majesty's said bounty, do therefore, worthy sir, desire you would accept our sincere and grateful thanks for transacting this affair so very much to our satisfaction, there being scarcely an instance previous hitherto, where the same has been paid to so late a date, which we cannot but attribute solely to your great care and tenderness for us, begging a continuance of your favour and interest in soliciting the procurement thereof for the future towards the relief and subsistence of us and our families, and may God reward your labour of love to us, and to this distressed church whose orthodox doctrine, exemplary discipline and peace have upwards of half a century been maintained and defended under the primitive zeal, happy government and influence of our good and truly venerable lord bishop, whose present indisposition by the divine assistance shall more firmly engage us not to relax our zeal for [80] the honour of God and his church.

We are reverend Doctor with the greatest sincerity and gratitude, your most obliged and most humble servants and brethren,

Robert Radcliffe.	Nathaniel Curghey.
Matthias Curghey.	Joseph Cosnahan.
James Wilks.	John Christian.
Paul Crebbin.	William Crebbin.
Nicholas Christian.	Thomas William Joseph Woods.
John Moore.	Robert Brew.
Samuel Gell.	John Quayle.

Nicholas Cowley, schoolmaster of Kirk Andrews.
James Waterson, schoolmaster of Castletown.
William Kewn, schoolmaster of Kirk Bride.

Kirk Michael, July 1st, 1754.

Memorandum: A copy was delivered to Dr Wilson on Monday the 20th July 1754 by me, James Wilks.

Modification of the clergy widows' fund's charter, 6 August 1754

[84][425] Whereas the fourth article comprised in a deed of trust touching a fund for the support of the distressed widows and orphans of the clergy of the Isle of Man, bearing date the twenty-sixth day of February in the year of our Lord one thousand seven hundred and forty and signed by the right reverend Thomas Sodor and Man, Doctor Stephen Hales and Doctor Thomas Wilson, trustees of the said fund, it is directed 'that if there shall be a surplusage after the payment of four pounds per annum to each widow, the same or such part thereof as shall be judged proper shall be applied towards keeping the orphans of clergymen to school, or towards putting them some honest employment'.

---

[425]Pp. 81-3 are chronologically out of order; see below.

Now I the said Thomas Wilson do hereby empower the present and all future stewards of the said trust, in the names of my father and the reverend Dr Stephen Hales, to give such part of the surplusage as they shall from time to time think necessary to the children as well as the orphans of clergymen, towards keeping them to school or putting them to some honest employment, taking the advice of the major part of their brethren in all such distributions, and subject likewise to the several rules laid down in the foresaid deed of trust. And I desire that this instrument may be recorded in the episcopal registry along with the other papers relating to this trust. Given under my hand and seal at Bishopscourt the sixth day of August in the year of our Lord one thousand seven hundred and fifty-four.

Signed and dated in the presence of us, Philip Moore, James Wilks, Thomas William Joseph Woods.

Thomas Wilson.

BISHOP MARK HILDESLEY (1755-72)

Letter from Mr Stephen Hales to Bishop Hildesley concerning the clergy widows' fund, 12 May 1755

[36] Dukes Court, St Martin's Lane. May 12, 1755.

My lord, Since I saw you, Dr Wilson told me he would send you copies of the papers relating to the £400 in the stocks for the use of the widows of the clergy in your diocese which are all enrolled in your office. As I think only £100 of it stands in my name, in what sum I forget, so if you think it proper, I may empower some proper person, by letters of attorney, to transfer it to you and whom else you shall think proper, that you may accept it before you leave London.

If I knew what fund it was in I would sign a letter of attorney empowering one Mr Willoughby an Exchange Alley broker, who is often at Teddington, to transfer it to you and whom else you shall name. As I remember, I signed a paper acknowledging the purport of this trust. I am, my lord, your lordship's obliged humble servant, Stephen Hales.

Pray respects to my lord of Durham. I go to Teddington this day at eleven and return only Saturday next hither. You may direct to me at Teddington, near Hampton Court.

[Note of Bishop Hildesley:] This I received whilst I was at the bishop of Durham's but do not remember whether I answered it or not, nor whether Dr Wilson at the sundry times I have seen him since ever made any mention or any proposal about transfer of the stock to M[ark] Sodor and Man.

Letter from the clergy to Dr Thomas Wilson, 20 August 1755

[81] To the Reverend Dr Thomas Wilson, prebendary of Westminster and rector of St Stephen's, Walbrook, London.

Reverend sir, We the clergy of this diocese being this day assembled do beg leave to acknowledge the perusal of a paragraph of your letter of the 25 June last to our worthy vicars-general, therein requesting our opinion and advice how the legacy of £100 left entirely to be disposed of to such pious uses for the benefit of this isle by our late right reverend diocesan (your worthy and pious father) as you would think must beneficial to the common good of your country and its church had best be applied. We, ever sensible and grateful for your many and generous favours, do humbly desire you would accept our best acknowledgments for this recent and repeated instance of your friendship to us and at the same time propose and recommend that the said legacy be laid out on a secure mortgage within this isle and that the interest thereof be applied towards the additional future support of the distressed widows and orphans of the clergy of this diocese, a noble charity first founded and brought to its present happy state by the generous contribution and indefatigable pains of your most worthy father and yourself, a charity founded on the most amiable principles and of the greatest utility, reflecting honour on those that laid the groundwork worthy the attention of all lovers of religion in general and the sacred order in particular, in itself most laudable and in its consequences most useful, by affording means to relieve the too often pressing wants of the otherwise afflicted and distressed.

[82] We also join with you in opinion that the legacy left by our late and right reverend diocesan to the poor of the several parishes mentioned in his lordship's will should be added to the charitable funds already established in said parishes and shall accordingly recommend the same to the wardens of our respective parishes, being fully persuaded that your proposal will be of more lasting benefit than if the same were immediately distributed among said poor.

Permit us also, worthy sir, to make our grateful acknowledgments for your purpose of leaving your father's books as a standing library for the perpetual use of us and our successors and for your intention of adding to it from time to time, a plan that will be a most lasting memorial of your good father, whose memory will be dear to us and our latest posterity. And in order that the same may be more extensively useful, we humbly recommend that the said library be fixed in the parish of Kirk Michael, a parish that may justly claim the honour of your nativity and his lordship's interment, a parish near the centre of the island where each of us and our successors may readily have recourse to and which library may be under the immediate inspection of our lord bishop for the time being. And would our narrow circumstances but afford it, we should cheerfully contribute towards building a house or enlarging and having the schoolhouse of said parish for their reception, to be under such rules and regulations as shall be judged most advisable for the future care and preservation of such a library.

We further crave your permission to make this public acknowledgment for your very assiduous application in our behalf, in remitting his majesty's royal bounty, hereby severally acknowledging to have received our respective proportions thereof from your order down to Christmas last.

[83] In these and all other previous instances of your friendship to us and our families and successors and to this church and nation we once more request that you would accept our grateful thanks, beseeching the author of all blessings to grant you all the happiness which this world affords. And after you have long and successfully laboured in his vineyard, may you and we be made partakers of the joys promised to those who do all the good they can in their generation.

We are reverend doctor with the highest regard and greatest sincerity and thankfulness your most obliged and humble servants and affectionate brethren, Robert Radcliffe, Matthias Curghey. Isle of Man, August 20th 1755.

James Wilks.

William Mylrea.

Nicholas Christian.

Samuel Gell.

John Christian.

Joseph Cosnahan.

John Moore.   William Crebbin.
Thomas William Joseph Woods.   Robert Brew.

Letter of welcome to the new bishop, 1 September 1755

[5][426] To the right reverend father in God Mark, by divine permission lord bishop
of Sodor and Man.

We your lordship's clergy this day assembled do with the greatest sincerity return
your lordship humble thanks for your paternal animadversions on the clandestine
marriages said to have been lately done within this diocese, and being sensible of
the fatal consequences of such irregular contracts (which we from our hearts do
abhor and detest) whereby the laws of God and the church are broken, the honour
and authority of parents and guardians violated, and contempt brought on our whole
order by the irregular acts of a very few, and an odium brought on the whole land
by their attempting to frustrate the wholesome laws of our neighbouring nations,
calculated by their wisdom upon just principles for their own preservation, moved
by these and other important reasons we do assure your lordship that we shall use
all means in our powers to strengthen your lordship's hands to bring to condign
punishment such as shall attempt to be guilty of such crimes and to preserve the
honour of this church and nation, whose wholesome discipline has been for ages
and hope shall be emulated by our neighbouring churches, and that your lordship
may have full testimony of our sincerity herein, we hereby severally and solemnly
engage ourselves and hereunto subscribe our names this first of September 1755.

Robert Radcliffe.   Joseph Cosnahan.
Matthias Curghey.   John Christian.
James Wilks.   William Crebbin.
William Mylrea.   Robert Brew.
Nicholas Christian.   Philip Moore.
John Moore.   Paul Crebbin.
[6] Samuel Gell.   Thomas Quayle.
Thomas William Joseph Woods.

Note: That the Reverend Messrs Robert Radcliffe, Philip Moore, Paul Crebbin and
Thomas Quayle not being present at the foresaid meeting of the clergy have since
notwithstanding voluntarily subscribed and engaged as the rest of their brethren
have before done. James Wilks, episcopal registrar.

    June 1, 1758. A copy hereof was given to the right reverend lord bishop of Man.
John W[ilks].

[8][427] Clergy assembled at Kirk Michael, September 1, 1755.

---

[426]Pp. 5-8 are out of chronological sequence.
[427]P. 7 is blank.

Thursday 10 June 1756

[3]⁴²⁸ Clergy present.

John Kippax, archdeacon, absent.
Robert Radcliffe,
Matthias Curghey, vicars-general.
Philip Moore.
William Mylrea.
John Quayle, indisposed.
Paul Crebbin.
James Wilks, episcopal registrar.⁴²⁹
John Moore.
Nicholas Christian.

Samuel Gell.
Nathaniel Curghey.
Joseph Cosnahan.
Thomas William Joseph Woods.
William Crebbin.
John Christian.
John Gill, indisposed.
Robert Brew.
Thomas Quayle.⁴³⁰

Our right reverend lord bishop proposing to admit the Reverend Mr Brew to the order of priesthood at the next ember season in September, as also Mr Daniel Gelling to the office of a deacon at said time, there appears no objection against them. Mr Gelling who is absent is to be acquainted of the [decision]. The public school of Peel being now vacant by the decease of the late Mr Teare, his lordship intends that the Reverend Mr Brew be master in his place.

[4] To the right reverend father in God Mark, lord bishop of Sodor and Man.

We the clergy of this diocese this day in convocation assembled, being deeply sensible of your lordship's regard for our well-being, of pastoral affection for us, do beg leave to return your lordship our hearty thanks for your expediting the payment of the royal bounty beyond what has been hitherto experienced by us, and we shall by the divine assistance endeavour to merit the continuance of your lordship's favours, of which we have still further proof by your lordship's zeal and readiness to promote our interest in the affair of the impropriation, and to bring our tedious suit to a happy and speedy conclusion. We at said time return your lordship our sincere and hearty thanks for your lordship's kind and affectionate charge and monitions this day delivered to us.

Robert Radcliffe.
Matthias Curghey.
Philip Moore.
William Mylrea.
Paul Crebbin.
John Moore.

Samuel Gell.
William Crebbin.
Joseph Cosnahan.
Thomas William Joseph Woods.
John Christian.
Thomas Quayle.

⁴²⁸Douglas, Manx National Heritage Library, MS 9756.
⁴²⁹Absent on the clergy's business.
⁴³⁰Archdeacon's curate at Castletown.

Nicholas Christian.   Robert Brew.
Nathaniel Curghey.

The right reverend diocesan at this convocation observed to the clergy that they will for the future keep to such a certain express form in their certificates of the diligence and fidelity of their ... schoolmasters, as shall be issued out by the episcopal registrar for that purpose, which ... anno 1740.

The bishop's letter about legislation against clandestine marriages, 7 March 1757

[9] To the reverend the vicars-general and the rest of the clergy of this Isle of Man.

My clergy having been pleased at my first coming amongst them to make a voluntary declaration of their abhorrence of the practice of clandestine marriages, which rendered this isle obnoxious to the censure and blame of our neighbouring countries, and likewise, at sundry times since signified their opinion that some stricter laws than any at present subsisting among us might be expedient for an effectual prevention of the like enormities, I thought, in justice to them, I can do no less than apprize our most reverend and worthy metropolitan of their sentiments, and of which in return I received his grace's particular approbation, together with his opinion for applying to our legislature here (as we are the only part of his majesty of Great Britain's dominions who enjoy the unlimited privilege of making our own laws) to take the matter into their consideration, in consequence of which advice jointly with that of some principal personages in England and Ireland, I accordingly made the proposal to our civil government assembled at Tynwald last summer and since that at Castletown, at both which times it appeared to meet with their unanimous assent, viz. That some additional law against the said scandalous practice of unauthorized marriages should be concerted, and a sketch was accordingly ordered to be drawn.

But whereas some differences in opinion have arisen concerning the proper and necessary penalty (as well with respect to natives as foreigners) to render such law effectual for the purposes referred to, and as I have assured my clergy of my unwillingness to approve of or consent to anything in the forming and enacting such law wherein they are so nearly concerned without their concurrence, and as it is a matter of the highest importance to have it well considered, I hereby earnestly desire and require that my brethren will give me a personal meeting at Kirk Michael on Thursday 22nd instant, with my prayers that our consultations may end to our mutual satisfaction and the [10] honour of God's church. I subscribe myself, gentlemen, your faithful brother and servant, Mark Sodor and Man. Bishopscourt, March 7, 1757.

March 8, 1757. A transcript hereof was forwarded by the sumner of Kirk Michael to Ballaugh at eight o'clock this morning. James Wilks.

Thursday 22 March 1757

[13][431] At a convocation holden at Kirk Michael, March 22nd, 1757. Clergy present:

Robert Radcliffe,
Matthias Curghey, vicars-general.
James Wilks, episcopal registrar.
Philip Moore.
William Mylrea.
John Moore.
Nicholas Christian.

John Christian.
Joseph Cosnahan.
Samuel Gell.
Thomas William Joseph Woods.
William Crebbin.
Thomas Quayle.
Daniel Gelling.

Absent:

Paul Crebbin, indisposed. Letter prays to be excused.
John Gill, indisposed and prays to be excused.
John Quayle, infirm.
Nathaniel Curghey.

[14] We the clergy of this isle whose names are hereunto subscribed being this day in convocation and having considered of an act proposed to be made by the legislature of this isle in order to prevent the practice of clandestine marriages, do approve of the said sketch and appoint the Reverend Robert Radcliffe, vicar-general, the Reverend Philip Moore, rector of Ballaugh, the Reverend William Mylrea, rector of Kirk Bride, and the Reverend James Wilks, vicar of Kirk Michael, to represent us before the said legislature at Castletown on Tuesday the 29th instant and lay the foresaid sketch before them. Witness our hands this 22nd March 1757.

Matthias Curghey.
John Moore.
Nicholas Christian.
Samuel Gell.
John Christian.
Thomas William Joseph Woods.

William Crebbin.
Robert Brew.
Thomas Quayle.
Daniel Gelling.
Joseph Cosnahan.

Sunday 29 April 1757

[15] At a convocation held at Balnyhown in Kirk German this 29th April 1757. Present: The bishop and the several gentlemen following.

Our said right reverend ordinary having of late received an extended draught of an act proposed by the legislature to be passed into a law for the more effectual prevention of clandestine marriages, which his lordship has this day communicated unto us, and we having considered the same, as well as some observations and

---

[431]Pp. 11-12 are blank.

queries made by his lordship relative to some amendments and alterations in said act, proposed to be laid before the legislature for their tender and judicious consideration, do approve of the said observations and queries hereunto annexed, and humbly request his lordship would be pleased to lay the same before the legislature for the purposes aforesaid, and use such other methods as his lordship shall judge most advisable concerning the premisses.

Robert Radcliffe.	John Christian.
Matthias Curghey.	Samuel Gell.
Philip Moore.	Joseph Cosnahan.
William Mylrea.	William Crebbin.
Paul Crebbin.	Thomas Quayle.
James Wilks.	Robert Brew.
John Moore.	Daniel Gelling.
Nicholas Christian.	

[19][432] Reverend sirs, Our right reverend lord bishop having lately received an extended draught of an act proposed to be passed for the better prevention of clandestine marriages, which his lordship having communicated to us, and he at our request being ready and willing to give his clergy another meeting on that head, we therefore think proper to signify the same unto you and hereby desire you would severally attend at Balnyhown in Kirk German on Friday the 23rd instant and when his lordship has convented to give you and us a meeting. We rest, reverend sirs, your affectionate brethren and humble servants, Robert Radcliffe. Matthias Curghey.

Kirk Michael, April 21, 1757. Examinatum per James Wilks, episcopi registrarium.
     Peel. April 23, 1757. Received at twelve o'clock and forwarded immediately to the Reverend Mr Radcliffe. Robert Brew.
     Kirk Patrick, April 23. Received in the evening and forwarded by the sumner to the vicar of Arbory to be sent to Rushen. Robert Radcliffe.
     Kirk Arbory, April 24, 1757. Received about prayer time in the morning and forwarded after prayers to the vicar of Rushen. John Moore.
     Rushen, April 25, 1757. Received by a wayfaring from Douglas at one o'clock in the afternoon and forthwith forwarded to the vicar of Malew. Nicholas Christian.
     [20] Malew. April 25, 1757. Received about 5 o'clock in the evening and forwarded immediately to the curate of Castletown. John Quayle.
     Castletown, eodem die. Received after five o'clock this evening and delivered immediately to the sumner of Malew to be forwarded to the Reverend Mr Crebbin, vicar of Santan. Thomas Quayle.
     Kirk Santan, April 26, 1757. Received and forwarded about eleven o'clock in the forenoon to the reverend the vicar of Kirk Braddan.

---

[432]Pp. 16-18 are blank.

Kirk Braddan. April 27, 1757. Received at seven o'clock in the morning and immediately forwarded to the reverend the vicar of Marown. Joseph Cosnahan.

Kirk Marown, April 27, 1757. Received about two o'clock in the evening. John Christian.

[22][433] To the reverend the curate of Kirk German, the vicars of Kirk Patrick, Rushen, Arbory and Malew, the curate of Castletown, the vicars of Santan, Marown and Braddan. These to be speedily forwarded by the several sumners and a note to be made of the time of receiving and transmitting the same [refers to above].

Thursday 7 June 1757

[25][434] Clergy present:

John Kippax, absent in England.	Joseph Cosnahan.
Robert Radcliffe.	John Christian.
Matthias Curghey.	Samuel Gell.
Philip Moore.	Nathaniel Curghey.
William Mylrea.	Thomas Woods.
John Quayle.	William Crebbin.
Paul Crebbin.	John Gill.[435]
James Wilks.	Robert Brew.
John Moore.	Thomas Quayle.
Nicholas Christian.	Daniel Gelling.

Exhibition of letters of orders

[27][436] To the several rectors, vicars, chaplains and curates of this diocese.

Reverend sirs, I am commanded by our right reverend ordinary to give you notice (which I hereby do) that his lordship, in conformity to the canon,[437] expects and requires you do respectively show and exhibit unto his lordship at Bishopscourt on Thursday the second of June next, being the day of our annual convocation, your letters of orders, institution and induction and all other your licences or faculties whatsoever, to the end his lordship may hereby get the better knowledge of the state of his diocese, and in case any of you, through indisposition or otherwise are lawfully hindered from attending said convocation, such absentee is to send his orders and other titles as above directed under seal to his lordship on said day to the ends aforesaid. I am, reverend sirs, your affectionate brother and humble servant, James Wilks, episcopal registrar, Kirk Michael, May 23, 1757.

---

[433]P. 21 is blank.
[434]Pp. 23-4 are blank.
[435]Indisposed, and prayed by letter to be excused.
[436]P. 26 is blank.
[437]1603/137. See Bray, *Anglican canons*, pp. 440-1.

Let these be speedily and carefully transmitted from one to another (by the several sumners) as following and a note made of the time of receiving and forwarding the same, that it may be known where the omission or neglect lies, if any such should happen.

To the reverend the rector of Ballaugh, the vicar of Jurby, curate of Andreas, rector of Bride, vicar of Lezayre, curate of Ramsey, vicars of Maughold, Lonan and Conchan, the chaplain of Douglas, the vicars of Braddan, Marown, Santan and Malew, the curate of Castletown, the vicars of Arbory, Rushen and Patrick, and the curate of German, who is to return these to the episcopal registry. James Wilks, episcopal registrar.

[28] 24 May 1757. Received 15 minutes after eight and forwarded immediately. William Mylrea, rector of Kirk Bride.

May 24, 1757. Received at ten o'clock in the forenoon and immediately forwarded. William Crebbin, vicar of Jurby.

24 May 1757. Received about six in the evening and forwarded forthwith. John Gill, curate of Kirk Andreas.

25 May 1757. Received about seven o'clock in the forenoon and forwarded immediately. Matthias Curghey, vicar of Lezayre.

Eodem die. Received about half an hour after eight in the forenoon and forwarded forthwith. Daniel Gelling, Ramsey.

25 May. Received about ten in the forenoon and forwarded forthwith by Thomas William Joseph Woods, vicar of Maughold.

May 26th. Received about eight o'clock in the morning and forwarded the same forthwith. Nathaniel Curghey of Lonan.

May 26th. Received at eleven o'clock in the forenoon and forwarded forthwith. Samuel Gell, vicar of Conchan.

27 May 1757. Received at eleven o'clock in the forenoon and forwarded immediately by Joseph Cosnahan, vicar of Braddan.

29 May 1757. Received and forwarded to the vicar of Santan. John Christian.

29 May 1757. Received after morning prayers and forwarded in the evening by Paul Crebbin.

30 May 1757. Received at church about ten o'clock and delivered to the curate of Castletown immediately after morning prayers by John Quayle, vicar of Malew.

[29] Castletown. 30 May 1757. Received about half an hour after one and forwarded immediately by Thomas Quayle.

Kirk Arbory, May 30, 1757. Received at night and forwarded next morning between seven and eight o'clock to the vicar of Rushen. John Moore.

Rushen, May 31, 1757. Received about ten o'clock in the forenoon and forwarded immediately to the vicar of Kirk Patrick, Nicholas Christian.

Patrick, May 31, 1757. Received about six o'clock in the evening and forwarded to the curate of German. Robert Radcliffe.

German, June 2, 1757. Received yesterday in the evening and delivered this day in convocation to the episcopal registrar by Robert Brew.

[31]⁴³⁸ The right reverend the lord bishop does now signify to his clergy in convocation his intention of holding a parochial visitation sometime this summer whereof previous notice to be given the several parishes that the several ministers may attend and discharge the duties of their office in this respect.

His lordship also signifies to the clergy that he purposes (God willing) to admit Mr Henry Corlett, academic student to the order of deacon next ember season and desires that if any of the clergy know of any lawful impediment they would signify the same in due time.

His lordship having likewise signified to the several clergy of his diocese by circular notice dated the twenty-third of last month that it was expected they should exhibit at this convocation their respective letters of orders, institutions, inductions, licences or other faculties whatsoever, to the end his lordship might thereby get the better knowledge of the state of his diocese and clergy, his lordship now directs that the said clergy exhibit the same accordingly, which is done in the manner hereafter laid down.

[32] Patrick. Reverend Robert Radcliffe vicar of Kirk Patrick, exhibited his:
1. Letters of priests' orders bearing date 21 April 1729.
2. Also his institution to said parish, dated 22 February 1729.
3. Mandate of induction, 23 February 1729.
4. Certificate of his being inducted, dated same day.

Lezayre. Reverend Matthias Curghey, vicar

1. 27 March 1727.   2. 3. 4. 12 February 1729.

Santan. Reverend Paul Crebbin.

1. 24 May 1730.   2. 3. 2 July 1731.   4. 6 July 1731.⁴³⁹

Ballaugh. Reverend Philip Moore, rector.

1. 23 September 1739.   2. 3. 10 July 1751.   4. 11 July 1751.

Bride. Reverend Mr Mylrea, rector.

1. 21 September 1746.   2. 3. 24 July 1754.   4. 29 July 1754.

Malew. Reverend John Quayle, indisposed, by his son Mr William Quayle.

1. 26 February 1713.   2. 3. 17 March 1739.   4. 15 April 1745.

---

⁴³⁸P. 30 is a covering note like that on p. 22.
⁴³⁹The text says 'May' but this must be a mistake.

Kirk Arbory. Reverend John Moore, vicar.

1. 20 September 1747.   2. 3. 6 July 1748.   4. 21 July 1748.

[33] Rushen. Reverend Nicholas Christian, vicar of Trinity, Rushen.

1. 21 September 1747.   2. 23 June 1748.
N.B. He neither exhibited a mandate nor certificate of induction, alleging he forgot
to take them with him.

Braddan. Reverend Joseph Cosnahan, vicar.

1. 23 September 1750.   2. Collation and institution. 4 October 1750.
3. 9 October 1750.   4. 16 October 1750.

Marown. Reverend John Christian, vicar of Kirk Marown.

1. 24 September 1752.   2. 3. 27 February 1753.   4. 5 March 1753.

Conchan. Reverend Samuel Gell, vicar.

1. 22 September 1745.   2. 3. 13 March 1748.   4. 25 May 1749.

Lonan. Reverend Nathaniel Curghey, vicar.

1. 25 September 1745.   2. 6 July 1753.
N.B. He exhibited neither a mandate nor a certificate of induction, alleging it
escaped his memory to take them with him.

Maughold. Reverend Thomas Woods, vicar.

1. 20 September 1747.   2. 3. 6 August 1754.   4. 21 October 1754.

Jurby. Reverend William Crebbin, vicar.

1. 23 September 1750.   2. 3. Collation and mandate 9 August 1751.
4. 19 May 1752.

[34] Andreas. Reverend John Gill, curate.

1. 24 September 1752.
Licence to preach and expound the Scriptures. 24 October 1751.

German. Reverend Robert Brew, curate.

1. 19 September 1756.
Licence to the cure of that parish 30 October 1756.

Castletown. Reverend Thomas [Quayle], curate.

1. 24 September 1752.

Ramsey. Reverend Daniel Gelling, curate.

Deacon's orders 19 September 1756.
Licence as curate 27 October 1756.

Michael. Reverend James [Wilks] vicar.

1. 29 May 1743.   2. 3. 16 March 1752.   4. 4 May 1752.

Memorandum. The several letters of orders, collations, institutions, mandates of inductions with their certificates annexed and other faculties as within and above mentioned being pursuant to the 137th canon ecclesiastical exhibited to our right reverend ordinary for his approbation, and the same being respectively allowed of, his lordship ordered me his registrar to endorse each and every of them as follows: '2 June 1757. Exhibitum James Wilks episcopi registraro' for which I received from each of the clergy a fee of 14d. for every such exhibit. James Wilks, episcopal registrar.

Thursday 18 May 1758

[37]⁴⁴⁰ Clergy present.

John Kippax, in England.⁴⁴¹
Robert Radcliffe,
Matthias Curghey, vicars-general.
Thomas Castley.⁴⁴²
Philip Moore.
William Mylrea.
John Quayle.⁴⁴⁴
Paul Crebbin.
James Wilks.
John Moore.
Nicholas Christian.

Joseph Cosnahan.
Samuel Gell.
Nathaniel Curghey, absent.
Thomas Woods.⁴⁴³
William Crebbin.
Robert Brew.
John Gill.
Thomas Quayle.
Daniel Gelling.
Henry Corlett, deacon.

---

⁴⁴⁰Pp. 35-6 are blank.
⁴⁴¹Infirm and unable to return.
⁴⁴²Academical professor and curate of Castletown.
⁴⁴³Indisposed and prays by letter to be excused.
⁴⁴⁴Indisposed and desires to be excused.

Qualifications for marriage or for being godparents

[39][445] That no person or persons whatever may be ignorant of the qualifications necessary to entitle them to marriage or to be admitted to stand as godfather or godmother, it is resolved and agreed upon in convocation and accordingly ordered that the third clause of the constitutions of 1703 be published in the several churches and chapels of this diocese upon the Lord's Day immediately after the Nicene Creed within two months after date hereof.

Which clause is as follows:

That no person admitted to stand as godfather or godmother, nor to enter into the holy state of matrimony, till they have received the holy sacrament of the Lord's Supper, unless being an orphan, there be a necessity for his speedy marriage; and this to be approved of and dispensed with by the ordinary for a limited time to fit himself for the sacrament; and where any of them are of another parish, they are to bring a certificate from their proper pastor.

A copy hereof is to be sent from the vicar of Kirk Michael to the rector of Ballaugh and so on in course from one clergyman to another, who are to take copies hereof in order to a publication, till the same comes round in usual manner to the episcopal registry. Mark Sodor and Man.
    June 11, 1758. Copied and forwarded. James Wilks.

Thursday 7 June 1759

[45][446] Clergy present.

John Kippax.[447]
Robert Radcliffe,
Matthias Curghey, vicars-general.
Thomas Castley, indisposed.
Philip Moore.[449]
William Mylrea.
Paul Crebbin.
James Wilks.
Nicholas Christian.
John Moore.

John Gill.[448]
Samuel Gell.
Joseph Cosnahan.
John Christian.
Thomas Woods.
William Crebbin.
Thomas Quayle.
Robert Brew.
Daniel Gelling.
Henry Corlett, deacon.

---

[445]P. 38 is blank.
[446]Pp. 40-4 are blank.
[447]He resides in England being unable through old age and infirmities to return to his charge.
[448]Indisposed, and by letter prays to be excused.
[449]In England by lord bishop's permission.

[46] At this convocation our right reverend lord bishop signified to his clergy that (the necessities of the church requiring) he intended to admit the Reverend Daniel Gelling, deacon, now curate of Kirk Andrews, into the sacred order of the priesthood, and Mr John Crellin, academic student into deacon's orders on Sunday next, being the tenth instant, and desired that if any of his clergy had or knew of any objection why they or either of them should not be ordained, they would signify the same to his lordship.

Memorandum: No objection offered.

His lordship also earnestly recommended to his clergy a due attention to the improvement and education of the growing youth of their several parishes, and ordered that pursuant to the orders and constitutions of 1703 they do for the future frequently visit the schools of their respective parishes, and to the end that it may be known whether the masters or mistresses of said schools do faithfully discharge their duty, his lordship enjoined that proper certificates be returned at the usual time by each minister in the following words, according to the purport of the right honourable Elizabeth Hastings' will, viz.

To the right reverend father in God .... lord bishop of Sodor and Man. My lord, I do hereby certify that according to the constitutions of 1703 I have visited the petty school of this parish A. B. licensed master/mistress, that the children under his/her care have been carefully taught and do improve in learning and good manners, are taught to say their prayers and catechism and do duly attend the public service of the church. Witness my hand this ... day of ... C. D., rector/vicar of ...

[47] And to the end that the wholesome discipline of the church may be duly observed, and that no person who is either under church censure or who has not received the holy sacrament of the Lord's Supper be admitted to enter into the holy state of matrimony (unless the ordinary for sufficient reasons shall think proper to dispense with the same for a limited time) his lordship requires that certificate be given by the several clergy of this diocese as they shall respectively be concerned, to every person demanding the same, in order to his or her obtaining solemnization of matrimony in the following terms (in case they merit such certificate and not otherwise) be the marriage either by banns or licence, viz.

I A. B., rector, vicar or curate of ... do hereby certify whom it may concern that C. D. of this parish hath received the holy communion according to the rites and ceremonies prescribed by the liturgy of the established Church of England, and that the said C. D. is not at this time to the best of my knowledge under any church censure. Witness my hand this ... day of ..... A.; B.

And when the marriage is solemnized by banns his lordship enjoins that such certificates be forthcoming as occasion may require.

And whereas upon sundry accounts, viz., of removals and other circumstances it may so happen that different degrees of evidence may offer or be wanting to the clergy for their due knowledge or intelligence of the facts in said certificate referred to, which they may be called upon to certify the truth of, for the better satisfaction [48] of the doubts they may possibly at any time be under in regard to what they may think, they can or cannot vouch for, his lordship has been pleased to signify and declare that where they cannot do it upon self-evidence (as may often happen to be the case) a moral certainty however obtained from any two credible persons (the parties themselves excepted) may suffice for satisfactory subscribing and issuing the said certificate without the necessity of any alteration in or deviation from the form hereby laid down.

His lordship also declared a great desire of having the church catechism printed in the Manx tongue by itself, to be distributed among the youth of the diocese that they may learn to say the same with propriety in their mother tongue, and earnestly recommend to the clergy that they use their best endeavours to improve the use and practice of the Manx tongue.

His lordship likewise expressed his desire of having the ordinary service of this church, together with the several occasional offices, translated into Manx by the Reverend Robert Radcliffe and Matthias Curghey, vicars-general, the Reverend Paul Crebbin, vicar of Kirk Santan, the Reverend James Wilks, vicar of Kirk Michael and the Reverend John Christian, vicar of Marown, and such translation agreed on by the foresaid gentlemen, to be forwarded to the rest of the clergy for their perusal and approbation so that all youths entering into holy orders may [49] have a copy thereof for their direction and use.

It was in like manner proposed by his lordship that a select number of the singing psalms be translated into Manx verse, fitted to the tunes used in churches, for the instruction and comfort of such persons as do not understand the English language, and such translation to be agreed on and approved of as above.

The bishop's complaint against the neglect of Good Friday, 4 April 1760

[55][450] To the reverend the instituted clergy of this isle of and diocese of Man.

Reverend sirs, I take this method of acquainting you how extremely I was aggrieved as well as surprised on this day morning to see the inhabitants of this isle in great numbers, after having been so lately and so signally the objects of a merciful providence, so soon forgetting their duties and obligations to heaven, as to lay aside all appearance of decent regard to the appointment of this one peculiar fast day, set apart by our church, for the solemn commemoration of the most interesting article of our holy religion, the death and sufferings of the Son of God for sinners!

The uncommon (at least to me uncommon) sight of men's following their ordinary occupations on this day, in yoking their cattle and tilling their land, etc., even in the face and neighbourhood of the church, during the whole time of divine service and celebration of the sacrament, and who, when spoken to about it, replied in their justification that 'it was the general practice throughout the isle' I must own, looked to me like an infatuated defiance of all rule, order and discipline.

---

[450]Pp. 50-4 are blank.

I am unwilling to direct the wardens of the several parishes (if they think their oaths and duty of their office do not oblige them) to present this flagrant instance of irreligious deportment, but I shall hope that you, my brethren, who are entrusted with the care of souls, will find yourselves as able as, I am persuaded, you are willing, and disposed to concur with me in the use of some salutary means 'to retrieve the reverence [56] due to this solemnity, which hath more or less from the earliest times in all Christian countries been paid to it, and more especially in the Church of England, who hath required it to be observed as a day of fasting and devotion, and to be sequestered from *all worldly business*. And surely no good Christian that is ready to celebrate any other fast when enjoined, on occasion of temporal calamities, would refuse or neglect to join in humiliation, assigned for much more weighty reasons, viz., for averting eternal vengeance!'

The several clergy are at liberty to make such use of the foregoing monition as they in their discretion shall judge most likely to answer the end for which it is intended. Given at Bishopscourt, Good Friday evening, April 4, 1760. Mark Sodor and Man.

N.B. A Jew of this isle was presented and fined for showing contempt to this day, notwithstanding the pretence of ignorance, a plea which Christians can in no wise be supposed capable of making.

[57] Kirk German. April 14, 1760. Received this monition at noon and forwarded about two o'clock to the reverend the vicar of Patrick. Robert Brew.

Kirk Patrick. April 14, 1760. Received about six o'clock and forwarded the next day to the vicar of Rushen by the sumner, by Robert Radcliffe.

Kirk Arbory, April 17, 1760. Received about one o'clock and immediately forwarded to the vicar of Rushen. John Moore.

Rushen. April 18, 1760. Received last evening and forwarded this morning. Nicholas Christian.

Kirk Malew, April 19, 1760. Received yesterday evening and forwarded this morning about eight o'clock. John Gill.

April 19, 1760. Received and forwarded to the vicar of Kirk Marown by Paul Crebbin, vicar of Kirk Santan.

Marown, April 21, 1760. Received yesterday and forwarded this morning as soon as transcribed to the reverend the vicar of Braddan. John Christian.

Kirk Braddan, April 21, 1760. Received about twelve o'clock and when transcribed, immediately forwarded to the reverend the vicar of Kirk Onchan. Joseph Cosnahan.

Kirk Onchan, April 21, 1760. Received about three o'clock and as soon as transcribed forwarded to the reverend the vicar of Lonan by Thomas Quayle.

Kirk Lonan, April 22. Received last night about nine o'clock and forwarded to the vicar of Kirk Maughold about eight this morning by Samuel Gell.

[58] Kirk Maughold. April 23, 1760. Received about noon and forwarded shortly after to the sumner to proceed as directed. Thomas William Joseph Woods.

Lezayre. April 24th. Received yesterday evening late and forwarded this day at twelve o'clock to the rector of Kirk Bride. Matthias Curghey.

April 25, 1760. Received late on Thursday evening and forwarded this morning early to the curate of Andreas. William Mylrea.

Kirk Andreas. April 25, 1760. Received about eight this morning and forwarded immediately after prayers to the vicar of Jurby. Daniel Gelling.

Ballaugh, April 25, 1760. Received about two o'clock this evening and forwarded as soon as transcribed. Henry Corlett for Philip Moore.

Jurby, April 26, 1760. Received yesterday evening and forwarded this morning. William Crebbin.

Thursday 29 May 1760

[65][451] Clergy present:

John Kippax.	Thomas Woods.
Robert Radcliffe.	William Crebbin.
Matthias Curghey.	Joseph Cosnahan.
Philip Moore.	Samuel Gell.
William Mylrea.	John Christian.
Thomas Castley.	Robert Brew.
Paul Crebbin.	Thomas Quayle.
James Wilks.	Daniel Gelling.
Nicholas Christian.	Henry Corlett, deacon.
John Moore.	John Crellin.[452]
John Gill.	Daniel Nelson.

[66] At this convocation our right reverend ordinary earnestly recommended to his clergy that they use their best endeavours to retrieve the reverence and respect due to good Friday, a day set apart by the church for the solemn commemoration of the death and passion of our Saviour.

His lordship also signified his intention of having a confirmation through the whole isle, sometime in the month of October next, whereof further previous notice to be given of the time and place where the youth of the several parishes are to attend.

His lordship also recommended that so many of the clergy as have not perambulated the bounds of their parishes for five years past would not fail to have a perambulation next year.

His lordship in like manner recommended to his two vicars-general and the four clergy of Rushen sheading, trustees of Mrs Catharine Halsall's charitable donations, that they meet sometime shortly to consider of ways and means to have the said will brought into execution, whereupon the said gentlemen have agreed to meet on this business at Balnyhown on Saturday the 21st instant.

The reverend John Gill, vicar of Malew, is appointed to preach at Tynwald.

---

[451]P. 59 is blank. P. 60 is a covering note as on p. 22. Pp. 61-2 contain another copy of the bishop's letter and pp. 63-4 are blank.
[452]Assistant chaplain of Castletown.

Modification to the prayer for the royal family, 11 November 1760

[67] To the reverend the rectors, vicars, chaplains and curates in the isle and diocese of Man.

Whereas since I sent off my directions concerning the prayers for the royal family, I have seen an order from the king and council of Great Britain, appointing that instead of the form as it now stands in the several parts of our liturgy, by the names there expressed, these following only shall be inserted, viz. 'her royal highness the princess dowager of Wales and all the royal family' of which the clergy of this diocese will be pleased to take notice and act accordingly. Given at Bishopscourt, November 11, 1760. Mark Sodor and Man.

Summons to a special convocation for the presentation of a loyal address to King George III, 3 January 1761

[73][453] To the several rectors, vicars and chaplains of this isle.

My brethren, As we are a part of the church and under sundry obligations to the crown of England, I believe you will with me judge it to be our duty to follow the example of other dioceses in addressing his present majesty on his accession to the throne of the British dominions. You are therefore hereby required personally to appear at a convocation to be held at Kirk Michael on Thursday the eighth instant in order to subscribe such address as shall then and there be agreed on to be transmitted to England. Given at Bishopscourt, January 3, 1761. Mark Sodor and Man.

Examined per James Wilks, episcopi registrarium.
[76][454] January 4, 1761. Forwarded to the curate of Ramsey at eight o'clock this morning. Matthias Curghey.
January 4, 1761. Forwarded this morning about nine o'clock. Daniel Nelson.
January 4, 1761. Received at eleven o'clock and sent away immediately to the sumner to proceed therewith. Thomas William Joseph Woods.
January 4, 1761. Received this evening at three o'clock and forthwith forwarded. Samuel Gell.
January 4, 1761. Received about 8 o'clock and forthwith forwarded. Thomas Quayle.
January 6, 1761. Received about one o'clock in the afternoon and returned to the episcopal registrar by me, Joseph Cosnahan.

---

[453]Pp. 68-72 are blank.
[454]P. 74 is blank and p. 75 is a cover note as on p. 22.

Thursday 8 January 1761

The loyal address

[77] To the king's most excellent majesty. The humble and dutiful address of the bishop, archdeacon and clergy of the isle and diocese of Man.

Most gracious sovereign, We your majesty's most dutiful and loyal subjects the bishop, archdeacon and clergy of the isle and diocese of Man, do with all humility and sincerity of heart, beg leave to approach your royal presence, to condole with your majesty the much lamented death of your royal grandfather. We of all others should be inexcusable were we insensible of the loss or forgetful of the favours of our late illustrious sovereign, during whose auspicious reign, the poor clergy of this diocese have constantly been partakers of his royal bounty, to the great comfort and support of themselves and families, who must for ever revere the memory of their prince, their father and benefactor. And we should think ourselves undeserving of the royal patronage and protection, did we not among the rest of your majesty's loyal subjects, with the deepest sense of duty and joy unfeigned, congratulate your majesty on your accession to the throne of your royal ancestors.

We also embrace this opportunity of expressing our thankful acknowledgments for the signal deliverance this isle in general was blessed with from the passages of a foreign enemy not long since, most happily and providentially subdued by one of his majesty's squadrons on the coast of this isle.

Bound therefore by every tie of gratitude and affection, our constant endeavours shall be to recommend ourselves [78] to the continuance of your majesty's royal favour by a faithful discharge of our duty in our several stations, and especially offering up our most ardent supplications to the throne of grace that your majesty's reign may be distinguished to the latest ages for the encouragement of true piety and virtue, for defending the faith, and extending its influence to the remotest of your dominions, that by the divine blessing on your majesty's arms, these realms and those of your allies may be established on the foundation of an honourable and lasting peace, that the great God may continue to multiply his favours on your majesty and every branch of the royal family, that he may long bless you with faithful and obedient subjects on earth, and crown you with immortal glory in heaven. Given under our hands this eighth day of January 1761.

Mark Sodor and Man.	[79] Thomas Woods.
William Mylrea, archdeacon.	William Crebbin.
Robert Radcliffe.	John Gill.
Matthias Curghey.	Joseph Cosnahan.
Philip Moore.	Thomas Quayle.
Thomas Castley.	John Christian.
Paul Crebbin.	Daniel Gelling.
James Wilks.	Henry Corlett.
Nicholas Christian.	John Crellin.
John Moore.	Daniel Nelson.
Samuel Gell.	

Examined per James Wilks, episcopi registrarium.

[81-2][455] London Gazette, *no. 10075, from Saturday January 31 to Tuesday February 3, 1761. Contains the above on the second page (with the signatures of the bishop and archdeacon only), followed by another loyal address from the House of Keys, dated 2 January 1761.*

Thursday 14 May 1761

[83] Clergy present.

William Mylrea.	Thomas Woods.
Robert Radcliffe.	William Crebbin.
Matthias Curghey.	Joseph Cosnahan.
Philip Moore.	John Christian.
Thomas Castley.	Samuel Gell.
Paul Crebbin.	Thomas Quayle.
James Wilks.	Henry Corlett.
Nicholas Christian.	Daniel Gelling.
John Moore.	John Crellin.
John Gill.	

Daniel Nelson, met with an accident and prayed to be excused per Mr Philip Moore.

[84] At this convocation the following orders were made and the oath or charge of the wardens and chapter-quest agreed on. The Reverend William Mylrea, archdeacon, is appointed to preach at Tynwald.

Rules for the wearing of clerical dress

[87][456] Whereas it has been observed that the habit of the clergy whereby they are properly to be distinguished from the laity and which generally secures that respect and regard due to their function, hath of late years been much neglected and disused, it is now expressly and indispensably required of the clergy of this diocese that for the future they do severally wear their proper habit and garb, and to prevent any misapprehension or doubt concerning the times and places they are bound to be so distinguished, I have thought fit to specify as follows:
    1. When convened by the ordinary on any occasion whatever.
    2. When or wherever they perform any duty belonging to their function.
    3. Whenever they are called or have occasion either by duty or business to attend in the spiritual court, and likewise whenever the government is assembled.

[455]P. 80 is blank.
[456]Pp. 85-6 are blank.

4. When or wherever they shall have occasion to wait on the lord of the isle or his representative, the governor for the time being, on any stated visit, either at home or abroad, it being a respect properly due to them, whether they expect it or not.

5. With regard to their travelling dress, whether on foot or horseback, it is expected that after the expiration of two months from the present date, no person in holy orders will, out of his own home or lands, appear in brown or light coloured clothes, but only in black or dark gray.

It is moreover to be wished, though not hereby absolutely enjoined, that the clergy, whose lot it is to reside or be often in towns, would more often than they usually do, wear their proper habit, as it would naturally tend to preserve the dignity and show that they themselves have a regard to, and are by no means ashamed of their function.

[88] 2. It is also hereby ordered that the office of public baptism be for the future administered according to the directions prescribed by the rubric of the church, and that the people be admonished accordingly.

3. That the catechizing and preparing the youth for confirmation be strictly observed, as the rubric, the canon and statute law of this land direct.

4. That one fixed form be observed for certifying the qualifications of catechumens for confirmation to be inscribed on the top of a single sheet of paper over the list of such as shall from time to time be competently prepared in the following words:

I do hereby certify our right reverend ordinary that I have carefully instructed and examined the several underwritten catechumens of the parish (town) of .... and do verily think that each and every of them are qualified for confirmation in the faith and doctrine of our holy religion, viz. A. B., C. D. Witness my hand this ...day of ... 17... A. B. rector/vicar/chaplain/curate of ....

5. And it is greatly to be desired and hereby enjoined that one at least of the sponsors of each catechumen do attend as a witness of their confirmation according to the rubric, unless sickness or some sufficient cause prevent.

6. And as the clergy's labour in the work of preparing the youth of their respective charges for confirmation will be greatly helped or otherwise by the previous instructions dispensed to their scholars by schoolmasters and mistresses, who being by the laws of the church under the cognizance and direction of the ordinary, the several clergy of this isle are hereby ordered to deliver or send to the ordinary, within one month after the date hereof, the names of all such persons both men and women as they know or believe to exercise or undertake the office of [89] teaching schools of any kind in any part of this diocese, in order that their character and qualifications may be inquired into and that they may be warned against

teaching anything but what is agreeable and not contrary to the doctrines and worship of the Church of England and by law established. See the seventy-seventh canon[457] and act of uniformity.[458]

The translation of the Prayer Book into Manx

And whereas the reverend Messrs Robert Radcliffe and Matthias Curghey vicars-general, the Reverend Paul Crebbin, vicar of Kirk Santan, the Reverend James Wilks, vicar of Kirk Michael and the Reverend John Christian, vicar of Marown, have been at commendable pains in translating a great part of the liturgy into the Manx tongue, which they have this day subscribed as by them approved of and delivered in convocation, it is hereby ordered that so much of said liturgy as is so translated, and no other, be used by the several junior clergy ordained since the year 1755 and by all such as shall thereafter be ordained till further orders be given to the contrary.

Catalogues of parochial libraries to be compiled

And to the end that the several parochial libraries of this diocese may be duly preserved, the ministers of the several parishes who have been inducted or licensed to their livings within these twelve months past are required to make a new catalogue of all the books belonging to their respective churches and deliver the same to the episcopal registrar, that in case any books are wanting, the same may be made good according to the purport of an act passed in the year 1734.

The churchwardens' oath and charge

And whereas several of the clergy and wardens have from time to time complained of the want of an uniform regular charge and oath to be administered and read to the wardens and chapter-quest, and such having been prepared and this day publicly read and approved of by the whole clergy in convocation assembled, it is hereby ordered that the said charge be henceforward observed and used on all occasions till ordered to the contrary, and that the clergy duly observe the orders and directions annexed to said charge in calling their parish officers together and forming their presentments.

Translating the Prayer Book into Manx

And in regard that a great part of the liturgy has already been translated into the Manx tongue and approved of as above mentioned [90] and that it is very desirable that work be annually proceeded in towards completing the whole, it is hereby recommended to the reverend Mr archdeacon, the Reverend Mr Moore, rector of Kirk Bride, the Reverend Mr Christian, vicar of Rushen, the Reverend Mr Moore,

---

[457]1603/77. See Bray, *Anglican canons*, pp. 370-1.
[458]14 Charles II, c. 4, 1662 (*Statutes of the realm* V, 364-70).

vicar of Kirk Arbory and the Reverend Mr Crebbin, vicar of Jurby, that they translate into the Manx tongue the Athanasian creed, the office of matrimony, the visitation and communion of the sick, the burial of the dead and commination office, and that they agree on the portions to be translated by each person, and return the same at the next convocation, subscribed and approved of by them and every of them. Mark Sodor and Man.

A copy of the foregoing order to be sent by the episcopal registrar to the rector of Ballaugh, and so on in usual course from one clergyman to another (who are to take copies) until the same be returned to the episcopal registrar, and the several clergy are to acquaint their respective congregations of the orders by us given with respect to baptisms, and persons attending the confirmation of their godchildren according to [the] rubric.

The churchwardens' oath and charge

[91] The oath or charge to be hereafter administered to the churchwardens and chapter-quest of this diocese.

First, if your minister and parish clerk do not their duty, you shall present them.
    Your minister's duty is:
    To read the service of the church on Sundays and holy days, soberly and distinctly, and in due time.
    To preach one sermon every Sunday (having no lawful impediment) in such language or tongue as shall be to the best satisfaction of the people.
    To catechize the youth of his parish every Sunday in the afternoon, and to explain some part of the church catechism after so plain and familiar a manner as may be to the edifying of the parishioners.
    To suffer none to come to the holy sacrament of the Lord's Supper until such time as they be confirmed (or in case of the lord bishop's absence or indisposition) they produce certificate from the archdeacon or vicars-general that they are duly qualified for confirmation.
    To visit the sick, to marry none without banns or licence, nor at any time but betwixt the hours of eight and twelve in the forenoon, and to live so soberly as to be a pattern of religion and virtue to his whole parish.
    [92] If he is not so, but a resorter of alehouses (more than for his honest necessity) or given to any other notorious vice, you are to present him.
    The clerk's duty is to ring the bells in due time, to attend the minister (when required) at the visitation of the sick, at the burial of the dead or baptizing of children, to raise the psalm when required by the minister or else to procure it to be done to the satisfaction of the minister.
    If he neglect herein or in any other duty incumbent on him, by the ancient custom of your parish, you are to present him.
    Secondly, if any of the parishioners profane the Lord's Day by habitually neglecting to come to church, by behaving themselves irreverently there, by resorting on that day to the alehouse, to gaming or sporting, or doing any works (except such as are of necessity or charity) you shall present them.

And for the due observance of holy days, if one out of every family, or two where the family is great, do religiously attend the service of the church at morning prayer, you are not to present them though they follow their lawful business as at other times, but if they do not come to church you shall present them.

If any moar, serjeant, proctor or any other person shall, on the Lord's Day, presume to receive any rent or sums of money, both he and the person paying such rent or sums of money are to be presented by you.

Thirdly, all parents, guardians and masters are to be presented if they do not send their children to be catechized when required to do so.

Fourthly, if any person pretends to sorcery, charms or witchcraft, or resort or seek to such pretenders, you shall present them.

You are likewise to present all such as commit fornication, adultery, incest or the like, known or upon common fame.

And forasmuch as it is observed that the great sins of cursing [93] swearing and taking God's name in vain are grown common, to the great scandal of the Christian religion and to the great grief and disquiet of all sober persons, you are therefore to present all such as are guilty of these crimes if they are of or above the age of fourteen years, and if under, you shall present their parents or guardians, as you will answer the contrary to god and his church for the breach of your oath, and you are to observe the same method in presenting the parents of those children under the age of fourteen years, who profane the Lord's Day by playing, gaming or sporting.

And whereas it is observed that many idle persons appoint meetings on Saturday night, which is generally spent in dancing even till after midnight, whereby they are rendered incapable of performing the duties of the following day, upon intimation hereof, you are to inquire who were the fiddlers of music and (for expedition's sake) present them, and as many more of the company as come within your knowledge.

Fifthly. If any legacies have been left to pious uses and have not been, or are not so employed, you shall present such as should dispose of them and do neglect or abuse their trust.

Sixthly. You are by your oath obliged to take care that the church and churchyard be kept in good repair. You are to provide good and legible books for the service of the church, a decent chalice and other vessels, with bread and wine for the sacrament, and to take care that marriages, christenings and burials be fully registered according to law and canon. If your chancel and church house be not kept in good repair, or if your minister resides not in his church house, you are to present.

Seventhly. If any encroach upon the churchyard or glebe land, you are to present them.

Eighthly, if the former churchwardens and questmen have not done their duty, you are to present them.

Ninthly, if you know of any will or decree concealed you are to discover the same to the court.

Tenthly. All persons at sixteen years of age ought to receive holy communion. If they do not, you are to [94] present them.

Eleventhly. If any cohabit as husband and wife not lawfully married, or any lawfully married do not cohabit, you are to present them.

Twelfthly. All such as pay not the church afore mentioned are to be presented.

Thirteenthly. The dogs are to be kept out of the church by the sumner; otherwise you are to present him.

Fourteenthly. If your school be not diligently kept, prayers read on Wednesdays and Fridays in Lent; you are to present.

Fifteenthly. You are to present all such as are given to drunkenness or tippling and such as carry tales from house to house, and that sow discord betwixt one person and another.

Sixteenthly. You are to see that the books for the use of the present and succeeding ministers be kept clean and in good order; otherwise you are to let the court know of it.

These articles are to be publicly read in church once in the quarter, viz., the first Sundays in January, April, July and October, that the people, as well as the parish officers, may be apprized of what crimes are presentable. And the wardens and chapter-quest are to meet the last Sunday in every month after evening prayers to set down in writing all matters they are bound by their oaths to present. And the foregoing articles to be read unto them by the ministers at every such meeting. And in case the wardens and chapter-quest neglect coming to church at such times in order to discharge their duty in this particular, the minister is required to present them. Given at Bishopscourt, this 16 May 1761. Mark Sodor and Man.

The correspondence concerning stricter observance of Ash Wednesday and Good Friday, now placed on record

[95] To the reverend the rectors, vicars, chaplains and curates of the Isle of Man.

Whereas in all small communities and societies of men professing or pretending to any sort of religion whatever, there are none but whose particular members are looked upon as bound to comply with some certain rules and appointments, without which all order and decency must be extinguished and everything run into confusion. Amongst others, those of the established Church of England have their well-known laws and constitutions to which its own members are obliged to conform, and to which his present majesty of Great Britain, the supreme head of our church here on earth, doth himself religiously conform, and hath signified by his declaration and example what he expects from his subjects. And whereas it hath been observed and lamented by all true friends to the welfare and prosperity of the church of Christ which hath happily subsisted in this isle and diocese of Man for several ages, that the inhabitants have of late appeared more than commonly neglectful of and in some instances showing open contempt to its public ordinances, and particularly to the two most solemn fast days, which have not only by the primitive church been ever observed with the strictest reverence and regard, but for which also the Church of England (of which we profess ourselves a part) hath accordingly prepared and set forth more than ordinarily solemn and devout offices. Now, for the better remedying the said scandalous abuses and for restoring the ancient and laudable attendance on the institutions of our holy religion, and more especially on the stated days set apart for fasting and humiliation, and to prevent, at least, their being so openly and notoriously desecrated and profaned, by persons following their occupations in the face of the church and in time of divine service on those days, I hereby signify and publish my most earnest request to our honourable and worshipful civil magistrates, and my express order to my reverend brethren, the clergy of this isle, that they will please to concur with me in taking such measures as shall be found and adjudged [96] most meet and expedient, and wherein I trust and pray we may do what will tend to the honour of God and his church, most agreeable to our obligations to the protection of providence and to the sentiments and approbation of all good Christians, particularly to the liege lord of this isle, as well as to our most excellent and religious king. Given at Bishopscourt 5 March 1761. Mark Sodor and Man.

This to be published at the usual time of morning service in all churches and chapels of this isle, on Sunday 15th instant March, being Palm Sunday, or the Sunday next before Easter.

To be copied, forwarded and returned to the ordinary with all convenient dispatch, and with due certificate of its coming to hand. And the sumners to have charge against delays.

[99][459] *Memorandum*. On Good Friday 1760. In returning from the sacrament at Ballaugh where I had been to assist the rector, I was eyewitness of three or four ploughs at work, and which had been so during the whole time of divine service and administration of the sacrament, within sight of the bishop and ministers and congregation, and this on the solemnest fast appointed by the laws of the established church of the whole year.

Question. If the Turks (as it seems they do) feast in contumely of Christ crucified, and a Jew was punished with fine for an irregularity or irreverence he was guilty of in his own house on this day, notwithstanding his plea of ignorance, what must be thought of or said for professed Christians who desecrate this day openly in the face of the sun, not barely by absence from the service of the church, but by a public contempt of that service, in following their worldly occupations, even whilst it is performing? A day had in the strictest regard and reverence by the primitive church, as being that particular day in the year on which Christians are required by the governors of the church to assemble in commemoration of the sufferings of a dying, crucified Saviour, therefore to be kept with fasting, which always implies a more than ordinary seclusion from business or pleasure. But such it seems is not the notion some Christians have of the nature or solemnity of any fast days, excepting such as are occasionally appointed for averting some temporal judgment.

For on Ash Wednesday 1761, upon my asking some of my nearest neighbours, whom I saw ploughing as I returned from divine service at the parish church, how they could answer it to their consciences to be attending their worldly affairs in that public manner, whilst the ministers and the rest of their fellow Christians were devoutly humbling themselves before God at the church? It was frankly answered

---

[459]Pp. 97-8 are blank.

that they thought 'there was no harm at all in their so doing'. And so they rest, as harmless members of the Christian church, whilst others for irregularities committed after the service of another fast day was over (though enjoined [100] by far less authority and sanction than the other two stated fasts) are obliged to confess their crime by open penance!

What I have further to remark or inquire into on this subject is how we shall account for the flagrant inconsistence of an absolute rest from worldly labour of the Christian husbandman on the day of Purification and Annunciation, and the notorious disrespect, not to say defiance to authority, not by absence from divine worship only, nor by following their occupations some parts of the day (which I presume they do not on any part of the two forementioned holidays) but by their doing it all the time the solemn service (the most solemn of any in the year) is performing.

That all holidays appointed by the church should have regard paid to them is not to be doubted or denied, by some of each family attending the public service, at least; but if we may judge from the several appointments of the several services, and will allow the compilers of our liturgy and the establishment of our ecclesiastical constitution to be as wise as some who (though members of the church) seem to think otherwise, the preference of solemnity is manifestly pointed out by the distinguishably extraordinary services of the two great feasts of Good Friday and Ash Wednesday, far beyond what is appointed for either of the two holidays of Purification and Annunciation, which have no proper Psalms and only single proper lessons, and those out of the Apocrypha.

On what account therefore it is that this opposite partiality is shown by the members, to that which has been so remarkably expressed towards other days by the governors of the church, and why it is that the wardens of the several parishes in this isle do so constantly and scrupulously present every the minutest slight or neglect shown to the solemnity of any part of an occasional fast day, whilst they as certainly take no notice of the most obnoxious profanation of every part of the two others the most solemn and stated, I am much at a loss to understand. It has been said the one has been ordered by our governors, and pray are not the other two, I will not say equally, but more authoritatively so? And if, in the order for an occasional fast, it is said 'the contemners of it shall be proceeded against [101] as the law directs' may we not ask what and where is that law which is not at least equally open against contemners of other fasts of no less, or as I have shown, of rather more importance (if there be any comparison) than this?

The heart of man we must readily allow is not within the scrutiny of mortal ken, as is his public behaviour. The latter, in all well-regulated societies, when notoriously repugnant to wholesome laws, is generally thought worthy the cognizance of the guardians and dispensers of those laws, especially, I say, where the breach of them is notorious and barefaced. And still, beyond all, will this hold good and desirable in the church and diocese of Man, which has long had the character and blessing of a more than ordinary attention to order and discipline, and where, therefore, less can be said in defence of connivance and relaxation, than in other places and countries, where regard to ancient laws of the church are not so professedly attended to.

I beg leave to refer my reasonings to the mature and deliberate consideration of my two worthy vicars-general, requesting their free remarks may be made upon them, and returned to me at their leisure with this paper, whereby they will greatly oblige their very affectionate friend and brother, Mark Sodor and Man. February 21, 1761.

[102] If anything can exceed the surprise and concern which are given to every serious, devout member of the established church, at seeing the contempt put upon two official prime fasts appointed by that church, it is the reasons and arguments urged in its alleviation or defence, viz.

1. General custom of the people of this isle to work throughout those days.
2. The late bishop and vicar-general Walker's example for it.
3. That prayers have been usually read on those days so early as eight in the morning, and no evening service at all on the said days.

N.B. The Jew that was fined in this isle for the disrespect shown to Good Friday in his own house, upon being charged with it by the officiating ministers of the town and parish, besides the plea of ignorance, that that was the Christians' day of humiliation, he moreover added as I am credibly informed, that it was the annual day of rejoicing among their people for the deliverance of the Jews from immediate destruction by Haman, who was the contriver of their ruin, being previously cut off, and that little could he think it a day which Christians devoutly set apart for remembering the death and crucifixion of their Saviour, when he saw so many of them at work as usual, and rolling the casks about the quay. *Pudet haec opprobia*, etc.

My lord, That the fasts and festivals of the church are enjoined to be religiously observed is granted. That there has been a great neglect of the due observation of such days is but too notorious to be denied. But that the said abuses may be remedied or prevented for the time to come, I concur and think it fitting that your lordship would be pleased to send a circular letter to your clergy, to be published in their several churches, requiring a strict observance of such days and then if the wardens neglect presenting the contemners of public authority, the court will proceed to such censure as the law directs. I am with all due respect, your lordship's most dutiful son and servant, Robert Radcliffe. Saturday February 28, 1761.

[103] The papers concerning the fast now intended some time ago to be placed on record. If Mr registrar has any duplicate originals that came to his hands, these may be returned to me; otherwise these three may be placed according to their dates, where such kind of orders are usually recurred to.

I would desire Mr Gelling's petition may be taken into consideration.

I am, Mr vicar-general's and your affectionate servant, Mark Sodor and Man. Friday morning, 15 May 1761.

Mr registrar will be pleased to give all convenient despatch to the circulation of the orders as the form of certificate for confirmation will soon be wanted.

The licensing of schoolmasters, 16 June 1761

[115][460] Whereas it is expressly contrary to the laws of our establishment for any person or persons whatever to engage in the business or employment of instructing youth without the approbation and licence of the ordinary of each respective diocese, notice is hereby given that all persons within this isle and diocese of Man not already licensed, who are desirous of entering or are now entered on the province of an instructor, upon producing a certificate, in the underwritten form, from the minister and wardens of the town or parish where they reside, may receive licence from the ordinary by applying for it. And all others who shall henceforth begin or continue to exercise the office of teaching youth without such licence and authority, must expect to be proceeded against according to law. The form of certificate required for entitling masters and mistresses to receive licences to teach and instruct youth in this diocese is to be set forth in the following words, viz.:

We whose names are underwritten, the minister and wardens of .... do hereby certify our right reverend ordinary that A. B. now applying for licence to teach school in our ...., so far as we know, or upon inquiry can learn, is a person of sober life and good behaviour, and qualified for what (he or she) undertakes, and that (he or she) doth hold and is determined or promises to teach no other doctrines or principles of religion than which are received and established in the Church of England, and we do accordingly recommend the said... to our right reverend ordinary for licence to teach young persons in our..., if he shall be fit or be pleased to grant the same. Witness our hands this.... .... rector, vicar, chaplain or curate.

This is to be copied and published the next Sunday after it comes to hand and the usual time of divine service in the morning, and certificate thereof to be returned to our registry. Given at Bishopscourt, 16 June 1761. Mark Sodor and Man.

[116] German. June 18, 1761. Received about eight o'clock in the afternoon and forwarded early the next morning to the vicar of Kirk Patrick by me, Henry Corlett.

Patrick, June 19, 1761. Received and forwarded to Rushen by me, Robert Ratcliffe.

Rushen, June 21st, 1761. Received this morning about eight o'clock and being Sunday, the same was published as within directed and forwarded to the vicar of Arbory immediately after evening service by me, Nicholas Christian.

Kirk Arbory, June 21, 1761. Received this evening and delivered to the vicar of Malew about twelve o'clock on the 22nd June. John Moore.

Kirk Malew, June 22, 1761. Received about noon and forwarded before two o'clock. Daniel Gelling.

Received the same day about three o'clock in the evening; sent to the sumner to be forwarded to Kirk Santan immediately, Thomas Castley.

---

[460]Pp. 104-6 are blank. Pp. 107-11 are out of chronological order; see below. P. 112 is a cover note as p. 22 and pp. 113-14 are blank.

Kirk Santan, June 24th, 1761. Received about twelve o'clock at noon and sent to the sumner to be forwarded to the reverend the vicar of Kirk Marown about five o'clock in the evening. Paul Crebbin.

Kirk Marown, June 25th 1761. Received about eight o'clock in the morning and forwarded before nine to the reverend the vicar of Braddan.

[117] Kirk Braddan, June 25th, 1761. Received at eight o'clock in the evening and forwarded before nine to the reverend the chaplain of Douglas. Joseph Cosnahan.

Douglas, June 25th 1761. Received this evening and forwarded next morning to the vicar of Kirk Onchan by me, Philip Moore.

Kirk Onchan, June 26th 1761. Received about one o'clock in the afternoon and forwarded forthwith to the vicar of Lonan by me, Thomas Quayle.

Kirk Lonan, June 26th. Received this evening about seven o'clock and forwarded next morning about five to the vicar of Kirk Maughold by me, Samuel Gell.

Kirk Maughold, June 27. Received at ten in the morning and forwarded before eleven to the chaplain of Ramsey. Thomas William Joseph Woods.

Ramsey, June the 27th. Received at one o'clock in the afternoon and forwarded at two to the vicar of Lezayre, John Crellin.

Lezayre, June 27th. Received about three o'clock in the afternoon and forwarded to Kirk Bride about five the same evening. John Gill.

Kirk Bride, June 28th 1761. Received about seven o'clock in the evening on the 27th instant and forwarded this day to the reverend Mr archdeacon immediately after evening service, having published the contents as within directed. Daniel Nelson.

[118] Kirk Andreas, 28 June 1761. Received about five o'clock in the evening and forwarded about half and hour after five to the vicar of Jurby. William Mylrea.

Jurby, 29th June 1761. Received about nine o'clock in the forenoon and forwarded per sumner within half an hour after. William Crebbin.

Ballaugh, 29th June, 1761. Received at eleven o'clock in the forenoon. Matthias Curghey.

Meeting of the trustees for the impropriations, 30 June 1761

[125][461] Dear Sirs, By direction of our right reverend ordinary notice hereby give you that the trustees concerned in the distribution of the annual sum due and payable on account of the impropriations at Easter last have appointed a meeting of the clergy and others concerned at Balnyhown in Kirk German on Tuesday the 30th instant by ten o'clock in the forenoon, when and where you and the schoolmasters of your several parishes (whom you are desired to acquaint herewith) are to attend in order to receive your dividends and to execute proper receipts for the same. I am, reverend sirs, your affectionate brother and humble servant, James Wilks, episcopal registrar. Kirk Michael, June 18, 1761.

[461]P. 125 is out of chronological order.

The bishop's call for a Manx translation of the Bible, 2 October 1761

[107] To the reverend the ministers of the several parochial churches in this isle and diocese of Man.

My good brethren, The more I have at any time considered and thought of the deplorable state of darkness and superstition the Christian church was for some years involved in, till the reformation in England took place for dispersing it in great measure amongst the people of the British dominions, with which, as we of this isle are ecclesiastically connected, it has been my earnest care and desire to remove everything that appeared to me to be still short of the contemplation of that great work in this part of the established church committed to my charge. Hence it is that I have, as you well know, been so zealously set upon rectifying that great absurdity St Paul so remarkably discourages in his epistles, the offering prayers and exhortations in a tongue unknown to the far greater part of a Christian congregation assembled for the worship of Almighty God, and having now (after long repeated entreaties) at last obtained by the joint assistance of some of my clergy, an uniform translation of the church service in the language of the country, which I trust, the junior part of my brethren will not fail of complying with the use of, and no other; I am led to take notice of another neglect, the correcting of which I apprehend would tend not a little to the edification and comfort of the greater part of the native inhabitants of this diocese, who are doubtless, many of them, capable and may in time be desirous of joining in, I mean, that delightful part of worship called psalmody, which, for want of proper authority to direct it otherwise, is at present everywhere throughout the isle, even in the country parish churches, set forth in English to a congregation the majority of which might as well be called upon to praise God in the Hebrew tongue, if the clerk was but master of it. I hereby think proper to order and enjoin that henceforward no more than one psalm or portion of a psalm in English be sung in any of the country churches on each Lord's Day or other holy day, which I think full sufficient for the use and gratification of the minority, who only can be supposed to understand it [108] waiting and hoping in the meantime for my reverend vicars-general being so good as to do their best to procure a Manx translation of some parts of the singing psalms, such as, after returning their approbation and recommendation, I may circulate an order for the use of in the churches and at the funerals in all the country parishes of this isle, without which order from the diocesan, they very well know, is to be expressly contrary to law to use or produce them in divine service.

And whereas I find some doubts have arisen among some of the clergy concerning the sense in which they are to observe my late injunction 'to instruct the people in a language they best understand', I here think fit more explicitly to declare my meaning to be that not every sermon preached in the country churches should be in the Manx tongue, but that, take the Sundays throughout the year, the English and Manx shall be proportioned to the capacities and talents of the congregation, for each respectively, as near as the minister can be able to compute, from his knowledge or inquiry.

This I take to be righteous, and the excess either way, if considerable, both cruel and unjust, and for which I might appeal to the conscience of any equitable person whatever, that does not think respect of persons in spiritual dispensations is to be had according to their temporal possessions or stations they hold in the external appearances of this world.

I am very sensible that the trouble of composing or transposing into Manx is rather more than the furnishing English discourses. For doubtless such to the young clerks, lately called out from a town school education, who find it difficult to recover their native tongue, yet I shall hope that from the motive of charity to the souls of the greater number committed to their charge, the reasonableness of the thing itself, the flagrant absurdity of the reverse, and the express [109] appointment of the ordinary, all taken and considered together will readily determine them to act in this point, as shall be most consonant to their duty, be the trouble of their strict regard to it what it will.

I take this opportunity to signify my permission to the clergy of my diocese (till I shall receive positive orders from our metropolitan) to insert 'our gracious Queen Charlotte' wherever the royal family are to be prayed for in our church service.

Commending all to whom these presents shall come to the divine blessing and favour, I rest, my reverend brethren, yours faithfully and affectionately in Christ Jesus, Mark Sodor and Man. Bishopscourt, October 2, 1761.

(This is to be circulated as directed but not required to be transcribed otherwise than, perhaps, such heads of it as everyone concerned shall think proper to take for memory's sake.)

I hope the clergy who agreed at our last convocation to undertake the translation of the rest of the occasional services in the liturgy then remaining undone have not been unmindful of such their engagement, and that they have had a meeting (as the other translators had) to ascertain each one's portion in the said work, and which, I trust, by this time is in great forwardness.

[111][462] Peel, October 6, 1761. Received about eleven o'clock and forwarded half an hour after to the vicar of Patrick, Henry Corlett, vicar of German.

Kirk Patrick, October 6, 1761. Received about one o'clock and forwarded that evening by the sumner to the vicar of Rushen.

Kirk Arbory. October 7, 1761. Received about one o'clock and forwarded to the vicar of Rushen at ten o'clock next morning, John Moore.

Kirk Christ Rushen, October 8, 1761. Received about five o'clock in the evening, forwarded to the vicar of Malew about eleven o'clock next morning, Nicholas Christian.

Castletown, October 9, 1761. Received about six o'clock in the evening and forwarded by the summoner early the next morning to the vicar of Santan. Daniel Gelling.

Kirk Santan. October 10, 1761. Received about twelve o'clock and sent to the sumner with all convenient despatch, to be forwarded to the reverend the vicar of Marown. Paul Crebbin.

---

[462]P. 110 is blank.

Kirk Marown, October 11. Received and forwarded by the sumner to the reverend the vicar of Kirk Braddan. John Christian.

Kirk Braddan, October 11, 1761. Received about five o'clock in the evening and returned to the episcopal registrar by me, Joseph Cosnahan.

The Manx psalter, 10 November 1761

[119] To the reverend the rectors and vicars of the parochial churches of the isle and diocese of Man.

My reverend brethren! It is with great pleasure I now find myself enabled to transmit to your hands some approved portions of psalmody translated into the language of the country we live in, which you'll be pleased carefully to transcribe either in the whole or in part, for the use of your respective congregations in the country.

I here think fit also to repeat my former order, that no more than one English psalm be sung at one service in any parochial country church where you have reason to believe the far major part of the congregation have no sufficient language but Manx, leaving it to your choice to use as many and as much of those I now send you as you shall think proper for the edification of the people, and as will not infringe too far on the time usually allowed for the rest of the service.

You will easily see the propriety, not to say necessity, of the lines of the psalms (at least those of common measure) being read to the congregation, many of which, who might be disposed to sing, not being able to read themselves, and which, till your clerks have made themselves masters of doing it distinctly and audibly, I promise myself your readiness to supply.

Being fully convinced that the Manx psalmody will tend greatly to the satisfaction and comfort of the greater part of the several flocks, hath made me think it my duty to appoint the use of it, and cannot therefore but wish you, by all means, to encourage and recommend it to them, to join in it, with heart and voice.

Commending you and your pious labours to the divine benediction and grace, I remain my reverend brethren, your affectionate friend and fellow servant in Christ, Mark Sodor and Man.

This to be copied and returned in the circuit as usual.

[120] November 10, 1761. Received and delivered to the vicar of Kirk German the same day by me, James Wilks, episcopal registrar.

November 16. Received in the evening and forwarded on the 20 at about nine o'clock in the morning to the vicar of Rushen. John Moore.

November 27th. Received last Sunday morning and forwarded this evening about three o'clock to the vicar of Malew. Nicholas Christian.

Received the 28th November and forwarded the 3 day of December 1761 to the vicar of Kirk Santan. Daniel Gelling.

Received December 4, 1761 and forwarded the seventh in the evening to the vicar of Kirk Marown by Paul Crebbin.

Received December 8, 1761 and forwarded the ninth in the evening to the reverend the vicar of Braddan, John Christian.

December 10th, 1761. Received about two o'clock in the afternoon and forwarded the next day to the reverend the vicar of Onchan, Joseph Cosnahan.

December 11th 1761. Received about four o'clock in the afternoon and forwarded early Monday following to the reverend the vicar of Lonan by Thomas Quayle.

December 14, 1761. Received about one o'clock in the afternoon and forwarded on Thursday following about seven o'clock in the morning to the reverend the vicar of Maughold by Samuel Gell.

Received December 17, 1761 about noon and forwarded to the reverend the vicar of Lezayre the nineteenth about nine in the forenoon by Thomas William Joseph Woods.

Received December 19th 1761 about noon and forwarded early on Thursday morning to the reverend the rector of Kirk Bride, by John Gill.

Received December 24, 1761 about ten o'clock at night and delivered to the sumner to forward it to the reverend Mr archdeacon on the 28th about four in the afternoon by Daniel Nelson.

Received December 29th 1761 about noon and forwarded early on Thursday morning the 31st instant to the reverend the vicar of Jurby, William Mylrea.

[121] Received about one o'clock at noon on December 31st 1761 and forwarded as directed on January 2nd 1762 at ten o'clock. William Crebbin.

January 2nd 1762. Received about noon and returned to the Reverend James Wilks, episcopal registrar. Matthias Curghey.

Thursday 15 April 1762[463]

[127][464] Clergy present.

William Mylrea.	Thomas Woods.
Robert Radcliffe.	William Crebbin.
Matthias Curghey.	John Christian.
Philip Moore.	Joseph Cosnahan.
Thomas Castley.	Samuel Gell.
Paul Crebbin.[465]	Thomas Quayle.
John Wilks.	Henry Corlett.
Nicholas Christian.	Daniel Gelling.
John Moore.	John Crellin.
John Gill, archdeacon's registrar.	Daniel Nelson.

---

[463] The Thursday in Easter week.
[464] Pp. 122-3 are blank; p. 124 is a cover note as p. 22. P. 125 is out of chronological order; see above. P. 126 is blank.
[465] Infirm and desired to be excused.

[129]⁴⁶⁶ At the convocation our right reverend diocesan signified to the clergy assembled that having occasion shortly to embark for England he hath thought proper, instead of waiting till Thursday in Whitsun week, to hold the annual convocation this day.

His lordship also directed that all persons whatever within this isle who teach school without licence be summoned to the next chapter court to show cause why they should not be proceeded against for presuming to teach without authority.

A letter from the archbishop of York to the bishop of Sodor and Man, 14 August 1762

[135]⁴⁶⁷ Bishopthorpe, August 14, 1762.

My good lord, When I had the honour of seeing your lordship here, in your discourse upon the state of religion in the Isle of Man, I was much surprised to find that the general practice was that the ministers in the public service of the church translated the Scriptures and the liturgy off hand out of English into the language of the island. The numberless inconveniences both to the minister and people, and more particularly the danger of injury to the tenor of the sacred writings and our excellent liturgy by such vague translations, must be very obvious and disagreeable to your lordship, whose constant care and earnest zeal for the cause of religion in your diocese is well known. It will be well worthy of your lordship to recommend and let me add my recommendation to some of the more experienced clergymen of the island to frame a plain translation of the liturgy which should be used uniformly throughout the diocese. It were to be wished too that such parts of the Scriptures as are the most necessary should be carefully translated by some able clergymen of the island, and that translation used also uniformly. I understand that at present the Gospel of St Matthew is the only part of Scripture translated into the language of the island, and that out of print now; I hope you will be able to have the four gospels and the Acts translated now and printed, and so go on through the whole by degrees. These translations should receive your lordship's approbation before they are used publicly. To print these requires more expense than can be expected from the inhabitants, and your lordship's Christian endeavours to procure a fund for this purpose will, I hope, meet with the success they deserve. [136] Books may be given for the public use of the parishes and sold to individuals at a low price to be fixed by your lordship. Some small religious tracts translated and dispensed among the lower ranks of people would be useful and you have made a good beginning to that purpose.

With regard to the language to be used in the public service in the church, it must differ according to the different circumstances of the parishes. We have one plain, general apostolical rule to guide us: 'Let all things be done to edifying decently and in order',⁴⁶⁸ and therefore for the souls' health of the flocks committed

---

⁴⁶⁶P. 128 is blank.
⁴⁶⁷P. 130 is blank. Pp. 131-3 are out of chronological order; see below. P. 134 is blank.
⁴⁶⁸1 Co. xiv. 40.

to their charge, the ministers ought to use the language of the island or English in proportion to the number of their flocks that understand the one or the other. And the mode of ascertaining the service in the most reasonable manner according to this proportion must be left to the determination of the bishop upon the representation of each minister.

This is the spirit of the law in Queen Elizabeth's time relating to the service in Wales, and it is now observed there according to the different circumstances of the different parishes. Indeed, no edification can there be in a minister's performing his duty in an unknown tongue, nor are there any means surer than the use of our established liturgy, if well understood, to create and cherish in us a sound spiritual and rational devotion. The people have a right to this and to every effort of that sincere affection for the salvation of souls, which is the true spring of all the industry and application which is required in a minister of the gospel of Christ.

To keep up a just sense of the Christian religion in our hearts and to fix in our minds a rational knowledge of it is the foundation of our reformation from popery, and to that purpose I trust that [137] there is due attention given to education under schoolmasters properly licensed. I hope the incessant workings of the papists have not introduced any of their schools amongst your people, which attempt is severely punishable by law, and would be of the utmost ill consequence both in a religious and civil light, which ought to be considered seriously by parents, who are often too fond of putting their children under the tuition of foreigners.

The good character your lordship gives of your clergy flatters our hopes and the good inclinations of the people make it much to be wished, that every means was taken to cultivate the plain knowledge and plain virtue of the lower sort, and to keep up their habits of religion, which is the most effectual means of maintaining their principles of religion. It were to be wished that the churches of the island were sufficiently repaired and enlarged and kept decent and clean. Whatever failing there may be in these respects, it is probably above the powers of the inhabitants to amend, which requires expense. If your lordship shall think of any method by a brief or otherwise to fulfil this good purpose, I will certainly do my utmost to co-operate with your lordship in this, and in every other of your pious intentions for the sake of our holy religion and the salvation of the souls committed to your charge. Allow me to be a fellow-labourer, always ready to give my most hearty recommendation, encouragement and assistance.

Remember my affectionate compliments to the clergy of your diocese. In all your and their truly Christian labours, my sincere wishes and prayers for your good success will attend you, always recommending you to the favour and protection of the Almighty.

Let me hear from you and believe me to be with the truest regard and esteem, my good lord, your affectionate brother and very humble servant, R. Ebor.[469]

[138] A true copy of a letter from the archbishop of York to the bishop of Man, Mark Sodor and Man.

---

[469]Robert Hay Drummond was archbishop of York from 19 September 1761 until his death on 10 December 1776.

Thursday 23 September 1762

[139] At a convocation of the clergy of the diocese of Sodor and Man at Kirk Michael, September 23, 1762.

Our right reverend diocesan having this day recommended to his clergy the prosecution of translating the remaining part of the Common Prayer Book into the Manx tongue, it is this day agreed upon by us whose names are subscribed, that in order to carry his lordship's recommendation into execution, that the reverend vicar-general Curghey and the reverend James Wilks, episcopal registrar, do allot to each of us a portion of the said Prayer Book and that we will use our best endeavours to complete such portion as soon as conveniently may be.

William Mylrea.
Robert Radcliffe.
Matthias Curghey.
Philip Moore.
Paul Crebbin.
Nicholas Christian.
John Moore.
John Gill.

Samuel Gell.
Thomas William Joseph Woods.
John Christian.
Daniel Gelling.
Thomas Quayle.
Henry Corlett.
Joseph Cosnahan.

[140] Pursuant to the within resolution we Matthias Curghey and James Wilks, clerks, have allotted to each of the clergy a portion of so much of the liturgy as remains untranslated into the Manx tongue, to be by them completed as soon as conveniently may be:

1. 1-4 Sundays in Advent, with Christmas Day, by Mr archdeacon.
2. St Stephen, St John, Innocents, Sunday after Christmas and Circumcision, vicar-general Radcliffe.
3. Epiphany; 1-4 Sundays after Epiphany, vicar-general Curghey.
4. 5-6 after Epiphany, Septuagesima, Sexagesima and Quinquagesima, Mr Wilks.
5. Ash Wednesday, 1-4 Lent, Mr Gill.
6. 5 Lent, Sunday-Wednesday before Easter, Mr Moore, Douglas.
7. Thursday before Easter, Good Friday, Easter Eve, Easter Day and Easter Monday, Mr Crebbin of Santan.
8. Easter Tuesday; 1-4 Sundays after Easter, Mr Christian of Rushen.
9. 5 Easter, Ascension, Sunday after Ascension, Whitsunday and Monday, Mr Moore of Arbory.
10. Whit Tuesday, Trinity Sunday, 1-3 Trinity, Mr Gell.
11. 4-8 Trinity, Mr Woods.
12. 9-13 Trinity, Mr Christian of Marown.
13. 14-18 Trinity, Mr Cosnahan.
14. 19-23 Trinity, Mr Quayle.
15. 24-25 Trinity, St Andrew, St Thomas, St Paul, Mr Gelling.
16. Presentation, St Matthew, Annunciation, St Mark, St Philip and St James, Mr Corlett.

17. St Barnabas, St John Baptist, St Peter, St James and St Bartholomew, Mr Crebbin of Jurby.

18. St Michael, St Luke, St Simon and Jude and all Saints, Mr Crellin.

Matthias Curghey.
James Wilks.

The clergy's assent to a translation of the Prayer Book and other matters, 12 November 1762

[131][470] To the right reverend father in God Mark, by divine permission lord bishop of Sodor and Man.

May it please your lordship to permit us the clergy of your lordship's diocese to express our most grateful acknowledgments of thanks for your lordship's paternal and truly Christian endeavours to promote and set forward the spiritual and temporal advantages of the people of your lordship's diocese in general; particularly for your earnest zeal in laying a foundation and disposing others to concur in raising contributions towards printing the liturgy of our church with some portion of the Holy Scriptures and other useful and good books (such as *The Christian Monitor*) in the Manx tongue.

And as your lordship has repeatedly heretofore and his grace our most reverend provincial has of late (in his grace's most kind and affectionate letter to your lordship) recommended an uniformity of expression in the liturgy to be used by all the clergy of this diocese, so we, as well from a sense of the expediency and great utility hereof, as from the duty we owe to his grace's and your lordship's recommendation, have unanimously agreed to undertake a plain translation of a large portion of the liturgy yet remaining untranslated into the mother tongue, to be revised by such of us as your lordship shall think proper to appoint for that purpose, and we are now severally engaged in performing our respective allotments thereof, and hope in a little time, by the divine assistance, to be able to present them to your lordship, which method, or such other as your lordship will be pleased to propose, we shall also take as speedily as may be in translating *The Christian Monitor*.

The favourable account your lordship was pleased to give of us to his grace, our most reverend and revered metropolitan, and the paternal and affectionate notice his grace has been pleased to take of us, in his grace's letter to your lordship, fill our hearts with the warmest sentiments of filial duty we owe to both, and impel us (with all submission and deference) to desire his grace would accept our most humble and unfeigned thanks, and your lordship (among your many other favours) to signify the same unto his grace.

We also crave leave with the highest sense of dutiful affection to acknowledge your lordship's goodness in devising a method for the good purposes of enlarging some of our churches, several of which, as your lordship well knows, are not sufficient for the reception [132] of one half of our congregations, to perform their

---

[470]Out of chronological order.

devotion with such decency of posture and composure of mind as befit Christian worshippers in the house of God, and herein we request your lordship would be pleased in our behalf to present our most humble and grateful thanks to their graces the most reverend the archbishops of Canterbury and York for their hearty concern for the good of this church, and to all others who, after their graces' example, have either countenanced or encouraged so good a work, and likewise to all such piously disposed personages as have contributed towards the laudable and beneficial undertaking of publishing the liturgy and other useful books in the Manx tongue, particularly to our most generous and liberal benefactors, the worthy members of the Society for Propagating Christian Knowledge, the reverend Dr Thomas Wilson, Sir John Thorold[471] and the worshipful board of Clothworkers Company.

We should be unmindful of our duty if we did not also render that tribute of thanks justly due to your lordship for your truly Christian labours, not only in composing your excellent catechetical conferences, heretofore circulated among us in manuscript, for our perusal and assistance, in the great and useful work of preparing the youth of our respective charges for confirmation, but also the great expense your lordship has been at in printing those conferences so judiciously calculated to preserve and increase the dear of God and a due sense of piety and true devotion among us, and likewise the Manx catechism with the list of contributions collected by the ever memorable Bishop Barrow for the better support and maintenance of the poor clergy and schoolmasters of this diocese, in like manner for expediting the new edition of our late right reverend lord bishop's exposition of the church catechism, printed by order of the late Mrs Catharine Halsall's executors.

Your lordship's truly apostolical concern and unabated vigilance for the welfare of this diocese has not been confined to spirituals only, but most generously extended to the temporal interests thereof, in endeavouring to open a door of charity for the relief of four poor clergymen's widows and orphans, from the Corporation of the Sons of the Clergy in our mother country, in trying whether there was not some possible room for the augmentation of our poor [133] livings from her majesty Queen Anne's bounty, in having our annuity payable by Lord Derby received with little or no expense through your lordship's influence, in settling several of our public charities on a clear and easy foundation and having others of them augmented beyond what they have been for some ages past.

For these and the many other accumulated instances of your lordship's paternal concern both for the spiritual and secular interest of this church and diocese, we once more request your lordship would be pleased to accept our most profound and dutiful thanks, humbly imploring the Almighty to prosper and succeed your labours, that we may long enjoy the blessing of your example and imitate that living pattern of true primitive Christianity, that orthodoxy may constantly be preserved and true piety more and more increase and flourish among us, and that after your lordship has long and successfully laboured in the vineyard of Christ, you and we may enjoy the happiness of those who turn many to righteousness is the hearty and earnest prayer of your lordship's most dutiful and obedient sons and servants,

---

[471] A well-known contemporary writer on religious themes. He died in 1775.

William Mylrea.
Robert Radcliffe.
Matthias Curghey.
Philip Moore.
Paul Crebbin.
Nicholas Christian.
John Moore.
James Wilks.
John Gill.

William Crebbin.
Thomas William Joseph Woods.
Samuel Gell.
Thomas Quayle.
Joseph Cosnahan.
Henry Corlett.
Daniel Gelling.
John Crellin.

Examined by James Wilks episcopal registrar. The original hereof given to the lord bishop of Sodor and Man this 12th November 1762 by me, James Wilks, episcopal registrar.

Thursday 26 May 1763

[145][472] Clergy present.

William Mylrea.
Robert Radcliffe.
Matthias Curghey.
Philip Moore.
Thomas Castley.
Paul Crebbin, infirm and unable to attend.
James Wilks.
Nicholas Christian.
John Moore.
John Gill, archdeacon's registrar.[473]

Thomas Woods.
William Crebbin.
Joseph Cosnahan.
John Christian.
Samuel Gell.
Thomas Quayle.
Henry Corlett.
Daniel Gelling.
John Crellin.
Daniel Nelson.

Orders and regulations presented at convocation

[147][474] Orders and regulations to be proposed and offered at the convocation, 1763.

1. All forms of certificates, recommendations, testimonials or any other relating to the clergy and schoolmasters and the government of the church, to be carefully entered in a book provided for that purpose in the registrars office, and such of the clergy or masters as have not copies to apply to the episcopal registrar for them.

    2. No schoolmasters to receive the annuities who, after notice given, continue to keep a public house.

    3. The sacrament of the Lord's Supper to be administered without fail in every parish church of this isle on each of the three festival days of Christmas, Easter and

---

[472]Pp. 141-4 are blank.
[473]Indisposed, and by letter desires to be excused.
[474]P. 146 is blank.

Whitsunday, unavoidable hindrance or disability of the incumbent excepted, and such hindrance to be certified to the ordinary.

4. Fair books to be had in every church, that no clergyman who may not be able to say the service by heart, be surprised and obstructed in performance of the duty of the day.

5. Prayer for the royal family to be altered and corrected with the pen in the church Common Prayer Books to avoid mistakes, as directed by the king's proclamation.

6. *The Manx liturgy and gospel of St Matthew to be revised and corrected for the press.*[475]

6/7. Accounts of public charities in this isle to be passed, and afterward annually at the convocation.

7/8. Preface to the confirmation office to be ready translated and wrote down for the minister to read when he attends the bishop in the performance of that office.

8/9. Archbishop's orders first and third to be read by the registrar and circulated, viz.

10. *Schoolmasters to be told not to come for their last annuities till notice given.*

11. *Preacher for Tynwald Day to be appointed.*[476]

[148] The archbishop's orders within referred to directed to the bishops of his province.

1. That you require of every person who desires to be admitted to holy orders that he signify to you his name and place of abode, and transmit to you his testimonial and certificate of his age, duly attested, with the title upon which he is to be ordained, at least twenty days before the time of ordination, and that he appear on Wednesday or at farthest on Thursday in ember week in order to his examination.

2. That you admit not any person to holy orders who having resided any considerable time out of the university, does not send to you with his testimonial, a certificate signed by the minister and other credible inhabitants of the parish where he so resided, expressing that notice was given in the church in time of divine service on some Sunday at least a month before the day of ordination, of his intention to offer himself to you to be ordained at such a time, and that upon such notice given, no objections have come to their knowledge, for the which he ought not to be ordained.

Letter of thanks to the Corporation of the Sons of the Clergy

[151][477] To the most reverend the archbishops, the right reverend the bishops and the rest of the worthy members of the court of assistants of the governors for relief of widows and children of clergymen.

---

[475]Deleted.
[476]Deleted.
[477]Pp. 149-50 are blank.

We the bishop, archdeacon, vicars-general and the rest of the clergy of the isle and diocese of Man this day assembled, beg leave to express our grateful sense and acknowledgments of the favours conferred on the petitioning widows of three of our clergy deceased in this diocese, by their being admitted on the list for receiving annual pensions of six pounds each.

A favour this, for which we never can be sufficiently thankful to heaven, and to our benefactors the worthy members of the corporation, to those especially who were the first principal movers and promoters of our cause.

The best return we can make, besides our humble thanks, is that of our ardent prayers for the prosperity and happiness of the corporation, and a promise of using our utmost care to deserve the continuance of the bounty already bestowed on our three supplicants, as well as the acceptance of future recommendations when occasion shall require. Done and subscribed at Bishopscourt in the Isle of Man this 26th day of May 1763.

Mark Sodor and Man.   Samuel Gell.
William Mylrea.   Thomas Quayle.
Robert Radcliffe.   John Christian.
Matthias Curghey.   Thomas William Joseph Woods.
Philip Moore.   Joseph Cosnahan.
[152] Thomas Castley.   William Crebbin.
Nicholas Christian.   Daniel Gelling.
John Moore.   Henry Corlett.
James Wilks.   John Crellin.

Examined per James Wilks, episcopal registrar.
N.B. The original hereof delivered to my lord bishop on order to be forwarded to the Corporation of Clergymen's Sons.

Distribution of The Christian Monitor in Manx, 4 November 1763

[155][478] To the reverend the clergy of the isle and diocese of Man.

I must entreat each and every of you to be very careful in the disposal of these truly useful books, entitled *The Christian Monitor* or *Ferraavee Chreestee*. That you deliver them to none, but such as, upon trial, you shall find has one in the family that can read intelligibly; who at least, you are fully persuaded, will, after a little use and application, be both able and disposed so to do.

I leave it to you, whether you shall take the trouble of sending me a list of those persons to whom you dispense them, but in case you so think fit, you may please at the same time to certify me what further number you may have occasion for.

The joyful and grateful sense, I understand, hath been shown and expressed by many people in several parts of this isle, upon hearing of the sundry Manx impressions being shortly expected, serves to confirm my conviction of the truth of

---

[478]Pp. 153-4 are blank.

my right worthy and right reverend predecessor's prophetic hopes, that such an undertaking would 'sometime prove a blessing to this country' and for which, I am sure we ought to be thankful to Providence, that has raised up friends and benefactors to assist in the article of expense attending the execution of so desirable and charitable a work.

May God vouchsafe to make it successful to the honour of his name and the spiritual emolument and edification of those for whose use it was intended! To which prayer, I trust, all sincere well-wishers to [156] the prosperity of our Sion will add a hearty Amen!

I am my dear and reverend brethren, your ever faithful and devoted fellow-servant in the great business of our common master, Mark Sodor and Man.

[P. S.] The Manx gospels, I hear, are very near, if not by this time quite finished, and shall be circulated as soon as they arrive.

This to be returned with an acknowledgment of the receipt of books to Mark Sodor and Man.

Those who receive the double books should be told that the Manx translation is at the end, which indeed ought to have been placed first.

You will be pleased to give notice to your congregation the next Sunday after your receipt of these books, when and where and on what terms they are to be distributed. And it also mayn't be amiss if you should from the pulpit recommend a careful and diligent use of them. Mark Sodor and Man.

[157] November 5, 1763. Received about eight o'clock this morning and forwarded to the Reverend Mr Radcliffe. Of *The Christian Monitors* I have received three and twenty, and of the exposition of the church catechism fifty-eight. Henry Corlett.

November 6, 1763. Received and forwarded to the vicar of Arbory. Robert Radcliffe.

November 9th. Received in the morning and despatched to the vicar of Rushen on the 10th. John Moore.

November 10th, 1763. Received about three o'clock in the evening and forthwith forwarded to the vicar of Malew. Nicholas Christian.

Malew, November 11, 1763. Received late last night and forwarded early this morning to the reverend vicar of Kirk Santan by Daniel Gelling.

Santan, November 11, 1763. Received about eleven o'clock in the forenoon and forwarded with all possible expedition to the reverend vicar of Marown, Paul Crebbin. Of *The Christian Monitor*, received two, and think that twenty-four more may be well dispensed within this parish.

Received 12th and forwarded the 14th to the reverend the vicar of Braddan. Of *The Christian Monitor* I have received twenty-four. John Christian.

Received the fourteenth and returned to the episcopal registrar by Joseph Cosnahan. Of *The Christian Monitors* I have received four dozen and of the exposition of the church catechism six books; shall yet have occasion for about twenty of the former and about fifty or sixty of the latter, and if after distribution as directed there be a surplus, they shall be carefully returned, with the names of the several persons to whom distributed.

[159][479] *Catalogue of the books belonging to the parochial library of Kirk German, 1763*[480]

Book of Homilies.
Allen's *Practical discourse on faith.*[481]
Craddock's *Knowledge and practice.*[482]
Bishop Hopkins' *Works.*[483]
Bray's *Catechetical lectures.*[484]
Nelson's *Feasts and fasts.*[485]
Parsons' *Christian directory.*[486]
Harmony between the psalms and other parts of Scripture.[487]
Abstract of the historical part of the Old Testament.[488]
Fox on the New Testament.[489]
Blair's *Sermons.* 5 volumes.[490]
Sherlock's *Discourses preached at the Temple.*[491]
Brett's *Independency of the church upon the state.*[492]
Sherlock's *Practical Christian.*[493]
The practical believer.[494]
Herbert's *Priest to the temple.*[495]
Account of the Society for Reformation of Manners.[496]
Bragge on the Parables, vol. 2.[497]

The above is a true catalogue of all the books delivered by the Reverend Mr vicar-general Radcliffe as the parochial library of Kirk German to me, Henry Corlett, vicar.

[479]P. 158 is a covering note as on p. 22.
[480]Books already mentioned (mainly in the 1725 list) are given their accession date only.
[481]Received in 1704.
[482]Received in 1705.
[483]Received in 1705.
[484]Received in 1705.
[485]Received in 1707.
[486]Robert Parsons (1546-1610) was an English Jesuit who wrote this in 1583. It was abridged by George Stanhope and published at London in 1703. How it got to German is unknown.
[487]One of the books of Edward Harley, received in 1736.
[488]The other book by Edward Harley, received in 1736.
[489]Francis Fox, *The New Testament explained* (London, 1722).
[490]Received in 1725.
[491]Properly *Discourses concerning the notes of the church* (London, 1687). How it got to German is unknown.
[492]Thomas Brett published this at London in 1717, at the height of the convocation dispute.
[493]Given in 1714.
[494]Given in 1699.
[495]Given in 1704.
[496]Given in 1703.
[497]Francis Bragge, *Practical discourses upon the parables of our blessed Saviour* (London, 1694).

The appointment of committees to revise the translation of the Prayer Book

[161][498] Resolved that the reverend Mr archdeacon, the reverend vicar-general Curghey, the Reverend Mr Wilks, the Reverend Mr Crebbin of Jurby and Mr Gill of Lezayre be appointed as a committee on the north side to revise and correct some of the portions of the liturgy translated into the Manx tongue in order to be printed.

Resolved also that the reverend vicar-general Radcliffe, the Reverend Mr Crebbin of Santan, the Reverend Mr Christian of Rushen, the Reverend Mr Christian of Marown and the Reverend Mr Moore of Douglas be appointed as a committee on the south side to revise and correct the remainder of the said portions.

Resolved likewise that said committees do meet once in each fortnight to proceed with this work, and that whenever any portion is under revisal, that the translator of such portion have notice to attend, and that the committee for the north division do meet at Ballaugh on Monday the 11th July next and that the committee for the south division do meet at Douglas on Monday the 27th June next for the first time, and that each committee at each meeting do make and subscribe and rule in writing, signifying the time and place of their next meeting.

Order for commemorating the death of the duke of Atholl, 1 February 1764

[175][499] To the reverend the rector of Ballaugh, the vicar of Jurby, the rectors of Kirk Andreas and Kirk Bride, the vicar of Lezayre, the chaplain of Ramsey, the vicars of Maughold, Lonan and Onchan, and the chaplain of Douglas.

Whereas it hath pleased the Almighty Ruler and Governor of the world in his wise providence to remove by death from all his earthly possessions, and among the rest, from the territories and dominions of this land of Man, our late liege lord his grace the duke of Atholl, whence, though we learn that there is no respect of persons with the supreme Lord and creator of all things, who takes away one and sets up another at his own good time and pleasure; yet, as the state of human nature necessarily requires subordination and difference of station, duties and obligations amongst fellow creatures of the same community, that loyalty and obedience which we owed the late prince and ruler of this isle whilst he lived, may remind us of our obligation also to pay some marks and tokens of grateful sentiment and honourable remembrance to him, now dead, and especially us of the clergy, who many of us stood doubly related to his grace as our lord and patron.

This comes therefore to order and require it of my reverend brethren the clergy of this diocese to take the first opportunity for publicly notifying to their respective congregations, that authentic intelligence is lately received of the death of the lord of this isle, the late duke of Atholl, and at the same time we recommend it to each and every of you to pay such regard to his grace's memory as to your judgment and consideration shall seem meet and due to the honour of that noble house.

Given at Bishopscourt, February 1, 1764. Mark Sodor and Man.

---

[498]P. 160 is blank.
[499]Out of chronological order.

[176] Ballaugh. February 6, 1764. Forwarded with all convenient speed to the vicar of Jurby, Matthias Curghey.

Jurby, February 6, 1764. Received and forwarded to the reverend the archdeacon, William Crebbin.

Andreas, February 7, 1764. Received at night 6th February and forwarded early the next morning 7th instant to Kirk Bride, William Mylrea.

Lezayre, 8th February. Received and forwarded forthwith to the chaplain of Ramsey. John Gill.

Ramsey 8th February 1764. Received at night and forwarded the next morning to the vicar of Kirk Maughold. John Crellin.

Kirk Maughold, February 9th, 1764. Received at seven o'clock in the evening and forwarded early next morning to the vicar of Kirk Lonan. Thomas William Joseph Woods.

Kirk Lonan. February 10th 1764. Received at twelve o'clock and forthwith forwarded to the vicar of Onchan. Samuel Gell.

Kirk Onchan, February 10th 1764. Received about half an hour before three in the afternoon and forthwith forwarded to the Reverend Mr Moore of Douglas. Thomas Quayle.

Received at noon February 11, Saturday. Douglas. Philip Moore.

Monday 12 March 1764

The loyal address to the duke and duchess of Atholl

[167][500] To their excellencies the most noble prince the duke of Atholl and Charlotte, duchess of Atholl, baroness Strange, etc, lady of the Isle of Man and the islands thereunto belonging. The humble address of the bishop and clergy of the diocese of Sodor and Man.

May it please your excellencies! We the bishop, archdeacon, vicars-general with the rest of the clergy of this diocese assembled, beg leave [by] the hands of our honourable and deservedly esteemed government to present this our address of condolence on the demise of our late liege lord the most noble James, duke of Atholl, your excellencies' predecessor, whose memory we have the justest reason to venerate and recognize with sentiments of unfeigned gratitude and regard, not only for his attention to the good government of this isle and the many salutary laws [had] and obtained during his rule over us, but also on account of his grace's having been, to many of us, our immediate patron and benefactor.

We at the same time take this opportunity to congratulate your excellencies on your accession to the honours and emoluments of the seignory, lordship and dominions of the Isle of Man and all other the isles and territories thereunto belonging, praying (as we especially by our godly function in duty bound) that your excellencies may [long] live to enjoy and provide for this government, over a loyal and obedient clergy and people, and that when it shall [please] the supreme Lord

---

[500]Out of chronological order.

and ruler of the universe to call [you] from the transitory glories of your high [station] upon earth, to partake of the more noble and permanent glories of another life, this ancient principality, with all [168] the hereditary dignities of your illustrious house, may successfully descend to your excellencies' latest posterity.

Done and subscribed in convocation at Kirk Michael in the Isle of Man this twelfth day of March 1764.

The arrival of the Manx gospels, 30 March 1764

[171][501] To the parochial clergy of this diocese.

My reverend brethren, This waits on you with great pleasure to signify my readiness to transmit to your hands a portion of the Manx gospels by such means as you shall contrive to convey them to you for the use of your parishioners so far as this first edition will extend.

I have likewise the satisfaction to acquaint you that our friends in England are still successfully exerting their endeavours for increasing the fund of contributions towards the expense of printing a larger and more correct edition of the holy oracles, and our excellent liturgy, when you shall be pleased to furnish them with matter for so truly Christian a work.

Whilst strangers and foreigners are thus zealously engaged in the service of this poor but very ancient church of Man, I have great confidence in my faithful clergy that they will not be wanting in their share of pains and study to promote the spiritual welfare of their respective charges, by helping to administer light to them that sit in darkness compared with what they will enjoy from an uniform translation of the Scriptures, of the New Testament [172] at least, and the public offices they are so ready to attend. I therefore do now once again find myself obliged in the name of our great Master, whose servants we are, to recommend it to you, my dear brethren, to take into consideration some method of proceeding with the liturgy already begun, and which our benefactors are so frequently inquiring after. Commending your willing labours in so pious and important an undertaking to the divine blessing and assistance, I remain, with my earnest prayers for the success of this, and whatever else may tend to the glory of God and the good of his church, reverend sirs, your affectionate friend and brother, Mark Sodor and Man.

N.B. It is earnestly requested of the clergy who have received the interleaved testaments that they will be so good as to insert freely their remarks on the blank pages as the best method that can be proposed for furnishing, from the whole, one correct edition, which will be much wanted, the number already printed being too small to answer the call for them.

[173] To all the officiating clergy in this isle. With respect to the form to be used, our new lieges' accession to their dominions, you'll be pleased to read: 'the lord,

---

[501]Out of chronological order.

the lady and government of this isle'. Given at Bishopscourt this thirtieth day of March, 1764. Mark Sodor and Man.

March 31st, 1764. Received and forwarded to the vicar of Jurby said day, Matthias Curghey.

March 31st, 1764. Received late in the evening and forwarded the day following, William Crebbin.

Received about five o'clock Sunday evening 1st April 1764 and forwarded about six the same evening to the curate of Kirk Bride. William Mylrea.

Received about seven o'clock Sunday evening 1st April 1764 and forwarded early the next morning to the vicar of Lezayre. Thomas Cubbon.

Received between seven and eight o'clock Monday evening 2nd April 764 and forwarded early the next morning. John Gill.

Received about one o'clock on Tuesday and forwarded on Wednesday morning to the vicar of Maughold by me, John Crellin. April 2nd, 1764.

[174][502] 1764, April 4th. Received this morning at nine o'clock and forwarded forthwith to the vicar of Kirk Lonan by Thomas William Joseph Woods.

April 5th 1764. Received last night and forwarded this morning at seven o'clock to the vicar of Onchan. Samuel Gell.

April 5th, 1764. Received this morning at ten o'clock and forwarded forthwith to the Reverend Mr Moore, chaplain of Douglas, by Thomas Quayle.

Came to hand April 5th and transmitted to the episcopal registrar the first opportunity by Philip Moore, Douglas.

The reply of the duke and duchess of Atholl, 11 April 1764.

[169][503] To the right reverend father in God Mark, lord bishop of Sodor and Man, the archdeacon, vicars-general and the rest of the clergy of the diocese.

My lord and gentlemen, The regard you express for the memory of the late duke of Atholl our worthy parent is highly obliging to us. We well know how much the good government and prosperity of the lordship and territories of Man was his study, and if in this and his other virtues we can follow his example, we shall reckon ourselves extremely fortunate.

It affords us the highest pleasure to observe that there is in the island at present a body of clergymen so respectable who by their example, as well as instruction, endeavour to promote piety, peace and true religion; your island, as far as history may be credited, early embraced Christianity, our warmest wishes are that it may still continue to flourish there as the solid basis of happiness to mankind. In these good purposes may you be useful instruments, and so far as our countenance or encouragement can contribute to your success, you may depend on both with the utmost alacrity, for however peculiar it may appear, yet to gentlemen of your learning and characters, and while we have so recent an instance of mortality under

---

[502]This page is also the cover, as p. 22.
[503]Out of chronological order.

our eye which naturally affects us with concern, we cannot help professing our sentiments to be that they who are the best members of society in this world are also best fitted for the next. Atholl, C. Atholl and Strange. Dunkeld, 11 April 1764.

The bishop's call for stricter church discipline

[179][504] To the reverend the parochial clergy of the isle and diocese of Man. Reverend brethren! It is a melancholy consideration in which I believe you will readily join with me to think what numbers of fellow Christians at almost every chapter court are presented for relapses into offences against the laws of that church of which they profess themselves members, and which they know, or ought to know, exclude such as are habitually guilty of them from the kingdom of heaven.

Give me leave therefore (not as thinking you particularly deficient in this duty but as we all stand in need more or less to be put in remembrance of it) to exhort you all for Christ's sake to exert your best endeavours to make the several delinquents that are now, or at any time, before you, sensible of the hazard they run of their precious and immortal souls, by the repetition of or continuance in a sin, so beneath the dignity of the human species, and so expressly contrary to the laws of the gospel institution, and to set forth to them and the rest of your hearers the heinous aggravation of giving a look to those appetites, common to brute creatures which Christians are allowed to gratify in the honourable estate of marriage.

It would, I think, be very profitable and instructive for your flocks if you would set yourselves to the frequent expounding the fifth chapter and the nine first verses of the six[th] to the Ephesians, and likewise the fifth chapter of the first epistle to the Corinthians, which, it is to be feared, not many of the Manx people are well acquainted with, for want of a new testament at hand in the mother tongue, and the very small chance they have of hearing them read publicly, by appointment in the course of the calendar. If an exact calculation was to be made how often or how seldom it falls to a Manx Christian's lot (who has little or no English) to receive a detail of the relative duties set forth in the two chapters above referred to, it could not fail to produce a serious and awakening reflection on the mind of any truly pious and compassionate pastor, whereby it would undoubtedly appear to him how desirable a blessing it would be to this church [180] to have a studied version of the epistles as well as gospels in the hands of the people, a Protestant people of the established Church of England, who being well disposed, would bid fair for becoming more than nominal Christians, from a frequent perusal of their duty so minutely and clearly specified in the writings of the apostles, which as we have no law that prohibits the use of them, renders their case, who have them not, the more grievous and lamentable. For although in the epistles there are confessedly some things hard and consequently not equally necessary to be understood by every reader, yet are there many more plain rules of Christian life and manners, as well as numerous texts, pointing out expressly the doctrine of salvation through the death and sacrifice of Christ, obvious enough to the lowest capacities of those who are able to read, if they had them but to read.

---

[504]Out of chronological order.

I earnestly pray God, who is the giver of all good gifts, to inspire every minister of his Word in this diocese with a feeling sense of the importance and necessity of the undertaking proposed, of furnishing the church of Man (the only church in the Christian world destitute of them) with the divine oracles in the vulgar tongue, a work which many worthy Christians abroad are cheerfully promoting by their liberal contributions.

Once more commending you to the influences of divine grace, and wishing you success in all your pastoral labours, I am, my reverend brethren, your faithful and affectionate fellow servant in Christ, Mark Sodor and Man. Bishopscourt, April 18, 1764.

N.B. Each of the clergy's remarks on the gospels and Acts of the Apostles lately printed are greatly wanted and earnestly desired in order for furnishing a new and larger impression.

[181] April 21st, 1764. Received at six o'clock in the evening and transmitted forthwith to the vicar of Jurby. Matthias Curghey, rector of Ballaugh.

April 21st, 1764. Received at seven o'clock in the evening and forwarded next day to the reverend the archdeacon. William Crebbin.

Received 23rd April at eight o'clock in the morning and about one in the afternoon forwarded to the reverend the rector of Kirk Bride. William Mylrea.

Received in the afternoon April 23 and transmitted to the vicar of Lezayre next morning by Philip Moore.

April 24th 1764. Received about eight o'clock in the morning and forwarded about three in the afternoon to the curate of Ramsey. John Gill.

Received in the afternoon of April 24th and forwarded about four the said afternoon to the vicar of Kirk Maughold. John Crellin.

Received April 24th in the evening and forwarded next morning to the vicar of Kirk Lonan by Thomas William Joseph Woods.

April 25th 1764. Received this evening and transmitted to the vicar of Kirk Onchan next morning by Samuel Gell.

April 26th 1764. Received in the evening and forwarded next morning to the reverend the chaplain of Douglas by Thomas Quayle.

April 27th 1764. Received in the afternoon and forwarded next morning to the reverend the vicar of Marown. Joseph Cosnahan.

Left at my house on Saturday 28th of April where it remained ever since, owing to my family's neglect in never acquainting me with the receipt of it. Forwarded this 2nd of May 1764 to the reverend the vicar of Santan by me, John Christian.

[182][505] May 2nd 1764. Received about six o'clock in the evening and forwarded next morning to the reverend the vicar of Malew by Charles Crebbin.

May 3, 1764. Received about ten o'clock in the forenoon and forwarded before eleven to the reverend the vicar of Arbory by Daniel Gelling.

May 3rd, 1764. Received about eleven and forwarded to the vicar of Rushen about... John Moore.

[505]This page is also the cover, as p. 22.

May 4, 1764. Received last evening and transmitted this morning to Mr vicar-general Radcliffe. Nicholas Christian.

May 5th. Received and transmitted to the vicar of German, the 7th. Robert Radcliffe.

May 9, 1764. Received about twelve o'clock and transmitted to the episcopal registrar by the reverend the rector of Kirk Bride, about five o'clock same evening. Henry Corlett.

Thursday 14 June 1764

[163][506] Clergy present.

William Mylrea.
Robert Radcliffe.
Matthias Curghey.
Philip Moore.
Thomas Castley.
Paul Crebbin.[507]
James Wilks.
Nicholas Christian.
John Moore.
John Gill.
William Crebbin.

Thomas Woods.
Joseph Cosnahan.
Samuel Gell.
John Christian.
Thomas Quayle.
Daniel Gelling.
Henry Corlett.
John Crellin.
Thomas Cubbon, deacon.
Charles Crebbin, deacon.

[164] At this convocation, his lordship signified his intention of ordaining the reverend Thomas Cubbon and the reverend John Crellin deacons into the sacred order of priesthood, and Mr Ewan Looney and Mr Charles Corlett into the order of deacons[508] the next ember season, and desired to know whether any of the clergy had any objection to said ordinations.

His lordship also most warmly commended to his clergy their due attention to and prosecution of that necessary work of translating the remainder of the New Testament into the vulgar tongue.

His lordship likewise directed that their graces the duke and duchess of Atholl's pious and affectionate answer to the bishop and clergy's address on their accession to the government of this isle be publicly read, which being done, it was resolved that the same be recorded.

Resolved also that the sum of one pound twelve shillings appropriated for the better support of the petty schoolmaster of Kirk Patrick out of the right honourable Lady Hastings' bounty for the year ending at Easter 1756, and the sum of three pounds four shillings to the petty schoolmaster of the parish of Jurby for the years 1762 and 1763 out of said charity be disposed of and distributed to such masters as have most faithfully discharged their duty (no certificates having been produced by

---

[506]P. 162 is blank.
[507]Indisposed and unable to attend.
[508]Neither of these seems to have served in the diocese.

any person performing the duty of schoolmaster in said parishes for said several years) according to the tenor and purport of her said ladyship's last will and testament.

Funds in the bishop's hands.

[165] Public monies for which the bishop looks on himself to be accountable, so soon as they are received by his agents and friends in London.

1. Royal bounty. Usually paid to James Heywood esquire. Of this there are now generally two quarters behind at the treasury.

2. Lady Hastings. Per William Young, schoolmaster at Yorkshire or his agent, Richard Lucas, merchant of Leeds.

3. Impropriations. Per John Blundel of Liverpool, esquire.

4. Corporation of Widows annuities. Per James Heywood, esquire.

5. Thompson's charity. Per Edward Woodcock, esq. or Mr Richard Townsend, Strand.

At an annual convocation holden at Bishopscourt, June 14, 1764, upon examining my lord bishop's accounts of receipts and payments of the royal bounty and Lady Hastings' charity down to Easter 1763, it appears that the whole has been paid off by his lordship except the sum of 3/4/0 of Lady Hastings' charity to the petty school of Jurby for the years 1762 and 1763 and the sum of 1/12/0 to Kirk Patrick for the year ending at Easter 1756, which have not been paid in regard no certificate has been produced of the schools being diligently kept, and therefore it is resolved that his lordship do dispose of said sum of 3/4/0 and 1/12/0 according to her ladyship's last will and testament.

Thursday 24 October 1765

[189][509] Clergy present:

William Mylrea.
Robert Radcliffe.[510]
Matthias Curghey.
Philip Moore.
Thomas Castley.
James Wilks.
Nicholas Christian.
John Moore.

Samuel Gell.
Joseph Cosnahan.
John Christian.
Thomas Quayle.
Daniel Gelling.
Henry Corlett.[511]
John Crellin.
Thomas Cubbon.

---

[509]P. 166 is blank. Pp. 167-9 are out of chronological order; see above. P. 170 is blank. Pp. 171-6 are out of chronological order; see above. P. 177 is blank and p. 178 is a cover, as p. 22. Pp. 179-82 are out of chronological order; see above. Pp. 183-8 are blank.

[510]The MS notes: 'Indisposed and desires to be excused.'

[511]The MS notes: 'His wife died yesterday.'

John Gill.[512]   Charles Crebbin.
William Crebbin.   Thomas Corlett.
Thomas Woods.   Robert Quayle.

[191][513] At this convocation the right reverend lord bishop recommended to his clergy diligently to revise the translation and impression lately made of the liturgy in the Manx tongue and to make their respective observations on such parts thereof as they upon due consideration think capable of amendment or alteration, and transmit the same to the episcopal registry in order that the next edition may be as complete and correct as possible. His lordship also enjoined his clergy to continue to pray for the government of this isle as usual until his lordship learns and signifies the form of words generally used for governors in his majesty's insular dominions of the like sort with this.

His lordship also signified his intention of having a parochial visitation throughout his diocese sometime the next spring or summer, when he will expect to find the several churches in good and decent repair, and require that a minute and particular account of the several charities and benefactions belonging to each parish be returned, specifying by whom and when given or left and to what uses, in whose hands and how secured, with the date of each deed of security for the same. And as to such charities and benefactions as are not limited to any particular parish, such as the royal bounty, Lady Hastings' charity which are in his lordship's hands and management, the fund for the support of the headmaster, the fund for support of clergymen's widows and orphans, and Mrs Halsall's charity, in the hands and management of others, his lordship appoints the reverend vicar-general Curghey, the reverend Mr archdeacon and the Reverend Mr Gill as a committee to inspect into the extent of security for said several funds and their application and to report the same within six months after date hereof, in order that said report may be recorded for the satisfaction of all concerned, and to the end the said committee may proceed according to the trust reposed into them, they are to fix time and place for the purposes aforesaid and are hereby vested with power to call upon and for such person [192] and papers as they shall judge necessary on the occasion.

His lordship likewise desired to know the opinion of this assembly whether it be expedient for them to address his majesty on the great change of affairs in this isle. It was resolved in the affirmative and that an address be drawn up accordingly, a copy whereof is hereunto annexed.

Resolved also that an address of thanks be drawn up and sent to the Society for Promoting Christian Knowledge for their zealous pains and interest exerted in behalf of this diocese in procuring an impression of the gospels and Acts of the Apostles as also of the Common Prayer Book in the Manx tongue for the benefit of the poor inhabitants of this isle.

His lordship also proposed that a new edition of the Common Prayer Book with a collection of the singing psalms be printed as soon as convenient in the Manx

[512]Indisposed, and by letter desires to be excused.
[513]P. 190 is blank.

tongue, and likewise the history of Joseph and his brethren, with the form of prayer generally made use of within this isle during the herring fishing season.

His lordship likewise directed (in order to prevent any failure or neglect of duty in the schoolmistress on the foundation of Mrs Halsall's charity in Castletown) that she be annually obliged to produce to the ordinary, the vicar's of the parish certificate of his care and assiduity, before she be entitled to receive the salary appropriated to that school.

His lordship in like manner directed that the several rector, vicars, chaplains and curates of this diocese for the future be called over and answer to their names at every chapter court or court of correction in their respective districts.

[193] His lordship signified to his clergy that he purposes (God willing) to ordain Mr James Oates, academic student, deacon next ember season, in order to assist the reverend Mr Christian vicar of Kirk Marown in the duties of his parish.

His lordship also directed the several parochial ministers to give their respective schoolmasters notice to attend at Kirk Michael on Friday the first of November next with certificates in the prescribed form, in order to their receiving their respective salaries, and

Finally directed the several clergy (as desired in the notice lately circulated) to signify what number of persons in their respective parishes are as yet unsupplied with Manx Common Prayer Books, which account is as underneath:

Lonan	36	German	36
Onchan	12	Michael	12
Douglas	36	Ballaugh	36
Braddan	24	Jurby	0
Marown	18	Andreas	0
Santan	20	Bride	12
Malew	60	Lezayre	24
Arbory	5	Ramsey	6
Rushen	12	Maughold	30
Patrick	· 0	TOTAL	379

The beforegoing orders to be circulated in usual manner and such parts thereof transcribed by the clergy as they shall judge necessary.

Thursday 22 May 1766

[197][514] Clergy present:

William Mylrea.	Samuel Gell.
Robert Radcliffe.	Joseph Cosnahan.
Matthias Curghey.	John Christian.
Philip Moore.	Thomas Quayle.
Thomas Castley.	Daniel Gelling.

[514]Pp. 194-6 are blank.

James Wilks, out of the isle.

Nicholas Christian.

John Moore.

John Gill.

William Crebbin.

Thomas Woods.

Henry Corlett.

John Crellin.

Thomas Cubbon.

Charles Crebbin.

Thomas Corlett.

Robert Quayle.

[199]515 At this convocation the right reverend the lord bishop most earnestly recommended to his clergy that they would, preferable to all things, attend to the completion of that part of the translation of the New Testament into the Manx language which yet remains untranslated, that the same be prepared for the press as speedily as possible, and that they, as soon as may be, afterwards deliver in their several remarks on the Manx liturgy.

His lordship also gives his clergy notice that for the future they are to pray for the governor of this isle in the prayer used before their sermon agreeable to the directions which his lordship has received from his grace the archbishop of York our metropolitan, on that head.

His lordship appoints Tuesday the tenth day of June next for meeting the trustees of the impropriate tithes at Balnyhown, and also appoints Thursday the nineteenth of the same month at Kirk Michael for the payment of the Lord Derby's money to the clergy, in case of the trustees' concurrence on their said meeting on the said tenth of June.

Resolved that the address of thanks which was resolved on by the clergy at the last convocation but hitherto deferred to be drawn up and sent to the Society for Promoting Christian Knowledge for their zealous pains and interest exerted in behalf of this diocese in procuring an impression of the gospels and Acts of the Apostles as also of the Common Prayer Book in the Manx tongue for the benefit of the poor inhabitants of this isle, be forthwith drawn up by the Reverend Philip Moore, rector of Kirk Bride and the Reverend John Gill, vicar of Lezayre in behalf of the clergy and forwarded to the said society through the hands of our right reverend lord bishop, whom they humbly request to forward the same to the said society.

Letter of thanks to the Society for Promoting Christian Knowledge

[201]516 To the honourable Society for Promoting Christian Knowledge.

We the archdeacon and clergy of the isle and diocese of Man having been favoured with the remarkable evidence of your tender and truly Christian regard for us and the people under our care and of your zealous assiduity in consequence thereof for the promoting their spiritual interest from the first moment our deplorable condition of being destitute of the sacred oracles in our native language was made known unto you by our right reverend and worthy diocesan the lord bishop of this isle, do

515P. 198 is blank.
516P. 200 is blank.

therefore beg leave to offer and lay before you our most grateful acknowledgment and sincere thanks for the several instances of your Christian zeal and labour of love, exemplified as well in your own generous contribution as in procuring so many other liberal subscriptions and contributions towards printing part of the Holy Scriptures for the sue of this diocese in its native language, and for your great expedition in having some time ago printed and transmitted unto us in the Manx tongue the four gospels, the Acts of the Apostles, the liturgy and *The Christian Monitor*, whereby we and the people committed to our charge have already experienced how mightily it would conduce towards the enlightening the minds and promoting the eternal welfare and happiness of the people of this isle to have the Holy Scriptures entire in their native language, could the same, by the blessing of God and the assistance of well-disposed Christians be in time accomplished.

We also beg leave to express our just sense of gratitude and joy for the kind and affectionate concern you feel for us and our people in the country parishes in your having in view and continuing your endeavours to extend the blessing still further, by your purpose to publish for the use of this diocese a complete edition of the New Testament or another impression of the liturgy with part of the singing psalms, the history of Joseph, the form of prayer used occasionally here in this isle at the season of the herring fishery, with some other small practical tracts, all which will be of the greatest utility to diffuse amongst our people a more general knowledge of divine [202] evangelical truths, and by the divine aid happily answer the well-intended views of the society, as well as the expectations of the generous subscribers to this great and good work, a work which, under the countenance and encouragement of the society, we have been greatly excited, on our parts as far as we are capable, to promote, by translating our several quotas of what has been already printed, and have now the comfort as well as pleasure to acquaint the society that the apostolic epistles are lately translated into the Manx language and will be ready for the press as soon as the society and our right reverend diocesan shall have taken measures for the same. In behalf of ourselves and the people of our respective charges we humbly request the society's acceptance of these our grateful sentiments and regard, in return for their generous benefaction and Christian zeal in encouraging this useful work, with our hearty prayers for the success of all their endeavours in the cause of God and his Christ, that the light of the Gospel may shine to the darkest regions of the earth, and the knowledge of redeeming love may be as extensive as the benevolent minds and intentions of the honourable society. Isle of Man, 22 May 1766.

William Mylrea.
Robert Radcliffe.
Matthias Curghey.
Thomas Castley.
Philip Moore.
Samuel Gell.
John Gill.
John Crellin.
John Christian.
John Moore.

Nicholas Christian.
Thomas Cubbon.
Joseph Cosnahan.
Henry Corlett.
Thomas Quayle.
William Crebbin.
Thomas William Joseph Woods.
[203] Thomas Corlett.
Robert Quayle.
Charles Crebbin.

The bishop's letter transmitting a paragraph of a letter he has received from Sir John Thorold, 5 May 1767

[207][517] To the reverend the archdeacon, vicars-general and the rest of the clergy of the isle and diocese of Man.

My reverend brethren! I herewith take leave to transmit to you a paragraph from our great and worthy benefactor Sir John Thorold's letter, whereby you will more and more perceive how zealous he is for the church of Man's being put on a level with other Christian countries, by having the whole sacred code in the hands of the people here. The Society for Promoting Christian Knowledge are so much of the same mind as to continue to solicit and receive large contributions towards the expense of printing, etc. as may appear by the papers that accompany this, without asking or expecting a single penny from the inhabitants of this isle.

I cannot therefore but think it my duty to refer it to your consideration whether you will not judge it expedient for you to join hand and heart in forwarding the work which is further desired of you, by our British friends, in such manner as the Manx language and the knowledge you have of it will admit.

My calling you together before my departure for England could have served no purpose but what may full as well be answered by my vicars-general, who will signify their inclination to give you a meeting in order for your agreeing together what portions each of you shall be disposed to engage in. I have already at sundry times said so much to you of the importance of an undertaking for furnishing your flocks with the divine oracles, that I conceive it unnecessary to add further solicitation to urge you to proceed in it.

Commending each and every of you to the divine blessing and guidance in this and all your labours for the glory of God and the good of his church here planted in this land, I remain, gentlemen, your affectionate brother and fellow servant in Christ, Mark Sodor and Man. Bishopscourt, May 5, 1767.

[208] Extract of a paragraph in a letter from Sir John Thorold, received 14 February 1767. After observing what he had heard of great numbers departing from the island, he proceeds as follows:

Those discouragements notwithstanding, it is hoped that the work of translating the Bible into the Manx language will be going forward without intermission. The cause is the cause of God, who will most certainly reward those who in different kinds of work labour in his vineyard. We are every moment hastening towards another world, into the happy part of which they must not enter who during the days of their sojourning in the present world, strive not to promote its welfare. O, that the gates of the celestial mansions, through the merits and mediation of our Melchizedek, King of Salem, may be open for our admission when our spirits shall be delivered from their earthly prisons and from this thick, dusky atmosphere.

---

[517]Pp. 204-6 are blank.

[209] Gentlemen, You see by the enclosed the great desire of our right reverend diocesan of having the Holy Bible translated into our mother tongue, and the great encouragement there is given for so laudable an undertaking. You are therefore desired to give us the meeting at Peeltown on Thursday the 21st instant, by ten o'clock in the forenoon, that we may consult and agree upon such measures as will be effectually conducive towards carrying on so great and good a work. We are, gentlemen, with all due respect, your faithful and affectionate brethren, Robert Radcliffe. Matthias Curghey. May 6, 1767.

To the reverend the rector of Ballaugh, the vicar of Jurby, the rectors of Andreas and Bride, the curate of Bride, the vicar of Lezayre, the chaplain of Ramsey, the vicars of Maughold, Lonan and Onchan, the chaplain of Douglas, the vicar of Braddan and his curate, the vicar of Marown and his curate, the vicars of Santan, Malew, Arbory, Rushen, Patrick, German and Michael, each of whom is desired to note on the back hereof the time the same is received and transmitted.

[210] Ballaugh. May 9, 1767. Received and transmitted to the vicar of Jurby at six o'clock this morning. Matthias Curghey.

May 9, 1767. Received and transmitted to the reverend the archdeacon at eight of the clock in the forenoon. William Crebbin.

Kirk Andreas, 9 May 1767. Received about half past twelve and transmitted about one to the vicar of Lezayre. William Mylrea.

Lezayre, 9 May 1767. Received about half past four and delivered about five in the evening to the curate of Kirk Bride. John Gill.

May the 9th 1767. Received and transmitted about half past five to the chaplain of Ramsey. Thomas Corlett.

Ramsey, May 9th. Received on Saturday night and transmitted on Sunday morning to the vicar of Maughold. John Crellin.

Kirk Maughold, May 10, 1767. Received at ten in the morning and forwarded to the vicar of Kirk Lonan in the evening. Thomas William Joseph Woods.

Kirk Lonan, May 10th. Received at night and transmitted next morning to the vicar of Onchan. Samuel Gell.

Kirk Onchan. May 11th. Received and transmitted to the chaplain of Douglas about five o'clock this evening. Thomas Quayle.

[211] Douglas, May 11, 1767. Received this evening and forwarded to Kirk Braddan next morning by me, Philip Moore.

Kirk Braddan, May 12, 1767. Received this morning and forwarded to Marown about eleven o'clock in the forenoon by me, Robert Quayle.

Marown, May 12th 1767. Received and forwarded to the Reverend Mr Cubbon, vicar of Santan. John Christian.

Kirk Santan. May 13, 1767. Received late in the evening and forwarded next morning to the vicar of Malew by me, Thomas Cubbon.

Kirk Malew, May 15th 1767. Received yesterday evening and forwarded this morning by me. Daniel Gelling.

Kirk Arbory. May 15, 1767. Received this morning and forwarded to the vicar of Rushen in the evening. John Moore.

Rushen, May 17, 1767. Received late last evening and forwarded immediately after morning service this day. Nicholas Christian.

Thursday 21 May 1767

The Manx Old Testament

[217][518] At a meeting of the clergy of the diocese of Man at Peeltown on Thursday the 21 May 1767. Resolved that so much of the Old Testament as is hereafter mentioned be by them translated into the Manx tongue, agreeable to the request of our right reverend ordinary, as following:

The book of :

Genesis:	archdeacon and vicar-general Radcliffe.
Exodus:	Henry Corlett.
Leviticus:	Mr Christian of Rushen.
Numbers:	Mr Crebbin of Jurby.
Deuteronomy:	Mr Moore of Arbory.
Joshua:	Mr Wilks of Michael.
Judges/Ruth:	Mr Quayle of Braddan, curate.
1 Samuel:	Mr Gell of Lonan.
2 Samuel:	Mr Cosnahan of Braddan, vicar.
1 Kings:	Mr Quayle of Onchan.
2 Kings:	Mr Christian of Marown.
1 Chronicles:	Mr Gelling of Malew.
2 Chronicles:	Mr Gill of Lezayre.
Ezra/Nehemiah:	Mr Cubbon of Santan.
Esther:	Mr Crellin of Ramsey.
Job:	Mr Corlett of Bride.
Proverbs:	Mr Woods of Maughold.
Ecclesiastes:	Mr Crebbin of Douglas, curate.
Song of Solomon:	Mr Clucas of Marown, curate.

The convocation records do not give any of the other translators of the Manx Bible. Those known are listed in the preface to Bible chasherick yn lucht thie. The Manx family Bible *(Onchan, 1979) and are as follows:*

Ezekiel:	*Nicholas Christian of Rushen.*
Daniel:	*Philip Moore of Kirk Bride.*
Minor Prophets:	*William Fitzsimmons, minister of episcopal chapel, Edinburgh.*[519]

---

[518]Pp. 214-16 are blank.
[519]Minister of Ayr Qualified Chapel (1771-6) and of Cowgate Qualified Chapel, Edinburgh (1776-99), where he was senior incumbent from 1795. In 1799 he was arrested and imprisoned on a charge of having helped four French prisoners escape from Edinburgh Castle.

1 Corinthians:	*William Mylrea of Kirk Andreas.*
2 Corinthians:	*Nicholas Christian of Rushen.*
1-2 Thessalonians:	*Daniel Gelling of Malew.*
Titus, Philemon:	*Samuel Gell of Lonan.*
1,2 Peter:	*Joseph Cosnahan of Kirk Braddan.*
1-3 John:	*Thomas Quayle of Onchan.*
Revelation 7-12:	*John Crellin of Ballure.*
Revelation 13-22:	*Henry Corlett of Kirk German.*

The other translators are unknown. The Gospel of Matthew appeared as early as 1748, to be followed by the four gospels and Acts in 1763 and the complete New Testament in 1767, which was reprinted in 1810, 1815 and 1825. The Old Testament appeared in 1773 and the complete Bible in 1775. It was reprinted in 1819 and again in 1979.

Thursday 26 November 1767

[223][520] Clergy present:

William Mylrea.	Samuel Gell.
Robert Radcliffe.	Joseph Cosnahan.
Matthias Curghey.	John Christian.
Philip Moore.[521]	Thomas Quayle.
Thomas Castley.	Daniel Gelling.
James Wilks.	Henry Corlett.
Nicholas Christian.	John Crellin.
John Moore.	Thomas Cubbon.
John Gill.	Charles Crebbin.[522]
William Crebbin.	Thomas Corlett.[523]
Thomas Woods.	William Clucas.

Accounts of the clergy widows' fund

[227][524] Fund for support of clergymen's widows. Account of receipts and disbursements from Easter 1753 to Easter 1766, by vicar-general Radcliffe, one of the stewards of that fund.

[228] The reverend Robert Radcliffe, vicar-general, one of the stewards for the management of the fund for support of clergymen's widows, etc. to the said fund, July 25th 1753.

To cash received from the late lord bishop, British 24/7/9; (Manx: 28/11/4½).

---

[520]Pp. 218-22 are blank.
[521]By letter to lord bishop, desires to be excused.
[522]Absent by permission.
[523]Absent by permission.
[524]Pp. 224-6 are blank.

Received also from his lordship a deed of mortgage bearing date October 3, 1749 on the lands of Captain Kaighin of Kirk Michael, for the principal sum of thirty pounds Manx, as also a bond of John Hughes, dated 6 June 1752 for the sum of forty-two pounds British, both which sums are part of the capital of this fund. N.B. Hughes' bond did not bear interest.

1754

To the profits of 300 pounds in the fund in England at 4/10/0 per annum. 13/10/0 British, is Manx 15/15/0.
    To the profits of Kaighin mortgage for three years ending Michaelmas 1751, 1752 and 1753 at 1/10/0 per annum. 4/10/0.
    Total: 48/16/4½.

1755

1.To contrabalance. 34/16/4½.
2.To the interest of the fund from England as Manx: 15/15/0.
3. To the interest of Kaighin's mortgage for the year ending Michaelmas 1754: 1/10/0.
4. Total: 52/1/4½.

1756

1. 33/1/4½   2. 15/3/4.   3. 1/10/0.   4. 52/13/6.
To the interest of 42 pounds British which had been in the hands of John Hughes and now sent the clergy from 30 July 1754 to 30 July 1755 at six percent per annum 2/10/4½ (Manx: 2/18/9½).

1757

1. 36/13/6.   2. 19/12/1½.   4. 56/5/7½.

1758

1. 40/5/7½.   2. 14/0/0.[525]   3. 4/8/9½.   4. 58/14/5.

[229] Contra.

1753-4

By cash paid to Mrs Gell, being an arrear paid to her ending Easter 1753: 2/0/0.
By cash paid to widows: Mrs Gell, Mrs Woods, Mrs Cosnahan. 4/0/0 each.
Subtotal: 14/0/0.

---

[525]A note says: 'reduced to 12/0/0 British'.

Balance: 34/16/4½.
Total: 48/16/4½.

1755

Cash to above three widows:	12/0/0.
To Mrs Gell, three quarters to Christmas 1755:	3/0/0.
Cash to Mrs Christian:	4/0/0.
Subtotal:	19/0/0.
Balance:	33/1/4½.
Total:	52/1/4½.

1756

Cash to Mrs Woods, Cosnahan, Allen, Christian:	16/0/0.
Balance:	36/13/6.
Total:	52/13/6.

1757

Cash to above widows:	16/0/0.
Balance:	42/14/5.
Total:	58/14/5.

[230] Receipts.

1759

1. 42/14/5.   2. 14/0/0.   4. 61/17/10¾.
Hughes interest to 30 July 1758. British 2/10/4½; (Manx 2/18/9½).
Further 3 months to 30 October 1758. 0/14/8¼.

    N.B. This forty-two pounds (Hughes) laid out in the hands of Samuel Nicholson of Peeltown in mortgage bearing date November 1, 1758 at five per cent and the interest thereof brought to next year's account.

1760

1. 45/17/10¾.   2. 14/0/0.   4. 63/16/10¾.
Nicholson, due 1 November 1759: 2/9/0.

1761

1. 39/16/10¾.   2. 17/19/0.   4. 57/15/10¾.

1762

1. 36/15/10¾   2. 17/19/0.   4. 54/15/10¾.

[231] Contra

1759

Paid to widows Woods, Cosnahan, Allen, Christian:	16/0/0.
Balance:	45/17/10¾.
Total.	61/17/10¾.

1760

Cash for above widows:	16/0/0.
Ditto for Mrs Quayle:	4/0/0.
Ditto for Mrs Curghey:	4/0/0.
Balance:	39/16/10¾.
Total:	63/16/10¾.

1761

Paid to five widows:	20/0/0.
Ditto to Mrs Christian, now Mrs Cosnahan, for one quarter ending Midsummer 1760, she having then remarried:	1/0/0.
Subtotal:	21/0/0.
Balance:	36/15/10¾.
Total:	57/15/10¾.

1762

Paid to six widows (plus Mrs Brew):	24/0/0.
Balance:	30/14/10¾.
Total:	54/14/10¾.

[232] Receipts

1763

1. 30.14/10¾.   2. 17/19/0.   4. 48/13/10¾.

1764

1. 22/13/10¾.   2. 17/19/0.   4. 40/12/10¾.

1765

1. 16/12/10¾.   2. 17/19/0.   4. 34/11/10¾.

1766

1. 10/11/10¾.   2. 17/19/0.   4. 28/10/10¾.

1767

1. 0/10/10¾.   2. 14/0/0.   4. 18/9/10¾.
Kaighin's mortgage to Michaelmas 1766: 1/10/0.
Nicholson's to November 1766: 2/9/0.

[233] Contra.

1763

Six widows :	24/0/0.
Cash paid to Mr Thomas Corlett on account of an arrear	
due to Mrs Parr, not settled till this year:	2/0/0.
Subtotal:	26/0/0.
Balance:	22/13/10¾.
Total:	48/13/10¾.

1764

Six widows:	24/0/0.
Balance:	16/12/10¾.
Total:	40/12/10¾.

1765

Six widows:	24/0/0.
Balance:	10/11/10¾.
Total:	34/11/10¾.

1766

Six widows, also Mrs Crebbin, she having commenced	
at Easter 1765:	28/0/0.
Balance:	0/10/10¾.
Total:	28/10.10¾.

[234] Arrears due to the several widows hereunder mentioned and yet unpaid though entered in the written account, viz.

To Mrs Christian, now Cosnahan, for the year ending Easter 1760:	4/0/0
Ditto to Michaelmas 1760:	1/0/0
Mrs Woods, one quarter ending Easter 1760:	1/0/0
Mrs Allen, 2 quarters ending ditto:	2/0/0

Mrs Curghey, one quarter ending Easter 1765:	1/0/0
Ditto one year ending Easter 1766:	4/0/0
Total owing at Easter 1766:	13/0/0

I do hereby acknowledge the above mentioned several sums to be due to the said several widows and do hereby promise to be accountable to them for the same. Witness my hand this 26 November 1767. Robert Radcliffe.

Witnesses present: John Gill; Joseph Cosnahan.

We whose names are subscribed, being appointed by order of the right reverend lord bishop to examine and report the before written account of the fund for support of clergymen's widows, having accordingly examined the same and the several vouchers offered in support thereof, do find the same to the best of our judgment to be just and regular, the above arrears of thirteen pounds being yet due to the several widows above mentioned, which said sum when paid and discharged will close the account to and for the year ending at Easter 1766, and this we give for our report in the premises, errors and omissions excepted. As witness our hands this 26 November 1767. William Mylrea, Matthias Curghey, John Gill.

At a convocation holden at Bishopscourt, November 26, 1767, the above report returned by the gentlemen whose names are subscribed to lord bishop. James Wilks, episcopal registrar.

Lawsuit for the fish tithes

[237][526] Whereas the Reverend Henry Corlett and James Parr, lessees of the lord bishop's fish tithes in the parish of Kirk German, some time ago prosecuted sundry boat masters in the said parish and town of Peel for withholding the legal tithe of herring by them and their boat crews respectively caught or killed, and obtained an order against them in the ecclesiastical court for the payment of full and legal tithe, bearing date 27 February 1767, from which said order they preferred their appeal to his excellency the governor and chancellor of this isle, who, on hearing the said appeal, affirmed the order aforesaid by decree bearing date 3 July 1767.

And whereas the said boat masters in contradiction to and subversion of the statute law of this land, are endeavouring to set up a new and unheard of custom of allotting only half a man's share as tithe, which in some cases will so far diminish and lessen the legal tithe as to reduce the same to the thirty-seventh fish, and in order to establish the said pretended custom have preferred their further appeal to his majesty in council and raised contributions of many of the fishermen in most of the parishes of this isle, and as it is apprehended that the several parochial clergy may be affected in their rights of fish tithes by the event of this suit, unless properly defended,

We therefore, the rectors and vicars of thirds, as also the vicars of pension, whose names are subscribed, do hereby request our right reverend ordinary that a proper defence be made herein, and do promise and oblige ourselves to contribute

---

[526]Pp. 235-6 are blank.

towards the expense of said suit in such proportion as the respective thirds of tithes belonging to us the rectors and vicars of thirds do bear to the whole tithes in the hands of the said lord bishop and of us the said rectors and vicars of thirds, and that the vicars of pension shall contribute in proportion to one half what shall be contributed by the vicars of thirds, his lordship and all concerned having now agreed, that in case any of us shall [238] be under a necessity to prosecute and defend the like rights in any of our respective parishes, that they will contribute towards such future suit, provided such suit be approved of to be good five of the senior clergy or a majority of them (the vicars-general always excepted).

William Mylrea.	Thomas William Joseph Woods.
James Wilks.	Philip Moore.
John Moore.	John Gill.
John Christian.	Nicholas Christian.
Thomas Quayle.	Joseph Cosnahan.
Thomas Cubbon.	William Crebbin.
Samuel Gell.	Daniel Gelling.

Modification to the grant made under the terms of the clergy widows' fund

[241][527] Resolved that whereas by a deed bearing date the 19th March 1744 for the settlement of a fund towards the support of the distressed widows and orphans of the clergy of this diocese, it is provided that the widows of all instituted clergymen within this diocese of Sodor and Man should receive yearly at two payments out of the charity in said deed mentioned the sum of four pounds British towards their maintenance during the time of their widowhood, and residence within this diocese, and it appearing by a resolution of convocation bearing date 4 June 1750 that the profits of said fund did not amount to the payment of four pounds British to each widow, and that it was then resolved they should for the future be paid at the rate of four pounds Manx per annum, till otherwise ordered, and the reverend vicar-general Radcliffe, one of the stewards and manager of said fund having this day returned an account of his management thereof for the time past to Easter 1766, and it appearing that the annual profits of said fund amounts only to the sum of seventeen pounds nineteen shillings which will not amount to the usual payment of four pounds per annum to each widow (who are now six in number) it is now resolved that the said widows shall receive only the sum of three pounds Manx for the year ending at Easter 1767 and so on yearly till otherwise ordered, and that the steward or manager of said fund shall annually at convocation return an account of the state of said fund. Mark Sodor and Man. November 26, 1767.

[242] William Mylrea.	John Christian.
Robert Radcliffe.	Joseph Cosnahan.
Matthias Curghey.	Thomas Quayle.
John Moore.	Daniel Gelling.

[527]Pp. 239-40 are blank.

Nicholas Christian.
James Wilks.
William Crebbin.

Henry Corlett.
Thomas Cubbon.
John Gill.

Thursday 21 April 1768

[245]⁵²⁸ Clergy present:

William Mylrea.
Robert Radcliffe.
Matthias Curghey.
Philip Moore.
Thomas Castley.
James Wilks.
Nicholas Christian.
John Moore.
John Gill.
William Crebbin.
Thomas Woods.
Samuel Gell.
Joseph Cosnahan.

John Christian.
Thomas Quayle.
Daniel Gelling.
Henry Corlett.
John Crellin.
Thomas Cubbon.
Charles Crebbin.
Robert Quayle.
Thomas Corlett.
William Clucas.
Ewan Christian.
William Fitzsimmons.

[246] At this convocation his lordship earnestly recommended to his clergy a steady perseverance in going through that great and useful work the translating into the mother [tongue] that portions of the Old Testament already undertaken by his clergy.

His lordship also recommended that as his excellency the governor of this isle should now be considered as his majesty's representative, so that particular regard and respect paid him in praying for him before sermon, which as to form his lordship leaves to the prudence and discretion of his clergy, until he learns in what manner the governors of others his majesty's islands abroad are prayed for.

That all the forms of certificates, etc., agreed upon and prescribed in convocation, be strictly attended to and observed.

That all the clergy of the country parochial churches do for the future, agreeable to our metropolitan's directions, make use of the Manx printed Common Prayer Book (whenever service is performed in Manx) and no other.

---

⁵²⁸Pp. 243-4 are blank.

Thursday 18 May 1769

[249]529 Clergy present:

William Mylrea.	John Christian.
Robert Radcliffe.530	Thomas Quayle.
James Wilks.	Daniel Gelling.
Matthias Curghey.	Henry Corlett.
Philip Moore.	John Crellin.
Thomas Castley.	Thomas Cubbon.
Nicholas Christian.	Charles Crebbin.
John Moore.	Thomas Corlett.
John Gill.531	William Clucas.
William Crebbin.	William Fitzsimmons.
Thomas Woods.	Ewan Christian.
Samuel Gell.	

[250] At this convocation our right reverend ordinary communicated and read a letter by his lordship lately received from the right honourable countess dowager Gower, signifying she had ordered the sum of five hundred pounds to be paid in towards carrying on and completing the great and useful work of printing the sacred Scriptures in the Manx tongue.

Resolved unanimously that the grateful thanks of this assembly be humbly given her ladyship for the great and noble benefaction, and that our right reverend ordinary would be pleased to communicate the same to her ladyship, in the name and behalf of this assembly.

And whereas the number of clergymen's widows within this diocese has increased so much that the fund appropriated for their support will not extend to the usual sum of 3/0/0 to each widow,

Resolved that the profits of said fund be distributed among said widows for the current and all succeeding years by the stewards thereof, share and share alike, until further order be made to the contrary.

His lordship signified to the clergy present that for the future he expected all testimonials, certificates, etc. requisite for ordination, institution, etc. be strictly agreeable to the laws and canons of the church, and that the same be presented in due time, and desired the clergy would inform future candidates for orders, etc. of the necessary requisites, or direct them to attend the episcopal registrar to that end.

His lordship also signified and ordered that the several schoolmasters be directed to procure the requisite forms of certificates to entitle them to their salaries, without which none would be paid unto them.

529Pp. 247-8 are blank.
530Indisposed and desires to be excused.
531Indisposed and prays to be excused.

He also earnestly recommended to his clergy a steady prosecution of the great work of finishing a translation of the Old Testament in the native tongue of the country.

He likewise signified his intention of admitting the Reverend Messrs William Clucas, Ewan Christian and William Fitzsimmons, deacons, into the sacred order of priesthood on Trinity Sunday next, and desired to know whether any of the clergy present had any objection against them or either of them. None offered.

The petition of Robert Radcliffe regarding the clergy widows' fund's accounts and the subsequent reply

[253][532] To the right reverend father in God Mark, by divine permission lord bishop of Sodor and Man.

The humble petition of Robert Radcliffe, one of the stewards of the fund for support of the widows and orphans of the clergy of this isle, showeth,

That your petitioner anno 1767 rendered an account of the several receipts and disbursements of this fund since it came into your petitioner's hands unto certain gentlemen of the clergy [constituted] as a committee to examine into and report unto your lordship of said fund, who reported the same accordingly, at which [time there] were several arrears due to and from him, which have since [been] called in and paid where due, as will appear by your petitioner's [accounts] and sufficient vouchers in support thereof, and whereas your petitioner is desirous that his foresaid accounts may pass and [be] approved of at next convocation,

Your petitioner humbly prays your lordship would be pleased either to examine foresaid accounts or otherwise appoint a committee of the clergy to examine and report such accounts, which are all closed to Easter 1769, so as that your petitioner may have his accounts passed and obtain a quietus so far, and as your petitioner is in an infirm state of health, that some other person may be appointed to undertake that business, and your petitioner shall ever pray, etc.

On consideration of this petition, we desire the clergy formerly appointed for the examination of all accounts touching public charities and benefactions belonging to this diocese, namely Mr archdeacon, Mr Curghey and Mr Gill, to examine the petitioner's accounts above mentioned and report the same unto us at our next convocation, to which end the petitioner is by himself or some other in his behalf to lay said accounts and all necessary vouchers before the committee in due time. Given at Bishopscourt, May 5th, 1769. Mark Sodor and Man.

[254] We whose names are subscribed being the committee appointed by our right reverend lord bishop to examine the accounts of the reverend Mr vicar-general Radcliffe as one of the stewards or managers of the fund for the support of the widows and orphans of the clergy of this isle, and to report the same to his lordship, having accordingly examined the said Mr vicar-general Radcliffe's accounts relative

[532]Pp. 251-2 are blank.

to the said fund, do find by the annexed receipts that he hath fully paid and discharged all the demands of the several clergymen's widows due at Easter last past, as also all that was due unto them for the several preceding years during which he was concerned as steward or manager of the said fund, and it also appears unto us, that after his having paid and discharged all their several demands to the aforesaid period, there remains a sum of seven shillings ten pence and three farthings belonging to the said fund undisposed of in his hands. This we return for our report in the premisses, as witness our hands this 18th day of May anno Domini 1769.

William Mylrea.
Matthias Curghey.
John Gill, vicar of Lezayre.

[255] An account of the said arrears due to the clergy widows of this isle as stated in vicar-general Radcliffe's account returned to record, as also of what has accrued due to Easter 1769, and likewise of the several payments made them and the balance now due, viz., to Easter 1769.

Due to Mrs Christian (now Cosnahan) for one year ending Easter 1760:	4/0/0
One quarter ending Midsummer 1760:	1/0/0
Total:	5/0/0
Due Mrs Woods. One quarter ending Easter 1766:	1/0/0
June 1, 1768, paid Mr Woods this balance:	1/0/0
Due Mrs Allen. Two quarters ending Easter 1766:	2/0/0
One year ending Easter 1767:	3/0/0
1768	3/0/0
1769	3/0/0
Total:	11/0/0
September 3, 1768, paid by your son George Allen:	2/0/0
Rests given her:	9/0/0
Due Mrs Curghey. One quarter ending Easter 1765:	1/0/0
1 year Easter 1766:	4/0/0
1767	3/0/0
1768	3/0/0
1769	3/0/0
Total:	14/0/0
February 8, 1768. Paid her by Reverend Mr Cosnahan:	4/0/0
January 24 1769. Paid her son Thomas Curghey:	4/0/0
March 10 1769. Paid her by Mr Henry Cosnahan:	4/18/0
Total:	12/18/0
Rests due her:	1/2/0

Due Mrs Cosnahan sr. One year ending Easter 1767:	3/0/0
1768	3/0/0
1769	3/0/0
Rests:	9/0/0
Due Mrs Quayle. One year ending Easter 1767:	3/0/0
1768	3/0/0
1769	3/0/0
Total:	9/0/0
January 16, 1768. Paid her by William Gargher:	3/0/0
April 3, 1769. Paid her by George Gargher:	3/0/0
Total:	6/0/0
Rests due her:	3/0/0
Due Mrs Brew in part for one year at Easter 1767:	1/5/6
1768	3/0/0
1769	3/0/0
Rests due:	7/5/6
Due Mrs Crebbin for one year at Easter 1767:	3/0/0
1768	3/0/0
1769	3/0/0
Total:	9/0/0
June 23, 1768. Paid by her son Rev. Charles Crebbin:	4/0/0
Rests due her:	5/0/0
Total due them:	39/7/6

[256] 1769, April 11. Received from vicar-general Radcliffe the sum of one pound five shillings and sixpence in full for my annuity as a clergyman's widow due at Easter 1767. Also the farther sum of three pounds in full of ditto, due at Easter 1768. Also the farther sum of three pounds in full of ditto due at Easter 1769, the whole amounting to seven pounds five shillings and sixpence and hereby do acquit him and the trustees of the fund for support of clergymen's widows to Easter last past. Witness by hand, Isabella Brew. Witness: James Wilks.

Similar attestations, same date and witness, from:

Ellinor Cosnahan, five pounds.
Ellinor Cosnahan for Anne Cosnahan, nine pounds.
Thomas Allen for Mary Allen, nine pounds.
[257] Isabel Curghey (my mark) 1/2/0.
William Quayle for Mary Quayle, three pounds.
William Crebbin for Jane Crebbin, five pounds.

[259][533] Robert Radcliffe's accounts:

Received:

1767

Balance remaining:	0/10/10¾.
Profits of the fund in England:	14/0//0.
Captain Kaighin's mortgage:	1/10/0.
Nicholson's mortgage:	2/9/0.
Total:	18/9/10¾.

1768

Balance:	0/9/10¾.
Profits:	17/19/0.
Total:	18/8/10¾.

1769

Balance:	0/8/10¾.
Profits:	17/19/0.
Total:	18/7/10¾.

1770

Balance:	0/7/10¾.

Contra:

1767

Paid cash to six widows at 3 pounds each:	18/0/0.
Balance this year:	0/9/10¾.
Total:	18/9/10¾.

1768:

Paid to six widows:	18/0/0.
Balance	0/8/10¾.
Total:	18/8/10¾.

---

[533]P. 258 is blank.

1769

Paid to six widows: 18/0/0.
Balance: 0/7/10¾.
Total: 18/7/10¾.

Thursday 7 June 1770

[263]⁵³⁴ Clergy present:

William Mylrea.   John Christian.
James Wilks,   Thomas Quayle.
John Moore, vicars-general.   Daniel Gelling.
Thomas Cubbon, official.⁵³⁵   Henry Corlett.
Matthias Curghey.   John Crellin.
Philip Moore.   Charles Crebbin.
Thomas Castley.   Ewan Christian.
Nicholas Christian.⁵³⁶   Thomas Corlett.
John Gill, ditto.   William Clucas.
William Crebbin.   Robert Quayle.
Thomas Woods.   William Fitzsimmons.
Samuel Gell.   Thomas Oates.

[264] At this convocation the ninth constitution of 1703 was publicly read and the latter part thereof, namely so far as relates to the visiting of schools, recommended and enjoined by the right reverend ordinary to be strictly observed by the several clergy of this diocese for the future.

And whereas by an account returned at convocation anno 1764 by our right reverend ordinary it appears that his lordship had then in hand several arrears of public charities and benefactions, particularly an arrear of Lady Hastings' charity to Jurby school (the same not having been legally or regularly claimed) for four years to Easter 1765 at 1/12/0 per annum, total 6/8/0; ditto impropriations at 2/10/0 per annum, total 10/0/0. Grand total: 16/8/0.

To Kirk Patrick school one year of Lady Hastings and impropriations to Easter 1756: 4/2/0.

To Kirk Bride school one year royal bounty to Easter 1763, total 3/0/0.

And his lordship taking into consideration the total want of a schoolhouse in some parishes and the bad state and condition of them in others, has by the advice of several of his clergy expended towards building a new schoolhouse in said parish of Jurby 16/0/0.

---

⁵³⁴Pp. 260-2 are blank.
⁵³⁵Archdeacon's registrar.
⁵³⁶Absent on particular business and desires to be excused.

Towards repairing the schoolhouse of Kirk Patrick 4/2/0.
Towards producing tables, forms, etc. at Kirk Bride 3/0/0.

It is the opinion and judgment of this assembly that the same has been prudently expended to useful purposes and answerable to the intention of the donors.

And whereas there remains in the hands of the Reverend Matthias Curghey late vicar-general, the sum of ten pounds or thereabouts, of money which was several years ago contributed towards defending the rights of the church by sundry well-disposed persons; after all persons within the said Mr Curghey's division who would receive their said contributions were gratefully and thankfully repaid, and as it is the misfortune [269] of the church to be at this time involved in a lawsuit for recovery of the tithe of herrings and other fish,

Resolved unanimously that the foresaid sum of ten pounds be deposited and paid into the hands of the reverend vicar-general Wilks to be by him applied towards the defence of the rights of the church now and for some time past unjustly invaded, and that the said vicar-general Wilks his receipt be a full discharge and indemnification to the said Reverend Mr Curghey for said sum.

[265-8] *A printed insert of the* London Gazette, *no. 11064, Tuesday 31 July to Saturday 4 August 1770. The first page contains the following:*

Isle of Man. July 14. On the fifth instant, the bishop of this isle gave a sermon in St John's chapel as usual, and afterwards at the head of the clergy, presented the following address to the governor, who after answering their address, proceeded with them to the Tynwald Hill, and went through the accustomed ceremonies and business of the day, which gave the utmost satisfaction to above ten thousand people present, and universally to the whole island, it being the first high court of Tynwald that has been holden there since the said island has been vested in his majesty.

To his excellency John Wood esquire, governor in chief and captain-general of the island and dominion of Man, and the dependencies thereof. The humble address of the bishop, archdeacon and the rest of the clergy of the isle and diocese of Sodor and Man.

May it please your excellency, We the bishop, archdeacon and clergy of the isle and diocese of Sodor and Man, animated with the warmest sentiments of duty, loyalty and affection to the person and government of our gracious sovereign, and the highest respect to your excellency, embrace this opportunity at this first and solemn court of Tynwald (since the royalties of this island were annexed to the imperial crown of Great Britain) to congratulate your excellency on the royal favour of being commissioned his majesty's vice-gerent in the government of this isle, and to felicitate this island in general on your excellency's happy appointment at the late revolution, as no circumstance could have been more favourable to the peace and happiness of the people committed to your care at that conjuncture, than his majesty's wise and seasonable continuance of your excellency to the government of this land, where your prudent and equable administration during several previous years had so justly endeared your excellency to all the inhabitants thereof.

Permit us therefore, sir, to participate in the general joy this day conspicuous in every face, to see their ancient, supreme, constitutional and so much wished for court of Tynwald restored to its former, or rather, superior dignity and importance, under your excellency's wise and judicious direction. And we beg leave to assure your excellency that we shall, by a faithful discharge of our duty in our respective stations, inculcate the strictest principles of loyalty and duty to his majesty, and cheerful obedience to all those put in authority under him, and more especially shall offer up our earnest supplications to the throne of grace, that the Supreme Director of all things would extend the blessings of peace and unity through this and every other part of his majesty's dominions, that your excellency's rule over us may be long, prosperous and happy, with health, honour and wisdom to discharge the arduous duties of your station, and that his majesty may never want so faithful a representative, the church so sincere a well-wisher, or this island so acceptable a governor.

Mark Sodor and Man.	Thomas Quayle.
William Mylrea.	Daniel Gelling.
James Wilks.	Henry Corlett.
John Moore.	John Crellin.
Thomas Castley.	Charles Crebbin.
Thomas Cubbon.	Ewan Christian.
Matthias Curghey.	Thomas Corlett.
Philip Moore.	William Clucas.
William Crebbin.	William Fitzsimmons.
Samuel Gell.	Robert Quayle.
Thomas Joseph Woods.	Thomas Oates.
John Christian.	

To which the governor returned the following answer:

My lord bishop, I am bound in duty to thank your lordship for your warm expressions of affection and loyalty to his majesty's person and government, as I am no less in [266] gratitude for your very favourable sentiments of my administration.

This public testimony of your regard for me, at the head of so respectable a body, on this great occasion, is of all things the most flattering, and must be so, when I consider your lordship's distinguishing judgment, when I know the sincerity of your love for the people of this island, and your unwearied endeavours to promote their happiness both here and hereafter.

Your applause, my lord, reflects a virtue on myself, and makes me proud indeed. Mr archdeacon and gentlemen of the clergy, Your zeal on this occasion calls alike for my most thankful acknowledgment, the exemplary conduct of your lives, your strict attention to the exercise of your sacred functions, leave me no room to doubt of your loyalty to the crown and your fidelity to my person. To deserve your esteem has ever been my peculiar study, to preserve it shall be my constant care. The same wise providence which has inspired your goodness will, I doubt not, teach me, as far as I am able, to encourage and to reward its labours.

Thursday 4 April 1771[537]

[271][538] Clergy present:

William Mylrea.	Thomas Quayle.
James Wilks.[539]	Daniel Gelling.
John Moore.	Henry Corlett.
Thomas Cubbon.	John Crellin.
Philip Moore.	Charles Crebbin.
Thomas Castley.	Ewan Christian.
Nicholas Christian.	Thomas Corlett.
John Gill.	William Clucas.
William Crebbin.	Robert Quayle.
Thomas Woods.	Thomas Oates.
Samuel Gell.	Nicholas Christian, jr.[540]
John Christian.	

[273][541] Resolved that the six senior clergy be appointed to draw up a proper answer to the fishermen's proposals forwarded to our right reverend ordinary by the worshipful Charles Lutwidge, receiver-general.

That the resolution entered into by our right reverend ordinary and the body of the clergy on the 26 November 1767 be renewed according to the original intention for the defence of the rights of the church.

That the several sums already contributed by the clergy and now remaining in the hands of the reverend vicar-general Wilks, be reserved as a common fund or stock for the defence of said rights, and that the clergy yet in arrear do pay in their proportions into the hands of said Mr Wilks within two months after date hereof.

Our right reverend ordinary has enjoined that the several clergy do on next Ascension Day perambulate the bounds of their respective parishes or so much of them as conveniently may be.

That the churchwardens and chapter-quest of each parish be called on once a month to form their presentments agreeable to the constitutions of 1703.

---

[537]Thursday in Easter week.
[538]P. 270 is blank.
[539]Vicar-general and episcopal registrar.
[540]Curate of Rushen.
[541]P. 272 is blank.

Thursday 11 June 1772

[275]⁵⁴² Clergy present:

William Mylrea.	Thomas Quayle.
James Wilks.	Daniel Gelling.
John Moore.	Henry Corlett.
Thomas Cubbon.	John Crellin.
Philip Moore.	Charles Crebbin.
Thomas Castley.	Ewan Christian.
Nicholas Christian.	Thomas Corlett.
John Gill.⁵⁴³	William Clucas.
William Crebbin.	Robert Quayle.
Thomas William Joseph Woods.	Thomas Oates.
Samuel Gell.	Nicholas Christian, jr.
John Christian.	

[277]⁵⁴⁴ It is resolved and agreed upon by us whose names are subscribed that the rights of the church be vigorously defended with respect to the tithe of herrings and other fish, and we hereby promise to contribute to whatever suit shall be carried on agreeable to the resolution in convocation of the 26 November 1767.

Mark Sodor and Man.	Thomas William Joseph Woods.
William Mylrea.	Samuel Gell.
James Wilks.	John Christian.
John Moore.	Thomas Quayle.
Thomas Castley.	Daniel Gelling.
Thomas Cubbon.	Henry Corlett.
Philip Moore.	John Crellin.
Nicholas Christian.	Charles Crebbin.
William Crebbin.	Ewan Christian.

⁵⁴²P. 274 is blank.
⁵⁴³Indisposed and prays to be excused.
⁵⁴⁴P. 276 is blank.

BISHOP RICHARD RICHMOND (1773-80)

Thanks to Dr Wilson for having added to the clergy widows' fund, 15 March 1773

[283]⁵⁴⁵ To the reverend Thomas Wilson, D. D., prebendary of Westminster.

Reverend sir, We the archdeacon and clergy of the isle and diocese of Man this day assembled beg leave to return our most grateful thanks and sincere acknowledgments for that fresh token of your benevolent regard and esteem for this your native country, signified to us in your letter of 10th January last to the reverend vicar-general Wilks, of adding 200 pounds more to the fund already established, chiefly by your most worthy father and yourself, towards the support of the poor clergymen's widows and orphans of this diocese, a fund though not very extensive in itself, yet has been the means of alleviating that extremity of distress they otherwise would have been unavoidably exposed to.

With you, sir, we are unanimously of opinion that the vesting the whole of this fund in the purchase of a landed estate within this island would, for many obvious reasons, be more eligible than suffering it to remain in any of the public funds, which are often of a fluctuating nature and beyond our comprehension. We have severally in our respective parishes made a strict inquiry for a proper purchase, and as yet are not able to find any we would recommend, and we shall continue to give every aid in our power to this desirable work. But should it so happen that a landed estate cannot be obtained, we would as the next most desirable purchase recommend some portion of the impropriate tithes, if approved of by you and by council learned in the law, as to the sufficiency of the title, hoping their graces of Atholl may be tender in their terms, as [284] such purchase is meant for a charitable purpose.

As to the fixing proper trustees and the qualifications of the recipients, we beg leave to refer those points to your own prudent consideration, who are already so well acquainted with the nature of this fund.

And to the end this business may be conducted with as little trouble as possible to you, we have appointed the reverend vicar-general Wilks and the Reverend Mr Moore, rector of Kirk Bride, to correspond with you and receive your directions in the affair, and to them, on whose prudence and discretion we much depend, we shall from time to time give the best information and intelligence touching a proper landed purchase, should any such offer.

Sincerely imploring the gracious disposer of all divine blessings that you may enjoy fullness of days (as did your much esteemed, venerable and right reverend

---

⁵⁴⁵Pp. 278-82 are blank.

father, whose memory is by us and will be revered in this isle to the latest ages) in health of body and mind and every other comfort of life, we beg leave with respect and esteem to subscribe ourselves, reverend sir, your much obliged and affectionate brethren,

William Mylrea.	Thomas William Joseph Woods.
James Wilks.	John Christian.
John Moore.	Thomas Quayle.
Philip Moore.	Daniel Gelling.
Thomas Castley.	Henry Corlett.
Nicholas Christian.	John Crellin.
William Crebbin.	Charles Crebbin.
Thomas Cubbon.	Ewan Christian.
Samuel Gell.	Thomas Corlett.

Peeltown, March 15, 1773. Examined by James Wilks, episcopal registrar. N.B. .The original forwarded to Dr Wilson.

The clergy's letter of welcome to Bishop Richmond, 15 March 1773

[287; 3][546] To the right reverend father in God Richard, by divine permission lord bishop of Sodor and Man.

May it please your lordship to permit us the archdeacon and clergy of your diocese this day assembled to congratulate your lordship on your appointment and consecration to this see, humbly imploring your lordship's blessing and prayers that we may walk worthy of the vocation whereunto we are called and prove faithful and diligent pastors of the flocks committed to our care. And it is our ardent prayer to the throne of grace for your lordship that true religion may be preserved under your government of this branch of the church of Christ, that true piety and virtue may increase and flourish among us, and that after you have long and successfully laboured in the vineyard of our common master, you may enjoy the happiness of those who turn many to righteousness.

We have through the favour of God been peculiarly happy under the guidance and direction of two eminently great patterns of religion, your lordship's immediate predecessors, each of whom contributed to rescue this ancient church of man from a distress it laboured under for a series of years, by being unavoidably plunged into a tedious and expensive lawsuit in the high court of chancery of Great Britain, from which it has by the blessing of God and the assistance of those worthy prelates and other friends been happily extricated.

[4] And that same good Providence, having of late years put it into the heart of our last worthy diocesan to lay a foundation for and excite other well-disposed Christians to concur in raising contributions towards printing the sacred oracles in

---

[546]This letter appears twice, once in Manx National Heritage Library, MS 9726, pp. 286-8 and again in MS 804C, pp. 3-5. Both page numberings are given here.

our native tongue, a blessing in this diocese unknown to ages past and whereof we are now in almost [288] full possession, the same being very near wholly completed, and towards making this sacred work so perfect as in our power we severally and cheerfully contributed by translating different portions thereof and submitting the same to the revision and correction of persons well qualified for that work.

We crave your lordship's permission to represent that the ashes of our former suit for the recovery of our rights were scarcely cold before the flame of a most vexatious litigation was kindled anew by the fishermen of this island, who having united themselves in one body, pertinaciously refuse to pay the tithe of herrings and other fish by them caught, and though these tithes are secured to the church by the sanction of the strongest laws, as well as by immemorial usage, yet by their making it a common cause they have broke in upon the rights of the see and also upon those of the parochial clergy, taking every litigious and procrastinating method which can be devised by the various measures of the law, appealing from every sentence and decree of our courts here to his majesty in council, and then deserting their appeals, which we have been obliged to pursue, on the last of which appeals his majesty was graciously pleased to award costs, yet as they apply the proceeds of the tithe to their defence and make it a common cause, they still [5] continue obstinate and unjustly involve us in fresh suits. And although we have great cause to lament the death of our late right reverend diocesan, our tender father and steady friend, yet we console ourselves with the pleasing hopes of your [289] lordship's aid and assistance, and of your having the countenance of his grace of Atholl, in protecting and preserving the rights of the church from the injurious attacks of those infatuated and misguided men, and restoring the peaceable and quiet enjoyment of the indubitable rights of the see and of the parochial clergy of your diocese, who are with most humbly duty to your lordship, your lordship's most obedient sons and servants,

William Mylrea, archdeacon.	Thomas William Joseph Woods.
James Wilks.	Thomas Quayle.
John Moore, vicars-general.	Daniel Gelling.
Philip Moore.	Henry Corlett.
Thomas Castley.	John Crellin.
Nicholas Christian.	Charles Crebbin.
William Crebbin.	Ewan Christian.
Thomas Cubbon.	Thomas Corlett.
Samuel Gell.	

Examined per James Wilks, episcopi registrarium. Peeltown, March 15, 1773.

NB: The original hereof sent to the right reverend lord bishop, then in London. Examined per Ewan Christian, episcopi registrarium.[547]

---

[547]This sentence appears only in MS 804C.

Philip Moore appointed as the clergy's representative to treat with Dr Wilson concerning the clergy widows' fund, 22 July 1773

[291][548] It having been represented unto us the archdeacon and clergy of the isle and diocese of Man that our worthy and benevolent friend and benefactor the Reverend Thomas Wilson, doctor of divinity and prebendary of Westminster, being desirous the Reverend Philip Moore, rector of Kirk Bride, should attend him shortly in Lancashire for us and in our behalf, to treat, settle and agree upon certain matters relative to some additions to be made to the fund appropriated towards the better support and maintenance of clergymen's widows and orphans within this isle,

We therefore, the said archdeacon and clergy this day assembled, reposing the utmost trust and confidence in the said Reverend Philip Moore, do hereby vest him with full power and authority (so far as in us lies) to treat, settle and agree with said Revered Doctor Wilson in all matters relative to the said fund, or any addition that shall be made thereto, and for us and in our name to sign, seal and execute [the] deed or instrument necessary for the better carrying the donor's pious and charitable intention into execution, ratifying and confirming whatever our commissioner, the Reverend Philip Moore, shall lawfully do or cause to be [done] in and about the premises as fully and effectually as if we were personally present. In witness whereof we have hereto subscribed our names at Kirk Michael, this 22nd July 1773.

William Mylrea.	Thomas Quayle.
James Wilks.	Daniel Gelling.
John Moore.	Henry Corlett.
William Crebbin.	John Crellin.
Samuel Gell.	Ewan Christian.
Thomas William Joseph Woods.	Thomas Corlett.
John Christian.	

Examined by James Wilks, episcopal registrar. N.B. The original hereof delivered to the clergy's commissioner, the Reverend Philip Moore.

Thursday 30 June 1774

[7][549] Clergy present:

William Mylrea.	Henry Corlett.
James Wilks.	Thomas Cubbon, official.
John Moore.	Charles Crebbin.
Thomas Castley.	Ewan Christian.
Philip Moore.	John Crellin.
Nicholas Christian.	Thomas Corlett.

---

[548]P. 290 is blank.
[549]Douglas, Manx National Heritage Library, MS 804C. Pp. 1-2 are blank. Pp. 3-5 are a copy of a letter in the previous MS (see above). P. 6 is blank.

William Crebbin.

William Clucas.[550]

Samuel Gell.

Robert Quayle.

John Christian.

Thomas Oates.

Thomas William Joseph Woods.

David Harrison.

Thomas Quayle.

John Clague.

Daniel Gelling.

[8] At this convocation it was proposed by the right reverend lord bishop that the most respectful and most grateful thanks of the bishop and clergy of the see and diocese of Man in convocation assembled should be presented to their graces the duke and duchess of Atholl for their generous and charitable benefaction in disposing of the impropriate tithes of Kirk Michael parish at a price much below their real value, and what they might undoubtedly have received for the same, in order that the said tithes might be appropriated to the use and purpose of augmenting the fund for the relief and better support of the widows and orphans of the clergy of the said isle and diocese of Man, and that the lord bishop should be requested to transmit to their graces the duke and duchess of Atholl the thanks of his clergy, together with his own, for this instance of their goodness and favour to the clergy of this diocese.

Resolved and agreed to by the whole assembly. A copy of the address of thanks is hereto annexed.

Thanks to the duke and duchess of Atholl respecting impropriate tithes

[9] May it please your graces to accept the most respectful and truly grateful thanks of the bishop and clergy of the isle and diocese of Man, this day in convocation assembled, for your generous goodness in consenting to dispose of your tithes in the parish of Kirk Michael for a sum much below their real value, and far short of what your graces might undoubtedly have received for them, in order to their becoming a fund for the relief and better support of the widows and orphans of the clergy of this diocese.

To those happy few who prefer the silent applause of their own hearts and the approbation of the searcher of all hearts to the praises, however just and deserved, of men, verbose acknowledgments and high, though well-founded commendations, all unacceptable; to your graces therefore we offer them not; but beg leave to assure you that we shall not fail to put up our constant and fervent prayers to the throne of grace, that the favour we now acknowledge, together with the other numerous instances of your piety towards God and your benevolence towards men, may be rewarded with [10] every blessing, both temporal and eternal. With the most profound respect we are (may it please your graces) your most obliged, most obedient and most humble servants.

Richard Sodor and Man.

Daniel Gelling.

William Mylrea.

Henry Corlett.

---

[550]Domestic chaplain to the lord bishop.

James Wilks,

John Moore, vicars-general.

Philip Moore.

Thomas Castley.

Nicholas Christian.

William Crebbin.

Samuel Gell.

John Christian.

Thomas William Joseph Woods.

Thomas Quayle.

Thomas Cubbon.

Charles Crebbin.

Ewan Christian.

John Crellin.

Thomas Corlett.

William Clucas.

Robert Quayle.

David Harrison.

John Clague.

Examined per Ewan Christian episcopi registrarium.

[11] Resolved also that the grateful thanks of the bishop and clergy should be presented to Lady Gower for her generous and charitable donation of three hundred pounds British towards enabling the Reverend Dr Thomas Wilson, prebendary of Westminster to fix an establishment for the better support and maintenance of the poor widows, orphans and children of the clergy of this diocese.

An address of thanks was immediately wrote and subscribed by his lordship and clergy and delivered to the Reverend Mr Moore, rector of Kirk Bride, to be forthwith transmitted to her ladyship, a copy of which is hereto annexed.

Letter of thanks to Lady Gower for her donation

Madam, If works of beneficence and charity are acceptable to the Supreme of all beneficent beings as sure they must, being the emanations of that divine Spirit which pervades the universe, upholding all things by the Word of his power and dispensing a certain proportion of happiness to all his creatures, this Almighty Lord of all must surely love those in a more especial manner who so much resemble himself in works of munificence and charity, whose lives, like those of your late noble father the earl of Thanet and your own (the faithful steward and pious dispenser of his princely liberalities) are solely devoted to doing good.

Deeply impressed with these sentiments and hearts overflowing with gratitude to our beneficent and pious benefactress, permit us the bishop, archdeacon, vicars-general and clergy of this isle and diocese of Sodor and Man [12] to lay at your feet our most sincere acknowledgments of thanks for your very generous donation of three hundred pounds towards enabling the Reverend Dr Thomas Wilson, prebendary of Westminster, to fix and establishment for the better support and maintenance of the poor widows, orphans and children of the clergy of this diocese, whose prayers and blessings, with ours, will for ever attend and follow you into those regions of peace and joy, where the good deeds of the charitable and beneficent are surely recorded and rewarded.

May the Almighty remember you and all our benefactors concerning this, and may you receive ten thousand times improved that joy and blessedness from the hand of God which the widow and fatherless receive from you.

Permit us madam to crave that the acknowledgment of our gratitude may be accepted as a testimony of that great esteem and regard with which we are, madam your most devoted and most obliged humble servants,

Richard Sodor and Man.	Thomas Cubbon.
William Mylrea.	John Crellin.
James Wilks.	Charles Crebbin.
John Moore.	Henry Corlett.
Philip Moore.	Daniel Gelling.
Thomas Castley.	Ewan Christian.
Nicholas Christian.	Thomas Corlett.
William Crebbin.	Thomas Oates.
Samuel Gell.	David Harrison.
Thomas Woods.	William Clucas.
John Christian.	John Clague.

[13] The reverend vicar-general Wilks, one of the stewards and manager of the late fund for the support of the widows and orphans of the clergy of this isle having moved that lord bishop might appoint a committee of the clergy for the examination of his accounts touching said fund, his lordship was thereupon pleased to appoint the reverend Mr archdeacon Mylrea, the reverend Mr vicar-general Moore and Mr Philip Moore, rector of Kirk Bride.

Exhibition of clergy papers

[16][551] His lordship having signified to the several clergy of his diocese by circular notice dated the twenty-seventh of last month that he required and expected that they would exhibit at this convocation their respective letters of orders, institutions, inductions, licences or other faculties whatsoever, his lordship therefore now directs that the said clergy exhibit the same, which is done accordingly, in the manner set down hereafter.

Kirk Andreas. Reverend Mr archdeacon William Mylrea rector, exhibited his:

1. Letters of priest's orders bearing date, 21 September 1746.
2. Institution to said parish, dated 18 July 1760.
3. Mandate of induction, the same date.
4. Certificate of his having been inducted, 12 August 1760.

Ballaugh. Reverend James Wilks, rector, exhibited his:

1. 29 May 1743.   2. 3. 16 September 1771.   4. 14 October 1771.

---

[551]Pp. 14-15 do not exist.

Arbory. Reverend John Moore, vicar, exhibited his:

1. 20 September 1747.   2. 3. 6 June 1748.   4. 21 July 1748.

Bride. The reverend Philip Moore, rector, exhibited his:

1. 23 September 1739.   2. 3. 10 July 1761.   4. 11 July 1761.

[17] Castletown. Reverend Thomas Castley A. M. exhibited his:

1. 5 June 1757.
Licence for being chaplain of Castletown, dated 31 January 1758.

Rushen. Reverend Nicholas Christian vicar, exhibited neither 1, 2, 3, or 4, alleging that he forgot that he was required by said circular letter to exhibit them at this convocation.

Jurby. Reverend William Crebbin vicar, exhibited his:

1. 3 October 1750.   2. 3. Collation and mandate, 9 August 1751.
4. 19 May 1752.

Lonan. Reverend Samuel Gell vicar, exhibited his:

1. 22 September 1745.   2. 3. 19 April 1759.   4. 3 July 1759.

Marown. Reverend John Christian vicar, exhibited his:

1. 24 September 1752.   2. 3. 27 February 1753.   4. 5 March 1753.

Braddan. Reverend Thomas William Joseph Woods, vicar, exhibited his:

1. 21 September 1747.   2. 3. Collation and institution 23 December 1768.
4. 6 April 1769.

[18] Kirk Onchan. Reverend Thomas Quayle, vicar,

1. 24 September 1752.   2. 3. 19 April 1759.   4. 3 July 1759.

Malew. Reverend Daniel Gelling, vicar,

1. 11 June 1759.   2. 3. 8 July 1761.   4. 23 July 1761.

German. Reverend Henry Corlett, vicar,

1. 15 February 1761.   2. 3. Collation and institution 4 March 1761.
4. 24 March 1761.

Maughold. Reverend Thomas Cubbon, vicar,

1. [2]7 June 1764.   2. 3. 7 March 1769.   4. 28 March 1769.

Santan. Reverend Charles Crebbin, vicar.

1. 28 February 1768.   2. 3. 7 March 1769.   4. 14 March 1769.

Patrick. Reverend Ewan Christian, vicar.

1. 21 May 1769.   2. 3. Collation and institution. 9 October 1769.
4. 18 October 1769.

[19] Kirk Michael. Reverend John Crellin, vicar,

1. 27 June 1764.   2. 3. 4 November 1771.   4. 11 November 1771.

Lezayre. Reverend Thomas Corlett, vicar.

1. 15 March 1772.   2. 3. 13 September 1773. 4. 21 September 1773.

Chaplains and curates

Reverend William Clucas, domestic chaplain to lord bishop.

1. 21 May 1769.

Reverend Robert Quayle, curate of Douglas exhibited neither letters of priest's orders or licence, alleging that he was in Dublin when said circular notice was given and that he was not made acquainted with the purport of it before he came to this convocation.

Reverend Thomas Oates, curate of Kirk Bride.

1. 15 March 1772.
Licence to be curate of the parish, date 5 May 1773.

Reverend David Harrison, chaplain of St Mark's chapel.

1. 30 November 1773.
Licence dated the same day.

Reverend John Clague, curate of Kirk Michael.

1. Letters of deacon's orders bearing date 30 November 1773.
Licence dated the same day.

Memorandum: The several letters of orders, collations, institutions, mandates of induction with their certificates annexed, and [20] other faculties as within mentioned being pursuant to the 137th canon ecclesiastical exhibited to our right reverend ordinary for his approbation, and the same being allowed of, his lordship ordered me his registrar to endorse each and every of them as followeth 'June 30, 1774. Exhibitum Ewan Christian, episcopi registrario' for which I received from each of the clergy a fee of 14d. for every such exhibit. Ewan Christian, episcopi registrarius.

Address to the king condemning the American rebellion, 23 October 1775

[21] The following address of the bishop and clergy of this isle and diocese having been transmitted to the earl of Suffolk, one of his majesty's principal secretaries of state, was presented to his majesty, which address his majesty was pleased to receive very graciously.

To the king's most excellent majesty. Permit, most gracious sovereign, the bishop and clergy of the isle and diocese of Man, few in number, inconsiderable in influence, and remote in situation, but in duty and affection to your sacred person, your family and government, equal to those of any diocese in your majesty's dominions, to express before you sentiments which, springing warm from their hearts, their coolest and most deliberate judgments also approve.

Fully sensible of our own unimportance, we should think it presumption to interrupt your majesty with the tender of our most humble duty, did not the circumstances of the time and the very culpable behaviour of some of our fellow subjects seem to call upon all persons, of all ranks and professions, 'high and low, rich and poor, one with another' to declare their abhorrence of the daring and unprovoked rebellion, begun and carried on, in several of your majesty's colonies, against the authority of the whole legislative power of Great Britain.

We profess the same passion for freedom, the same steady adherence to our just and legal rights, which is pretended to be the object in pursuit by the advocates of nominal liberty and real licentiousness, but we know not, nor expect any true liberty, except under the guardianship of the laws; and we know not, and hope never to know, any other guardians of the laws, than our sovereign and his two houses of parliament.

[22] That the decided, unthinking many are (as is usual in such cases) misled and deceived by the designing and ambitious few we are fully persuaded, and that the former may have their eyes opened, their errors removed and (then) their faults forgiven, and the latter be brought to a speedy repentance, or their deserved punishment, we earnestly pray.

Our prayers and our hearts are, alas, all we have to offer to your majesty, but those, because sincere, will by you, sire, not be disdained.

May the present disturbance be the only one that shall ever disquiet your royal and benevolent mind, may it be short as the transient storm, and be succeeded by an unruffled balm, a long and glorious sunshine; may all your subjects, both at home and abroad, be duly sensible of the blessings they enjoy under your just and gentle rule! And may they express their grateful sense of these blessings by unfeigned piety towards their God, and undissembled loyalty to their king. May your majesty's enemies (who, if your subjects, are enemies to their country) 'be clothed with rebuke, with shame and dishonour! But upon your own royal head, and on those of your posterity, may your crown flourish, till all human empire shall be no more.' Castletown, Isle of Man, October 23rd 1775.

Richard Sodor and Man.
William Mylrea, archdeacon.
James Wilks, vicar-general.
John Moore, vicar-general.
Thomas Cubbon, official.
Philip Moore.
Ewan Christian, episcopal registrar.
William Clucas.

John Christian.
Charles Crebbin.
Robert Quayle.
Thomas William Joseph Woods.
Thomas Quayle.
Samuel Gell.
Thomas Castley.

In the name of themselves and the rest of the clergy of the diocese. Examined per Ewan Christian, registrarius episcopi.

The bishop's letter to the clergy, 6 May 1776

[23] To the reverend the clergy of the diocese of Man.

Reverend brethren, When I went to England in the last spring, I hoped and fully purposed to have returned early enough in the summer to have met you in convocation, though not precisely at the time appointed for holding that assembly, and although detained by unavoidable business a full month longer than I expected, I should still have been able to have realized that my hope and design, had not an accidental hurt received in my journey not only detained me yet near a month more, but rendered me moreover so lame that for several weeks after my landing in the island I was not able to undergo the smallest fatigue. This disappointment (however) made me more anxiously wish for such a degree of health and strength as might enable me to meet you in convocation at the time directed by the ecclesiastical constitutions of 1703, viz., on the Thursday in the approaching Whitsun week. But none of you (I suppose) are ignorant that by a succession of gouty attacks I have been confined nearly the whole winter to my house, and by the last severe and most painful fit have been lamed to such a degree as to be to this day unable to get downstairs. In this condition, I have nothing to do, but with humble resignation to submit to the chastening hand of the all-wise and all-merciful disposer of health and sickness, of life and death; hoping from his favour to regain by gradual (though probably slow) steps, such a measure of strength as may enable me to hold a convocation sometime in the month of July, which nothing but absolute inability shall prevent me from doing, and of the day fixed for said convocation, you may depend on receiving such timely notice as may prevent inconvenience to any of you, from your attendance thereupon.

I take this opportunity of acquainting you (which information, you my brethren, I am sure will receive with the same pleasure with which I give it) that the most respectable Society for Promoting Christian Knowledge to which this church is (as

I doubt not, ye are all very sensible) under the highest obligations, are now engaged in [24] printing off a large impression, Manx on one side, English on the other, of the valuable treatise upon the sacrament of the Lord's Supper composed by my ever honoured, ever revered predecessor, the excellent Bishop Wilson. The Society are also printing off 2000 Common Prayer Books in a smaller size, for the use of your congregations, and fifty copies in quarto, for your own use in your reading desks, all which shall be distributed as soon after they come to the island, as possible. I have expressed and shall take all opportunities to express your thanks, together with my own, for this continuing and abounding labour of love shown by this excellent Society to our little diocese, in which outward expressions of thanks as well as in inward sentiments of gratitude, ye will all, I am satisfied, cordially join with, reverend sirs, your most affectionate brother and very humble servant, Richard Sodor and Man.

P. S. The order herewith forwarded relative to parish clerks, schoolmasters and mistresses, you will be pleased to execute without delay. Peeltown, 6th May 1776.
Examined per Ewan Christian registrarium episcopi.

The bishop's letter against unauthorized preaching and teaching, 16 July 1776

[25] To the several rectors, vicars, chaplains and curates within the isle and diocese of Man.

Reverend brethren, Whereas we have been informed that several unordained, unauthorized and unqualified persons from other countries have for some time past presumed to preach and teach publicly, hold and maintain conventicles, and have caused several weak persons to combine themselves together in a new society and have private meetings, assemblies and congregations, contrary to the doctrine, government, rites and ceremonies of the established church and the civil and ecclesiastical laws of this isle,

We do therefore (for the prevention of schism and the establishment of that uniformity in religious worship which so long hitherto subsisted among us) hereby desire and require each and every of you to be vigilant and use your utmost endeavours to dissuade your respective flocks from following, or being led and misguided by such incompetent teachers, and to exhort, incite and invite them devoutly to read and consider the Holy Scriptures, to attend constantly and reverently the blessed sacraments, their parish church and the ghostly advice of their own minister, by which they will be better and more comfortably instructed in the means of grace and salvation than by the crude, pragmatical and inconsistent, if not profane and blasphemous *ex tempore* effusions of those pretenders to the true religion, and if afterward they regard not the truth, but obstinately and wilfully persist in error, then to know and find out the names of such persons within your respective parishes and chapelries as attend the public instructions of the said disorderly and unqualified teachers, or frequent the said conventicles, meetings, assemblies and congregations, and if upon due inquiry and certain information you discover, or consistently with your own knowledge know that any licensed schoolmaster, mistress, parish clerk or any other person who holds or enjoys [26] any place, office or employment by licence from us or our predecessors, that you signify and make known unto us in writing the name or names of such schoolmaster, mistress, parish clerk or any other person who holds or enjoys any place, office or employment under episcopal licence as aforesaid within one moth after the receipt hereof, as also unto our reverend vicars-general or one of them, the name or names of any other person or persons within your respective parishes or chapelries who attend the public instructions of the said teachers, or frequent the said conventicles, meetings, assemblies or congregations, within the above limited time.

And we likewise further desire and require each and every of you in case any of the above mentioned, unordained, unauthorized and unqualified teachers shall at any time hereafter offer to be a partaker of the Holy Communion in any of your respective churches or chapels, that you repel him or them so offering and the minister so repelling them or any of them to give an account of the same unto us within fourteen days after at the farthest, as is directed by the rubric in this behalf. Given at Peeltown the 16th day of July 1776. Richard Sodor and Man.

P. S. Let these be forwarded in the usual manner if the time of receiving and forwarding the same be noted by each of you.

You will also take a copy thereof and publish it *plena ecclesia* in English and Manx at the usual time in your respective churches or chapels, the Sunday next after your receipt thereof.

Examined per Ewan Christian registrarium episcopi.

Letter from the clergy to the first crown governor, (no date)[552]

[27] To his excellency John Wood, esquire, governor, chancellor and captain-general of this isle.

May it please your excellency, We the bishop, archdeacon and the rest of the clergy of the isle and diocese of Man, desire to offer to your excellency our very respectful congratulations on your return to the exercise of your government in this island, and to express our hopes that you have brought with you and our sincerest wishes that you may continue to possess such a share of health as may prevent the cares of government from being burdensome to your excellency, and may enable you to enjoy the satisfactions of life, with that true relish which, without the blessing of health, is not to be hoped for.

Your excellency's equitable and gentle rule over this country has justly endeared you to the people of all ranks and all professions therein, and has rendered your health and welfare a matter of general concern to them all, but by persons of no rank and profession can they more earnestly be wished and prayed for than by those who have the honour to subscribe themselves, with the greatest respect, sir, your excellency's most obedient and most humble servants,

---

[552]John Wood was recalled in 1777, so the letter must date from before that year.

Richard Sodor and Man.
William Mylrea.
James Wilks.
John Moore.
Philip Moore.
Thomas Castley.
William Crebbin.
Thomas William Joseph Woods.
Nicholas Christian.
John Christian.
Ewan Christian.

William Clucas.
Thomas Quayle.
Daniel Gelling.
Henry Corlett.
Thomas Cubbon.
Charles Crebbin.
David Harrison.
Thomas Corlett.
Robert Quayle.
Thomas Oates.
John Clague.

Examined per Ewan Christian, episcopi registrarium.

Thursday 19 September 1776

[28] At a convocation held in St John's chapel in the parish of Kirk German on the 19th day of September anno Domini 1776. Clergy present:

William Mylrea.
James Wilks.
John Moore.
Thomas Castley.
Philip Moore.
Nicholas Christian.
William Crebbin.
Samuel Gell.[553]
John Christian.
Thomas William Joseph Woods.
Thomas Quayle.
Daniel Gelling.

Henry Corlett.
Thomas Cubbon, official.
Charles Crebbin.
Ewan Christian.
John Crellin.
Thomas Corlett.
William Clucas.
Robert Quayle.
Thomas Oates.
David Harrison.
John Clague.
John Parr.

[29] At this convocation the right reverend the lord bishop nominated and appointed the Reverend Mr William Mylrea, archdeacon and rector of Kirk Andreas, the reverend Mr John Moore, vicar-general and vicar of Kirk Arbory, and the reverend Ewan Christian, episcopal registrar and vicar of Kirk Patrick, a committee to inspect and examine the accounts, bills of costs, etc., of the reverend vicar-general Wilks relative to certain lawsuits for the recovery of legal fish-tithe, wherein James Parr of Peeltown, the Reverend Henry Corlett, vicar of Kirk German, and the said Mr Wilks were plaintiffs, and to report the same unto his lordship as soon as conveniently may be, to which end his lordship desired the said Mr Wilks to lay said accounts and all necessary vouchers before the said committee. Ewan Christian, episcopal registrar.

---

[553]Absent owing to indisposition.

His lordship likewise nominated and appointed the reverend Messrs John Christian, vicar of Marown, Thomas William Joseph Woods, vicar of Kirk Braddan, and Thomas Quayle, vicar of Kirk Onchan, a committee to inspect and examine the accounts of the reverend vicar-general Wilks relative to the fund for the support and maintenance of the widows and orphans of the clergy of this isle and to report the same unto his lordship before the next convocation. Ewan Christian, episcopal registrar.

His lordship likewise nominated and appointed the above mentioned Reverend Messrs John Christian, Thomas William Joseph Woods and Thomas Quayle a committee to inspect and examine the accounts of the reverend vicar-general Moore respecting the management of Mrs Catharine Halsall's bounty and to report the same unto his lordship before the next convocation. Ewan Christian, episcopal registrar.

Thursday 15 October 1778

[30] At a convocation holden in St Peter's chapel in Peeltown on Thursday the 15th day of October in the year of our Lord 1778.

The right reverend father in God Richard by divine permission lord bishop of this diocese, being though not dangerously, yet so far indisposed as to be altogether unable without hazard of increasing his indisposition to be personally present in this convocation, presides and is represented in the said convocation by the reverend Mr William Mylrea, archdeacon of the said diocese, as appears by the following authentic copy of a commission given and granted to the said archdeacon for that purpose, viz.

Commission to the archdeacon to preside at the convocation

Richard by divine permission lord bishop of Sodor and Man to the Reverend Mr William Mylrea, archdeacon of the said diocese, greeting,

Whereas circular notice hath been given to you and the clergy of this diocese to meet in convocation in St Peter's chapel in Peeltown precisely at the hour of eleven o'clock in the forenoon of Thursday the fifteenth instant, and that since the circulation of the said notice we have been and still continue to be so much indisposed as to be entirely unable (without the risk of increasing our indisposition) to attend at the said convocation, therefore know you and all others whom it may concern, that we do by these presents nominate, constitute and appoint you the said Mr William Mylrea to represent us, and for us and in our place and stead to preside in the said convocation, and do invest you with full power to treat and give your wholesome advice and directions respecting such business as shall be proposed, to consent to those [31] things which shall there seem expedient, or dissent from such things as shall seem inconvenient, and further to do for us what the nature of the said convocation shall demand and require. In testimony whereof we have hereunto subscribed our name and affixed our seal episcopal this fourteenth day of October in the year of our Lord one thousand seven hundred and seventy-eight.

Richard Sodor and Man. Examined by Ewan Christian, episcopal registrar.

Clergy present:

William Mylrea.
John Moore.
Ewan Christian, vicar-general.
Philip Moore.[554]
Daniel Gelling.
Thomas Cashley.
Nicholas Christian.
William Crebbin.
Samuel Gell.[555]
John Christian.
Thomas William Joseph Woods.

Thomas Quayle.
Henry Corlett.
Thomas Cubbon.
Charles Crebbin.
John Crellin.
Thomas Corlett.
William Clucas.
Robert Quayle.
Thomas Oates.
David Harrison.
John Clague.

[32] At this convocation it is resolved that the sum of 31/6/3¼ being a balance of the contributions of the clergy towards the defence of the rights of the church agreeably to certain acts of convocation dated respectively 26 November 1767, 7 June 1770, 4 April 1771 and 11 June 1772, which balance is now in the hands of the reverend vicar-general Christian, to be paid by the same vicar-general to the several contributors or their representatives in proportion to their respective contributions. William Clucas, episcopal registrar.

The reverend Messrs John Christian, Thomas William Joseph Woods and Thomas Quayle, being a committee appointed at the last convocation to inspect, examine and report the state of the accounts of the Reverend John Moore, vicar-general relative to Mrs Catharine Halsall's charity, having neglected to do so, are at this convocation (by their own consent) re-elected and appointed a committee for the said purpose and within one month from this day to report to the right reverend the lord bishop all receipts and disbursements of the said charity. William Clucas, episcopal registrar.

The reverend Messrs Thomas Cubbon and William Clucas are appointed a committee to audit the accounts of all receipts and disbursements of the charity towards the support and maintenance of the widows, children and orphans of the clergy for the year ending at Easter last past, and have accordingly audited and approved of the same. William Clucas, episcopal registrar.

---

[554]Absent owing to indisposition.
[555]Absent owing to lameness.

BISHOP GEORGE MASON (1780-3)

Thursday 7 June 1781[556]

A precept for convocation, 1781[557]

Douglas, 21st May 1781.

The several rectors, vicars, chaplains and curates within the diocese of Man.

Reverend gentlemen, I am directed by the right reverend the lord bishop to inform you that his lordship purposes (God willing) to hold a convocation in the schoolhouse in the parish of Kirk Michael upon Thursday in Whitsun week next, where you are required to convene by eleven o'clock in the forenoon of the same day, if not prevented by indisposition or some other sufficient cause, and to bring along with you as usual, copies of your parochial registers of marriages, baptisms and burials attested by yourselves and churchwardens, and commencing from your last returns made of your respective registers. And his lordship also desires that if any of you have any business to be transacted or any matter or thing to be proposed, discussed or resolved upon in said convocation, that he will expect to be made acquainted therewith in writing at least one week before, otherwise his lordship must be excused from attending thereto. I am, gentlemen, your most obedient humble servant, Calcott Heywood, episcopal registrar.

P. S. Let these be forwarded in the usual manner and as expeditiously as possible.

Braddan, May 21, 1781. Received at two o'clock afternoon, and forthwith forwarded to the reverend vicar of Marown by Thomas William Woods.
Kirk Marown, May 21st, 1781. Received about five o'clock in the afternoon and forwarded immediately to the chaplain of St Mark's by Thomas Christian, vicar of Marown.
St Mark's, May 21st, 1781. Received about eight o'clock P. M. and forwarded early next morning to the reverend vicar-general Crebbin by David Harrison.
Santan, May 22nd, 1781. Received at seven o'clock in the morning and forwarded immediately to the Reverend Mr William Clucas, vicar-general. Charles Crebbin.

---

[556]For the summons to this convocation, see the appendix.
[557]This document, found among the loose ecclesiastical papers in the Manx National Heritage Museum, was published in the *Journal of the Manx Museum* IV (1938-40), p. 18, as a model of the summonses or 'precepts' issued for convocation.

Malew, May 22nd, 1781. Received in the afternoon and forwarded forthwith to the reverend Mr Castley. William Clucas.

Castletown, 22nd May 1781. Received about eight o'clock at night and forwarded immediately to the Reverend Mr Moore of Kirk Arbory by me, Thomas Castley.

Kirk Arbory, May 23, 1781. Received at about eleven o'clock and forwarded immediately to the vicar of Rushen, John Moore.

Rushen, May 23, 1781. Received about one of the clock P. M. and forwarded to the vicar of Kirk Patrick. Nicholas Christian.

Kirk Patrick, 24th May, 1781. Received about eleven o'clock in the forenoon and forwarded to the Reverend Mr Corlett, vicar of Kirk German, by Ewan Christian.

Peeltown, May 24th, 1781. Received about two o'clock P. M. and forwarded to the Reverend Mr Clague, curate of Kirk Michael, by Henry Corlett.

Kirk Michael, May 25th 1781. Received at nine o'clock last night and forwarded this morning by six o'clock to the Reverend Mr Gelling, rector of Ballaugh, per me, John Clague.

St Mary's, Ballaugh. May 25, 1781. Received at eight o'clock in the morning and forwarded forthwith to the reverend vicar of Jurby by me, Daniel Gelling.

Jurby, May 25th, 1781. Received about ten of the clock in the forenoon and forwarded immediately to the reverend Mr archdeacon by William Crebbin.

Kirk Andreas, 25th May 1781. Received in the evening and delivered to the curate of Kirk Bride. William Mylrea.

Kirk Bride, 25th May 1781. Received late in the evening and delivered to the sumner to be forwarded as usual. Daniel Mylrea.

Lezayre, May 26, 1781. Received in the morning about nine o'clock and forwarded immediately to the Reverend W. [sic] Crellin. John Moore.

Ramsey, 26th May 1781. Received at ten in the morning and forwarded forthwith to Reverend Mr Cubbon. John Crellin.

Kirk Maughold, May 26, 1781. Received about two o'clock P. M. and forwarded to the Reverend Mr Gill, vicar of Lonan, by Thomas Cubbon.

Kirk Lonan, May 27th, 1781. Received at nine o'clock in the forenoon and forwarded at one P. M. to the Reverend Mr Quayle, vicar of Conchan, by me, Samuel Gell.

Onchan, May 27th, 1781. Received about three o'clock in the afternoon and forwarded about four to the Reverend Mr Moore, chaplain of Douglas, by me, Thomas Quayle.

Douglas, May 27th, 1781. Sunday evening. Received and returned to the episcopal registrar next morning by me, Philip Moore.

[33] Clergy present:

William Mylrea.	Thomas Quayle.
Charles Crebbin.	Henry Corlett.
William Clucas.	Thomas Cubbon.
Philip Moore.	Ewan Christian.
Thomas Castley.	John Crellin.

Daniel Gelling.

John Moore.

Nicholas Christian.

William Crebbin.

Thomas William Joseph Woods.

Samuel Gell.

Thomas Christian.

Robert Quayle.

[34] David Harrison.

John Clague.

Daniel Mylrea.

John Moore.[558]

The clergy's address of welcome to the new bishop

To the right reverend father in God George, by divine permission lord bishop of Sodor and Man, at his primary convocation held on Thursday in Whitsun week, June the 7th, 1781.

We the archdeacon and clergy of this isle embrace this happy occasion to congratulate your lordship, the whole community and ourselves on your promotion to the episcopal dignity of this diocese, promising ourselves from your equanimity and moderation in this high and arduous function the mutual and peaceable enjoyment of all the blessings which such virtues have a tendency to secure to us, during your presidency in the church of God, and that all the inhabitants of this land, high and low, rich and poor, one with another, may long and happily rejoice in seeing the work of the Lord prosper in your hands, in this sequestered part of our great master's vineyard, to the conservation and cultivation whereof your lordship has been so providentially appointed.

That your lordship's name may be transmitted to posterity with dignity and honour, we conclude this our respectful address in the words of a sacred author: 'God give thee wisdom in thine heart to judge his people in righteousness.'[559] Amen.

William Mylrea.

Charles Crebbin.

William Clucas.

[35] Henry Corlett.

Thomas Cubbon.

John Crellin.

Robert Quayle.

John Clague.

Daniel Mylrea.

Philip Moore.

Daniel Gelling.

Samuel Gell.

John Moore.

William Crebbin.

Ewan Christian.

Thomas Quayle.

Examined by William Clucas, episcopal registrar.

At this convocation it was resolved and agreed by the whole assembly that the most respectful thanks of the bishop and clergy of the isle and diocese of Man in

[558]Officiating minister at Lezayre.

[559]1 Ch. xxii. 12.

convocation assembled should be presented to Dr Wilson for his donative of his father's works[560] to the parochial libraries of this isle and other benefactions to the church of Man.

A copy of the address of thanks is hereunto annexed.

Letter of thanks to Dr Wilson for his many benefactions

To the reverend Dr Wilson, prebendary of Westminster, etc.

At this primary convocation holden at Bishopscourt on Thursday in Whitsun week 1781 under the presidency of the right reverend father in God Dr George Mason, lord bishop of this diocese, we the archdeacon and clergy of this isle with his lordship assembled take the opportunity of this our solemn meeting to testify his lordship's and our own most grateful sense of your many accumulated favours to the diocese wherein you were born, and of which your most venerable father was a most illustrious luminary for more than half a century.

Your establishment of a fund for the better support of our poor clergymen's widows and children claims our most grateful and [36] affectionate acknowledgments, an institution first planned by your excellent father and yourself and of which you have the pleasure to see the happy and blessed effects.

Our next tribute of gratitude is due for your generous donative of your own father's life and works to the parochial libraries of this isle, now possessed of another treasure of sacred knowledge and that primeval piety of which the right reverend author was so bright an example.

The promise of an hundred guineas for the improvement and enlargement of our many incompetent churches and chapels is another instance of your great regard for the honour of God and the good of this diocese which with most grateful hearts we unanimously acknowledge, beseeching the Almighty to bless the remainder of your days with ease and comfort, and finally to reward all your acts of beneficence and charity with our great Master's cheerful compensation of 'well done good, etc.'[561]

William Mylrea.	Thomas Quayle.
Charles Crebbin.	Henry Corlett.
William Clucas.	Thomas Cubbon.
Philip Moore.	John Crellin.
Daniel Gelling.	Thomas Christian.
Samuel Gell.	Robert Quayle.
John Moore.	David Harrison.
William Crebbin.	John Clague.
Ewan Christian.	Daniel Mylrea.

Examined by William Clucas, episcopal registrar.

---

[560]Edited by C. Cruttwell and published in two volumes (London, 1781).
[561]Mt. xxv. 21.

[37] The Reverend Messrs Thomas Quayle and John Crellin are appointed a committee to audit the accounts of all receipts and disbursements of the charity towards the support and maintenance of the widows, children and orphans of the clergy for the years 1779, 1780 and 1781. William Clucas, episcopal registrar.

Thursday 23 May 1782

[38] Clergy present:

William Mylrea
Charles Crebbin,
William Clucas, vicars-general.
Philip Moore.
Daniel Gelling.
Thomas Castley.
John Moore.
William Crebbin.
Thomas William Joseph Woods.
Samuel Gell.
Thomas Quayle.

Henry Corlett.
Thomas Cubbon.
Ewan Christian.
John Crellin.
Thomas Christian.
John Clague.
Robert Quayle.
David Harrison.
[39] Daniel Mylrea.
John Moore.
John Bridson.

Thursday 12 June 1783

[40] Clergy present:

William Mylrea.
William Clucas,
Charles Crebbin, vicars general.
Daniel Gelling.
John Moore.
William Crebbin.
Thomas William Joseph Woods.
Samuel Gell.
Thomas Quayle.
Henry Corlett.
Thomas Cubbon.

Ewan Christian.
John Crellin.
Thomas Corlett.
Thomas Christian.
John Clague.
David Harrison.
Robert Quayle.
Daniel Mylrea.
John Moore.
John Bridson.

BISHOP CLAUDIUS CRIGAN (1784-1813)

Thursday 19 May 1785

[41] Clergy present:

William Mylrea.
John Moore,
Ewan Christian, vicars-general.
John Crellin.
Thomas Castley.
Daniel Gelling.
William Clucas.
William Crebbin.
Samuel Gell.
Thomas Quayle.
Henry Corlett.
Thomas Cubbon.

Charles Crebbin, indisposed.
Thomas Corlett.
Robert Quayle.
Thomas Christian.
John Clague.
Julius Cosnahan.
Daniel Mylrea.
John Moore.
John Bridson.
John Christian.
David Harrison.

[42] At this convocation the Reverend Daniel Gelling, Thomas Quayle and John Crellin, episcopal registrar are appointed a committee to inspect, examine and report the state of the accounts of the Reverend John Moore, vicar-general relative to Mrs Catharine Halsall's charity and to give his lordship satisfaction as to the receipts and disbursements.

Whereas several of the wardens of this diocese represent it as a grievance that they are obliged to present on common fame, as also such persons as do not attend divine service on holy days, the reverend Messrs John Crellin, episcopal registrar, Daniel Gelling and Henry Corlett are appointed a committee to represent this to the legislature, as soon as other matters of a similar nature are ready to be laid before them, for their consideration and amendment.

Thursday 8 June 1786

[44][562] At a convocation at St Peter's church in Peeltown on Thursday [8 June] 1786.

Clergy present:

William Mylrea.
John Moore.
Ewan Christian, vicars-general.
John Crellin, episcopal registrar.
Thomas Castley.
Daniel Gelling.
William Clucas.
William Crebbin.
Samuel Gell.
Thomas Quayle.
Henry Corlett.
Thomas Cubbon.

Charles Crebbin.
Thomas Corlett.
Robert Quayle.
Thomas Christian.[563]
John Clague.
David Harrison.
John Moore.
Daniel Mylrea.
John Bridson.
John Christian.
John Gell.

Thursday 30 May 1787

[45] At a convocation holden at Peeltown on the thirtieth day of May, 1787. Clergy present:

William Mylrea.
John Moore.
Ewan Christian.
John Crellin.
Thomas Castley.
Daniel Gelling.
William Clucas.
William Crebbin.
Samuel Gell.
Thomas Cubbon.

Charles Crebbin.
Thomas Corlett.
Robert Quayle.
John Clague.
David Harrison.
John Moore.
Daniel Mylrea.
John Bridson.
John Gell.
John Christian.

An address to the dowager duchess of Atholl

At the said convocation the following address was agreed on:

To her grace the duchess dowager of Atholl, etc., etc., etc., May it please your grace, We the archdeacon and clergy of the diocese of Sodor and Man beg leave to approach your grace, [46] and to allude to the intimation conveyed by your grace

---

[562]P. 43 is blank.
[563]Suspended, absent.

to the reverend Mr archdeacon in the year 1784 respecting your appointment of the right reverend father in God Claudius, lord bishop to this then vacant diocese.

The sanction of your grace's signature has ever justly influenced our opinions in favour of the prelate recommended and appointed to govern the church of Man, and now, in addition to this, that the experience of three years has enabled us to form a complete judgment of his lordship's character, we are happy in having it in our power to notify to your grace from our annual synod that his lordship's learning and abilities, his activity and zeal in the pastoral duties, his exemplary piety as a prelate, his tempered vigilance and moderation as a ruler over this church, reflect honour on your grace's appointment and deservedly engage him a place as well in the affections of his clergy as in the catalogue of his venerable predecessors.

May your grace's noble family fully enjoy every happiness and blessing that must result from the election of faithful and true pastors for this church is the sincere prayer of your grace's humble servants.

William Mylrea.	Robert Quayle.
John Moore.	John Moore.
Ewan Christian.	Thomas Cubbon.
Thomas Castley.	John Clague.
Daniel Gelling.	Daniel Mylrea.
Thomas Quayle.	David Harrison.
William Crebbin.	[47] John Bridson.
John Crellin.	John Gell.
Henry Corlett.	John Christian.
Thomas Corlett.	William Clucas.

Thursday 10 May 1788

At a convocation holden at St Peter's church in Peeltown on Thursday the tenth of May 1788. Clergy present:

Reverend and right honourable Lord George Murray, archdeacon, absent.

John Moore,	Charles Crebbin.
Ewan Christian, vicars-general.	Thomas Corlett.
John Crellin, episcopal registrar.	Robert Quayle.
Thomas Castley.	Thomas Christian, suspended.
Daniel Gelling.	John Clague.
William Clucas.	David Harrison.
William Crebbin.	John Moore.
Samuel Gell.	[48] Daniel Mylrea.
Thomas Quayle.	John Bridson.
Henry Corlett.	John Gell.
Thomas Cubbon.	

At this convocation the Reverend John Crellin, episcopal registrar, and the Reverend Daniel Gelling were appointed a committee to inspect and examine and also to report the state of the accounts of the Reverend John Moore, vicar-general, relative to Mrs Catharine Halsall's charity, and to satisfy his lordship as to the receipts and disbursements.

Also the Reverend John Crellin, episcopal registrar and the Reverend Henry Corlett appointed a committee to audit the account of all receipts and disbursements of the charity established for the support and maintenance of the widows, children and orphans of the clergy, and report the same to his lordship.

Whereas no certificate has been returned by any of the vicars save the vicar of Lonan of the completion of the repairs ordered at his lordship's late visitation, his lordship has indulged the wardens, who have been remiss, with the space of three months from the fifteenth of May instant, when certificate is to be returned that said repairs are perfected.

His lordship intimated at this convocation that he purposed admitting Mr Nicholas Christian, one of the students at Castletown to the order of a deacon, to which the clergy consented.

Letter of congratulation sent to the king on his recovery, 31 March 1789

[49] To the king's most excellent majesty. We the bishop and clergy of the isle and diocese of Man beg leave to offer your majesty our most warm and respectful congratulations on your recovery from the bed of sickness, an event as it has diffused an universal joy through every rank of your subjects, so it has engaged our particular gratitude to the Almighty for having restored you to the ardent prayers of your people.

Remote as we are in situation from your majesty, we happily feel ourselves as within the sphere of your royal influence, favour and protection, circumstances that render your health and welfare objects of the greatest concern to us, and it is our most fervent prayer that to the blessing of restored health by which God has been graciously pleased to enable your majesty to resume the reins of government, he may add an increasing vigour of body and mind to support the cares thereof.

We beg leave further to represent that the protection your majesty has during your reign as head of the national church afforded to our national establishment, and the pious zeal you have ever uniformly manifested in the discharge of the duties of Christianity and in the display of the virtues of that holy profession, whilst [50] they merit our warmest admiration cannot fail of producing the most blessed and beneficial effects through your extensive empire.

That your majesty may long, very long continue to constitute the happiness of your most amiable consort, of your most illustrious family, and of your loyal and affectionate people, shall ever be the devout prayer of your majesty's most dutiful and truly affectionate subjects. 31 March 1789.

Thursday 4 June 1789

Clergy present:

Lord George Murray, absent.
John Moore.
Ewan Christian.
John Crellin.
Thomas Castley.
Daniel Gelling.
William Clucas.
Samuel Gell.
Thomas Quayle.
Henry Corlett.
Thomas Cubbon.

Charles Crebbin.
Thomas Corlett.
Robert Quayle.
[51] John Clague.
David Harrison.
John Moore.
John Bridson.
Daniel Mylrea.
John Christian.
John Gell.
Nicholas Christian.

At this convocation holden June 4, 1789, the reverend vicar-general Christian, the Reverend John Crellin episcopal registrar, and the Reverend Thomas Cubbon are appointed a committee to examine Peter J. Heywood esquire's bill on account of soliciting a bill in parliament respecting the agreement between his grace the duke of Atholl, the right honourable the earl of Derby and the clergy relative to the impropriate fund, and to report to his lordship what they think necessary to be done, and what answer is to be given to said Mr Peter John Heywood on the occasion.

Application made on said day by the Reverend Mr Nelson for a removal of his suspension, which his lordship, upon inquiry, did not think fit should take place, on account of certain irregularities lately committed by him, but a ray of hope held out.

The accounts of the reverend Messrs Moore and Christian, vicars-general, not audited since the directions given at last convocation in 1787, to be forthwith examined and reported by the persons then appointed.

Thursday 27 May 1790

[52] Clergy present:

Lord George Murray.
John Moore.
Ewan Christian.
John Crellin.
Thomas Castley.
Daniel Gelling.
William Clucas.
John Gell.
Thomas Quayle.
Henry Corlett.
Thomas Cubbon.

Charles Crebbin.
Thomas Corlett.
Robert Quayle.
John Clague.
David Harrison.
John Moore.
Daniel Mylrea.
John Gell.
Nicholas [Christian].
Henry Maddrell.

At this convocation, resolved that the trustees of the widows' fund and Mrs Catharine Halsall's charity meet on the first day of July next to audit the accounts and to consider what may be necessary to be done respecting the repairs of a house in Castletown, a gift from her.

[53] The Reverend Thomas Christian, vicar of Marown, having quitted the retirement enjoined on him by his lordship and returned to the scene of his former unfortunate connections, has this day promised to repair to Kirk Bride and submit himself to the guidance and direction of his brother-in-law the Reverend Mr Clucas during the period of his probation.

Application was this day made by the Reverend Mr Nelson for a removal of his suspension, which his lordship is not disposed to do, having heard of some late irregularities omitted by the said Mr Nelson.

Thursday 16 June 1791

Clergy present:

Lord George Murray, absent.	Robert Quayle.
John Moore.	John Clague.
Ewan Christian.	[54] David Harrison.
John Crellin.	John Moore.
Thomas Castley.	John Bridson.
Daniel Gelling.	Daniel Mylrea.
William Clucas.	John Christian.
William Crebbin.	John Gell.
Samuel Gell.	Nicholas Christian.
Thomas Cubbon.	Henry Maddrell.
Charles Crebbin.	Hugh Stowell.[564]
Thomas Corlett.	

Ordered that the trustees of Mrs Catharine Halsall's charity do meet at Castletown on the chapter court day next ensuing in order to view the houses there bequeathed by her, and to consider whether it may not be proper to rebuild them.

Thursday 31 May 1792

[55] Clergy present:

Lord George Murray, absent.	Robert Quayle.
Ewan Christian,	John Clague.
William Clucas, vicars-general.	David Harrison.
John Crellin.	John Christian.
Thomas Castley.	John Bridson.
David Gelling.	Daniel Mylrea.

---

[564]Student at Castletown.

William Crebbin, absent.
Samuel Gell, absent.
Thomas Cubbon.
Charles Crebbin.
Thomas Corlett.

John Gell.
Nicholas Christian.
Henry Maddrell.
Hugh Stowell.

[56] Resolved...
Ordered as last year respecting the houses left by Mrs Catharine Halsall,
whether it may not be proper to rebuild them.
Agreed by the clergy that they will allow Mrs Hannah Barnsley one year to pay
the arrears of royal bounty due, or that Mr Quayle shall set the time as he may best
think fit.

Thursday 23 May 1793

[57] Clergy present:

Lord George Murray.
Ewan Christian,
William Clucas, vicars-general.
John Crellin.
Thomas Castley.
Daniel Gelling.
Henry Corlett.
William Crebbin.
Samuel Gell, indisposed.
Thomas Quayle.
Thomas Cubbon.
Charles Crebbin.
Thomas Corlett.
Robert Quayle.

John Clague.
David Harrison, indisposed.
John Christian.
John Bridson.
Daniel Mylrea.
John Gell.
Nicholas Christian.
Henry Maddrell.
Hugh Stowell.
John Clague, sick.
John Cannell.
Joseph Stowell.
John Gelling.[565]

Thursday 12 June 1794

Called over 12 June 1794. Absent ut anno priore.

Thursday 28 May 1795

Absent 1795: William Crebbin, Samuel Gell, Lord George Murray. Read 1795.

[565] An incomplete note begins: 'These three [Cannell, Stowell, Gelling] this year 1793...'.

Thursday 19 May 1796

Read 1796. Absent, [William] Crebbin, [Samuel] Gell.

[58] Read 19 May 1796.

Lord George Murray, the vicars of Jurby, Lonan and Santan absent owing to indisposition.

[59] Matters discussed at convocation, 19 May 1796.

His lordship having good reason to believe that the parochial clergy, lose some hundreds of pounds annually by neglecting to institute a suit against Lord Derby to recover from his lordship an equivalent for the present increased value of the impropriate tithes, the bishop therefore desires the clergy may as soon as possible return to him such an accurate statement of the present value of the said tithes as may stand the test of a legal investigation.

His lordship also desires that the clergy may in a fortnight or three weeks at farthest return to him the number of the poor in their respective parishes, distinguishing the aged and infirm from such as are able by their honest endeavours to contribute something towards their own subsistence. Also the amount of the funds in each parish or town for the support of the poor, with the average amount of their annual collections.

And whereas we find from sad experience that the censures of the church have proved ineffectual to suppress the sins of adultery and fornication, we wish to take the sense of the clergy, whether it might not be advisable to adopt another mode of punishing such offenders, by proposing it to the legislature to enact a law empowering the bishop and vicars-general [60] to commute their censures for a pecuniary fine, to be proportioned (at the discretion of the said spiritual judges) to the circumstances of the offending parties, and such fines to be levied and paid to the vicar and wardens to be by them applied to the relief and support of the poor of that parish where one or both offenders reside. Approved.

And whereas several of the wardens of this diocese represent it as a grievance that they are obliged by their oath to present on common fame, as also all such persons as do not attend divine service on holy days, whether it would not be proper to represent this to the legislature for their consideration and amendment. Approved.

Whereas Mr Thomas Christian, vicar of the parish of Marown, was by our sentence dated 14 August 1786 suspended *ab officio et beneficio sine die* for being found guilty of fornication with Evelyn Kelly, and that instead of pursuing a course of penitent behaviour, he hath since rather given himself over to a reprobate mind, by relapsing into the same crime with the same woman and others, the bishop desires the opinion of his clergy whether, after bringing such a reproach upon [61] the church of God and the sanctity of the ministry, the said Thomas Christian ought not to be degraded from the ministry of this church? His degradation agreed to.

The reverend Robert Quayle, vicar of Kirk Braddan, having branded his character with a mark of infamy by subscribing a paper writing purporting that he had maliciously and slanderously belied the reverend Mr Thomas Whitehurst. The sentiments of the clergy were intended to be required on his lordship's return, but that he had given his lordship solemn satisfaction that he had an author for what he had said with respect to that gentleman.

It having been suggested by some of the trustees at the last convocation that from the great expense likely to attend such a work, it would be less to the advantage of the objects of the trust to rebuild than to dispose of the concerns at Castletown bequeathed by Mrs Catharine Halsall now in ruins. The trustees now to fix a day for meeting shortly, in order to carry into execution any measure desirable to be adopted to make the said concerns productive as soon as possible.

The chapter court at Castletown, viz. June the second, 1796, fixed for the meeting.

[62-4] *A fair copy of the above.*

Thursday 8 June 1797

[58][566] Read 1797. Lord George [Murray] absent. Also vicars of Jurby, Lonan and Onchan.

Things to be settled.

Mrs Halsall's charity on a day to be appointed at the chapter court.

Mr Edward Moore to be agreed with by the vicar-general at chapter court respecting the services done by the late Reverend Philip Moore in the widows fund.

Thursday 31 May 1798

[65] Clergy present:

Lord George Murray, absent.
Ewan Christian.
William Clucas.
John Crellin.
Thomas Castley.
Daniel Gelling.
William Crebbin, absent.
Samuel Gell, absent.
Henry Corlett.
Thomas Cubbon.
Charles Crebbin.
Thomas Corlett.

Robert Quayle.
John Clague.
David Harrison.
John Christian.
John Bridson.
Daniel Mylrea.
John Gell.
Nicholas Christian.
Henry Maddrell.
Hugh Stowell.
John Clague.

Joseph Stowell, student at Castletown.
James Gelling, student at Castletown.
[Thomas] Kewley, student at Castletown.

[566]Out of chronological order.

There is no further record of any convocation held in Bishop Crigan's time. The statutory dates for them are given below, and the ones which were probably held (but have left no record) are in **bold type.**

Thursday 16 May 1799
Thursday 5 June 1800
Thursday 28 May 1801
Thursday 10 June 1802
Thursday 2 June 1803   (The bishop was probably off the island.)
Thursday 24 May 1804
Thursday 6 June 1805
Thursday 29 May 1806
Thursday 21 May 1807
Thursday 9 June 1808
Thursday 25 May 1809
Thursday 14 June 1810
Thursday 6 June 1811
Thursday 21 May 1812

The 1813 date (10 June) fell during an interregnum and so the convocation was not held.

BISHOP GEORGE MURRAY (1814-27)

Thursday 2 June 1814

According to the *Manks Advertiser* of Saturday 4 June (p. 2), a convocation was held at St George's, Douglas, at which John Nelson, vicar of Jurby, was the preacher. Afterwards, the bishop entertained the clergy to lunch at castle Mona.

Thursday 18 May 1815
Thursday 6 June 1816
Thursday 29 May 1817

No records survive for convocations on these statutory dates, though the bishop is known to have been in the island at that time.

Thursday 14 May 1818
Thursday 3 June 1819
Thursday 25 May 1820
Thursday 14 June 1821

The above are the statutory dates, but the bishop was probably off the island in 1818, 1819 and 1821.

Wednesday 26 June 1822

[66] Clergy present:[567]

Daniel Mylrea, archdeacon.
*Thomas Cubbon, vicar-general.
Thomas Stephen, vicar-general.
Joseph Brown, episcopal registrar.
*Hugh Stowell.
*David Harrison.
*James Gelling.
*Henry Maddrell.
*John Nelson.
*Thomas Howard.

Bowyer Harrison.
*Thomas Thimbleby.
*Robert Brown.
John Christian.
Philip Corlett.
William Duggan.
William Gill.
John Gell.
William Corrin.
*George Stickler Parsons.

---

[567]Certain names are asterisked, but the significance of this is not clear.

*Edward Craine.
*John Cottier.
*John Edward Harrison.
*Alexander Gelling.
*Joseph Qualtrough.
*William Christian.

*Thomas Kewley.[568]
John James Gelling.
Samuel Gelling.
John Thomas Clarke.
*James Crebbin, deacon.

Thursday 22 May 1823
Thursday 10 June 1824
Thursday 26 May 1825
Thursday 18 May 1826
Thursday 7 June 1827

The above are the statutory dates, but the bishop was off the island in 1824 and 1825, and probably also in 1826.

---

[568]He and the next three are listed as 'academic students'.

BISHOP WILLIAM WARD (1828-38)

No convocation was held in 1828 (29 May) because the bishop had not yet arrived in the island.

Thursday 13 August 1829

Daniel Mylrea, archdeacon, absent from illness.
John Nelson, vicar-general.
Benjamin Philpot, vicar-general, absent in England.
Joseph Brown
Henry Maddrell
Hugh Stowell, absent in England.
James Gelling
Thomas Stephen
Joseph Qualtrough
John Edward Harrison
Thomas Howard
Edward Craine
Alexander Gelling
William Christian, suspended (absent).
Bowyer Harrison
William Corrin
William Duggan
Thomas Kewley
Robert Brown, absent.
George Stickler Parsons
Archibald Holmes
John Thomas Clarke
Samuel Gelling
William Gill, curate of Malew
James Crebbin, curate of St George's
John Cannell, curate of Bride
Lewis Geneste, curate of Ballaugh
Robert Money Chatfield, domestic chaplain to the bishop.
John Wright, absent.
Francis Broderick Hartwell.
A. Harford Locking, Somersetshire.
I. Ditcher Kingswood, Gloucestershire.

Thursday 3 June 1830
Thursday 26 May 1831
Thursday 14 June 1832
Thursday 30 May 1833

These are the statutory dates for convocation, though no records have survived.

Friday 17 October 1834[569]

Archdeacon Philpot.
Vicars-general [John] Nelson
and [Francis] Hartwell.
Hugh Stowell.
*Henry Maddrell.
James Gelling.
Thomas Stephen.
Thomas Howard.
Edward Craine.
*John Edward Harrison.
*Alexander Gelling.
Joseph Qualtrough.
Joseph Brown.
Bowyer Harrison.
*William Corrin.
Thomas Kewley.

William Gill.
William Carpenter.
*Robert Brown.
Archibald Holmes.
George Stickler Parsons.
*John Thomas Clarke.
William Drury.
Samuel Flood.
[v] *William Duggan.
Samuel Gelling.
Daniel Nelson.
John White.
John Gell, supernumerary.
John Cannell, supernumerary.
*John Stowell, supernumerary.
*Edward John Brookes.[570]

Thursday 11 June 1835

No record has survived of this convocation, if one was indeed held.

Thursday 26 May 1836[571]

Memorial of the bishop of Sodor and Man to his majesty's commissioners appointed to consider the state of the established church with reference to ecclesiastical duties and revenues, 1836

I feel myself called upon thus publicly to address your honourable board, as the only way open to me of recording my most solemn remonstrance and protest against

---

[569]This and the following convocations to 1848 are recorded on loose sheets which are attached to Manx National Heritage Library, MS 804C, but not numbered.
[570]Curate of Kirk Andreas.
[571]Reprinted from W. F. Ward, *The Isle of Mann and the diocese of Sodor and Mann* (Douglas, 1837), appendix III. The bishop's memorial was the fruit of a meeting of the clergy at Kirk Michael on 15 March 1836, which was then circulated around the island in May and almost certainly discussed at the annual convocation, though that is not recorded in the acts.

that recommendation of your second report, by which provision is made for the future annexation of the present see of Sodor and Man to that of Carlisle. Since in my opinion this union of the two sees would be highly inconvenient to both, and most detrimental to the spiritual, as well as to the social interests of that people, over whom the providence of God has placed me, I should consider myself wanting to my duty, did I ever silently concede the point, or cease to press it upon the attention of the church, so long as my life offers an impediment to its accomplishment.

Although this proposition has now become prospectively the law of the land, there are two reasons, which induce me to bring it before the board at this present time. I am informed by an eminent legal authority, that your commission did not extend to the Isle of Man, and that therefore so much of the act of last session, as refers to that island, is virtually repealed, and must be re-enacted under a new commission; but even if this were not the case, there is, I apprehend, a power vested in your honourable board of altering or modifying any of its former recommendations: it is under the hope therefore, that the proposition affecting the Isle of Man may be reconsidered on either the one or the other of these grounds, that I beg to lay before your honourable board my own views of this question in as strong a light, as is consistent with the respect due from me to his majesty's commissioners.

I propose, in the first place, to give some reasons for the preservation of its ancient privileges to the Isle of Man, and afterwards to consider in their order all the objections, which have been urged on the other side.

The first reason for the preservation of that bishopric rests upon its antiquity; there are authentic records of an almost uninterrupted succession of insular bishops for more than 1400 years.

Secondly, from its geographical position the Isle of Man is entitled to retain its bishop.

Thirdly, as a distinct people, the Manx are entitled to continue in the enjoyment of this among their other ancient privileges: their laws, ecclesiastical and civil, are different from those of England; their legislative and executive government is distinct from, and their legislative independent of, the English; the church therefore, as well as the state, requires a distinct governor.

Fourthly, the constant presence of the bishop is necessary as head of the council, the principal branch of the legislature in the island, and as leading trustee of all the insular charities; these are duties, which cannot be exercised by an archdeacon, or any other deputy.

Fifthly, there is another reason, in some measure connected with the last, which should have some weight, when we are making new laws for an old people, and invading their long-established rights. The bishop is one of the principal resident gentlemen in the island, whose station in society, whose connexions in England, and whose property give him the power of befriending the necessitous, and that the more effectually, because, from living among them, he knows their wants and their characters, from personal observation.

In the sixth and last place, from reasons moral and religious a resident bishop should be retained in that island. His presence there has necessarily a great moral influence upon society in all ranks, because his authority extends to all ranks. But most especially would the absence of the bishop affect the interests of religion: the bishops of Sodor and Man have hitherto maintained those interests almost single-handed. There is not a church or chapel, nor an institution for the advancement of learning, which is not a monument of the careful munificence, and charitable exertions of some bishop of the island. Not to speak of more ancient remains, the *monitus locorum* of ruder, but not less pious ages; since the restoration

Bishop Barrow founded parochial schools in every parish, and also a free-school in Castletown for the purposes of general education. He also left an estate to provide for the education and partial support of the clergy: besides which, he raised funds in England for the purchase of the impropriate tithes, then in the hands of Lord Derby, since then recovered back from the clergy by the duke of Atholl after fifty years possession, and now vested in the crown.

Bishop Wilson, the second great benefactor of the island since the restoration, obtained by law from the Derby estates what was then considered an equivalent, but which does not now return more than a fourth part of the original value of the tithes. Besides the blessings resulting from the personal superintendence of so watchful an overseer for more than half a century, Bishop Wilson built churches and chapels proportioned to the population at that time, founded public libraries in every parish, and in all respects made his diocese a model not only for the Church in England, but for the whole Christian church throughout the world.

Bishop Hildesley trod worthily in his footsteps, and left the Manx a precious legacy in the Bible and the liturgy, translated, under his care, into their own language. Succeeding bishops have built, or caused to be built, both churches and chapels. But it was impossible for the bishops to find means for the building of churches, equal to the extraordinary increase of the population, before the attention of the English public had been, as it now is, generally drawn to the subject: notwithstanding therefore the exertions of my predecessors, when I came to the see nine years ago, I found that the population of the island had increased so rapidly, having more than doubled itself since the time of Bishop Wilson's death, that local means were wholly inadequate to furnish the necessary church accommodation: I had recourse, therefore, to English charity, and succeeded in raising funds sufficient for the building and rebuilding of eleven new churches and chapels. A proposition also made by me for a more extensive application of the funds arising from the trust estate left by Bishop Barrow, met with cordial assent, and a vigorous co-operation on the part of my co-trustees, and the principal gentlemen of the island, the consequence of which was the establishment of a college upon the estate, which his majesty has graciously permitted to be called King William's College; it already contains nearly 200 students.

I mention these circumstances, which refer to myself, because I am well assured, that if any benefits have accrued, or are likely to accrue to the Isle of Man from any exertions made by me, those benefits are the necessary consequence of my personal superintendence, and freedom from other duties: had I been resident at Carlisle, encumbered with the cares of that diocese, and with parliamentary duties, none of those works (even had they been projected) could have been carried into effect. The same causes also must have operated to have diminished the exertions of Bishops Barrow, Wilson, Hildesley, and all the other bishops of that island, had this annexation taken place before their day: Bishop Wilson's government could not, in that case, have called forth that eulogium of the Lord Chancellor King, that 'if the ancient discipline of the Church were lost, it might be found in all its purity in the Isle of Man'.

If such have been the advantages resulting to the Isle of Man from the presence of its own bishop within its own shores, it is certainly a hard, if not an unjust, thing to deprive an ancient and a loyal, though a poor, people of their undoubted rights without the most obvious necessity. I looked, therefore, in the report of your honourable board for some reasons of weight sufficient to justify the proposed change. Without detracting from those advanced either in number or importance, I hope to shew you, that you have acted in this matter, on grounds insufficient in themselves, and inapplicable in the present case.

The following are the words of the report: 'We are of opinion that the bishopric of Sodor and Man may, without inconvenience, be united to that of Carlisle.' Since these words stand the first in order, I must call your attention to an inconsistency in the report, which they suggest. Speaking in your first report of the proposed union of Bristol and Llandaff, you say: 'If this plan be adopted, it cannot be denied, that the interposition of the Bristol Channel between the two divisions of the diocese will produce some inconvenience, and that the bishop will be resident at a considerable distance from the greater part of his diocese.' Again, in your second report, you say: 'When the union of the sees of Bristol and Llandaff was recommended, we were not insensible to the inconveniences attending that arrangement, and the representations, which have since been made to us against it, have operated so strongly on our minds, as to induce us, on reconsideration, to relinquish that plan.' Those representations, I am informed, came from the people of Bristol and Llandaff, who laid before the board the great inconveniences which would arise from the fact of the Bristol Channel dividing the proposed diocese. To these representations you very reasonably yielded; yet a few lines only further on it is given as the opinion of the board, that the bishoprics of Man and Carlisle, between which intervenes, not the estuary of a river, but a wide sea, of a navigation confessedly the most difficult and dangerous to be found round the coasts of the United Kingdom, 'may be united without inconvenience'. This is surely inconsistent with your own expressed opinion, 'that the interposition of the Bristol Channel between two divisions of a diocese would produce some inconvenience; an inconvenience sufficiently great to induce you to relinquish the plan'. Is it not also inconsistent with your objection to a bishop being resident at a considerable distance from a great part of his diocese? Does there not appear an inconsistency in the statements, that the sees of Bristol and Llandaff, on account of the Channel, cannot, but that the sees of Man and Carlisle, notwithstanding the sea, can be united without inconvenience? 'Convenient' is certainly not the word most applicable to the proposed measure; for looking at it merely as an arrangement of expediency, the inconvenience of that arrangement forces itself upon our notice in whatever way we view it; not only as regards the clergy and the people of the Isle of Man, but also the bishop of Carlisle.

I have myself always found it exceedingly difficult and inconvenient to exercise an efficient control over my diocese during my occasional absence in England, although I am intimately acquainted with all its peculiar circumstances, and am free from all other episcopal duties. I assume, therefore, that it would be much more difficult and inconvenient for a bishop of Carlisle, who could never be supposed to have the same opportunities of local information, as a resident bishop must necessarily possess; and who has, moreover, duties already sufficiently onerous, without the addition of those resulting from such an appendage as that of the Isle of Man to Carlisle. To the inconvenience of such an addition, the bishop of Exeter, when speaking on this subject in the house of lords, has borne ample testimony. He said he could speak from personal experience; the Scilly Islands had been lately added to his diocese; and although he gladly took them under his charge, rather than suffer them to remain without a bishop, yet the inconvenience attending his superintendence of them could only be known by one, who had experienced it: at that very time he was in great perplexity as to the right course to pursue; either he must defer his visitation to those islands till another summer, a delay which would be greatly prejudicial to the interests of the church there, or he must neglect some most important duties in other parts of his diocese.

Such are the inconveniences attending the annexation of the Scilly Islands to the diocese of Exeter — islands small in themselves, and of little importance compared with the Isle of Man. These inconveniences, however, were unavoidable; it was necessary, that those islands should have a bishop. But with the Isle of Man the case is far different: the bishop of Carlisle is not called upon to receive under his care this most inconvenient appendage to his present large diocese, because the people of that island are destitute of a spiritual overseer; but an independent bishopric of fourteen hundred years duration is to be swept from the English Church, an important and populous island is to be deprived of its own complete system of civil and ecclesiastical government, principally, as it would appear, for the purpose of making an addition to the see of Carlisle. The only other reason advanced in your report rests upon the same ground of territory. You say, that 'the Isle of Man contains only eighteen parishes, over which the archdeacon, who is resident, and has a respectable income, can exercise an effectual superintendence'. With reference to this it has been said, that the commissioners in equalizing the ecclesiastical divisions of England and Wales could not overlook the Isle of Man. But in the first report, in which the new divisions were all proposed, you did overlook it; for Carlisle received considerable additions, but the diocese of Sodor and Mann was not mentioned; and in the map of England and Wales, attached to the report, the Isle of Man only is left uncoloured, as though it had nothing to do with the ecclesiastical divisions of England and Wales: this is the point, to which I wish to call your attention.

The diocese of Sodor and Mann does not interfere with any of the English dioceses; the arrangements for the re-division of those sees were all made without reference to the Isle of Man. It is doubtless perfectly right, that the twenty-six ecclesiastical divisions of England and Wales should be made more equal; but it does not therefore follow, that the twenty-seventh bishopric, separated geographically, morally, civilly, and for 1400 years ecclesiastically, from the other twenty-six, should be abolished, because it is smaller than the rest. For although the diocese of Sodor and Man is small in comparison with the English bishoprics, yet the assumed advantage of a new division of territory is not a sufficient reason for destroying a sacred institution of 1400 years' duration, unless it can be shown that such an institution is either useless, or that it interferes with other necessary arrangements. I have already shown, that it is not useless: neither does it interfere with other necessary arrangements, because they were all originally made without reference to it; and from its geographical position it never can. One only reason can be urged on the ground of territory, that abstractedly speaking (for we must speak of the Isle of Man abstractedly from England) the diocese of Man is too small, and its territory unworthy the undivided care of so high a dignitary as a bishop.

The history, however, of the Christian church in its earliest and purest days, sufficiently refutes such an opinion. Such was not the opinion of the pious founder of that bishopric in 440. Such has not been the opinion of succeeding ages. Such was not the opinion of the great and good Bishop Wilson, who, when he was offered an English bishopric, refused to accept it. 'My wife', he said, 'is poor, but I will not forsake her in my old age.' The Isle of Man was not thought unworthy of his care by that primitive bishop, the benefit of whose learned labours is now reaped by the whole Christian world. Such, again, is not the opinion of the late bishop, who declared last session in his place in the house of lords, that, from fourteen years' experience, he considered the retention of its separate bishopric as essential to the well-being of the church in the Isle of Man.

My own opinion is sufficiently expressed in this memorial. But it is said, that the people of the island are indifferent as to the loss of their resident bishop, because they have sent up no petitions on this subject. Your honourable board is aware, that the archdeacon, the clergy, and the great body of respectable inhabitants have memorialized both his majesty and the board: and if the interested, the indifferent, and the disaffected would rejoice in the bishop's absence, there cannot be brought forward a stronger argument for his retention; for those, who most require the coercive power of either the civil magistrate, or the spiritual overseer, are not the first, but the last, who will make a voluntary effort to retain that power among them. Much has been said lately in England against the non-residence of the clergy, and his majesty charges the commissioners, 'that the best mode should be devised of providing for the cure of souls, with a special reference to the residence of the clergy on their respective benefices'; but, notwithstanding, you now propose to deprive the Isle of Man of its peculiar privilege of a bishop, with his clergy, constantly resident, and to supply his place by an archdeacon.

But is it not a degradation of the episcopal character? Is it not an indignity cast upon our apostolic office, to say, that an archdeacon can effectually fulfil the superintending duties of that office? An archdeacon is only *primus inter pares*; he is not a spiritual overseer; that people, therefore, whose resident bishop is supplanted by an archdeacon, lose whatever spiritual advantage is to be gained by the presence of a spiritual overseer. I trust that your honourable board will now see, that this proposition is not defensible on the ground of 'territory'. With regard to the episcopal 'revenues' of the see of Man, the board, of course, saw the injustice of alienating them for the benefit of Carlisle: you will also, I think, see the injustice, as well as the impolicy, of scattering those revenues among the inferior clergy. It is surely impolitic to admit the principle, that, if the clergy of a certain diocese be poor, they may claim the episcopal revenues, because there is not a diocese in the united church, to which this principle would not be applicable; and it is dangerous to tempt men with expectations which they ought not to desire to see realized. In this case, however, such a measure would be unjust towards the people, even should it in a temporal point of view benefit the clergy.

I have already shown the great advantages derived to the people from the residence of their own bishop among them; their forefathers purchased these advantages for them, by dedicating a portion of their property to his support to take this portion, therefore, and apply it for the benefit of any other order of the ministers of the church, would be unjust, not only to the present, but to all future generations of Manxmen. But to the clergy themselves this proposed benefit would be more specious than real; they are doubtless very poor, but they would not be compensated by the small portion they could each receive, at the most £50 or £60, from the subdivision of the bishop's revenues, for the loss of the only person of rank or property among them — far from gaining the comforts or the influence property, they would still remain poor; while, by this scattering of all its revenues, the church would lose the important station it now holds in all insular affairs. There is a source indeed, from which the clergy might receive temporal benefit, without spiritual detriment, either to themselves or the people. I have already mentioned certain impropriate tithes, once the property of the clergy, but now vested in the crown. To gain these tithes for the poor clergy, I have not hesitated to employ the most urgent importunities with every successive government during the last nine years. Could I live to see this boon granted, and the insular church secured in all her rights and privileges, I should go down to my grave without a doubt of her future welfare and prosperity.

From the prospect of what might be, I revert with pain to the proposition of your honourable board. When I first heard of your intention, I looked anxiously for some benefit proposed, as likely to accrue either to the Isle of Man, to Carlisle, or to the church generally, thinking that the church of Man had an undoubted right to expect such a reason at your hands; but I looked in vain — neither in the report, in the house of lords, nor elsewhere, was any such reason advanced.

Could the diocese of Sodor and Man have been made in any way subservient to the relieving of any English bishop, from the burden of too oppressive duties, even to its own detriment, my voice should not have been raised against such an arrangement. But when you take from the church of Man her spiritual father, you take that which does not enrich you, but makes her poor indeed: when therefore I can see or hear of no possible advantage, either to the church generally, or to the sees of Man or Carlisle, in particular; but the contrary to all, to the church generally the loss of a bishop; to Carlisle a great additional burden; to the Isle of Man great temporal and spiritual loss for the present, and a gloomy prospect for the church in future. When I see an ancient institution disturbed, without any plea of improvement, when I see a bishopric, coeval with the church itself, about to abolished, and that to the detriment of the church — when I am told, that those revenues, which, in a former age, independent islanders set apart for the support of their own bishop, are either to be alienated from the soil to a foreign bishop, or perverted to other uses than those, for which they were originally granted when I enquire into the authority, with which this was done, and find, that his majesty's commissioners have so far departed from the spirit, if not from the letter, of his majesty's instructions, which demanded 'the suggestion of such measures as might be most conducive to the efficiency of the established church', as actually to diminish, rather than to increase the number of its chief officers; and when, to accomplish this, I find, they have carried their powers across the sea to an island, to which their commission did not extend: when I hear this defended on grounds, which, even were they tenable, which they are not, would be altogether insufficient to warrant the disturbing of any ancient institution, much less to sanction the extinction of an independent church, which ages have hallowed, and which the great Head of the church has blessed in a peculiar manner, both in its bishops, its priests, and its people – when I see and hear all this, and remember that the providence of God has appointed me overseer and guardian of that church; and that I am responsible to him, if, through wilful neglect, or treacherous dereliction of my duty, that portion of his vineyard should suffer any hurt, either in the present or the future time; I should indeed be wanting in the duty which I owe, not only to my church, but to yourselves, did I cease to press this most solemnly upon your consciences, that this is not a mere question of convenience or of inconvenience, but, that in this and every act to which you put your hands, is involved the welfare of many million souls. You are intrusted with the interests of the fairest proportion of Christ's church – our sovereign is bound by the most solemn oath to preserve those interests in their full integrity – he has committed his conscience into your keeping – he has charged you to suggest such measures only, as shall 'be most conducive to the efficiency of the established church'.

Can you then, unwarranted by any pretext of improvement, venture to remove the mar of God from before the altar, where he has ministered without reproach, for 1400 years? Can you answer to your God for dismembering his church? Can you answer to your king, for detracting from the efficiency of the church by diminishing the number of its officers? Can you answer to the Bishops of the church for weakening their order, and adding to, rather than lightening their burdens? Will you one day be able to answer to future generations of Carlisle and the Isle of Man, for leaving them to the divided care of one spiritual overseer, when, but for your arrangement, they would have for ever continued to enjoy, each their ancient spiritual privileges, and their birthright? Can you persevere in this, and be at peace? God, and your own consciences alone can tell; but this others can tell also – the whole church is witness to me, that you have not been left unwarned – thus far I have done my duty – perhaps I may appear to some to have exceeded my duty be it so – the praise of God is of more value than the praise of man. I will never cease to repeat the warning with the greater earnestness, as the approach of my death hastens the accomplishment of this measure – to avert the threatened calamity from my church I am prepared to make any sacrifice, even of friendship; for I believe most solemnly, that in a very few years after the removal of the bishop, the name only of a church will be left to her, and her empty walls will stand as sad memorials of an arrangement, needless and uncalled for in itself, burdensome to Carlisle, and destructive to her own best interests. But it shall be never said that the last of this long line of bishops stood by with folded arms, without an effort, in the name of God, to arrest the stroke, before it fell.

While, then, my many years give serious warning, that I must speak as a dying man, and when I tell you that, after all other earthly cares are forgotten, my fears for this the church of my affections will add a pang to my dying hour, I have a good hope, that my words will not pass unheeded, but that the church of Man may even yet be spared, as a memorial of happier days, that are passed, and as an earnest of brighter days to come.

Thursday 18 May 1837

The statutory day for convocation; there is no record of one having been held.

Thursday 7 December 1837

Petition of Manx clergy for the preservation of the see of Sodor and Man.

To the right honourable the lords spiritual and temporal, the humble petition of the archdeacon and undersigned clergy of the diocese of Sodor and Man for the preservation of their bishopric as a distinct and independent see, showeth,

That whereas by an act of the late parliament, commonly called the English Church bill, it has been determined by the civil power, on the removal of the present bishop of Sodor and Man, to annex his diocese to the see of Carlisle, your petitioners beg leave humbly to represent that, in their judgment, such an annexation would be inconvenient and injurious, not to say uncalled for and unjust. With great inconvenience would the bishop of Carlisle receive so burdensome an addition to his duties, and be obliged, most probably, in advanced age, and with a large family and establishment, to cross and recross continually a wide channel, confessedly one of the most stormy and dangerous near the British shores. With equal inconvenience would his clergy and laity be able to communicate with him, either personally or by post, during two-thirds of every year, on those numberless matters, in which, as bishop of their insular church, head of its council, and leading trustee of its college, schools, and various charities, he would have to be consulted. Hence your petitioners are fully persuaded that embarrassment to all classes in the island, from its legislature down to its poor, and consequences injurious to their temporal and spiritual welfare, would inevitably arise from a non-residence of its bishop, so large, necessitated, and authorized, as must follow from the annexation of this see to Carlisle.

Such an arrangement, therefore, they earnestly deprecate being carried into effect; the rather, as it appears to them uncalled for by any serious ecclesiastical advantage. To remove an ancient landmark, to sink an independent bishopric almost coeval with Christianity itself, they would deem, under any circumstances, a grave measure, justifiable only from the extreme exigency of the case, but here the exigency seems all the other way. The Isle of Man is rapidly increasing in population and importance, and in consequent requirement and employment of a resident diocesan. Never were his presence, advice and ministrations in the church and council of his people, so urgent as in the present day. To secure his services and benison, independent islanders of a former age, at the same time that they enjoined his residence by statute law, rendered it easy and honourable by baronial dignity and liberal emoluments. Having made this provision for an independent bishop of their own, that their posterity should be deprived of him, in their hour of the greatest need, your petitioners humbly represent would at least be hard, they even venture to think unjust. Their constitution would be infringed, their statute law would be broken, England's compact with them would be violated, and their own episcopal revenues would be either abstracted from the soil, or converted to other ends than those for which they were plainly given.

And for risking all these evils, your petitioners humbly submit that no imperious necessity has been shown, or can be made out. A diocese which filled the hands of an apostolic Wilson, cannot reasonably be deemed too small, especially when its population is more than doubled since his day; the duties of that diocese could not with propriety and adequacy be discharged by the archdeacon; and as to enriching its parochial clergy by the spoils of their bishopric, your petitioners dislike the principle, and dread the example; they affect not indeed to conceal that the vicars of the diocese are in straitened, in very straitened, in lamentably straitened circumstances, from which they humbly solicit, and would gratefully accept, honourable relief; but they disclaim a wish to procure temporal advantage at the expense of spiritual loss.

And they beg respectfully to suggest, that there seems an opening by which, without trenching on the independency; of their bishopric, themselves and their large families might be placed in comparative comfort through the benevolent intercession of your lordships with the crown. Would her majesty be graciously pleased to increase the value of the ten vicarages in her majesty's gift to £150 a year out of the insular crown tithes at her majesty's disposal, since the bishop would increase the four in his gift to, the same amount, and the like arrangement might be made with his successors, the whole body of the parochial clergy in the island would be placed more nearly in that situation of temporal disembarrassment which is so all but indispensable to their integrity and usefulness. If, therefore, by an act of your right honourable house, the apprehended evils to this island could be averted, and the boon here suggested procured, your petitioners would rejoice, and thank God, and ever pray, &c.

There was no convocation in 1838 owing to the interregnum.

BISHOP JAMES BOWSTEAD (1838-40)

Thursday 23 May 1839

Benjamin Philpot, archdeacon.
Francis Broderick Hartwell, vicar-general, absent in England.
Alfred Philips, prinicipal of King William's College.
Robert Dixon, vice-principal of King William's College.
John Nelson, absent.
Thomas Howard.
Henry Maddrell.
Thomas Stephen.
Edward Craine, absent.
John Edward Harrison.
Alexander Gelling.
Joseph Qualtrough.
Joseph Brown, episcopal registrar.
Bowyer Harrison.
William Corrin.
William Duggan, minister of Marown.
William Gill
Samuel Gelling
Bobert Brown, absent.
John Lamothe Stowell, absent.
George Stickler Parsons
Archibald Holmes
John Thomas Clarke
William Carpenter
John Cannell
Thomas Caine
John Gell
Henry Joseph Stevenson, Mariner's chapel, absent.
Daniel Nelson, archdeacon's official.
William Drury, curate of Andreas.
Edward Qualtrough, curate of German.
John Qualtrough, curate of Lezayre, not well.
Thomas Pump Drake, curate of St Barnabas
William Kermode.

The convocation is also recorded in the Manx Sun *of Friday 31 May 1839 (p. 4).*

BISHOP HENRY PEPYS (1840-1)

Thursday 11 June 1840

John Cecil Hall, archdeacon.
Francis Broderick Hartwell, vicar-general.
Alfred Philips, principal of King William's College, absent.
Robert Dixon, vice-principal of King William's College, absent.
John Nelson, absent.
Thomas Howard, at a funeral.
Henry Maddrell, archdeacon's registrar.
Thomas Stephen.
Edward Craine, late.
John Edward Harrison.
Alexander Gelling, absent.
Joseph Qualtrough, late.
Joseph Brown, episcopal registrar.
Bowyer Harrison
William Corrin
William Duggan
William Gill
Samuel Gelling
Bobert Brown, at a funeral.
John Lamothe Stowell
George Stickler Parsons
Archibald Holmes
John Thomas Clarke
William Carpenter, off the island.
John Cannell
Thomas Caine
John Gell
Henry Joseph Stevenson
Daniel Nelson, supernumerary and official, off the island.
Thomas Drury, curate of Andreas, off the island.
Edward Qualtrough, curate of Dalby
John Qualtrough, curate of Sulby
Thomas Rump Drake, curate of St Barnabas
William Kermode, curate of Lezayre
Maurice Fitzgerald Day, curate of St George's
William Christian, absent.

According to the Manx Sun *of Friday 19 June 1840 (p. 4) the bishop delivered a charge at the convocation.*

BISHOP THOMAS VOWLER SHORT (1841-6)

With the coming of Bishop Thomas Vowler Short to the Isle of Man, the convocation took on a new life. The bishop preached an annual charge, which he had printed and distributed well beyond the confines of the diocese. The commencement of the Tithe commutation act, 1839 *also meant that receiving the tithe account became an annual feature of the meeting. For this edition, the preconization lists are abridged, giving only the names of the absentees and of the unbeneficed clergy (the others will be found in the clergy lists at the end of the volume). The tithe accounts have also been consolidated and presented in a separate table (see the end of the second volume).*

Thursday 19 May 1842

Absent or late:

Henry Maddrell, archdeacon's registrar, absent, unwell.
Edward Craine, late on account of a funeral.
Alexander Gelling, absent.
William Duggan, late.
George Stickler Parsons, absent with permission.
William Carpenter, off the island.
John Gell, sent apology on account of old age.
George Caesar Stephen, absent, unwell.

Unbeneficed clergy:

Francis Broderick Hartwell, vicar-general.
Robert Dixon, principal of King William's College.
Joseph George Cumming, vice-principal of King William's College.
Thomas Francis Reed, Mariners' church.
William Christian, curate of Lonan and Maughold.
William Kermode, curate of Lezayre.
William Bell Christian, curate of St John's.
Gilbert Hervey, curate of Malew.
Andrew Williamson, curate of St Barnabas.
John Howard, curate of St Mary, Castletown, absent.
William Tait, curate of St George's.

Daniel Nelson, archdeacon's official, supernumerary for the north part of the diocese.
Edward Qualtrough, supernumerary for the south part of the diocese; absent.

N.B. The vicarage of Patrick not noticed above, the late vicar the reverend Thomas Stephen having died 29 April.

The service began at eleven o'clock. Mr Brown of Kirk Michael, episcopal registrar, read prayers. Reverend Thomas Howard, rector of Ballaugh, preached. The bishop delivered the following charge, sitting at the altar in the chapel (see below). The bishop then took off his robes and sat on a chair with a table in the chapel, in his gown and cassock.

1. With regard to the Oeil Voirey, or service on Christmas Eve, the bishop consulted the clergy whether, as Bishop Ward had directed the clergy not to hold these, which order had not been generally obeyed, it would now be better to discontinue the service, or to try to put a stop to the irregularities which had occasioned the order of Bishop Ward?

It was agreed that it was better, when the incumbent thought fit, to have the service and to put an end to the evil customs which had been allowed to creep in.

2. The bishop distributed copies of a paper to be filled up at the quarterly visitations of the parochial schools, and requested the clergy to be regular in making this return.

3. Some conversation took place with regard to the parochial church libraries which appear generally to have fallen into utter decay. The question was as to whether it would be better to try to re-establish them or to consolidate them into two libraries, one at the south and the other at the north. That in the south is already in course of formation, at the college library, to which the clergy have free admission, and from which they may borrow books. Some of the clergy seemed to wish for libraries at the glebe houses, others for the establishment of a clerical library for the north. The bishop offered the use of any of his own books to the clergy, but nothing was decided.

4. A petition was presented from the sumners who formerly had the tithe of the second house in consideration of their trouble in collecting the vicar's tithe, and who, as all notice of this had been omitted in the Tithe Act, prayed for a compensation. The clergy were of opinion that the sumners having now no trouble in collecting the tithe, could have no just ground for any remuneration from the clergy.

5. Some discussion took place as to the way in which the quarterages of schoolmasters were paid (the children pay extra for arithmetic and writing, whereas every child ought from the first to be instructed in both these, and this form of payment disorganizes the school, and prevents the master from adopting the newest and best methods of teaching). One or two of the clergy promised to try whether any better scale of payments could be adopted.

6. Objections were raised to the custom of calling auctions after divine service, as being inconvenient and unseemly. But it was found to be legally required in some cases, and the clergy agreed to the propriety of quietly discountenancing it as much as possible.

7. The tithe agent (Mr S. Harris)'s accounts were examined and approved.

8. The bishop distributed white paper books to such of the clergy as agreed to make entries in them relative to the history and concerns of their several cures. Thomas V. Sodor and Man.

Thursday 8 June 1843

Absent or late:

Francis Broderick Hartwell, vicar-general, unwell.
Edward Craine, sent an excuse.
Joseph Qualtrough, late.
William Corrin, his daughter dangerously ill.
Samuel Gelling, absent on account of the badness of the weather.
John Cannell, absent, ill.
John Gell, infirm.
George Caesar Stephen, absent; the weather, unwell.

Unbeneficed clergy:

Thomas Francis Reed, Mariners' church.
Robert Dixon, principal of King William's College.
Joseph George Cumming, vice-principal of King William's College, off the island.
Daniel Nelson, archdeacon's official, curate of Andreas, unwell.
William Christian, curate of Lonan and Maughold.
William Bell Christian, curate of St John's.
Gilbert Hervey, curate of Malew.
Andrew Williamson, curate of St Barnabas.
John Howard, curate of St Mary's.
John Fry Garde, curate of Bride.
Edward Qualtrough, supernumerary, unwell.

The service began at eleven o'clock. Mr Brown of Kirk Michael read the prayers. The Reverend William Gill of Malew preached. The bishop delivered the following charge (see below). The bishop then took off his robes and sat on a chair with a table, in the chapel in his gown.

1. There was much conversation on the subject of the charge, viz., ecclesiastical discipline. And it was agreed on all hands that it could only be carried out by the care of the several parishes.

2. Mr Harris' tithe account was presented and approved.

3. The bishop was sorry to state that the parochial school quarterly returns had been very inadequately made, and requested that greater regularity might be observed.

4. The clergy who had promised to try the plan of a regular and weekly payment to schoolmasters reported that they had not from circumstances been able to give the question a fair trial.

5. Few of the clergy reported much progress as to their entries in the parochial books, but several others requested to have such books sent to them.

6. The bishop begged the clergy to observe that he was ready to confirm in any parish when notice was given him of catechumens ready for confirmation. He requested that the candidates might not be younger than sixteen.

7. Much conversation took place as to the state of the parsonages and a prospect was held out of rebuilding those of Lezayre, by the Reverend J. H. Lamothe, Patrick, by the Reverend A. Holmes, St Luke's Baldwin and St Jude's Andreas, in which the bishop promised to assist the diocesan association.

Vicar-general Corlett promised to draw up a form for presentments and directions for churchwardens, which during the year were printed. Thomas Vowler Sodor and Man.

Note attached to the tithe account.

The agent cannot account for the several sums still due to the several recipients, until matters now in dispute are settled, either by the clerk of the rolls or some other competent authority, there having been in two or three cases errors in the composition book and properties entered twice for the same tithe. S. H. Jr.

Thursday 11 July 1844

Absent or late:

Edward Craine, unwell.
Alexander Gelling, unwell.
John Thomas Clarke, off the island.
John Gell, unwell.
George Caesar Stephen, prevented by business.

Unbeneficed clergy:

Francis Broderick Hartwell, vicar-general.
Robert Dixon, principal of King William's College, off the island.
Joseph George Cumming, vice-principal of King William's College.
Daniel Nelson, archdeacon's registrar, curate of Andreas.
William Christian, curate of Lonan and Maughold.
William Bell Christian, curate of St John's, off the island.
Gilbert Hervey, curate of Malew, off the island.
Andrew Williamson, curate of St Barnabas.
John Frye Garde, curate of Bride.
John Congreve, curate of St George's, off the island.
Isaac Brittain, curate of Jurby.
Edward Qualtrough, supernumerary, off the island.

At this convocation, the bishop gave notice:

1. That he was always ready to confirm any catechumens in any parish, of which due notice was given him, and that he wished the catechumens to be of the age of sixteen years.

2. That as letters of orders had never been exhibited since he came to the diocese, if any of the clergy would bring them to convocation 1845 they would be registered free of expense.

3. That the entering the names of the reputed fathers of illegitimate children was illegal, unless they had been affiliated.

4. With regard to the copies of parochial registers returned at convocation, it appeared on inquiry that some clergymen had made the return for the civil year January 1[to] December 31st, some from Easter to Easter, some from convocation to convocation, and that some had not included burials int heir returns. It was therefore ordered that copies of registers be made out, including all the baptisms, burials and marriages for the last year ending December 31st and returned to convocation annually, so that for the future the copies are to be made out including the civil year January 1[to] December 31st.

5. The clergy were requested to try to induce their congregations to join audibly in the psalms and responses in church.

6. The archdeacon was requested to report officially as to the state of parsonage houses.

7. The clergy were requested to make entries in their parochial books, and the bishop promised to provide such books for those clergymen as had not received them.

8. The clergy were requested not to neglect to make from time to time perambulations of their several parishes that the boundaries might be duly ascertained.

9. The clergy were requested to make the school returns for their several parochial schools.

10. Mr Harris the agent had not sent in the account of the tithe collection.

Thursday 15 May 1845

Absent or late:

Edward Craine, unwell.
Bowyer Harrison, unwell.
Robert Brown, at a funeral.
John Henry Lamothe, unwell.

Unbeneficed clergy:

Francis Broderick Hartwell, vicar-general, unwell.
Robert Dixon, principal of King William's College.
Joseph George Cumming, vice-principal.
Daniel Nelson, archdeacon's official.

William Christian, curate of Lonan and Maughold.

John Frye Garde, curate of German.

Isaac Brittain, curate of Jurby, in England.

Alexander Watt, curate of St George's.

Gilbert Hervey, curate of Malew.

Philip Dowe, curate of St Barnabas.

Robert Faulkner Wood, curate of St George's.

Edward Qualtrough, supernumerary.

Charles Trollope, curate of Lezayre.

The clergy were requested to report at the next convocation as to the state of their several parishes with regard to family prayers.

I promised to prepare an address which is hereunto appended. Thomas V. Sodor and Man.

The letters of orders, etc.

His lordship having at the convocation held at Bishopscourt on Thursday the 11th July 1844 intimated that as letters of orders had never been exhibited since he came to the diocese, if any of the clergy would bring them to convocation 1845 they would be registered free of expense. Pursuant to the said intimation and the 137th canon ecclesiastical at the convocation holden at Bishopscourt on Thursday in Whitsun week, viz., the 15th May 1845, letters of orders as undermentioned were exhibited to his lordship, approved of and endorsed by the episcopal registrar.[572]

Andreas:	Joseph Christian Moore, deaconed by the bishop of Lichfield and Coventry 2 November 1828 and priested by Hereford 20 December 1829.
Arbory:	Alexander Gelling. Crigan, May 1809; Crigan, December 1811.
Ballaugh:	Thomas Howard. Crigan, 1 October 1807; Crigan, May 1809.
Braddan:	Crigan, June 1812; Crigan, March 1816.
Bride:	John Nelson. Crigan, December 1803; Crigan, February 1804.
German:	John Lamothe Stowell. Oxford, 28 August 1825; Durham, 17 September 1826.
Jurby:	John Edward Harrison. Crigan, October 1806. Crigan, 1 October 1807.
Lezayre:	John Henry Lamothe. Chester, 15 December 1839; Chester, 13 December 1840.
Lonan:	Joseph Qualtrough. Crigan, October 1803; Crigan, October 1806.
Malew:	William Gill. 29 September 1820; 4 December 1824.
Marown:	William Duggan: Murray, March 1819; Murray, June 1820.
Maughold:	Bowyer Harrison. Murray, November 1815; Murray, November 1816.
Michael:	Joseph Brown. Crigan, 1 October 1807; 24 December 1807.

[572]The name of the ordaining bishop is attached in each case.

Onchan:	Edward Craine. Crigan, May 1809; Crigan, March 1810.
Patrick:	Archibald Holmes. Murray, March 1824; Short, February 1826.
Rushen:	William Corrin. Murray, August 1817; Murray, May 1819.
Santan:	Samuel Gelling. Murray, July 1821; February 1826.
Principal:	Robert Dixon. Deaconed at St Catharine's Hall, Cambridge, 15 January 1832 and priested at Bristol, 3 March 1833.
Vice-principal:	Joseph George Cumming: 17 April 1836.
St George's:	Francis Broderick Hartwell. July 1829; April 1830.

Chaplains:

St Barnabas:	William Carpenter.
St James:	George Caesar Stephen. June 1840; July 1841.
St John's:	William Bell Christian. June 1840; July 1841.
St Jude's:	William Drury. June 1832; March 1833.
St Luke's:	Thomas Caine. 8 February 1835; 27 March 1836.
St Mark's:	John Thomas Clarke. Murray, June 1820; Murray, July 1821.
St Matthew's:	John Cannell. Murray, February 1827; Murray, November 1828.
St Paul's.	William Kermode. Bowstead, 24 March 1839; Pepys, 14 June 1840.
St Stephen's.	John Qualtrough. Chester, 19 November 1837; Bowstead 24 March 1839.

Curates:

Andreas:	Daniel Nelson: Ward, March 1831; March 1833.
St Barnabas:	Philip Dowe: deacon – 21 July 1844.
St George's:	Alexander Watt: 21 July 1844; 2 March 1845.
St George's:	Robert Faulkner Ward: deacon 29 December 1844.
German:	John Frye Garde: 18 December 1842; 21 July 1844.
Jurby:	Isaac Brittain: deaconed 21 July 1844.
Lezayre:	Charles Trollope: deacon, 11 May 1845.
Malew:	Gilmour Harvey: deacon 15 November 1840.
Maughold:	William Christian. Crigan, October 1811; Crigan, March 1816.
Supernumerary:	Edward Qualtrough: deacon, 28 February 1836; priest at Chester, 19 November 1837.

Thursday 4 June 1846

Absent or late:

Edward Craine, unwell.
John Edward Harrison
Alexander Gelling, late from an accident.
Francis Broderick Hartwell, unwell.
George Caesar Stephen, absent.
Daniel Nelson, archdeacon's registrar, at a funeral.

New curates:

Charles James Stewart, German.
Arthur Brereton Perceval, St Barnabas
John Barton, St Mary, in England.
Edward Qualtrough, supernumerary.

The bishop owes up to this time six pounds five shillings and sixpence to the royal bounty and Lady Elizabeth Hastings' trust, to go to building parsonage house.

Received from the Right Reverend Thomas Vowler Short, lord bishop, towards completing the new vicarage house Kirk Michael, the balance remaining in his lordship's hands belonging to the royal bounty and Lady Elizabeth Hastings' trust, at convocation 4th June 1846, being six pounds five shillings and sixpence, as witness my subscription the 14th October 1846. Joseph Brown, vicar of Kirk Michael.

BISHOP WALTER AUGUSTUS SHIRLEY (1846-7)
BISHOP ROBERT JOHN EDEN (1847-54)

Bishop Shirley died just over three months after his consecration, and was replaced only days before the 1847 convocation by Bishop Eden.

Thursday 27 May 1847

The tithe account is all that survives.

Thursday 18 May 1848

Absent or late:

John Cannell, absent.
George Caesar Stephen, absent.
William Corrin, unwell.
John LaMothe Stowell, late.
William Drury, absent.

St Barnabas was vacant.

After morning prayers read by his lordship's chaplain the vicar of Michael, the reverend Edward Forbes B. A., chaplain of St George's, Douglas, preached a sermon from Acts vi. 4.

The names of the clergy were then called over, when his lordship then pronounced an eloquent and appropriate charge to the clergy, which they unanimously prayed his lordship to publish.

The venerable archdeacon then read a congratulatory address from the clergy of the diocese to his lordship, for which his lordship, in the most feeling manner, thanked the archdeacon and clergy.

His lordship afterwards consulted the clergy on the propriety of passing an act of Tynwald for making better provision for parochial schoolmasters and for making further regulations for the better government for the parochial and other schools in the Isle of Man.

His lordship also laid before the clergy Mr Harris the tithe accounts as before 1847, which year and the next to e[piscopal] r[egistrar]...

His lordship having by circular notice dated 22 April 1848 signified that he expected and required the several clergy of his diocese to exhibit at this convocation their respective letters of orders, institutions, induction and all other licences or faculties whatever pursuant to the 137th canon ecclesiastical, the same were exhibited [accordingly in the manner set down hereafter.][573]

Andreas. The venerable Joseph Christian Moore, A. M. rector.

1. Deacon   2 November 1828.
2. Priest   20 December 1829.
3. Instituted   17 April 1844.
4. Inducted   20 April 1844.

Arbory. Reverend Alexander Gelling, vicar.

1. 4 May 1809.   2. 10 December 1811.   3. 4 March 1816. 4. 19 March 1816.

Braddan. Absent, Reverend William Drury.

German. Reverend John LaMothe Stowell, vicar.

1. 28 August 1825.   2. 17 September 1826.   3. Collated 28 March 1839.

Jurby. Reverend John Edward Harrison, vicar.

1. 15 October 1806.   2. 1 October 1807.   3. Collated 4 April 1818.

Lezayre. Reverend William Bell Christian, A. M., vicar.

1. 14 June 1840. 2. 1 August 1841.   3. 7 July 1845.   4. 12 July 1845.

Lonan. Reverend Joseph Qualtrough, vicar.

1. 28 February 1803.   2. 15 October 1806.   3. 1 April 1824.

Malew. Reverend William Gill, vicar[-general?] and surrogate. 1 February and 29 June 1847.

1. 29 September 1820.   2. 4 December 1824.   3. 7 September 1830.
4. 28 September 1830.

Marown. Reverend William Duggan, vicar.

1. 21 March 1819.   2. 24 June 1820.   3. 7 December 1840.
4. 26 December 1840.

[573]Supplied from the draft copy.

Maughold. Reverend Bowyer Harrison, vicar.

1. 30 November 1815. 2. 3 November 1816. 3. 4 April 1818.
4. 14 April 1818.

Michael. Reverend Joseph Brown, A. M., vicar. Episcopal registrar and surrogate.
1 February and 29 June 1847.

1. 1 October 1807. 2. 24 December 1807. 3. 4. 4 April 1818.

Onchan. Reverend John Howard, vicar. No exhibits.
Patrick. Reverend Archibald Holmes, vicar. No exhibits.
Rushen. Reverend William Corrin, vicar. Unwell. No exhibits.

Santan. Reverend Samuel Gelling, vicar.

1. 25 July 1821. 2. 25 February 1826. 3. 24 June 1835. 4. 25 June 1835.

Ballaugh. Reverend Thomas Howard, rector. No exhibits.

Bride. Reverend Daniel Nelson, rector.

1. 27 March 1831. 2. 31 March 1833. 3. 19 November 1847.
4. 22 November 1847.

St George's. Reverend Edward Forbes, B. A., chaplain.

1. 29 January 1840. 2. 29 December 1840. 3. 1 November 1847.
4. 19 November 1847.

St Jude's. Reverend John Qualtrough, chaplain and curate of Andreas.

1. 19 November 1837. 2. 24 March 1839. 3. 10 February 1848.
4. 17 February 1848.

St Mary's. Reverend George Stickler Parsons, government chaplain.

1. 24 June 1820. 2. 25 July 1821. Licence, 19 September
               1827.

St Mark's. Reverend John Thomas Clarke, chaplain.

1. 3 January 1822. 2. 1 November 1822. Licence, 27 October 1828.

St Matthew's. Reverend John Cannell, chaplain, absent.

St Luke's, Reverend Thomas Caine, chaplain.

1. 8 February 1835.   2. 27 March 1836.   Licence, 13 November
1840.

St James. Reverend George Caesar Stephen, chaplain. Absent.

St Paul's. Reverend William Kermode, chaplain, surrogate. 10 December 1847.

1. 24 March 1839.   2. 14 June 1840.   Licence, 12 October 1843.

St John's. Reverend John Frye Garde, chaplain.

1. 16 December 1842.   2. 21 July 1844.   Presentation, 27 December 1845.

The Dhoon. Reverend William Christian, chaplain. No exhibits.
St Barnabas, vacant.

Jurby. Reverend Charles Trollope, curate.

1. 11 May 1845.   2. 19 August 1846.   Licence, 19 August 1846.

Malew. Reverend Gilmour Harvey, curate. No exhibits.

German. Reverend Charles James Stewart, deacon. Curate B. Voddy, German.

1. 4 April 1848.

St Mary's. Reverend John Barton, curate.

1. 5 April 1846.

Andreas. Reverend William Hawley, curate.

1. 4 July 1847.   Licence, 5 July 1847.

Sulby. Reverend Edward Brailsford, curate.

1. 4 July 1847.

Lezayre. Reverend Thomas Street Millington, curate.

1. 19 March 1848.   Licence, 20 March 1848.

St George's. Reverend John Flowers Sergeant, curate.

1. 9 April 1848.   Licence, 10 April 1848.

Supernumerary. Reverend Edward Qualtrough.

1. 28 February 1836.   2. 19 November 1837.

The college.

Reverend Robert Dixon, A. M., principal and dean.

1. 15 January 1832.   2. 3 March 1833.

The Reverend Joseph George Cumming, A. M., vice-principal and curate.

1. −   2. 17 April 1838.

Endorsed: 'May 18, 1848. Exhibited, Joseph Brown, episcopal registrar.' Received 14d. for each exhibit.

Lezayre.	Royal bounty to Baldwin:	11/0/1.
Braddan.	Royal bounty to St Mark's:	7/1/3/0 or 7/12/5.
Onchan.	Royal bounty to St John's:	7/13/0 or 7/12/5.

Wednesday 30 May 1849

Absent or late:

Alexander Gelling, unwell.
John Thomas Clarke, unwell.
John Frye Garde, late − preaching to Friendly Society.
Edward Qualtrough, absent at Peel, preaching to the Friendly Society.

New curates:

William Hawley, Andreas.
Edward Brailsford, Sulby.
Thomas Street Millington, Lezayre.
John Thomas Serjeant, St George's.
Joseph Mayor, jr. Rushen.
William Gill, jr. Michael.

The bishop delivered a charge and the Reverend J. Alcock of St Barnabas preached a sermon.[574]

[574]*Manx Sun*, Wednesday 6 June 1849, p. 4.

Wednesday 22 May 1850

Absent or late:

Alexander Gelling, absent
Joseph Qualtrough, absent
John Thomas Clarke, absent
George Caesar Stephen, absent
John Frye Garde, absent
Edward Qualtrough, absent; at Friendly Society.

New curates:

John Flowers Serjeant, St Goerge's
Joseph Mayor jr., Rushen, absent
William Gill, jr., Michael, absent
Joseph Preston Ward, Sulby
Thomas Fenton, Laxey
Robert Airey, Lezayre
Henry Hardy, Jurby
William Drayton, minister of St Thomas, Douglas.
Thomas Street Millington, Lezayre.

The Reverend Joseph Brown, episcopal registrar and vicar of Michael, read the prayers. The Reverend William Corrin, vicar of Rushen, preached. The episcopal registrar having called over the names of the clergy, the bishop delivered an eloquent and appropriate charge to the clergy. Statement of tithe for crop 1849 by Samuel Harris jr., tithe agent, was read and approved. Afterwards a long discussion took place regarding the irregular entires and returns and copies delivered to the deputy episcopal registrar of baptisms, marriages and burials of several parishes and chapelries, and which by his lordship's directions were not received at the spring chapter court, not being in the form and schedules of an act for the better regulating parish and other registers of baptisms, marriages and burials in the Isle of Man. The episcopal registrar was directed to receive and keep the several returns till his lordship had an opportunity to consult with his excellence the lieutenant governor, etc., on the subject.

After dinner the episcopal registrar paid to or for the several recipients entitles thereto the royal bounty, Lady Elizabeth Hastings' donations and his lordship's stipend to his curates or vicars of pension. At the same time, the agent distributed the impropriate fund and Mrs Catherine Halsall's, etc., charities entitled to receive the same.

Thursday 19 June 1851[575]

Absent:

Alexander Gelling, his son ill.
Archibald Holmes, off the island.
John Cannell, his daughter dead.
George Caesar Stephen
John Flowes Sarjeant, off the island.
Hugh Colman Davidson, curate of St Mary's.

New curates:

Richard Moss, curate of Rushen.
Matthew Nisbet Thompson, curate of Lezayre.
Richard Cattley of Worcester College, Oxford, to be curate of Onchan.

Thursday 24 June 1852

Absent:

John Edward Harrison, unwell.
Alexander Gellling, unwell.
John Cannell, in England.
George Caesar Stephen
Gilmour Harvey

William Kermode of St Paul, Ramsey, preached a sermon.[576]

Thursday 8 September 1853

Absent:

Daniel Nelson
John Edward Harrison
Alexander Gelling
Joseph Henry Gray, off the island.
John Thomas Clarke, off the island.
John Cannell, off the island.
Robert Airey
Richard Cattley

---

[575]This was actually the Thursday of Trinity Week.
[576]*Manx Sun*, Saturday 26 June 1852, p. 4.

New curates:

George Bennett, Laxey
William Kelly, Andreas
Lloyd Stewart Bruce, Dhoon and Maughold
George William Langstaff, St Barnabas
William Maxwell Smith, Lonan
John Strickland, Rushen, absent, at a burial.

Also present was Benjamin Philpot, rector of Great Cressingham, Norwich and formerly archdeacon of Sodor and Man.

The service commenced at eleven o'clock. The Reverend Joseph Brown, episcopal registrar, read prayers. The lord bishop and the archdeacon read the communion service and administered the Lord's supper to thirty-six clergy present and to Lady Auckland and three daughters. Afterwards the bishop and clergy adjourned for twenty minutes, and on their return the names of the clergy were called over by the registrar, after which the archdeacon for himself and the clergy of the diocese addressed his lordship, congratulating him on his safe return to the island, deploring the accident that had caused his absence, hoping and praying that Almighty God may speedily restore him to perfect health and preserve him many years, to be a protection and comfort to his family and a blessing to his diocese.

His lordship rose up and in the most affectionate manner returned his thanks to the archdeacon and the clergy for their congratulation, commiseration and kind wishes, and hoped that with God's blessing and the clergy's co-operation, his endeavours for the good of the diocese would be beneficial. A letter of thanks to Dr Short, bishop of St Asaph, for the munificent donation of one thousand pounds for the charity of the widows and orphans of those clergymen who have, as incumbents or under the bishop's licence, officiated in the island, to be called Mrs Short's money, was signed by the bishop, archdeacon and clergy present and given to the episcopal registrar to record, and to send an office copy to the bishop of St Asaph.

The gift of the abbey and part of ground adjoining, it was stated, has been granted by the Reverend William Perceval Ward for the purpose of erecting an asylum, chapel and school room, but which cannot be done till the expiration of Miss Stowell's lease and the lord bishop was requested and agreed to write a letter of thanks to Mrs Ward.

The episcopal registrar produced receipts from the several rectors of the royal bounty, Lady Elizabeth Hastings' donation and the bishops curates or vicars of pension.

The bishop read a letter which he had received from Mr Peters, announcing the gift of a pair of spectacles of Bishop Wilson's as an heirloom to the diocese. The vicar of Michael mentioned that he possessed Bishop Hildesley's walking stick and would give it to be added to his lordship's collection.

A question was asked as to the custom of fixing tombstones. Also a question was asked about the desirableness of fixing subjects of examination by the diocesan inspector. This matter was left to the inspector.

Tuesday 18 October next was fixed for the consecration of Marown church.
Tuesday 18 October in the afternoon for consecrating German new burial ground.
Thursday 27 October for the consecration of St Thomas' church, Douglas.
Sunday morning 23 October, a confirmation at Malew church.
Sunday evening 23 October a confirmation at Rushen church.
Sunday morning 6 November, a confirmation at Ballaugh church.
Sunday evening 6 November, a confirmation at Jurby church.
Confirmations in Lonan and Onchan to take place in December, no day yet fixed on.

Wednesday 14 June 1854

Absent:

Alexander Gelling, unwell.
George Caesar Stephen, at a funeral.
Gilmour Harvey, off the island.
George William Langstaff, off the island (curate of St Barnabas).

New curates:

William Maxwell Smith, Michael.
John Strickland, Rushen.
Hugh Stowell Gill, Baldwin.
John Purdon Stoute, Braddan.
William Linton Thompson, Sulby.

Horatio Powys, rector of Warrington, Lancashire and bishop-elect was present.

The archdeacon preached the sermon. The rumour that the new bishop had Tractarian tendencies was without foundation.[577]

---

[577]*Manx Sun*, Saturday 17 June 1854, p. 4.

BISHOP HORATIO POWYS (1854-77)

Thursday 31 May 1855

Absent:

John Edward Harrison, unwell.
Alexander Gelling, unwell.
Thomas Caine, preaching to Friendly Society.
Edward Forbes, off the island from ill health.
John Purdon Stoute, unwell.

New curates:

William Maxwell Smith, Michael.
Henry Grattan White, Ballaugh.
Henry Thomas Adamson, St Barnabas.

Thursday 15 May 1856

Absent:

John Edward Harrison, unwell.
Alexander Gelling, unwell.
John Lamothe Stowell, duty at church.
Edward Forbes, abroad in ill health.
John Cannell, unwell.
Charles James Stewart, off the island.
Benjamin Philpot Clarke, doing duty.

The bishop delivered his charge and celebrated holy communion.[578]

Thursday 4 June 1857

Absent:

Thomas E. Brown, vice-principal of King William's College.
John Edward Harrison, unwell.
Alexander Gelling, unwell.

[578]*Manx Sun*, Saturday 17 May, 1856, p. 4.

Edward Forbes, not on the island.
John Thomas Clarke, absent.
John Cannell, absent.
William Richard Ick, not on the island.

New curates:

William Richard Ick, St George's.
Edward Gomersall Charlesworth, Michael.
William Lloyd Jones, St Thomas.
Francis Richard Swallow, Foxdale.
Thomas Fletcher, St Barnabas.
George Dawes, St Luke's.
William Charles Sparrow, St Mary's.

Wednesday 2 June 1858

Distribution of the royal bounty up to 3 April 1858:

We the undersigned clergy and schoolmasters of the diocese of Sodor and Man entitled to a distributive share of the royal bounty, do hereby acknowledge to have received from the Reverend Joseph Brown, episcopal registrar, the sums affixed to our respective names, being our dividends for four quarters of the royal bounty, ending 5 April 1858.

Percentage	Parish	Sum rec'd	Date	Name
1	Arbory	0/17/10¾	2/6	Gelling
13	Baldwin	11/12/8	19/6	Dawes
8	German	7/3/2	2/6	Stowell
11	Jurby	9/16/10¾	1/6	Harrison
5	Sulby	4/9/5¾	1/6	Christian
7	Marown	6/5/3¼	11/6	Duggan
1	Maughold	0/17/10¾	1/6	Harrison
9	Rushen	8/1/0¾	2/6	Corrin
9	Santan	8/1/0¾	2/6	Gelling
9	St John	8/1/0¾	4/6	Garde
9	St Mark	8/1/0¾	2/6	Clarke
3	Andreas	2/13/8¼	2/6	Moore
3	Ballaugh	2/13/8¼	2/6	Howard
3	Bride	2/13/8¼	2/6	Nelson
3	Castletown	2/13/8¼	2/6	Gill
3	Douglas	2/13/8¼	7/6	Cannell
3	Ramsey	2/13/8¼	2/6	Kermode

Remainder indivisible		0/0/1¾		
100		89/9/9.		

Received from the honourable and right reverend Horatio, lord bishop of Sodor and Man, by the Reverend Joseph Brown, episcopal registrar, one pound fourteen shillings and four pence sterling each, being our stipend of two pounds Manx, as bishop's vicars of pension as curates of Jurby and German. Witness our subscriptions the say and date preceding our respective signatures.

1 June 1858   Henry Hardy, for J. E. Harrison.
2 June 1858   Thomas Howard, for J. L. Stowell.

Tuesday 24 August 1858

A brief convocation was held following the consecration of the new chapel at Bishopscourt. No business was transacted.[579]

Thursday 19 May 1859

Absent:

Alexander Gelling
Thomas Caine
John Thomas Clarke
John Cannell, unwell.
Charles Hill, not on island.
William Lloyd Jones, in England.
Charles Douglas, duty.

New curates:

William Lloyd Jones, St Thomas.
Charles Douglas, Michael.
William Charles Sparrow, St Paul's
Samuel Sharp Walker, Andreas
William French Clay, Lezayre.

Royal bounty as previous year.

---

[579]*Manx Sun*, Saturday 28 August 1858, p. 4 and Saturday 4 September 1858, p. 4, which contains a full account of the consecration of the chapel.

Thursday 31 May 1860

Absent:

John Lamothe Stowell
Thomas Caine
John Cannell
Samuel Simpson
William Hawley
Hugh Ashworth Stowell
Charles Hill

New curates:

Samuel Sharp Walker, Andreas
Thomas Howard Gill, Malew
John Wadsworth, St Mary
Edward Snepp, St George's
Joseph Bellamy, Michael.

Royal bounty as before.

Thursday 25 July 1861

Absent:

Daniel Nelson
William Drury
John Howard
Thomas Caine
James Butler Kelly, episcopal registrar.
[John] Thomas Clarke
John Cannell
Samuel Simpson
Edward Ferrier
Gilmour Harvey
Hugh Ashworth Stowell
John Leach
Edward Snepp

Royal bounty as before. At this convocation there was some controversy surrounding the introduction of high church practices (such as the hearing of confessions) at Kirk Michael and Jurby. The bishop supported the vicars there, but the convocation was more lukewarm and the two vicars had to reaffirm their loyalty to the Prayer Book.

Thursday 12 June 1862

No absences recorded on the roll, but three (unnamed) reported in the *Manx Sun*.[580]

New curates:

Robert H. Cardew, St Thomas.
Edward William Kissack, Andreas.
J. J. S. Moore, St Olave's.

Royal bounty as previous year. The Reverend J. B. Kelly read the prayers and the Reverend R. W. Aitken read the lessons.

Thursday 28 May 1863

Absent:

Thomas Caine, on duty.
Edward Snepp, on leave.
John Thomas Clarke, with leave.
John Cannell, on leave.
Edward Ferrier, on leave.
Charles Hill, on leave.
Hugh Coleman Davidson, on leave.
Robert H. Cardew, unwell.

New curates:

Thomas Booth Lee, Lezayre
Charles M. Speke Mules, Michael
James Robert Ffoliott, Braddan

Vicar general: Richard Jebb
Episcopal registrar: Samuel Harris.

According to the Manx Sun *of Saturday 11 July 1863 (p. 5), this convocation passed a resolution at the bishop's request, asking him to prepare a canon which would restore the ancient custom of the Manx church praying for the legislature of the island. The convocation was adjourned to 6 July 1863, to enable the canon to be prepared. The resolution was proposed by Thomas Howard, rector of Ballaugh and seconded by William Gill, vicar of Marown, as follows:*

[580]Saturday 14 June 1862, p. 4.

Resolved that the bishop be requested to prepare a canon to restore the ancient custom of the Manx church in praying for the legislature of this isle during public worship, and that convocation be adjourned to St John's, July 6th 1863 at 10 o'clock, for the purpose of considering the wording of such canon when prepared.

Monday 6 July 1863

According to the Manx Sun *of Saturday 11 July 1863 (p. 5), the bishop presented his proposed canon, as follows:*

In the name of our great Master the Lord Jesus Christ, and to the glory and increase of his kingdom among men.

We, the bishop, archdeacon, vicar-general and clergy of this isle agree to revive the ancient custom of the Manx Church in offering up a special petition, during divine service, for the temporal rulers of this isle; and to this end we oblige ourselves hereafter to resume the practice of adding in the litany, after the words: 'the lords of the council and all the nobility' the following words: 'and with them, the lieutenant-governor, the legislature and all persons in authority in this isle.'

Further, in the clause of the litany relating to 'the kindly fruits of the earth, etc.' to which Bishop Wilson of blessed memory, in convocation, June 1705, added the words: 'and restore and continue to us the blessings of the sea', to omit the words 'and restore' as no longer applicable to the special occasion on which these words were ordered to be used.

The bishop said that he would proceed with the changes only if the convocation was unanimous, but there were several people who doubted the legality of what was proposed. The archdeacon had submitted the following paper, dated 26 June 1863:

With respect to the proposed new canon, the undersigned begs leave to submit for consideration the following queries preliminary:

First, whether the clergy of this diocese are not precluded by the subscriptions and declarations by each at ordination or upon licence or institution, from entertaining any proposal for alterations or additions to the liturgy of the church as by law established?

Second, how far is the question affected by the fact that this diocese is a part of the province of York? The act of uniformity [1662] was fully accepted by the convocation of the province of York. Can the synod of any one diocese make a change without reference to the metropolitan see?

Third, whether in any alteration of our uses in common prayer the concurrence of the civil power is indispensable? So in Bishop Wilson's order for the petition in the litany concerning 'the blessings of the sea' it is expressly stated in the original to have been made with the approbation of the civil government. There has been no governor-in-chief in this island since the duke of Atholl's time. The Tynwald court of the Isle of Man, including therein the lieutenant-governor, is only a part of the civil government – her majesty the queen of England being lady of Man, holding

Man as a fief under her own crown. Can there be any movement made in such a matter without licence first had from our sovereign lady the queen?

Fourth, will the words in the last part of the canon of 1703 for the making of such orders and constitutions as shall from time to time be found wanting cover so much as the making of a canon for what is virtually an alteration in the Book of Common Prayer?

Fifth, can it be ascertained from the records when and where the practice of specifically naming in the Manx liturgy the lord and lady and the rulers of this island (they being so named as of the nobility of the realm) was discontinued, and why it was so discontinued, as the words are in the Manx Prayer Book printed at London in 1765, but omitted in that printed in 1777. The act of revestment was passed in January 1765.

Joseph C. Moore, rector of Andreas and archdeacon.

Both the bishop and the vicar-general assured them that they could make whatever changes they wished, since neither the act of 25 Henry VIII, c. 19 nor the act of uniformity (1662) applied in the Isle of Man. This view was supported by the reverends J. B. Kelly, J. H. Gray, W. Hawley and John Howard, who all quoted ancient precedents for the insertion of prayers into the liturgy. The Reverend W. Gill also recalled that this had been done in 1832 and in 1845, but thought that it was the wrong time for the Manx church to strike out on its own and that the whole question of its relationship to the wider Church of England, including the applicability of English church legislation to the diocese, should be reviewed. The archdeacon still had his doubts, and so the bishop persuaded the clergy to drop their proposals, so as not to give the impression of being divided on a matter of public prayer.

Thursday 19 May 1864

At a convocation of the clergy of the diocese of Sodor and Man at Bishopscourt on Thursday in Whitsun week, May 19th 1864, Samuel Harris esq., having intimated his intentions to resign his office as tithe agent in consequence of his having been appointed high bailiff of Douglas, it was resolved and determined by the whole body of the clergy that there be tendered to Mr Harris the hearty and unanimous thanks of the recipients of tithe rent charge and the rest of the clergy for the kind and efficient manner in which for many years he has discharged the duties of tithe agent, and that this document be placed on record in the episcopal registry. Witness our hands this 19th May 1864. Signed by the bishop and clergy.

Thursday 29 June 1865[581]

Absent:

Robert Dixon
Samuel Gelling
John Stowell, off the island.
John Howard
Thomas Caine
Henry Hardy
John Cannell
John Turnbull
William Heaton
Richard Child Willis
Charles Hill
Benjamin Philpot Clarke
Hugh Coleman Davidson
Frederick Greer, St Thomas
George Savage, Marown.

The bishop talked about 'the careful introduction of music' as an aid to public worship. The clergy objected to the imposition of rates for the lunatic asylum on their tithes and passed a resolution to submit a formal objection to this. The royal bounty was distributed and the tithe account was discussed.

Thursday 27 July 1865

A special convocation was held at St John's chapel to elect a proctor for the York convocation. It was presided over by the archdeacon and the following were present:

William Gill
Hugh Stowell Gill
Archibald Holmes
Thomas Henry
John Howard
Robert Aitken
John Qualtrough
John Stowell
John Garde.

---

[581]According to newspaper reports, the annual meeting was postponed to this date because of the bishop's poor health.

A motion was proposed by Archibald Holmes and seconded by John Stowell, and William Gill was duly elected.[582]

Thursday 21 June 1866

Absent:

Thomas Caine.
Hugh Stowell Gill, off the island.
Robert Wesley Aitkin, off the island.
William Heaton.
Benjamin Philpot Clarke.
Edward Ferrier, clerical duites.
Robert Airey
John Cannell.
Joseph Bellamy.

The bishop alluded in his charge to certain irregularities in the parish of Braddan and indicated that he wanted to put a stop to incestuous marriages there. He had made inquiries about the misappropriation of money collected for the poor, which had been poorly invested, and he indicated that the total sum was something under £700 a year.

Later the royal bounty was distributed and the tithe account was presented. The bishop said he was upset at the apathy shown towards the Diocesan Society, which had raised less than £200 the previous year. He had therefore applied for funds to the Curates' Aid Society and suggested launching an appeal for more money to be raised locally.

Thursday 13 June 1867

Absent:

Daniel Nelson, unwell.
Thomas Caine, at home.
William Heaton, consigned with a cold.
Benjamin Philpot Clarke, on duty.
William Hawley, off the island.

---

[582]*Manx Sun*, Saturday 29 July 1865, p. 4.

Thursday 4 June 1868

Absent:

Thomas Howard, rector of Ballaugh.
John Cannell
Joseph Bellamy

The bishop spoke in his charge about the prospect of the disestablishment of the Church of Ireland, and warned the clergy that a similar fate could befall the Manx church. He appealed to the clergy to rally against this eventuality. He also feared that the royal bounty might be withdrawn, as there had been indications to that effect in some comments made in the British parliament.

At this convocation, the bishop accused William Drury, the vicar of Braddan, of improper conduct with respect to the closure of St Thomas' church in Douglas and said: 'The vicar of Braddan has displayed his imbecility by entrusting his case to a malicious and unscrupulous lawyer.' The lawyer in question was Alfred Adams, one of the most respected members of the Manx bar, who initiated an action for slander against the bishop. The bishop offered to apologize, but Mr Adams withdrew his suit and the matter was allowed to drop. Unfortunately, the bishop then interpreted this as a climbdown by Mr Adams and wrote to the clergy accordingly. The result was that an attack was made on the bishop in the legislative council (8 July 1868) and his proposal to separate the Douglas churches from the parish of Braddan was subsequently defeated.

The Lady Elizabeth Hastings fund was also discussed, and questions were asked about who was entitled to draw on it. The clergy expressed their dissatisfaction that John Garde had been the object of a suit for recovery of rates on his tithe, in support of the lunatic asylum. Mr Garde had won his case locally but there was the threat of an appeal to the privy council, in which case a special convocation would be summoned to formulate a co-ordinated response.

Questions were also asked about the impropriate fund, but as the matter was soon to come before the chancery court, it was felt that to publish details would be prejudicial to the case.[583]

Tuesday 8 December 1868

A special meeting of convocation was held to elect a proctor for the York convocation. William Gill was elected as before, though there was a formal protest against the bishop's ruling that only the incumbents of the seventeen ancient parishes had the right to vote. The vicar-general had added the royal chaplains of St John's and St Mary's (Castletown) to this number, but Mr Gray complained on behalf of the unbeneficed clergy, who were summoned to the meeting but denied the right to vote. The Reverend John Qualtrough of Arbory said he was going to petition the house of keys against the posting of public notices on church doors.

---

[583] *Manx Sun*, Saturday 6 June 1868, p. 4.

This was unanimously supported by the other clergy. The convocation was presided over by the archdeacon, and present were:

John Qualtrough
William Drury
William Gill
Hugh Stowell Gill
John Garde
Gilmour Harvey
John Gray
William Hawley
John Corlett
Robert Airey
Dr Jones-Scott
H. C. Davidson
W. S. Moses
J. White-Matthews
George Paton
Thomas Caine
Frederick Moore[584]

Thursday 20 May 1869

Thomas Howard
William Drury, duty.
John Howard, ill.
Robert Wesley Aitken, off the island.
Thomas Henry, off the island.
John Frye Garde, off the island.
John Cannell.

According to the Manx Sun *of Saturday 22 May 1869 (p. 4), the archdeacon raised the matter of funeral fees, which were thought by some to be too high. It was decided that the law stating that no-one could dig a grave in the churchyard without the vicar's permission would be enforced, and that all coffins would lie at least three feet below the surface.*

The bishop's charge referred to the enforced closure of St Thomas' church, which remained unresolved and had been referred to the ecclesiastical commissioners in England for a decision. The bishop mentioned that he had been attacked personally over this when the division of Braddan parish had been discussed in the house of keys and blamed this on the vicar of Braddan. He also attacked Alfred Laughton, a young lawyer who had made the charges against the

---

[584]*Manx Sun*, Saturday 12 December 1868, p. 4.

bishop at the legislative council meeting in 1868.[585] *This led Laughton to sue the bishop for libel and the case was heard at Ramsey on 15 February 1870. On 15 March 1870 it was announced that the bishop had won the case, on the ground that his remarks to convocation were privileged and not subject to libel actions against them.*

It was reported that Tynwald was investigating the condition of churchyards. The tithe account was presented and forms were distributed for making application to Lady Elizabeth Hastings' fund. It was also stated that difficulties had been created for the impropriate fund because it had not been properly administered in the past. In particular, two laymen had to be appointed as trustees, and after some searching, the lieutenant-governor had finally named Mr E[dward] M[oore] Gawne and Mr E[dward] C[urphey] Farrant.

On the asylum rate question, Mr H. S. Gill and Mr J. Qualtrough proposed setting up a committee to protect the clergy's interests in the matter. The clergy were happy to pay this rate on their vicarages and glebe lands, but not on their tithes. These two men and Mr J. Garde were appointed to be the said committee.

This convocation also discussed a complaint which had been made about the high funeral fees charged by the clergy. It was pointed out that sometimes clergy were kept waiting for as much as four hours, and in future notice would be given that they would wait for a 'reasonable time' only. It was also agreed to enforce the law which said that no-one could dig a grave in a churchyard without the vicar's permission, and that there should be at least three feet of soil above every buried coffin.[586]

Thursday 9 June 1870

Curates present: Henry Grattan White, Ballaugh.
                          George Paton, Maughold.
                          Thomas Davis, Maughold.
                          Richard Lloyd, Lezayre.
                          Frederick Greer, Braddan.
                          Theophilus Talbot, German.
                          Thomas William Dinwoody, Andreas.

Absent: Thomas Howard, unwell.
                          Bowyer Harrison, unwell.
                          John Cannell.

The bishop declined to give a charge because of his recent illness and the still unresolved dispute with the vicar of Braddan over St Thomas' church in Douglas.

---

[585]For Laughton's version of events, see F. A. Laughton, *High-bailiff Laughton's reminiscences* (Douglas, 1916), pp. 130-7. The book was reprinted in 1999. Alfred Laughton (1828-1911) was an Englishman who moved to the Isle of Man, where he was admitted to the bar in 1850. He became a lifelong member of St George's church, Douglas.
[586]*Manx Sun*, Saturday 22 May 1869, p. 4.

The royal bounty of £89/9/0 was distributed as usual, as were the tithe earnings. The finances of the Curates' Aid Society were in some disarray because the lay committee supposedly set up for collecting subscriptions was not functioning properly. The vicar of Kirk Michael asked whether parochial schools could be used for other purposes and was told by the bishop that the chancery court had investigated the matter thoroughly but could come to no final decision unless the trust deeds of the various schools concerned could be produced.

The impropriate fund required two laymen on the committee, and after consultation with the duke of Atholl and the lieutenant-governor, the latter appointed Edward Moore Gawne and E. C. Farrant. Hearings would be held on 13 June and the clergy were invited to make submissions to the committee.

Some of the clergy mentioned the great inconvenience caused in their parishes by the ending of Sunday funerals, which had been common there. It was declared that traditionally the family decided the day and the incumbent the time when a funeral would take place, and it was hoped that in future steps could be taken to avoid inconvenient Sunday funerals.

They also discussed the burden imposed on them by the charge they were liable to pay for the upkeep of the lunatic asylum. The clergy all agreed to support each other in any suit against one of them to collect this rate, and it emerged that Mr Ingram, the vicar of Kirk Michael had one pending against him. An appeal fund was started. The trustees of the Lady Elizabeth Hastings fund also discussed that.

It was further noted that the vicar of Braddan did not stay for lunch and that the bishop was looking exceptionally tired.[587]

Thursday 1 June 1871

Absent:

Thomas Howard, unwell.
John Lamothe Stowell
Thomas Caine.
Henry Hardy, unwell.
William Ingram, unwell.
John Cannell, unwell.
George Paton, unwell.
William Heaton, funeral.

At this convocation, Thomas Wortley Drury, who was bishop of Sodor and Man from 1907-11, was ordained, and a sermon was preached on Matthew xx. 1 by Wyndham Hutton, vicar of Lezayre. The bishop did not deliver a charge, claiming that he was inhibited by a legal obligation from doing so. A committee was also appointed to raise funds for the Curates' Aid Society, since without local contributions no grant would be forthcoming.

[587]*Manx Sun*, Saturday 11 June 1870, p. 4.

The reverends E. Ferrier and H. S. Gill were appointed secretaries for the south of the island, and W. M. Hutton and W. C. Ingram for the north.

The Reverend H. S. Gill reported that the Reverend W. C. Ingram had been sued for non-payment of lunatic asylum rates on his tithe, but had won his case in the deemster's court. It was reported that the attorney-general was supportive of the clergy in their action against payment of this rate.

It was also reported that Reverend W. Drury was the only clergyman not to stay for lunch.[588]

Thursday 23 May 1872[589]

Curates present:	Henry Grattan White, Ballaugh.
	Joseph Bellamy, Lonan.
	James Hamilton Edmunds, Cronk-y-voddy.
	Frederick Greer, St George's, Douglas.
	James Elkey Pattison, Lezayre.
	Frederick Moore, Foxdale.
	Thomas William Dunwoody, Andreas.
	Theophilus Talbot, St Olave's, Ramsey.
	Thomas Wortley Drury, Braddan.
Absent:	Thomas Howard
	Daniel Nelson
	William Drury
	John Howard, unwell.
	Wyndham Hutton, off the island.
	John Cannell, chaplain of St Matthew's
	George Paton
	Thomas Charles Langton, unwell.

At this convocation, William Ingram, vicar of Kirk Michael and the bishop's domestic chaplain, read morning prayer, and the bishop celebrated holy communion. The bishop subsequently stated that he had not issued a charge since 1869, because of the ongoing dispute over St Thomas, Douglas. He expressed the hope that both sides in that dispute, having aired their respective opinions, would put past differences behind them and restore harmony. He also responded to a memorial signed by most of the clergy, and agreed to lift his ban on the ordination of non-graduates. He paid tribute to the late William Gill, vicar of Malew, and urged all the parishes to insure their churches and parsonages against fire. The clergy then proceed to elect William Kermode, vicar of Maughold, as their representative in the York convocation. The proposed priesting of Thomas Drury

---

[588] *Manx Sun,* Saturday 3 June 1871, p. 4.
[589] As reported in the *Manx Sun,* 25 May 1872, p. 4 and in the *Isle of Man Times and General Advertiser,* same date, p. 4.

at this convocation was postponed because of a complaint to the effect that he had been preaching in a non-conformist chapel (Dalrymple Memorial Chapel) without the bishop's permission.[590]

The bishop said that he was pleased with the standard attained by recent confirmation candidates. It was also announced that the affairs of the Curates' Aid Society, the Impropriate Fund and the Lady Hastings' Charity were all in good order. The royal bounty of £89/9/0 and the tithe revenue were both distributed as usual.

The bishop also spoke about the appeal which he intended to make against his conviction for libel against Alfred Laughton, over the affair of St Thomas' church. He complained that he had not been supported by the clergy, but no support was forthcoming in response to this complaint. The suit against the vicar of Braddan had been resolved in the bishop's favour and he would soon be consecrating the church and appointing an incumbent.[591]

Archdeacon's visitation.

The archdeacon announced that he would conduct an island-wide visitation of the parishes, and asked that parishioners should be invited to participate. At the convocation he asked for:

1. A detailed report on the condition of the church, schools, etc., especially regarding the walls, roof, spouting, windows and doors.

2. A detailed report on the burial ground (walls, gates, depth of graves, etc.)

3. A list of all articles needed for the proper performance of divine service (books, surplices, collecting boxes, font, communion plate, a clean linen altar cloth and the ordinary altar coverings.)

4. A catalogue of all registers, noting the date at which each begins and ends.

5. A terrier of glebe lands, and any other emoluments attaching to the benefice.

6. A statement of any charities that had accrued to the parish since 1869.

7. A report of the state and condition of the glebe house and premises.

8. The amount of church insurance policies.

Tithe suit.

After the passing of the asylum act[592] deemster Stephen had ruled that the clergy tithe was not rateable for the purpose of supporting the asylum, but this had been contested by the asylum committee. For several years the bishop, the archdeacon and one or two clergy had paid under protest, but the matter had now gone to law and would be decided shortly.[593]

---

[590]The charge was false and Mr Drury was priested shortly afterwards.

[591]The Braddan church act, 1871 made the division of the ancient parish legal (*Acts of Tynwald*, IV, 1-4).

[592]In 1866. (*Acts of Tynwald*, III, 422-5).

[593]The clergy lost their appeal on 15 July 1872.

Thursday 5 June 1873[594]

Curates present: Henry Grattan White, Ballaugh.
Frederick Greer, Braddan.
Frederick Moore, Patrick.
Thomas Charles Langton, Braddan
David Morgan, Maughold.
Frederick Bickerton Grant, Rushen.
Joshua Jones, principal of King William's College.
Edward Scott, vice-principal of King William's College.
Hugh Coleman Davidson of King William's College.

Absent: Thomas Howard
John LaMothe Stowell
John Cannell
John Qualtrough
Robert Airey
George Paton
John Bellamy
Thomas William Dunwoody (off the island).

The bishop asked the clergy to state whether or not they wanted a confirmation in the coming year. He did not give a charge, and asked that the conflicts of the past should be forgotten. He further suggested an annual gathering of church choirs at Bishopscourt, which was agreed to, a committee being set up for that purpose.

The royal bounty of £89/9/0 was distributed as usual and the clergy were invited to raise matters for discussion, though none did. The tithe earnings were distributed as usual. The impropriate fund was in good order. The bishop also announced that no schools would be transferred to the education board before 1 July 1873.[595]

Curates' Aid Society

Mr W. Ingram gave a full report of the society's activities in the country as a whole before mentioning the diocese in particular. He reminded the convocation that in 1866 the society had agreed to grant £300 towards the maintenance of clergy, provided that the diocese could raise another £200. In that year, £473 was raised and £400 was distributed to the following churches: Baldwin, Cronk-y-voddy, Sulby, Laxey, Grenaby, Dhoon, St Paul Ramsey, Dalby, Foxdale and Port St Mary (Rushen). Currently there was a clergyman working at Port St Mary, but Dalby was vacant. The clergy asked for a supernumerary to be appointed to cover

---

[594]As reported in the *Manx Sun*, 7 June 1873, pp. 4-5. (The paper is misdated 6 June 1873.)
[595]The education board came into existence following the passing of the elementary education act, 1872 (*Acts of Tynwald*, IV, 57-94).

*the north, where extra pulpit supply was difficult to obtain. The archdeacon
proposed a vote of thanks to Mr Ingram which was seconded by Mr H. S. Gill and
carried unanimously.*

The tithe suit

*Mr H. S. Gill reported that after judgement had been given against the clergy on
15 July 1872, he had consulted the attorney-general, who advised him to seek
counsel from Mr Manistey in London. Mr Gill had asked Mr Manistey:*
    1. Whether the tithe rent was rateable.
    2. If so, whether it had been legally valued.
    3. Whether an appeal was advisable.
    *Mr Manistey had replied that the tithe rent was not rateable, that no question
of fairness could be raised about the valuation and that an appeal was most
certainly advisable. The appeal had gone forward, at the bishop's expense. Mr
Shaw of the Manx bar agreed with Mr Manistey's view. The clergy were asked to
contribute to the appeal fund as follows:*
    Vicars: *£4/10/0 each*
    Rectors: *£9/0/0 each*
    Archdeacon: £31/0/0
    Bishop: *£45/0/0*

Churchwardens

*The bishop asked for the following words to be added to the churchwarden's oath:
'using sound discretion according to the best of their ability'. This was agreed
unanimously.*

The meeting concluded with greater harmony than had been seen for many years.

Thursday 28 May 1874

Absent: Thomas Howard
        Daniel Nelson
        John Qualtrough
        Edward Kissack
        Edward Ferrier
        John Hamilton Edmunds
        Stephen Nathaniel Harrison
        William Hawley
        Frederick Greer
        Thomas Drury, curate of Braddan
        Frederick Grant, curate of Rushen.

Royal bounty[596]

This totalled £89/9/0 and was distributed as follows:

£2/13/8	*to Douglas, Ramsey, Castletown, Bride, Ballaugh, Andreas.*
£7/3/2	*to German.*
£9/16/10	*to Maughold.*
£11/12/6	*to Sulby chapel.*
£16/19/10	*to St Mark's chapel.*
£19/13/7	*to Cronk-y-voddy.*
£8/1/0	*to Santan.*

The tithe suit before the privy council

The appeal was now ripe for hearing, though there was still some time to reach a compromise which would put the matter on the right footing. The clergy thanked the bishop for bringing the matter before the trustees of the impropriate fund, who had been able to recoup the legal costs incurred by the vicars bringing the suit. This meant that there was enough money in hand to meet the legal expenses which would be incurred if the suit were to be heard.

Lady Hastings' Fund

The vicar of Onchan asked whether he could apply for a grant from the fund if his school came under the Board of Education, with the result that the catechism was under threat there. Several other clergy remarked that they had experienced no difficulty with the Board over this. The bishop said that he had investigated the matter thoroughly, and that as long as the catechism was taught and the other stipulations laid down in the trust deed were observed, the grant could and would be made to schools in the Board's care.

Curates' Aid Society

Mr W. C. Ingram had resigned from Kirk Michael and sent the following letter to the bishop:

Kirk Michael, 21 March 1874.

My dear lord bishop, on leaving your diocese I shall have to resign my office of organizing secretary of this society in the Isle of Man. That my successor in this office may be fully informed as to the present condition of the society's work here, I wish to lay before your lordship a statement with which you may furnish him on his appointment.

---

[596]The details of the convocation were published in the *Manx Sun*, 30 May 1874, p. 5, from which the following account has been taken.

1. In 1866 a block grant of £300 a year was made to your lordship for the diocese, on condition that a sum of not less than £200 was yearly raised to meet it. The work of raising this yearly sum of £200 was carried on with varying success until 1871, when it was resolved at convocation that certain of the clergy should be appointed to assist your lordship in their work. Messrs H. S. Gill, E. Ferrier, W. H. Hutton and W. C. Ingram were accordingly elected by convocation. Subsequently, Mr F. Hutton was added to this number of local secretaries, and I was accredited by the committee in London as the society's agent here.

The organization thus adopted has, I am thankful to say, proved successful, as is shown by the fact that the sums raised have been in:

1871:   £184/10/4
1872:   £201/4/6
1873:   £219/10/7.

I may say that this latter sum would have been greater, but for much illness and domestic sorrow which has during the year fallen to the lot of the two southern secretaries. Amongst others, the attorney-general's subscription has not been collected, but I am given to understand that it will be forthcoming in the list for 1874.

Your lordship will see that since the present organization has been at work the amount raised has increased year by year, and the *rate of increase is also increasing*. It is not therefore in the least degree unreasonable to expect that the amount raised in 1874 will be £250 or very little short of it.

2. It is a further matter of satisfaction that the stipends of the curates working under these grants has been considerably increased. The grants rated for 1874 give to all priests-in-charge of outlying districts a minimum stipend of £120 and a house.

3. This list of grants made for 1874 is now secured by a resolution of the committee for three years upon the further condition that, in addition to the £200, there be also raised a sum of not less than £50 a year for the society's general fund.

I cannot but think that this condition is perfectly just and right. During the last seven years the society has granted us £2100 without receiving in return anything worth speaking of for its general fund. It is only reasonable that the committee should now look for us to do something in return for this great liberality. I do not anticipate the slightest difficulty as to the raising of this extra sum of £50 per annum. As I said before, I believe the subscriptions, etc. this year will amount to £250 without any special appeal.

4. I should like, however, here to point out where and how I think more money might be raised. Your lordship will see by the reports that Laxey, Grenaby, Port St Mary and Baldwin and other places have contributed yearly a decreasing sum. Now I think that if the people of these districts really cared for the ministrations of the church, they would, if their duty in this matter were fairly pointed out to them, subscribe more liberally to this fund than they now do.

I would suggest that the clergy of these districts, in receipt of grants, should be requested either to have a quarterly collection, say at the ember seasons (a plan which, as the reports show, answers well at Foxdale, St John's, Cronk-y-voddy and other places), or that they should interest their people in the work and obtain a number of subscribers for small sums (a plan which, as the reports show, answers well at The Dhoon, Sulby and elsewhere). I feel quite sure that if the clergy will but try to interest their people in their work, there will be no difficulty whatever as to the raising of this sum. The advantage of having the grants secured at their present rate for the next three years is of course very great, and should stir us up to renewed zeal.

5. The report for 1873 is now in the press and will be ready to be laid before the clergy at convocation. I have been in the habit of sending a copy of it to every subscriber whose name appears in the list. I should strongly recommend this practice to be continued.

The Home Mission Field is published on 1 January, 1 April, 1 July and 1 October, and in it are acknowledged all sums received in London before the fifteenth of each preceding month. All remittances by local secretaries should therefore be made before that date, and then I should strongly advise a copy of this publication being sent to each subscriber whose name appears. This has been my practice and I believe it has a good result. These publications will be supplied from the office in London to the organizing secretaries. I am, my lord, your lordship's faithful servant, W. C. Ingram.

Rev. R. Airey proposed and Rev. H. S. Gill seconded a vote of thanks to Mr Ingram for his five years of hard work. The message would be conveyed to him by the bishop.

Further correspondence on this subject

7 Whitehall, London SW, 6 March 1874.

My lord, the committee has lately had the applications for renewal of grants for 1874 from the several parishes and districts in your lordship's diocese under its consideration, and also your lordship's list of recommended grants. The committee has carefully noted the amount which can in each case be locally raised to meet the society's grant and I am desired to say it has renewed the grants with a view of securing to each curate (being in priest's orders) a minimum stipend of £120 per annum. I am further directed to say that the committee, in renewing these grants, thinks it desirable to enter into a fresh concordat with your lordship, as it thinks the time has now arrived when the diocese should endeavour to take upon itself the duty of raising a larger proportion of the stipends.

Under the old arrangement – that in force since 1867 – which the committee notices has worked most satisfactorily, the society guaranteed grants to the amount of £300, on condition that £200 should be raised in the diocese to meet such grants (thus securing a total sum of £500 for distribution in the diocese) and that collections should be made and associations formed in behalf of the society's general fund. Also, under this arrangement, if any of the grants were not drawn by reason of vacancies of curacies, three-fifths of such undrawn grants reverted to the society's general fund and two-fifths to the local fund. The committee now proposes that it should make grants for 1874 to the amount of £500, made payable by quarterly instalments, on condition that not less than £250 is raised for the society's general fund and remitted by half-yearly instalments at Midsummer and Christmas in each year, and in advance of payment of grants for the quarters then ending, to 7 Whitehall; and further, that any grants not drawn should revert to the society's general fund.

The committee, in the hope of giving a greater degree of security to the diocesan arrangements, desires me to say that it hopes to be able to renew this grant of £500 annually, on these new terms, for two more years, viz., 1875 and 1876, but it proposes at the end of that period to reconsider the grant with a view to a readjustment of the conditions to the then circumstances of the diocese. It hopes by that time the diocese will be willing to take a larger proportion of the stipends upon itself, thus setting the society at liberty to that extent to help other parishes. The society's general regulations with respect to grants are to be observed, and the annual forms of application for renewal of grants to be sent in annually as usual. I am, my lord, your lordship's faithful servant, Arthur I. Ingram, secretary.

The bishop's reply:

Bournemouth, 20 March 1874.

Sir, I have been prevented by indisposition replying sooner to your official annunciation of 6 March, from which it appears that the CAS has agreed to renew the grants to my diocese for the current year and resolved to continue them for 1875-6 on the terms of the original concordat with me, subject to the alterations stated in your letter, viz., that an amount of not less than £250 will be required from the diocese as subscriptions to the general fund of the society instead of £200 as heretofore, in order to secure a grant of £500 to be distributed in such proportions as to secure to each recipient, being in priest's orders, in augmentation of income otherwise secured to him, such a grant as will raise his stipend to £120 per annum, and that all undrawn grants shall revert to the society's general fund.

I need not repeat my expressions of gratitude to the society for what it has enabled me to do during the last seven years in the Isle of Man, and I regret that a larger amount than £219/10/7 has not been collected there during the last year for the general fund of the society. After having drawn more that £2000 during that period of seven years from the funds of the society, I consider it perfectly right and just that the original concordat with me should be revised as porposed, considering the great and increasing demands upon the general funds of the society by other English dioceses, but as no previous notice has been given of the intended change, and as one quarter of the present year has already expired, I should feel grateful to the committee of the society if it would allow me to suggest that the new arrangement should not be carried into operation before 1 January 1875, though I feel myself bound to increase the amount to be collected during the present year if possible. Believe me, yours faithfully, Horace Sodor and Man.

The secretary's reply:

16 April 1874

My lord, your lordship's letter of 20 March was read to the committee at its meeting on 14 April, when it was unanimously resolved that in consideration of the society reserving £500 for grants in the diocese of Sodor and Man, the minimum contribution to its general fund required from the diocese for the current year 1874 be £200 instead of £250 as already announced, but that the other considerations named in the secretary's letter of 6 March be confirmed. I am, my lord, your lordship's faithful servant, Arthur Ingram, secretary.

Many suggestions were then made as to how to raise subscriptions:
  1. Appoint a paid collector.
  2. Divide the diocese into four districts, in order to bring the appeal closer to the people (the bishop's suggestion).
  3. Continue the present system and appoint four new secretaries (the archdeacon's suggestion). This was the course adopted.
  F. N. Hutton (St Thomas, Douglas), G. Paton (Ramsey), H. S. Gill (Malew), Gilmour Harvey (Santan), B. P. Clarke (Marown) were appointed with power to add a lay assistant and to elect an organizing agent to replace Mr Ingram. It was suggested that they should convene as soon as possible.

Confirmations

The bishop announced that he planned to hold an annual confirmation in October for the parishes of Braddan, Douglas and Onchan, and to institute a regular pattern of visitations at which confirmations might take place. He asked whether any of the clergy required a confirmation, and the archdeacon replied that he desired one at Andreas.

Marriage licences

J. L. Stowell, vicar of Kirk German, was appointed as surrogate for Peel district on the resignation of Mr Ingram and following a petition from the citizens of Peel asking for a more local surrogate. To avoid irregularities, the bishop had instructed the vicar-general to circulate the following:

In order to prevent in future any irregularities in granting marriage licences, you are hereby authorized and directed to require three clear days' notice by one or other of the contracting parties, through the clergyman of the parish in which either resides, or by some friend authorized to do so in their behalf, of their intention to apply to you for a licence to marry under the provisions of the act of Tynwald promulgated. By order of the bishop. S. Harris, registrar.

After some discussion of possible difficulties, the new arrangements were accepted by the clergy.

Incumbents' Sustentation Fund

Rev. H. S. Gill mentioned this society, newly formed by the Marquis of Lorne, designed to raise the clergy stipend to a minimum of £200. He encouraged all eligible incumbents to apply for a grant.

Saturday 23 January 1875

A meeting of the clergy was held at St James' Hall (Dalby). It had been summoned by the archdeacon, who absented himself because of his membership of Tynwald, leaving Rev. William Drury, vicar of Braddan, in the chair.

Present:

William Drury
Hugh Stowell Gill
William Kermode
Thomas Caine
Benjamin Clarke
Edward William Kissack
Wyndham Madden Hutton
Gilmour Harvey
Robert Airey
William Thomas Hobson
Francis Hutton
William Hawley
Edward Ferrier
George Paton
Stephen Nathaniel Harrison
John Corlett
Frederick James Moore
Charles Thomas Langton
Joseph Bellamy
Frederick Grier, curate of St George's.
[Benjamin William] Ricketts, curate of St Paul's, Ramsey.
Frederick Grant, curate of Rushen.
Robert Gawne Brearey, curate of Malew.

There was a preliminary debate about the advisability of admitting reporters. A vote was taken and it was narrowly agreed that they should be admitted, but they voluntarily abstained and the Rev. H. S. Gill later gave the following report to the press.[597]

---

[597]The meeting is recorded in the *Manx Sun*, 30 January 1875, p. 5.

A meeting had been held in Liverpool on Friday 8 January 1875 to discuss the possibility of creating a new bishopric for that town. One suggestion was that the diocese of Sodor and Man should be formally extended to include Liverpool, and that the bishop's revenue should form part of the endowment of the new see. This was supported by Rev. Dr Joshua Jones (later Hughes-Games), then principal of King William's College, who suggested that £1000 of the bishop's income could be used to augment poor livings in the Isle of Man and the rest applied to the endowment of the see.[598] When news of this meeting reached the Isle of Man there was a swift and almost entirely negative reaction. The meeting of the clergy, though not officially a convocation, acted as such, as the following documents indicate.

Letter from Mrs Cecil Hall.

The Reverend F. Hutton read the following letter from Mrs Cecil Hall.

16 Finch Road, Douglas, 23 January 1875.

As the widow of your late loving and beloved archdeacon, allow me to address you. We gloried in being called to a land where the holy Bishop Wilson laboured, whose memory is cherished not only here but in England and America, who when twice offered bishoprics in England, refused, saying: 'he would not leave his wife because she was poor'. The scheme of robbery propounded at the Liverpool meeting, to confiscate the revenues of our ancient see for the benefit of the wealthy merchant princes of modern Tyre has, I rejoice to say, raised such a storm of indignation among all classes throughout the land, that if the clergy be but true to their church, I have no fear of the result. But they must make no compromises, nor be tempted by the holding out the prospect of an addition to their livings, nor sell their birthright for a mess of pottage, however faint and hungry they may be; for if they do, most surely they will not inherit the blessing. Let them, though weak, stand firm in the Lord and in the power of his might, and say fearlessly, be the consequences what they may: 'The Lord forbid it me that I should give the inheritance of my fathers unto thee!'[599] You have heard of a similar attempt to annex the diocese of Sodor and Man to England, which, even after the bill was passed, God defeated through the instrumentality of English churchmen. The falsehood now propagated, that the Manx clergy and laity are desirous of the Liverpool arrangement, will be, I trust, refuted by you, as you will win the respect and admiration of those whose commendation is worth having. That the Great Head of the church may prosper your efforts is the prayer of your sincere friend, F. A. Hall.

---

[598]See *Manx Sun*, 16 January 1875, p. 3 for a full report.
[599]1 Ki. xxi. 3. Naboth's reply to King Ahab, who wished to purchase his vineyard.

Resolutions

The following resolutions were then proposed and carried unanimously.

It was moved by the Reverend H. S. Gill and seconded by Reverend B. P. Clarke:

Resolved that this meeting, having heard with surprise and indignation of a proposal recently made at Liverpool for the union of this diocese with a new diocese of Liverpool in order that an endowment may be in part provided for the proposed new bishopric out of the episcopal revenues of this see, which revenues inalienably belong to the church thereof, reprobate such proposal as a scheme of injustice and spoliation, and as one most injurious to the interests of the church in this island.

It was moved by the Reverend G. Harvey and seconded by Reverend W. Kermode:

Resolved that petitions be presented to the two houses of parliament and to the Tynwald court, representing the injustice and inexpediency of the proposed union, and praying that the diocese of Sodor and Man — the oldest existing diocese in the British Isles — may be preserved intact.

The form of the petitions

The humble petition of the undersigned clergy of the diocese of Sodor and Man showeth:

That your petitioners have heard that a movement is now being made in the town of Liverpool for the erection of such town into a bishop's see, and for the incorporation with the proposed new see of the diocese of Sodor and Man, with the view of obtaining the episcopal revenues of such diocese for the endowment in part of such new see.

That this diocese is the most ancient existing bishopric in the British Isles, that the proposed union, if effected, would be the virtual abolition of this diocese, an abolition which your petitioners apprehend would be regarded by the embers of the Church of England at large with extreme abhorrence and regret.

That the pecuniary advantage which the wealthy borough of Liverpool would gain by the proposed appropriation in whole or in part of the Manx episcopal revenue, would be far outweighed by the inconvenience arising from the necessary absence of the bishop of the new see from time to time in the discharge of his duties in the Isle of Man, while on the other hand, to require the bishop of Man to undertake the charge of such a large and distant population as that of Liverpool, would be practically to deprive the Manx church of any efficient supervision.

That the promoters of the proposed new see urge as a reason for its creation the great extent of the diocese of Chester, of which Liverpool is a part, and the separation of the diocese into two very distant portions by the estuary of the Mersey. That the proposed united diocese would consist of two portions, separated by seventy miles of the Irish Channel, portions widely different in all respects, by reason of the Isle of Man being a distinct kingdom, under a separate civil government and legislature (of which the bishop is ex-officio a member) and having ecclesiastical laws in many respects different from those of England.

That it has been suggested that the proposed union might be effected without the application of the whole of the episcopal revenue to the endowment of the new see, a portion thereof being appropriated to the augmentation of the poor livings in this island. That your petitioners admit that most of the livings in this island are very poor, but on this head your petitioners adopt the following language of their predecessors, in a petition for the house of lords in 1837, to prevent the then-intended union of this diocese with that of Carlisle: 'As to enriching their parochial clergy by the spoils of their bishopric your petitioners dislike the principle, and dread the example; they affect not indeed to conceal that the vicars of the diocese are in... very straitened... circumstances, from which they... would gratefully accept honourable relief; but they disclaim a wish to procure temporal advantage at the expense of spiritual loss.'

Wherefore your petitioners humbly entreat your honourable house to resist any attempt which may be made to deprive them of their bishopric. And your petitioners will humbly pray, etc.

Further resolutions

It was moved by the Reverend H. S. Gill and seconded by Reverend R. Airey:

Resolved that the petitions now read be adopted and signed, with the understanding that the last paragraph in such petitions respectively does not commit the clergymen who sign the same to any expression of opinion on the questions of a redistribution of the revenues of the church within this island.

It was moved by the Reverend B. P. Clarke and seconded by Reverend F. P. B. N. Hutton:

That the cordial thanks of this meeting be tendered to Mrs Cecil Hall for the interest which she has shown on this occasion, as ever, in the welfare of the Manx church.

BISHOP WILSON'S PAROCHIAL LIBRARIES

There is a list extant (in Dr Wilson's hand) giving the titles of forty books which he or his friends gave to parochial libraries in the diocese.[600] *It has recently been printed in M. Perkin,* A directory of the parochial libraries of the Church of England and the Church in Wales *(London: Bibliographical Society, 2004) p. 443. All but two of these books are mentioned in the convocation records, which also give the dates of acquisition by the libraries. Items 1-27 and 29-34 are in the inventoried list produced in 1725 and printed on pp. 159-61 above. Wilson's handlist is reproduced here with the corresponding numbers in the 1725 inventory (where applicable) and the year of acquisition. More detailed information is provided for the others.*

1.	19	(1705)
2.	18	(1705)
3.	17	(1705)
4.	3/14	(1699, 1705)
5.	2	(1699)
6.	5	(1699)
7.	4	(1699)
8.	6	(1699)
9.	7	(1699)
10.	9	(1699)
11.	8	(1699)
12.	10	(1699)
13.	16	(1705)
14.	12	(1704)
15.	22	(1707)
16.	21	(1707)
17.	13	(1704)
18.	1	(1699)
19.	15	(1704)
20.	25	(1707)
21.	20	(1707)
22.	24	(1707)
23.	11	(1703)
24.	26	(1707)
25.	23	(1707)
26.	27	(1707)

[600]Douglas, Manx National Heritage Library, MD 15072.

27.   28   (1714)
28.   William Law's *Christian Perfection*, given in 1729.
29-33.   29   (1725)
34.   30   (1725)
35.   Bishop Wilson on *The Lord's Supper*, given in 1734.
36.   Francis Fox, *The New Testament explained*, given in 1735.
37.   Edward Harley's *Abstract*, given in 1736.
38.   Edward Harley's *Harmony*, given in 1736.
39.   Bishop Wilson's *An essay towards an instruction for Indians, explaining the most essential doctrines of Christianity* (London, 1740).
40.   Henry Hammond, *The New Testament...compared with the original Greek...and illustrated with critical and explanatory notes, etc.* (London, 1736).

The last two are not mentioned in the records and it is uncertain when they were given to the libraries, though it was probably in 1740 or 1741. Most of the books survive in at least one or two copies, which can now be found in the Manx National Heritage Library.

BISHOPS IN THE ISLE OF MAN

The origins of Christianity in the Isle of Man are extremely obscure, though it appears that in earliest times the church there was closely linked to, and dependent on Ireland. In the eleventh century the island had bishops who were theoretically suffragans of York, though part of the Scottish hierarchy. But about 1134 the king of Norway created a new diocese, consisting of his possessions in the western isles of Scotland ('Suðre øyar', the 'southern isles'; anglicized as Sodor), and of the Isle of Man. The diocese was a suffragan see of Nidaros (Trondheim) from 1153, but after the isles passed to the kingdom of Scotland in 1266 this link became increasingly formal and was last mentioned in 1441. In 1387 Scottish support for the Avignon pope during the great schism (1378-1417) led to the deprivation of the bishop of Sodor and Man, who supported Rome, but the latter retained the Isle of Man and was subsequently recognized as a suffragan of Canterbury. In 1541 the English parliament passed a statute (33 Henry VIII, c. 31) attaching the diocese of Sodor and Man (effectively only Man) to the province of York. N.B. Names in square brackets are of bishops who were appointed but either not consecrated or not installed in possession of the see.

Man (York)

Roolwer	1079?
William	1079?
Hamond	1079?-95?

Sodor and Man (Nidaros from 1153/Scotland from 1266)

Wimund	1134/8-48?
[Nicholas	1148?]
John	1152
Gamaliel	1154-66?
Ragnald	1166-70?
Christian	1170-90?
Michael	1188/94-1203
Nicholas	1210-17
Reginald	1217-26?
[Nicholas of Meaux	1219-24/5?]
John, son of Hefare	1226?
Simon	1226-48
[Laurence	1248]
Richard	1253-75
[Gilbert	1275]

Mark	1275-1303
Alan	1305-21
Gilbert MacLelan	1324-26/7?
Bernard	1327/8-31?
[Cormac Cormacii	1331]
Thomas de Rossy	1331-48
William Russell	1349-74
John Don(e)gan	1374-87

Sodor and Man (English; unattached)[601]

John Don(e)gan	1387-92
John Sproten	1392-?
Conrad	1402
Theodore Bloc	1402-?
John Burgherlin	1425-?
Richard Payli (Pulley)	1429-?
[John Burghersh	1433-?]
John Seyre (Feyre)	1435-?
Thomas Burton	1455-8
Thomas Kirkham	1458-?
Richard Oldham	1478-85
Hugh Blackleach	1487-?
Hugh Hesketh	1513-?
John Howden	1523-?

Sodor and Man (York)

Robert	?-1546
Henry Man	1546-56
Thomas Stanley	1555-70
John Salisbury	1570-3
John Meyrick	1576-99
George Lloyd	1599-1605
John Philips	1605-33
William Forster	1633-5
Richard Parr	1635-44[602]

[601] A letter of Pope Callistus III dated 11 July 1458 recognizes York as the metropolitan see of Sodor and Man, a fact which the *New Catholic Encyclopedia* takes to mean that that was the date on which the diocese was 'transferred' from Nidaros (Trondheim) to York. Even if that were the papal intention, however, it did not register in York, and the diocese was not formally attached to the northern province until 1542.

[602] Supposedly died towards the end of 1643 but was still alive and functioning as bishop on 20 February 1644 (see Manx Episcopal Wills, vol. 10). He probably died before the end of the old style year 1643 (24 March 1644).

Samuel Rutter	1661-3
Isaac Barrow	1663-70
Henry Bridgman	1671-82
John Lake	1682-4
Baptist Levinz	1684-93
[Henry Finch	1693-?][603]
Thomas Wilson	1698-1755
Mark Hildesley	1755-72
Richard Richmond	1773-80
George Mason	1780-3
Claudius Crigan	1784-1813
George Murray	1813-27
William Ward	1828-38
James Bowstead	1838-40
Henry Pepys	1840-1
Thomas Vowler Short	1841-6
Walter Augustus Shirley	1846-7
Robert John Eden	1847-54
Horatio Powys	1854-77
Rowley Hill	1877-87
John Wareing Bardsley	1887-92
Norman Dumenil John Straton	1892-1907
Thomas Wortley Drury	1907-12
James Denton Thompson	1912-24
Charles Leonard Thornton-Duesbury	1925-8
William Stanton Jones	1928-42
John Ralph Strickland Taylor	1943-54
Benjamin Pollard	1954-66
George Eric Gordon	1966-74
Vernon Sampson Nicholls	1974-83
Arthur Henry Attwell	1983-9
Noel Debroy Jones	1989-2003
Graeme Paul Knowles	2003-

[603]Not effective.

LORDS OF MAN

Norse

Ketil Flatnef	*c.* 850-70
Tryggvi	*c.* 870-?
Asbjørn Skerjablesi	?
Ragnall (Ragnald)	913-21
Mac Ragnall I	921-40?
Mac Harold	?-977
Godred I	977-89
Sigurd	989-1014
Thorfinn	1014-60
Mac Ragnall II	1060
Godred II	*c.* 1060-70
Fingal	1070-9
Godred I (III)	1079-95
Lagman	1095-6
Donald	1096-8
Magnus I	1098-1103
Olaf I	1103-53
Godred II (IV)	1152-8
Sumerled	1158-64
[Reginald	1164]
Godred II (IV) restored	1164-87
Reginald I	1187-1226
Olaf II	1226-37
Harold I	1237-48
Reginald II	1249
Harold II	1249-50/2?
Magnus II	1252-65

Scottish

Alexander III	1266-86
Margaret	1286-90

English

Richard de Burgh	1290
John Balliol	1293-6
Anthony Bek	1298-1311

Henry de Beaumont	1310
Piers Gaveston	1311
Henry de Beaumont restored	1311-12

Scottish

Thomas Randolph	1313-?

English

William Montague I	1333-44
William Montague II	1344-93
William le Scrope	1393-9
Henry Percy	1399-1405
Sir John Stanley I	1405-14
Sir John Stanley II	1414-37
Thomas I, Lord Stanley	1437-59
Thomas II	1459-1504
Thomas III	1504-21
Edward	1521-72
Henry	1572-93
Fernando	1593-4
[Crown administration	1594-1610]
William I	1610-42
James I	1642-51
Thomas (IV)	1652-60
Charles	1660-72
William II	1672-1702
James II	1702-36
James III	1736-64
John	1764-5

British

George III	1765-1820
George IV	1820-30
William IV	1830-7
Victoria	1837-1901
Edward VII	1901-10
George V	1910-36
Edward VIII	1936
George VI	1936-52
Elizabeth II	1952-

GOVERNORS AND LIEUTENANT-GOVERNORS OF THE ISLE OF MAN

Governors

1405?	Michael Blundell
1417	John Litherland
1422	John Walton
1428	Henry Byron
?	?
1496	Peter Dutton
1497	Abbot Henry Radcliffe
1504	Ralph Rushton
1511	John Ireland
1518	John Fazakerley
1521	Thomas Danport
1522	John Ireland (again)
1527	Henry Stanley
1532	John Fleming
1536	George Stanley
1545	William Stanley
1552	Henry Stanley
1570	Edward Tarbrook
1576	John Harmer
1580	John Sherbourne
1592	Cuthbert Gerard
1593	William Stanley
1594	Randolph Stanley
1595	Thomas Gerard
1596	Piers Legh
1599	Cuthbert Gerard
1600	Robert Molyneux
1609	John Ireland
1623	Sir Frederick Leige
1626	Edward Holmewood
1627	Sir Charles Gerard
1628	Edward Christian
1639	Foulkes Hunckes
1640	John Greenhalgh
1651	Philip Musgrave
1651	Colonel Robert Dunkinfield
1652	Matthew Cadwell
1656	William Christian

1659	James Chaloner
1660	Robert Nowell
1664	Bishop Isaac Barrow
1673	Henry Nowell
1677	Henry Stanley
1678	Robert Heywood
1690	Roger Kenyon
1693	William Sacheverell
1696	Nicholas Sankey
1701	James Cranston
1702	Charles Stanley
1703	Robert Mawdesley
1713	Charles Stanley
1718	Alexander Horne
1723	John Lloyd
1723	Thomas Horton
1736	James Murray
1744	Patrick Lindsey
1751	Basil Cochrane
1761	John Wood
1773	Henry Hope
1775	Richard Dawson
1777	Edward Smith
1790	Alexander Shaw
1793	John Murray, fourth duke of Atholl
1804	Lord Henry Murray
1805	Cornelius Smelt

Lieutenant-governors

1830	Cornelius Smelt (continued)
1832	Colonel John Ready
1845	Honourable Charles Hope
1860	Francis Conant-Piggott
1863	Lord Henry Brougham Loch
1882	Sir Spencer Walpole
1893	Sir Joseph Ridgeway
1895	Lord John Henniker-Major
1902	Lord Raglan
1918	Major-General Sir William Fry
1925	Sir Claude Hill
1932	Sir Montagu Butler
1937	Vice-Admiral the Earl Granville
1945	Air Vice-Marshal Sir Geoffrey Rhodes Bromet
1952	Sir Ambrose Dundas Flux Dundas
1959	Sir Ronald Herbert Garvey
1966	Sir Peter Hyla Gawne Stallard

1974 Sir John Warburton Paul
1980 Rear Admiral Sir Oswald Nigel Cecil
1985 Major-General Lawrence New
1990 Air Marshal Sir Lawrence Jones
1995 Sir Timothy Daunt
2000 Ian David Macfadyen

THE PARISHES AND CHAPLAINCIES OF THE ISLE OF MAN

Ancient parishes

Most of the parishes are crown livings, which means that until 1765 they were in the gift of the lords of Man and from 1765 to 1825 of the dukes of Atholl. Parishes where the bishop is patron are marked with an asterisk (*).

North side	Oldest registers
Sheading of Ayre	
Andreas (rectory)	1666
Bride (rectory)	1693
Lezayre	1696
Sheading of Michael	
Ballaugh (rectory)	1598
Jurby*	1606
Michael	1611
Sheading of Glenfaba	
German*	1667
Patrick*	1714
South side	
Sheading of Garff	
Conchan (Onchan)	1627
Lonan	1718
Maughold	1647
Sheading of Middle	
Braddan*	1626
Marown	1622
Santan (Santon)	1690

Sheading of Rushen

Arbory	1652
Malew	1649
Rushen	1670 (lost); 1709

Chaplaincies

Chaplaincies are in the gift of the rector or vicar of the parishes in which they are situated. Those that became parishes in their own right acquired the bishop as their patron, with the sole exception of Douglas, St Ninian, where the patron is the Church Pastoral Aid Society.

Alphabetical order

All Saints, Douglas	1898	Braddan
Baldwin, St Luke	1840	Braddan
Ballure	1712	Maughold; became Ramsey South in 1822.
Castletown	1701	Rushen; parish from 1921.
Cronk y Voddy	1852	Patrick.
Dalby, St James	1839	German.
Dhoon	1840	Maughold.
Foxdale	1850	German; parish from 1881.
Laxey	1856	Lonan; parish from 1917
Ramsey South, St Paul	1822	Maughold; parish from 1904.
St Barnabas	1832	Braddan; parish from 1869; closed 1957.
St George	1781	Braddan; parish from 1878.
St John	1820	Patrick; parish from 1949.
St Jude	1841	Andreas, dissolved in 2005.
St Mark	1772	Malew.
St Matthew	1708	Braddan; parish from 1879.
St Ninian	1913	Braddan; parish from 1913.
St Olave	1870	Lezayre; parish from 1881.
St Thomas	1849	Braddan; parish from 1872.
Sulby, St Stephen	1839	Lezayre.

Chronological order

Chaplaincies

1701	Castletown
1708	St Matthew
1712	Ballure (to 1822, then Ramsey South)
1772	St Mark
1781	St George
1820	St John
1822	Ramsey South, St Paul

1832	St Barnabas
1839	Dalby, St James
1839	Sulby, St Stephen
1840	Dhoon
1840	Baldwin, St Luke
1841	St Jude
1849	St Thomas
1850	Foxdale
1852	Cronk y Voddy
1856	Laxey
1870	St Olave
1898	All Saints, Douglas

New Parishes

1869	Douglas, St Barnabas (closed in 1957 and united to St George).
1872	Douglas, St Thomas.
1878	Douglas, St George.
1879	Douglas, St Matthew.
1881	Ramsey North, St Olave.
1881	Foxdale.
1904	Ramsey South, St Paul.
1913	Douglas, St Ninian.
1917	Laxey.
1921	Castletown.
1949	St John (the Baptist).

CHRONOLOGICAL LIST OF THE CLERGY BY PARISHES

The information for this list was gleaned from a variety of sources. By far the most useful is J. D. Gelling, A history of the Manx church, 1698-1911, *which also gives the assistant curates of each parish. For the earlier period, W. Harrison,* The diocese of Sodor and Man, *Manx Society Studies XXIX (Douglas, 1879) has been used, but with great caution. J. Chaloner,* A short treatise of the Isle of Man, *ed. J. G. Cumming, Manx Society Studies X (Douglas, 1864) gives a most useful list of the clergy in 1653. For the period since 1911, successive issues of* Crockford's Clerical Directory *have been the principal source.*

Archdeacons and rectors of Andreas (to 1938).

Laurence	1247
Domnall	1257
Macaboy	1270
Cormac	1320
Patrick	1408
Gilbert	1482
Thomas Clerk	1497
John Walles	1513
? Gostellaw (Gorstyllaw)	1534
Gilbert de Latham	1544-52
Christian	?
Richard Gorstyllaw	1557-77
Hugh Holland	1577-87
John Phillips	1587-1633
John Broxop	1634-43
Samuel Rutter	1643-52/60
[John Harrison	1652-60][604]
Jonathan Fletcher	1660-9
William Urquhart	1669-87
John Lomax	1687-95
Archippus Kippax	1696-1700
Christopher Marsden	1700-1
Vacant	1701-3
Samuel Wattleworth	1703-18
Robert Horrobin	1719-27
John Kippax	1727-60

---

[604]*Locum tenens* during Samuel Rutter's (self-imposed?) exile. He went to Bride in 1660.

William Mylrea	1760-87
Lord George Murray	1787-1803[605]
Lord Charles Aynsley	1803-8
Honourable George Murray	1808-14
Daniel Mylrea	1814-32
Benjamin Philpot	1832-9
John Cecil Hall	1839-44
Joseph Christian Moore	1844-86
Joshua Hughes-Games	1886-95
Hugh Stowell Gill	1895-1912
John Kewley	1912-38

Archdeacons

Charles Vincent Stockwood	1938-58
Ernest Henry Stenning	1958-64
Edward Brown Glass	1964-78
Arthur Ashford Clague	1978-82
David Albert Willoughby	1982-96
Brian Harold Partington	1996-2005
Brian Smith	2005-

Andreas

Henry Maddrell	1938-53
Robert John Cannell	1953-9
Charles Alfred Cannan	1959-64
Edward Brown Glass	1964-78 (archdeacon)
Frederick Stanley White	1978-94
Roderick Charles Geddes	1994-2003
Peter Upton-Jones	2003-4

See Lezayre.

Arbory

Alan of Whithorn	1291
Dominic Kenneth	1370-2
Mactyr	1372-5
Ayg Mac Peter	1375
Thomas Symeyn	1571-6
Thomas Orman	1576-7
James Smyth	1577-80
Edward Callow	1580

---

[605]He resigned the archdeaconry in 1801, and Daniel Mylrea was appointed to it. Mylrea did not become rector of Andreas until 1814.

Alexander Stevenson	1580-1
John Stevenson	1581-5
Vacant	1585-1609
Thomas Norris	1609-23
Thomas Harrison	1623-8
Robert Norris	1628-50
John Crellin	1650-70
Vacant	1670-80
Samuel Robinson	1680-1712
Robert Parr	1713-23
Vacant	1723-6
Charles Wattleworth	1726-8
John Quayle	1728-48
John Moore	1748-91
John Christian	1791-1815
Alexander Gelling	1816-59
John Qualtrough	1859-75
William Thomas Dinwoody	1875-6
Frederick Grier	1876-80
Charles Thomas Langton	1880-90
John Kewley	1891-1912
Frederick William Stubbs	1912-37
Norman Hemingway	1937-57
Cecil Vivian Curtis	1957-67
Harry Waterhouse	1969-72
Geoffrey Buckroyd Clayton	1972-97
Christopher Andrew Quine	1999-

Baldwin, St Luke

Thomas Caine	1840-53
Hugh Stowell Gill	1853-6
George Dawes	1856-9
Robert Airey	1859-64
Benjamin Philpot Clarke	1864-5
William Frederick Drury	1866-8
Edward William Kissack	1868-9
Charles Thomas Langton	1869-80
William Appleton	1880
Samuel Gasking	1880-2
Hugh Kinred	1882
Richard Jones	1882-9
George Thomson	1889-91
Mordaunt Laidlaw Warren	1891-4
Robert William Watson	1894-9
Samuel Butterton	1899-1902
Francis Iles	1903-6
Robert Lewin Cain	1906-9

Frank Whittaker	1910-13
John Gerald Francis Burnet	1913-14
Vacant	1914-23
John Arthur Holden	1923-7
Alfred Henry Lloyd Davies	1928-30
Vacant	1930-3
William Osborne Allison	1933-5
Vacant	1935-9
William Henry Saunders	1939-44
George Gilbert Gresswell	1944-8
Vacant	1948-52
Alan Holland Doyle	1952-5
Henry Saunderson	1955-74

See Braddan.

Ballaugh

Donald M'Corkyll	1408
Philip Hoggett	1576-80
Donald Callow	1580
Edward Baguley	1580-1
Vacant	1581-98
Nicholas Thompson	1598-1640
Robert Parr	1640-73
Charles Parr	1673-81
Henry Lowcay	1681-1700
Vacant	1700-3
William Walker	1703-29
William Bridson	1729-51
Philip Moore	1751-60
Matthias Curghey	1761-71
James Wilks	1771-7
Daniel Gelling	1777-1801
Daniel Mylrea	1802-14
Hugh Stowell	1814-35
Thomas Howard	1836-76
William Kermode	1877-90
Edward Kissack	1890-7
Thomas Redfearn Kneale	1897-1934
Kenneth George Gates	1934-8
Thomas Elliott	1938-49
William Vernon Walmsley	1949-59
James Henry Platt	1960-6
David Lumgair	1967-70
Theodore John Childs	1970-7
John Drury Gelling	1977-92
John Laurie Evans	1993-6

| Cyril David Rogers | 1997- |

Ballure, St Catherine

John Parr	1688-91
Vacant	1691-1712
James Knipe[606]	1712-47
Thomas William Joseph Woods	1747-54
Daniel Gelling	1754-61
John Crellin	1761-71
John Bridson	1771-83
Daniel Mylrea	1783-5
John Bridson	1785-8
Nicholas Christian	1789-90
Henry Maddrell	1790-1803
William Sturt	1803-4
Robert Craine	1804-7
Thomas Howard	1807-9
Alexander Gelling	1809-16
Bowyer Harrison	1816-16
John Kaye	1816-19
Philip Corlett	1819-22

See Ramsey South, St Paul.

Braddan

Alexander Stevenson	1575-6
John Moore	1576-82
William Crowe	1582-1603
Edward Moore	1603-8
Robert Cottier	1609-23
Robert Oates (Otte)	1623-4
John Thompson	1624-33
Patrick Thompson	1633-89
Vacant	1689-91
John Bridson	1691-3
John Woods	1693-6
Robert Fletcher	1696-1704
John Curghey	1704-33
John Cosnahan	1733-50
Joseph Cosnahan	1750-68
Thomas William Joseph Woods	1768-86
Julius Cosnahan	1786
John Moore	1786-91

[606]Schoolmaster, not ordained but licensed by the bishop.

Robert Quayle	1792-1809
Thomas Howard	1810-36
Robert Brown	1836-46
William Drury	1847-87
Frederick James Moore	1888-1912
William Andrew Rushworth	1912-50
Bertram George Kelly	1950-65
Kenneth Liley	1965-74
Leslie Hayes	1974-8
David Charles Post	1978-9
Clifford David Bradley	1979-84
Roger Harry Horne	1985-8
Harold Aldridge	1989-95
Philip Scott Frear	1995-

Bride

Donald Nigel	? - 1377
Malcolm Ysaye	1377
Patrick	1408
John Moore	1582-1609
John Thompson	1609-14
William Crowe	1614-23
Charles Cowill	1623-38?
Samuel Hinde	1638?-60
John Harrison	1660-86
John Christian	1687-98
Vacant	1698-1700
John Parr	1700-23
Robert Parr	1723-9
Matthias Curghey, sr.	1729-54
William Mylrea	1754-60
Philip Moore	1760-83
William Clucas	1783-98
John Crellin	1798-1808
John Bridson	1808-16
Thomas Cubbon	1817-30
John Nelson	1830-47
Daniel Nelson	1847-75
John Qualtrough	1875-9
Edward William Kissack	1879-90
Charles Langton	1890-4
Daniel Cowley	1895-1913
Sidney Botwood	1913-19
James Hampton Cain	1919-41
William Grange Sumner Duckworth	1941-8
John Herbert Jones	1948-55
William Edward James Cringle	1955-61

George Wilson	1962-6
Alaister McDougall Barr	1967-71
Geoffrey Kershaw	1971-5
Arthur Raymond Thomas Clode	1975-8
John Harold Sheen	1978-97
James Alan Heslop	1998-9
Peter John Upton-Jones	2000-

Castletown, St Mary

Hugh Holland	1577
James Makon	1701-19
Robert Horrobin	1719-25
John Kippax	1727
William Ross	1727-54
Vacant	1754-8
Thomas Castley	1758-1807
Joseph Brown	1807-18
Thomas Thimbleby	1818-27
George Stickler Parsons	1827-55
Edward Ferrier	1855-96
Edward Henry Leatham Locke	1896-1921
William Nathaniel Carter	1922-9
Henry Maddrell	1930-8
John Herbert Brereton Sewell	1938-47
Henry Fraser Crennell	1947-9
Henry Smith Whittaker	1949-55
Edward Brown Glass	1955-64
Rudolf William Henry Dawson Murrray	1964-72
Joseph Marshall Payne	1972-8
Peter Shepherd Wilson	1978-83
William Norman Kelly	1984-92
Simon Timothy Michael Rex Dean	1992-2005

Cronk y Voddy

John Fry Garde	1852-4
Charles James Stewart	1854-7
Christopher Tennant Taylor	1857-8
Henry Hardy	1858
John Corlett	1859-65
James Edmunds	1866-75
Edward Collet	1875-6
Joseph Kyte	1876-9
Herbert Robert Finnis	1879-80
John Burnaby Stephenson	1880-2
Hugh Kinred	1882-95
Alfred George Bowerman	1895-1906

William Kerr Smyth	1906-8
Henry Eaves	1908-10
Samuel Sidebotham	1911-13
Thomas Bache	1913-15
Frederick Arthur Betts	1915-17
Arthur Evelyn Nelson	1918-22
Harold Stone Hitchen	1922-4
Frederick James Hirst	1924-6
Vacant	1926-33
William Charles Cato Symonds	1933-6
John Richard Crone Gamble	1937-8
Vacant	1938-41
Wilfred George	1941-6
Charles Vincent Stockwood	1948-58

See German.

Dalby, St James

William Kermode	1839-40
George Caesar Stephen	1840-58
Charles Hill	1858-68
Joseph Kyte	1868-72
Vacant	1872-81
Charles Marston Barnes	1881-8
Charles Henry Brocklebank	1888-90
Harry Creswell Pigot	1890
Norman King	1890-2
William Callahan	1892-4
Edward Henry Leatham Locke	1894-6
William Henry Gibson	1896-8
William Whalley	1898-1903
Thomas Williams	1903-7
Hampton Robinson	1907-9
Frederick Shippham	1909-10
Arthur Pearson Bradshaw	1911-14
Vacant	1914-19
Thomas Herbert Hastings	1919-22
George Thomas Ball-Knight	1922-5
Charles Percy Stammers	1925-7
Wilfred Percy Beard	1927-9
Joseph Phillips	1929-32
Alexander Wigan Buckley	1932-8

See Patrick.

Dhoon

William Christian	1840-50
Thomas Fenton	1850-2
Lloyd Bruce	1853-5
Samuel Hill	1855-8
Hugh Ashworth Stowell	1858-69
Jonathan Akroyd	1869-72
Stephen Nathaniel Harrison	1873-89
Richard Jones	1889-91
William George Rolston	1891-1907
George William Gregson	1907-13
Robert Ferguson	1914-58

See Maughold.

Douglas, All Saints

Under Douglas, St George from 1898 to 1996. Now under Douglas, St Thomas.

Douglas, St Barnabas

William Carpenter	1835-48
John Alcock	1848-52
Joseph Henry Gray	1852-69
Henry Sutton	1870-2
William Thomas Hobson	1872-95
Frederick John Landsell	1896-1903
George Edward Craven	1904-9
Frederick William Stubbs	1909-12
Henry Shenston	1912-17
Isaiah Rostron	1917-21
Frederick Arthur Betts	1922-4
Robert Harrison Mayoh	1924-8
Harold Stone Hitchen	1929-34
Eric Douglas Geddes	1934-8
Henry Saunderson	1938-50
James Ernest Broadbent	1951-7

Closed in 1957.

Douglas, St George

Charles Crebbin	1781-1817
John Christian	1817-27
Benjamin Philpot	1827-32
Thomas Howard	1832-6
Francis Broderick Hartwell	1836-46
Edward Forbes	1847-59

William Hawley	1859-77
Henry Armstrong Hall	1877-80
John Edward Beauchamp George	1880-91
Robert Benjamin Baron	1891-1906
John Campbell	1907-8
Robert Daniel Kermode	1908-19
William Charles Jordan	1919-25
Arthur John Talbot Easter	1925-7
Charles Vincent Stockwood	1927-48 (archdeacon from 1938)
Jack White	1948-53
Percival Charles Halls Matthews	1953-80
David Albert Willoughby	1980-96 (archdeacon)
Brian Harold Partington	1996-2004 (archdeacon)
Brian Smith	2005- (archdeacon)

Douglas, St Matthew

Samuel Robinson	1708-14
Peter Lancaster	1714-16
Anthony Halsall	1716-32
Thomas Birkett	1732-6
Philip Moore	1736-65
Charles Crebbin	1765-9
Robert Quayle	1770-91
Nicholas Christian	1791-7
Hugh Stowell	1797-1802
John Kewley	1802-10
Joseph Qualtrough	1810-16
Robert Brown	1817-32
John LaMothe Stowell	1832-5
Samuel Gelling	1835
John Cannell	1835-73
Thomas Arthur Taggart	1874-1909
Hugh Selwyn Taggart	1909-26
Theodore Henry Egbert Japing	1927-32
Lewis Cecil Watson	1932-42
William Wood	1943-54
Bernard Burnett	1954-76
Kenneth Reginald Court	1976-84
Duncan Whitworth	1984-

Douglas, St Ninian

Disney Charles Woodhouse	1913-15
Henry Cameron McNeil	1915-28
Edwin James Towndrow	1928-32
Walter Whitfield Williams	1932-45

Reginald James Benson	1945-55
Frank Hamer	1955-65
William Bolton	1965-75
Graham Gregory	1975-91
Warren Adamson	1991-3
Garth Clews Grinham	1994-2001
Brian Darbyshire	2002-

Douglas, St Thomas

William David Carter	1849-51
Samuel Simpson	1851-61
Church closed during dispute	
Francis Pierpoint Burton Norman Hutton	1872-7
Marmaduke Washington	1877-81
John Nathaniel Quirk	1881-2
Ernest Bickersteth Savage	1882-1914
Reginald Bradley Jolly	1914-20
Nathaniel John Poole	1920-31
Ernest Barker	1931-43
Frederick Ingram Cox	1943-8
William Grange Sumner Duckworth	1948-54
George Parr	1954-9
John Herwald Rice Glynne Jones	1960-72
Dermot Nichols Bowers	1972-88
Alec John Smith	1988-92
Sidney Eric Mourant	1992-6
Alan John Fitch	1997-2002
Ernest Pettengell	2003-

Foxdale

Joseph William Kewley	1850-4
Francis Swallow	1856-8
John Leech	1859-64
Frederick James Moore	1864-75
William Hart	1876-7
Thomas Bates	1877-9
Eustace William Cochrane	1879-1900
George Packer	1900-3
Frederick William Stubbs	1903-9
Robert Lewin Cain	1909-16
Frederick Arthur Rawcliffe	1917-21
Frederick Arthur Betts	1921-2
Arthur Kenyon	1922-34
Henry Saunderson	1934-8
George Ernest Williams	1939-46

William Henry Saunders	1946-9
William Edward James Cringle	1949-55
William Percy Allen	1957-61
Brian Horace Kelly	1961-4
John Richard Claude Hamilton	1964-6
Charles Henry Milton-Smith	1966-72
Norman Stanley Saul	1972-7
Brian Harold Partington	1977-96

See Patrick.

German

Morice	1408
Philip Hoggett	1575-6
Alexander Stevenson	1576-80
John Cosnahan	1580-1608
Robert Moore	1608-21
William Cosnahan	1621-30
Hugh Morrey	1330-3
John Harrison	1633-52
Thomas Harrison	1652-61
Henry Lowcay	1661-80
John Woods	1680-2
Samuel Wattleworth	1682-1703
Vacant	1703-10
Matthias Curghey	1710-29
John Woods, jr.	1730-40
John Craine	1741-2
Vacant	1742-4
James Wilks	1744-52
Robert Christian	1752-4
Vacant	1754-8
Robert Brew	1758-60
Henry Corlett	1761-1801
James Gelling	1801-38
John LaMothe Stowell	1839-80
Henry Dening	1880-1
James George Williams	1881-9
Daniel Scurr Cowley	1890-5
George Ensor	1895-6
Edward Rainbow	1897-1907
Walter Lewis	1907-14
Norman Veitch Scorer	1914-17
William Hudson	1917-22
William Henry Willetts	1922-5
Edward Thomas Pakenham	1926-31

Edgar Lionel Morris	1931-66
James Henry Platt	1966-9
Herbert Alexander McCullough	1970-7
Brian Horace Kelly	1977-2004

St John (the Baptist)

William Gill	1820-4
Samuel Gelling	1824-33
William Drury	1833-4
John Gell	1834-45
William Bell Christian	1845
John Fry Garde	1845-65
John Corlett	1865-1909
Sidney Botwood	1909-13
Vacant	1913-19
Frederick Arthur Betts	1919-20
Charles Alfred Cannan	1921-4
Frederick Cecil Cotes	1924-6
Frederick Appleton	1926-30
Clarence Gordon Felix Justin Wentner	1930-3
William Charles Cato Symonds	1933-6
Vacant	1936-41
Wilfred George	1941-6
Charles Vincent Stockwood	1948-58
William Thomas Dixon	1959-77
Brian Harold Partington	1977-96

See Patrick.

St Jude

William Drury	1841-7
Daniel Nelson	1847
John Qualtrough	1848-59
George Bishop	1859-65
Benjamin Philpot Clarke	1865-9
Edward William Kissack	1869-72
James Seely Wilkinson	1872-88
Thomas Redfearn Kneale	1888-93
Robert Bibby Blakeney	1893-4
Adrian Rolleston	1894-1913
John Gerald Francis Burnet	1914-17
James Arthur Cooil	1917-34
David Wilson	1934-7
Gideon Davies	1938-40
John Herbert Jones	1940-8

Thomas Stanley McPherson	1949-52
William Ernest Barker	1952-6
Wilfred George	1956-67
Victor Dawes	1967-73
Frederick Stanley White	1975-89

See Andreas. The parish was dissolved on 6 March 2005.

Jurby

Roland	1291
Donald	1408
John Cosnahan	1575-80
Philip Hoggett	1580-5
John Stevenson	1585-1603
John Clarke	1603-45
William Crowe	1645-98
John Christian	1698-1747
Samuel Gell	1747-8
Vacant	1748-51
William Crebbin	1751-1803
John Nelson	1803-18
John Edward Harrison	1818-58
Henry Hardy	1858-75
Frederick James Moore	1875-8
Joseph Bellamy	1879-91
Henry Wilson	1891-5
Frederick William Stubbs	1895-1903
William Whalley	1903-5
Henry Shenston	1905-12
George William Gregson	1913-31
Norman Hemingway	1931-7
John Richard Crone Gamble	1938-46
Wilfred George	1946-67

See St Jude.

Laxey

Hugh Stowell Gill	1856-9
Matthew Pierpoint	1859-61
Joseph Bellamy	1861-78
Robert Gawne Brearey	1878-81
Theodore Charles Chapman	1881-4
Henry Lionel James	1884-5
Claud Reade	1885-7

John Morris Spicer	1887-95
Charles Henry Leece	1895-7
William Edward Davies	1897-1904
William Henry Gibson	1904-16
Robert Lewin Cain	1916-26
Benjamin Webster	1926-30
Sidney Benson Botwood	1930-47
Frank Hamer	1947-9
Joseph Lloyd	1950-6
Ernest Shufflebottom	1957-9
George Gilbert Gresswell	1959-70
John Percy Hebden	1970-84
William Henry Scattergood	1984-92
Clement Upton	1993-6
William Harrison Martin	1997-

Lezayre

Michael	1408
William Norris	1571-85
William Crowe	1603-14
Silvester Crowe	1614-24
Edward Crowe	1624-56
Charles Coole	1656-60
John Thompson	1660-7
Samuel Robinson	1667-81
Robert Parr	1681-1712
Vacant	1712-14
Henry Allen	1714-27
William Bridson	1728-9
Matthias Curghey, jr.	1729-61
John Gill	1761-72
Thomas Corlett	1773-1803
Henry Maddrell	1803-42
John Henry LaMothe	1842-5
William Bell Christian	1845-61
Edward Snepp	1861-3
Thomas Henry	1863-9
Wyndham Madden Hutton	1869-77
Clement Carus Wilson Shepheard	1877-8
Arthur Bridgman	1879-1909
James Hampton Cain	1909-19
Robert Daniel Kermode	1919-39
Gordon Sayle	1939-46
Jonathan Edward Cowley	1947-50
John Richard Crone Gamble	1950-4
Peter Weir	1955-8

William Sealey Robertson	1958-69
Arthur Ashford Clague	1969-82 (archdeacon)
Leslie Victor Henry	1983-6
Colin John Fleetney	1986-91
Brian Edward Shepherd	1991-2002
Vacant	2002-4
Gordon Frank Barker	2004-

Lonan

William Norris	1585-1627
James Moore	1627-53
Charles Parr	1653-73
Thomas Thwaites	1674-86
John Taubman	1686-1725
Robert Radcliffe	1725-35
Edward Moore	1735
Vacant	1735-53
Nathaniel Curghey	1753-9
Samuel Gell	1759-1802
Hugh Stowell	1802-14
Thomas Cubbon	1814-17
David Harrison	1817-24
Joseph Qualtrough	1824-53
Thomas Caine	1853-78
Frederick James Moore	1878-88
James Seely Wilkinson	1888-95
John Quine	1895-1940
Gideon Davies	1940-4
William Sealey Robertson	1944-53
Walter Edward Brooke	1953-9
Thomas Herbert Woodward Copner	1959-75
Donald Albert Wilson	1975-80
John Percy Hebden	1980-4

See Laxey.

Malew

John Hugh	1368
Donald Nigel	1370-7
Malcolm Ysaye	1377
Richard Byderosse	1408
Harlefson	1560-74
Thomas Norris	1574-1606
William Watterson	1606-8

Edward Caloe	1609-10
Thomas Norreys	1610-30
John Cosnahan	1630-3
Robert Parr	1633-40
Thomas Parr	1641-95
John Woods	1696-1739
John Quayle	1739-58
John Gill	1759-61
Daniel Gelling	1761-77
William Clucas	1778-83
David Harrison	1783-1817
William Christian	1817-30
William Gill	1830-71
Hugh Stowell Gill	1871-95
John Morris Spicer	1895-1919
Sidney Benson Botwood	1919-30
Robert Higginson Reid	1931-2
Henry Saunderson	1932-4
Henry Smith Whittaker	1934-49
William Henry Saunders	1949-56
Thomas Bertie Jenkins	1956-72
Joseph Marshall Payne	1972-82
Ernest William Fisher	1984-93
Michael Frederick Roberts	1993-

St Mark

David Harrison	1772-83
John Moore	1783-6
John Gell	1786-1809
Patrick Kneale	1809-14
Edward Craine	1814-20
William Duggan	1820-7
John Thomas Clarke	1827-64
Thomas Howard Gill	1864-5
Robert Airey	1865-74
John Mitchell	1874-6
Frederick Grant	1876-8
Benjamin Lupton	1878-91
Charles Kroenig	1891-6
Arnold John Holmes	1897-1903
Robert Halstead	1903-4
Henry Hickin	1905-12
Vacant	1912-18
Arthur Kenyon	1918-22
Frederick Woodhouse Gelling	1922-5
Frederick Appleton	1926-8

Frederick John Colepeper	1928-32
Henry Saunderson	1932-6
Gideon Davies	1936-8
John Herbert Jones	1938-40
George William Herbert Hulme	1941-6
George Samuel Smith	1946-8
Vacant	1948-53
James Barnes	1953-5

See Malew.

Marown

John Gell	1576-1603
Thomas Norris	1603-5
Lewis Norris	1605-18
John Norris	1618-23
William Oates	1623-77
Robert Fletcher	1677-96
Vacant	1696-1701
Ewan Gill	1701-13
William Bridson	1713-27
Matthias Curghey	1728-9
Vacant	1729-34
Thomas Christian	1734-52
John Christian	1753-79
Thomas Christian	1780-99
John Bridson	1799-1808
Thomas Stephen	1809-27
William Duggan	1827-62
Robert Wesley Aitken	1862-9
Benjamin Philpot Clarke	1869-1903
Archibald Edward Clarke	1903-34
Harold Stone Hitchen	1934-6
Wilfred George	1936-46
Sidney Benson Botwood	1947-53
Clifford Alwyn Parkinson	1955-8
Neville Shaw Vaughan	1958-72
David Albert Willoughby	1972-80
David Bush	1980-7
Arthur Malcolm Convery	1987-2004
Ian Davies	2005-

Maughold

John Stevenson	1576-80
John Christian	1580-1614

John Thompson	1614-24
Thomas Allen	1625-42
William Oates	1642-60
Robert Allen	1660-3
Vacant	1663-6
Thomas Allen	1666-1726
Henry Allen	1727-46
Thomas Allen	1746-54
Thomas William Joseph Woods	1754-68
Thomas Cubbon	1769-1814
John Edward Harrison	1814-18
Bowyer Harrison	1818-71
William Kermode	1871-7
Gilmour Harvey	1877-8
Henry Grattan White	1878-94
James Seely Wilkinson	1895-8
Robert Daniel Kermode	1898-1908
John Grasett Pope	1908-20
Ernest Andrew Stafford Young	1920-7
Henry Maddrell	1928-30
Robert John Cannell	1930-53
William Grange Sumner Duckworth	1954-73
Brian Horace Kelly	1973-7
Norman Stanley Saul	1977-90
David John Green	1990-

Michael

Donald Crahan	1571-85
Thomas Preston	1585-1605
Philip Leighe	1605-9
Hugh Cannell	1609-64
Vacant	1664-72
Samuel Wattleworth	1672-7
Edward Nelson	1677-86
Henry Norris	1686-1717
Vacant	1717-35
John Allen	1735
Edward Moore	1735-51
James Wilks	1752-71
John Crellin	1771-98
Daniel Mylrea	1799-1802
Nicholas Christian	1802-8
Thomas Harrison	1808-18
Joseph Brown	1818-60
James Butler Knill Kelly	1860-4
William Clavell Ingram	1864-74

Robert Airey	1874-8
Ernest Bickersteth Savage	1878-82
William Hawley	1882-93
Alfred Morris	1894-1913
Henry Devall	1913-22
Edward Thomas Pakenham	1922-6
Charles Alfred Cannan	1926-59
John Francis Foster	1959-64
Ronald Robert Pierpoint Rigby	1965-72
John Drury Gelling	1972-92

See Ballaugh.

St Olave (North Ramsey)

William David Carter	1847-8
Thomas Millington	1848-50
Robert Airey	1850-8
William Clay	1858-61
John James Stevenson Moore	1861-3
Thomas Lee	1863-5
George Paton	1865-6
Henry Barff	1866-7
Walter Awdrey	1867-70
Theophilus Talbot	1870-4
Edward Curwen	1874-5
Charles Buckley	1876-8
Robertson Bardell	1878-9
William Morris	1879-96
Charles Hopkins	1896-1903
Arthur Kingston Dearden	1903-4
William Edward Davies	1904-17
Charles Vincent Stockwood	1918-27
Walter Stanley Senior	1927-30
Halford William Young	1930-50
Edward Brown Glass	1951-5
Thomas Whitehead Taylor	1956-61
William Edward James Cringle	1961-80
John Harold Sheen	1980-97

See Bride.

Onchan (formerly Conchan)

Richard	1408
John Moore	1566-75

Henry Gell	1575-80
John Oates (Otte)	1580-1647
Vacant	1647-50
John Woods	1650-80
Thomas Robinson	1680-6
Ewan Gill	1686-1701
William Gell	1701-48
Samuel Gell	1748-59
Thomas Quayle	1759-98
John Cannell	1798-1809
Edward Craine	1810-47
John Howard	1847-92
Stanley Kermode	1892-1904
Walmsley Stanley	1904-8
Robert Wakeford	1908-33
Henry Gordon	1933-8
John Duffield	1938-70
Dennis Baggaley	1971-96
Nicholas Anthony Wells	1997-2003
Arthur Malcolm Convery	2004-

Patrick

William Craine	? - 1575
Philip Hoggett	1575-6
Alexander Stevenson	1576-80
John Cosnahan	1580-1608
Edward Moore	1608-21
William Cosnahan	1621-30
Hugh Morrey	1630-33
John Harrison	1633-52
Thomas Harrison	1652-61
Henry Lowcay	1661-77
Samuel Wattleworth	1677-1703
Matthias Curghey	1703-29
Robert Radcliffe	1729-69
Ewan Christian	1769-1808
Nicholas Christian	1808-11
John Cottier	1812-27
Thomas Stephen	1827-42
Archibald Holmes	1842-65
John Fry Garde	1865-77
William Hawley	1877-82
Hugh Davidson	1882-97
Hugh Kinred	1897-1921
Edward Henry Leatham Locke	1921-9
Benjamin Webster	1930-7

David Wilson	1937-45
Thomas Herbert Woodward Copner	1945-59
William Charles Turner	1959-63
Henry Hall	1965-8
Brian Harold Partington	1968-96
Paul Jonathan Bennett	1996-2000
Geoffrey Breffitt	2001-

Ramsey South, St Paul

Philip Corlett	1822-5
Archibald Holmes	1825-42
William Kermode	1843-71
George Paton	1871-1900
Henry Thomas Devall	1900-11
Mark Wilks Harrison	1911-46
Gordon Sayle	1947-52
Arthur Harold Mock	1952-64
John Francis Foster	1964-79
Percy Campbell Cox	1980-2
Brian Paish Brownless	1982-7
David Brereton Foster	1987-91
Peter Charles Robinson	1992-9
Norman David Greenwood	1999-

Rushen

William	1408
James Smyth	1574-7
Vacant	1577-81
Alexander Stevenson	1581-8
Daniel Gell	1588-94
William Watterson	1594-1606
John Corkhill	1606-38
John Keig	1638-52
John Thompson	1652-60
Richard Thompson	1660-91
John Parr	1691-1700
Vacant	1700-3
Matthias Curghey	1703-13
Thomas Christian	1713-27
Vacant	1727-9
John Quayle	1729-39
Vacant	1739-48
Nicholas Christian	1748-82
John Clague	1782-1816
Joseph Qualtrough	1816-24

William Corrin	1824-59
Hugh Stowell Gill	1859-71
Edward William Kissack	1872-9
Arthur Allwork	1879-81
Frederick Francis Tracey	1881-5
Charles Dawes	1885-7
Blundell Browne	1887-93
Thomas Redfearn Kneale	1893-7
Charles Henry Leece	1897-1927
Albert Ridings	1927-32
John Duffield	1932-8
William Benjamin Farrer	1939-48
George Gilbert Gresswell	1948-59
William George Ellis Squire	1959-64
John Drury Gelling	1964-77
Donald Andrew	1977-82
Frederick Hinton Bird	1982-2003
Norma Jean Cole	2004-

Santan (Santon)

Donald	? -1291
Odo	1291
Alexander Stevenson	1571-5
Vacant	1575-81
Edward Baguley	1581-97
Robert Moore	1597-1614
William Cosnahan	1614-18
John Cosnahan	1618-52
Vacant	1652-6
Edward Crowe	1656-67
Hugh Cosnahan	1667-91
John Cosnahan	1691-1724
Vacant	1724-31
Paul Crebbin	1731-64
Thomas Cubbon	1765-9
Charles Crebbin	1769-1817
John Nelson	1818-27
Thomas Kewley	1827-35
Samuel Gelling	1835-65
Gilmour Harvey	1865-77
Henry Grattan White	1877-8
Robert Airey	1878-89
John Kirkby	1890-1
Richard Jones	1891-1931
William Hornby	1931-8
Frederick Woodhouse Gelling	1938-49

Edward Jones	1950-4
Edward Bertie Gregory	1954-70
David Lumgair	1970-2
James Myrtle Cotter	1973-8

Served from Braddan (1978-88) and from Arbory since 1988.

Sulby, St Stephen

John Qualtrough	1839-48
Edward Brailsford	1848-9
Joseph Preston Ward	1849-51
Matthew Thompson	1851-3
Edward Qualtrough	1853
William Thompson	1853-5
William Kelly	1855-8
John Corlett	1858-9
James Orchard Stuart	1859-60
Robert Wesley Aitken	1860-2
Samuel Sharpe Walker	1862-5
James Eckley Pattison	1865-78
William John Canton	1878-82
Charles Bell	1882-5
William Blakeney	1885-9
Sidney Swan	1889-90
James Gardner	1891-2
Archibald Edward Clarke	1892-1903
Percy Brown	1904-6
Alfred George Bowerman	1906-29
William Charles Cato Symonds	1929-33
Wilfred George	1933-6
George Ernest Williams	1936-9
William Sealey Robertson	1939-44
William Henry Saunders	1944-6
Vacant	1946-52
William Percy Allen	1952-7
John Richard Claude Hamilton	1958-64

See Lezayre.

Vicars-general

1570-5	William Craine		1570-85	John Moore
1575-80	Henry Gell			
1580-1626	William Crow		1585-1627	William Norris
1626-64	Hugh Cannell		1627-40	Nicholas Thompson
			1640-67	Robert Parr

(1647-53	James Moore)[607]			
1664-95	Thomas Parr	1667-86	John Harrison
1695-1703	Samuel Wattleworth	1686-98	John Christian
1704-33	John Curghey	1698-1712	Robert Parr
		1712-29	William Walker
		1729	Robert Parr
		1729-40	John Woods
1733-50	John Cosnahan	1740-51	Edward Moore
1750-69	Robert Radcliffe	1751-70	Matthias Curghey
1769-78	James Wilks	1770-80	John Moore
1778-80	Ewan Christian	1780-4	Charles Crebbin
1780-4	William Clucas	1784-91	John Moore
1784-1808	Ewan Christian	1791-8	William Clucas
		1799-1808	John Crellin
		1808-11	Nicholas Christian
1808-27	Thomas Cubbon	1812-24	Thomas Stephen
		1824-8	William Roper
1827-35	John Nelson	1828-31	Benjamin Philpot
1835-61	Thomas Corlett	1831-46	Francis Hartwell
		1847-71	William Gill[608]
1861-84	Richard Jebb		
1884-1903	Samuel Harris		
1903-6	Charles Thomas Cheslyn Callow		
1906-32	Cyril Tomlinson Wynn Hughes-Games		
1932-48	Ramsey Johnson		
1948-73	Frank Johnson		
1973-96	Peter William Stanley Farrant		
1996-	Clare Faulds		

Episcopal registrars

1580-1609	John Cosnahan
1609-26	Hugh Cannell
1626-38	William Cosnahan
1638-41	John Keig
1641-2	John Harrison
1642-51	Thomas Parr
1651-65	Thomas Norris[609]
1658-79	Richard Fox
1679-84	Robert Parr
1684-95	Samuel Wattleworth

[607] Acted as a third vicar-general.

[608] This appears from the 1848 convocation, but he is not known to have exercised the function of vicar-general.

[609] He and his successor seem to have overlapped for a number of years.

1696-1739   John Woods
1739-73   James Wilks
1773-8   Ewan Christian
1778-80   William Clucas
1780-4   Calcott Heywood
1784-99   John Crellin
1799-1814   William Kewley
1814-18   Thomas Allison
1818-57   Joseph Brown
1858-62   James Kelly
1863-1903   Samuel Harris

Office altered to diocesan registrar in 1880 and combined with that of vicar-general in 1884.

Archdeacon's registrar (official)

1682?-90   John Christian
1690-8   Samuel Wattleworth
1698-1726   Charles Wattleworth
1726-35   Edward Moore
1735-50   Robert Radcliffe
1751-70   John Gill
1770-1808   Thomas Cubbon
1808-35   Henry Maddrell
1835-47   Daniel Nelson
1847-71   Robert Henry Lace Brown
1871-84   Thomas Callow

Merged with the above when the probate and matrimonial jurisdictions were secularized in 1884.

Principals of King William's College

1833-8   Edward Wilson
1838-41   Alfred Philips
1841-65   Robert Dixon
1866-86   Joshua Hughes-Games
1886-99   Frank Bridgeman Walters
1900-12   Edwin Hone Kempson
1913-30   Edward Cunliffe Owen
1930-5   George Herbert Harris
1935-58   Sydney Ernest Wilson
1958-79   Geoffrey Ripon Rees-Jones
1979-89   Paul Kneen Bregazzi
1989-96   Stuart Alker Westley
1996-2000   Peter Kerr Fulton-Peebles

2000-   Philip David John

Vice-principals of King William's College

1833-41   Robert Dixon (afterwards principal)
1841-55   Joseph George Cumming
1855-61   Thomas Edward Brown
1861-4   John Turnbull
1864-86   William Heaton
1886-1913   Vacant
1913-26   Hilaro Howard Wathen Dickson
1926-30   William Gilchrist Wilson
1935-7   Joseph David Dallin Paul
1944-53   Canon Ernest Henry Stenning
1955-60   Stanley Boulter
1964-5   Basil Christian Altham Hartley

The traditional office of vice-principal was altered in 1965 to become a stepping-stone to a headship in another college. As such, it survived to 1985 and was occupied by the following:

1966-70   David Lowell Curtis
1971-5   Charles Ian MacMillan Jones
1975-80   Frank Staniland McNamara
1980-5   Nigel Arthur Halfpenny

INDEX OF THE CLERGY (ALPHABETICAL)

Name	Parish	Date(s)
Adamson, Warren	Douglas, St Ninian	1991-3
Airey, Robert	St Olave	1850-8
	Baldwin, St Luke	1859-64
	St Mark	1865-74
	Michael	1874-8
	Santan	1878-89
Aitken, Robert Wesley	Sulby, St Stephen	1860-2
	Marown	1862-9
Akroyd, Jonathan	Dhoon	1869-72
Alan of Whithorn	Arbory	1291
Alcock, John	Douglas, St Barnabas	1848-52
Aldridge, Harold	Braddan	1989-95
Allen, Henry	Lezayre	1714-27
	Maughold	1727-46
Allen, John	Michael	1735
Allen, Robert	Maughold	1660-3
Allen, Thomas	Maughold	1625-42
Allen, Thomas	Maughold	1666-1726
Allen, Thomas	Maughold	1746-54
Allen, William Percy	Sulby, St Stephen	1952-7
	Foxdale	1957-61
Allison, William Osborne	Baldwin, St Luke	1933-5
Allwork, Arthur	Rushen	1879-81
Andrew, Donald	Rushen	1977-82
Appleton, Frederick	St John (the Baptist)	1926-30
	St Mark	1926-8
Appleton, William	Baldwin, St Luke	1880
Awdrey, Walter	St Olave	1867-70
Ayg Mac Peter	Arbory	1375
Aynsley, Lord Charles	Andreas	1803-8
Bache, Thomas	Cronk y Voddy	1913-15
Baggaley, Dennis	Onchan	1971-96
Baguley, Edward	Ballaugh	1580-1
	Santan	1581-97
Ball-Knight, George Thomas	Dalby, St James	1922-5
Bardell, Robertson	St Olave	1878-9
Barff, Henry	St Olave	1866-7

Barker, Ernest	Douglas, St Thomas	1931-43
Barker, Gordon Frank	Lezayre	2004-
Barker, William Ernest	St Jude	1952-6
Barnes, Charles Marston	Dalby, St James	1881-8
Barnes, James	St Mark	1953-5
Baron, Robert Benjamin	Douglas, St George	1891-1906
Barr, Alaister McDougall	Bride	1967-71
Bates, Thomas	Foxdale	1877-9
Beard, Wilfred Percy	Dalby, St James	1927-9
Bell, Charles	Sulby, St Stephen	1882-5
Bellamy, Joseph	Laxey	1861-78
	Jurby	1879-91
Bennett, Paul Jonathan	Patrick	1996-2000
Benson, Reginald James	Douglas, St Ninian	1945-55
Betts, Frederick Arthur	Cronk y Voddy	1915-17
	St John (the Baptist)	1919-20
	Foxdale	1921-2
	Douglas, St Barnabas	1922-4
Bird, Frederick Hinton	Rushen	1982-2003
Birkett, Thomas	Douglas, St Matthew	1732-6
Bishop, George	St Jude	1859-65
Blakeney, Robert Bibby	St Jude	1893-4
Blakeney, William	Sulby, St Stephen	1885-9
Bolton, William	Douglas, St Ninian	1965-75
Botwood, Sidney Benson	St John (the Baptist)	1909-13
	Bride	1913-19
	Malew	1919-30
	Laxey	1930-47
	Marown	1947-53
Bowerman, Alfred George	Cronk y Voddy	1895-1906
	Sulby, St Stephen	1906-29
Bowers, Dermot Nichols	Douglas, St Thomas	1972-88
Bradley, Clifford David	Braddan	1979-84
Bradshaw, Arthur Pearson	Dalby, St James	1911-14
Brailsford, Edward	Sulby, St Stephen	1848-9
Brearey, Robert Gawne	Laxey	1878-81
Breffitt, Geoffrey	Patrick	2001-
Brew, Robert	German	1758-60
Bridgman, Arthur	Lezayre	1879-1909
Bridson, John	Braddan	1691-3
Bridson, John	Ballure	1771-83
	Ballure	1785-8
	Marown	1799-1808
	Bride	1808-16
Bridson, William	Marown	1713-27
	Lezayre	1728-9
	Ballaugh	1729-51

Chapman, Theodore Charles	Laxey	1881-4
Childs, Theodore John	Ballaugh	1970-7
Christian	Andreas	c. 1550?
Christian, Ewan	Patrick	1769-1808
Christian, John	Maughold	1580-1614
Christian, John	Bride	1687-98
	Jurby	1698-1747
Christian, John	Marown	1753-79
Christian, John	Arbory	1791-1815
Christian, John	Douglas, St George	1817-27
Christian, Nicholas	Rushen	1748-82
Christian, Nicholas	Ballure	1789-90
	Douglas, St Matthew	1791-7
	Michael	1802-8
	Patrick	1808-11
Christian, Robert	German	1752-4
Christian, Thomas	Rushen	1713-27
Christian, Thomas	Marown	1734-52
Christian, Thomas	Marown	1780-99
Christian, William	Malew	1817-30
Christian, William	Dhoon	1840-50
Christian, William Bell	St John (the Baptist)	1845
	Lezayre	1845-61
Clague, Arthur Ashford	Lezayre	1969-82
Clague, John	Rushen	1782-1816
Clarke, Archibald Edward	Sulby, St Stephen	1892-1903
	Marown	1903-34
Clarke, Benjamin Philpot	Baldwin, St Luke	1864-5
	St Jude	1865-9
	Marown	1869-1903
Clarke, John	Jurby	1603-45
Clarke, John Thomas	St Mark	1827-64
Clay, William	St Olave	1858-61
Clayton, Geoffrey Buckroyd	Arbory	1972-97
Clerk, Thomas	Andreas	1497
Clode, Arthur Raymond Thomas	Bride	1975-8
Clucas, William	Malew	1778-83
	Bride	1783-98
Cochrane, Eustace William	Foxdale	1879-1900
Cole, Norma Jean	Rushen	2004-
Colepeper, Frederick John	St Mark	1928-32
Collet, Edward	Cronk y Voddy	1875-6
Convery, Arthur Malcolm	Marown	1987-2004
	Onchan	2004-
Cooil, James Arthur	St Jude	1917-34
Coole, Charles	Lezayre	1656-60

Copner, Thomas Herbert Woodward	Patrick	1945-59
	Lonan	1959-75
Corkhill, John	Rushen	1606-38
Corlett, Henry	German	1761-1801
Corlett, John	Sulby, St Stephen	1858-9
	Cronk y Voddy	1859-65
	St John (the Baptist)	1865-1909
Corlett, Philip	Ballure	1819-22
	Ramsey South, St Paul	1822-5
Corlett, Thomas	Lezayre	1773-1803
Cormac	Andreas	1320
Corrin, William	Rushen	1824-59
Cosnahan, Hugh	Santan	1667-91
Cosnahan, John	Jurby	1575-80
	German	1580-1608
	Patrick	1580-1608
Cosnahan, John	Santan	1618-52
Cosnahan, John	Malew	1630-3
Cosnahan, John	Santan	1691-1724
Cosnahan, John	Braddan	1733-50
Cosnahan, Joseph	Braddan	1750-68
Cosnahan, Julius	Braddan	1786
Cosnahan, William	Santan	1614-18
	German	1621-33
	Patrick	1621-33
Cotes, Frederick Cecil	St John (the Baptist)	1924-6
Cotter, James Myrtle	Santan	1973-8
Cottier, John	Patrick	1812-27
Cottier, Robert	Braddan	1609-23
Court, Kenneth Reginald	Douglas, St Matthew	1976-84
Cowill, Charles	Bride	1623-38?
Cowley, Daniel Scurr	German	1890-5
	Bride	1895-1913
Cowley, Jonathan Edward	Lezayre	1947-50
Cox, Frederick Ingram	Douglas, St Thomas	1943-8
Cox, Percy Campbell	Ramsey South, St Paul	1980-2
Crahan, Donald	Michael	1571-85
Craine, Edward	Onchan	1810-47
Craine, Edward	St Mark	1814-20
Craine, John	German	1741-2
Craine, Robert	Ballure	1804-7
Craine, William	Patrick	? - 1575
Craven, George Edward	Douglas, St Barnabas	1904-9
Crebbin, Charles	Douglas, St Matthew	1765-9
	Santan	1769-1817
	Douglas, St George	1781-1817

Crebbin, Paul	Santan	1731-64
Crebbin, William	Jurby	1751-1803
Crellin, John	Arbory	1650-70
Crellin, John	Ballure	1761-71
	Michael	1771-98
	Bride	1798-1808
Crennell, Henry Fraser	Castletown	1947-9
Cringle, William Edward James	Foxdale	1949-55
	Bride	1955-61
	St Olave	1961-80
Crowe, Edward	Lezayre	1624-56
	Santan	1656-67
Crowe, Silvester	Lezayre	1614-24
Crowe, William	Braddan	1582-1603
	Lezayre	1603-14
	Bride	1614-23
Crowe, William	Jurby	1645-98
Cubbon, Thomas	Santan	1765-9
	Maughold	1769-1814
	Lonan	1814-17
	Bride	1817-30
Curghey, John	Braddan	1704-33
Curghey, Matthias, sr	Patrick	1703-29
	German	1710-29
	Bride	1729-54
Curghey, Matthias	Rushen	1703-13
Curghey, Matthias, jr	Marown	1728-9
	Lezayre	1729-61
	Ballaugh	1761-71
Curghey, Nathaniel	Lonan	1753-9
Curtis, Cecil Vivian	Arbory	1957-67
Curwen, Edward	St Olave	1874-5
Darbyshire, Brian	Douglas, St Ninian	2002-
Davidson, Hugh	Patrick	1882-97
Davies, Alfred Henry Lloyd	Baldwin, St Luke	1928-30
Davies, Gideon	St Mark	1936-8
	St Jude	1938-40
	Lonan	1940-4
Davies, Ian	Marown	2005-
Davies, William Edward	Laxey	1897-1904
	St Olave	1904-17
Dawes, Charles	Rushen	1885-7
Dawes, George	Baldwin, St Luke	1856-9
Dawes, Victor	St Jude	1967-73
Dean, Simon Timothy Michael		
Rex	Castletown	1992-2005

Gamble, John Richard Crone	Cronk y Voddy	1937-8
	Jurby	1938-46
	Lezayre	1950-4
Garde, John Fry	St John (the Baptist)	1845-65
	Cronk y Voddy	1852-4
	Patrick	1865-77
Gardner, James	Sulby, St Stephen	1891-2
Gasking, Samuel	Baldwin, St Luke	1880-2
Gates, Kenneth George	Ballaugh	1934-8
Geddes, Eric Douglas	Douglas, St Barnabas	1934-8
Geddes, Roderick Charles	Andreas	1994-2003
Gell, Daniel	Rushen	1588-94
Gell, Henry	Onchan	1575-80
Gell, John	Marown	1576-1603
Gell, John	St Mark	1786-1809
Gell, John	St John (the Baptist)	1834-45
Gell, Samuel	Jurby	1747-8
	Onchan	1748-59
	Lonan	1759-1802
Gell, William	Onchan	1701-48
Gelling, Alexander	Ballure	1809-16
	Arbory	1816-59
Gelling, Daniel	Ballure	1756-61
	Malew	1761-77
	Ballaugh	1777-1801
Gelling, Frederick Woodhouse	St Mark	1922-5
	Santan	1938-49
Gelling, James	German	1801-38
Gelling, John Drury	Rushen	1964-77
	Michael	1972-92
	Ballaugh	1977-92
Gelling, Samuel	St John (the Baptist)	1824-33
	Douglas, St Matthew	1835
	Santan	1835-65
George, John Edward Beauchamp	Douglas, St George	1880-91
George, Wilfred	Sulby, St Stephen	1933-6
	Marown	1936-46
	Cronk y Voddy	1941-6
	St John (the Baptist)	1941-6
	Jurby	1946-67
	St Jude	1956-67
Gibson, William Henry	Dalby, St James	1896-8
	Laxey	1904-16
Gilbert	Andreas	1482
Gilbert de Latham	Andreas	1544-52
Gill, Ewan	Onchan	1686-1701
	Marown	1701-13

Harrison, John	Patrick	1633-52
	German	1633-52
	Andreas	1652-60
	Bride	1660-86
Harrison, John Edward	Maughold	1814-18
	Jurby	1818-58
Harrison, Mark Wilks	Ramsey South, St Paul	1911-46
Harrison, Stephen Nathaniel	Dhoon	1873-89
Harrison, Thomas	Arbory	1623-8
Harrison, Thomas	Patrick	1652-61
	German	1652-61
Harrison, Thomas	Michael	1808-18
Hart, William	Foxdale	1876-7
Hartwell, Francis Broderick	Douglas, St George	1836-46
Harvey, Gilmour	Santan	1865-77
	Maughold	1877-8
Hastings, Thomas Herbert	Dalby, St James	1919-22
Hawley, William	Douglas, St George	1859-77
	Patrick	1877-82
	Michael	1882-93
Hayes, Leslie	Braddan	1974-8
Hebden, John Percy	Laxey	1970-84
	Lonan	1980-4
Hemingway, Norman	Jurby	1931-7
	Arbory	1937-57
Henry, Leslie Victor	Lezayre	1983-6
Henry, Thomas	Lezayre	1863-9
Heslop, James Alan	Bride	1998-9
Hickin, Henry	St Mark	1905-12
Hill, Charles	Dalby, St James	1858-68
Hill, Samuel	Dhoon	1855-8
Hinde, Samuel	Bride	1638?-60
Hirst, Frederick James	Cronk y Voddy	1924-6
Hitchen, Harold Stone	Cronk y Voddy	1922-4
	Douglas, St Barnabas	1929-34
	Marown	1934-6
Hobson, William Thomas	Douglas, St Barnabas	1872-95
Hoggett, Philip	German	1575-6
	Patrick	1575-6
	Ballaugh	1576-80
	Jurby	1580-5
Holland, Hugh	Castletown	1577
	Andreas	1577-87
Holden, John Arthur	Baldwin, St Luke	1923-7
Holmes, Archibald	Ramsey South, St Paul	1825-42
	Patrick	1842-65
Holmes, Arnold John	St Mark	1897-1903

Kermode, Robert Daniel	Maughold	1898-1908
	Douglas, St George	1908-19
	Lezayre	1919-39
Kermode, Stanley	Onchan	1892-1904
Kermode, William	Dalby, St James	1839-40
	Ramsey South, St Paul	1843-71
	Maughold	1871-7
	Ballaugh	1877-90
Kershaw, Geoffrey	Bride	1971-5
Kewley, John	Douglas, St Matthew	1802-10
Kewley, John	Arbory	1891-1912
	Andreas	1912-38
Kewley, Joseph William	Foxdale	1850-4
Kewley, Thomas	Santan	1827-35
King, Norman	Dalby, St James	1890-2
Kinred, Hugh	Baldwin, St Luke	1882
	Cronk y Voddy	1882-95
	Patrick	1897-1921
Kippax, Archippus	Andreas	1696-1700
Kippax, John	Castletown	1727
	Andreas	1727-60
Kirkby, John	Santan	1890-1
Kissack, Edward William	Baldwin, St Luke	1868-9
	St Jude	1869-72
	Rushen	1872-9
	Bride	1879-90
	Ballaugh	1890-7
Kneale, Patrick	St Mark	1809-14
Kneale, Thomas Redfearn	St Jude	1888-93
	Rushen	1893-7
	Ballaugh	1897-1934
Knipe, James	Ballure	1712-47
Kroenig, Charles	St Mark	1891-6
Kyte, Joseph	Dalby, St James	1868-72
	Cronk y Voddy	1876-9
LaMothe, John Henry	Lezayre	1842-5
Lancaster, Peter	Douglas, St Matthew	1714-16
Landsell, Frederick John	Douglas, St Barnabas	1896-1903
Langton, Charles Thomas	Baldwin, St Luke	1869-80
	Arbory	1880-90
	Bride	1890-4
Laurence	Andreas	1247
Lee, Thomas	St Olave	1863-5
Leece, Charles Henry	Laxey	1895-7
	Rushen	1897-1927
Leech, John	Foxdale	1859-64

Leighe, Philip	Michael	1605-9
Lewis, Walter	German	1907-14
Liley, Kenneth	Braddan	1965-74
Lloyd, Joseph	Laxey	1950-6
Locke, Edward Henry Leatham	Dalby, St James	1894-6
	Castletown	1896-1921
	Patrick	1921-9
Lomax, John	Andreas	1687-95
Lowcay, Henry	German	1661-80
	Patrick	1661-77
	Ballaugh	1681-1700
Lumgair, David	Ballaugh	1967-70
	Santan	1970-2
Lupton, Benjamin	St Mark	1878-91
Macaboy	Andreas	1270
Mactyr	Arbory	1372-5
Maddrell, Henry	Ballure	1790-1803
	Lezayre	1803-42
Maddrell, Henry	Maughold	1928-30
	Castletown	1930-8
	Andreas	1938-53
Makon, James	Castletown	1701-19
Marsden, Christopher	Andreas	1700-1
Martin, William Harrison	Laxey	1997-
Matthews, Percival Charles Halls	Douglas, St George	1953-80
Mayoh, Robert Harrison	Douglas, St Barnabas	1924-8
McNeil, Henry Cameron	Douglas, St Ninian	1915-28
M'Corkyll, Donald	Ballaugh	1408
McCullough, Herbert Alexander	German	1970-7
McPherson, Thomas Stanley	St Jude	1949-52
Michael	Lezayre	1408
Millington, Thomas	St Olave	1848-50
Milton-Smith, Charles Henry	Foxdale	1966-72
Mitchell, John	St Mark	1874-6
Mock, Arthur Harold	Ramsey South, St Paul	1952-64
Moore, Edward	Braddan	1603-8
	Patrick	1608-21
Moore, Edward	Lonan	1735
	Michael	1735-51
Moore, Frederick James	Foxdale	1864-75
	Jurby	1875-8
	Lonan	1878-88
	Braddan	1888-1912
Moore, James	Lonan	1627-53

Moore, John	Onchan	1566-75
	Braddan	1576-82
	Bride	1582-1609
Moore, John	Arbory	1748-91
Moore, John	St Mark	1783-6
	Braddan	1786-91
Moore, John James Stevenson	St Olave	1861-3
Moore, Joseph Christian	Andreas	1844-86
Moore, Philip	Douglas, St Matthew	1736-65
	Ballaugh	1751-60
	Bride	1760-83
Moore, Robert	Santan	1597-1608
	German	1608-21
Morice	German	1408
Morrey, Hugh	Patrick	1630-3
	German	1630-3
Morris, Alfred	Michael	1894-1913
Morris, Edgar Lionel	German	1931-66
Morris, William	St Olave	1879-96
Mourant, Sidney Eric	Douglas, St Thomas	1992-6
Murray, Honourable George	Andreas	1808-14
Murray, Lord George	Andreas	1787-1803
Murray, Rudolf William Henry		
Dawson	Castletown	1964-72
Mylrea, Daniel	Ballure	1783-5
	Michael	1799-1802
	Ballaugh	1802-14
	Andreas	1814-32
Mylrea, William	Bride	1754-60
	Andreas	1760-87
Nigel, Donald	Bride	? - 1377
	Malew	1370-7
Nelson, Arthur Evelyn	Cronk y Voddy	1918-22
Nelson, Daniel	St Jude	1847
	Bride	1847-75
Nelson, Edward	Michael	1677-86
Nelson, John	Jurby	1803-18
	Santan	1818-27
	Bride	1830-47
Norreys, Thomas	Malew	1610-30
Norris, Henry	Michael	1686-1717
Norris, John	Marown	1618-23
Norris, Lewis	Marown	1605-18
Norris, Robert	Arbory	1628-50

Norris, Thomas	Malew	1574-1606
	Marown	1603-5
	Arbory	1609-23
Norris, William	Lezayre	1571-85
	Lonan	1585-1627
Oates, John	Onchan	1580-1647
Oates, Robert	Braddan	1623-4
Oates, William	Marown	1623-77
Oates, William	Maughold	1642-60
Odo	Santan	1291
Orman, Thomas	Arbory	1576-7
Packer, George	Foxdale	1900-3
Pakenham, Edward Thomas	Michael	1922-6
	German	1926-31
Parkinson, Clifford Alwyn	Marown	1955-8
Parr, Charles	Lonan	1653-73
	Ballaugh	1673-81
Parr, George	Douglas, St Thomas	1954-9
Parr, John	Ballure	1688-91
	Rushen	1691-1700
	Bride	1700-13
Parr, Robert	Malew	1633-40
	Ballaugh	1640-73
Parr, Robert	Lezayre	1681-1712
	Arbory	1713-23
	Bride	1723-9
Parr, Thomas	Malew	1641-95
Parsons, George Stickler	Castletown	1827-55
Partington, Brian Harold	Patrick	1968-96
	Foxdale	1977-96
	St John (the Baptist)	1977-96
	Douglas, St George	1996-2004
Paton, George	St Olave	1865-6
	Ramsey South, St Paul	1871-1900
Patrick	Andreas	1408
Patrick	Bride	1408
Pattison, James Eckley	Sulby, St Stephen	1865-78
Payne, Joseph Marshall	Castletown	1972-8
	Malew	1972-82
Pettengell, Ernest	Douglas, St Thomas	2003-
Phillips, John	Andreas	1587-1633
Phillips, Joseph	Dalby, St James	1929-32
Philpot, Benjamin	Douglas, St George	1827-32
	Andreas	1832-9
Pierpoint, Matthew	Laxey	1859-61

Pigot, Harry Creswell	Dalby, St James	1890
Platt, James Henry	Ballaugh	1960-6
	German	1966-9
Poole, Nathaniel John	Douglas, St Thomas	1920-31
Pope, John Grasett	Maughold	1908-20
Post, David Charles William	Braddan	1978-9
Preston, Thomas	Michael	1585-1605
Qualtrough, Edward	Sulby, St Stephen	1853
Qualtrough, John	Sulby, St Stephen	1839-48
	St Jude	1848-59
	Arbory	1859-75
	Bride	1875-9
Qualtrough, Joseph	Douglas, St Matthew	1810-16
	Rushen	1816-24
	Lonan	1824-53
Quayle, John	Arbory	1728-48
Quayle, John	Rushen	1729-39
	Malew	1739-58
Quayle, Robert	Douglas, St Matthew	1770-91
	Braddan	1792-1809
Quayle, Thomas	Onchan	1759-98
Quine, Christopher Andrew	Arbory	1999-
Quine, John	Lonan	1895-1940
Quirk, John Nathaniel	Douglas, St Thomas	1881-2
Radcliffe, Robert	Lonan	1725-35
Radcliffe, Robert	Patrick	1729-69
Rainbow, Edward	German	1897-1907
Rawcliffe, Frederick Arthur	Foxdale	1917-21
Reade, Claud	Laxey	1885-7
Reid, Robert Higginson	Malew	1931-2
Richard	Onchan	1408
Ridings, Albert	Rushen	1927-32
Rigby, Ronald Robert Pierpoint	Michael	1965-72
Roberts, Michael Frederick	Malew	1993-
Robertson, William Sealey	Sulby, St Stephen	1939-44
	Lonan	1944-53
	Lezayre	1958-69
Robinson, Hampton	Dalby, St James	1907-9
Robinson, Peter Charles	Ramsey South, St Paul	1992-9
Robinson, Samuel	Lezayre	1667-81
Robinson, Samuel	Arbory	1680-1712
Robinson, Samuel	Douglas, St Matthew	1708-14
Robinson, Thomas	Onchan	1680-6
Rogers, Cyril David	Ballaugh	1997-
Rolleston, Adrian	St Jude	1894-1913

Rolston, William George	Dhoon	1891-1907
Ross, William	Castletown	1727-54
Rostron, Isaiah	Douglas, St Barnabas	1917-21
Rushworth, William Andrew	Braddan	1912-50
Rutter, Samuel	Andreas	1643-52/60[610]
Saul, Norman Stanley	Foxdale	1972-7
	Maughold	1977-90
Saunders, William Henry	Baldwin, St Luke	1939-44
	Sulby, St Stephen	1944-6
	Foxdale	1946-9
	Malew	1949-56
Saunderson, Henry	Malew	1932-4
	St Mark	1932-6
	Foxdale	1934-8
	Douglas, St Barnabas	1938-50
	Baldwin, St Luke	1955-74
Savage, Ernest Bickersteth	Michael	1878-82
	Douglas, St Thomas	1882-1914
Sayle, Gordon	Lezayre	1939-46
	Ramsey South, St Paul	1947-52
Scattergood, William Henry	Laxey	1984-92
Scorer, William Veitch	German	1914-17
Senior, Walter Stanley	St Olave	1927-30
Sewell, John Herbert Brereton	Castletown	1938-47
Sheen, John Harold	Bride	1978-97
	St Olave	1980-97
Shenston, Henry	Jurby	1905-12
	Douglas, St Barnabas	1912-17
Shepheard, Clement Carus Wilson	Lezayre	1877-8
Shepherd, Brian Edward	Lezayre	1991-2002
Shippham, Frederick	Dalby, St James	1909-10
Shufflebottom, Ernest	Laxey	1957-9
Sidebotham, Samuel	Cronk y Voddy	1911-13
Simpson, Samuel	Douglas, St Thomas	1851-61
Smith, Alec John	Douglas, St Thomas	1988-92
Smith, Brian	Douglas, St George	2005-
Smith, George Samuel	St Mark	1946-8
Smyth, James	Rushen	1574-7
	Arbory	1577-80
Smyth, William Kerr	Cronk y Voddy	1906-8
Snepp, Edward	Lezayre	1861-3

[610]Left Andreas in 1652 but did not resign the living until 1660.

Spicer, John Morris	Laxey	1887-95
	Malew	1895-1919
Squire, William George Ellis	Rushen	1959-64
Stammers, Charles Percy	Dalby, St James	1925-7
Stanley, Walmsley	Onchan	1904-8
Stephen, George Caesar	Dalby, St James	1840-58
Stephen, Thomas	Marown	1809-27
	Patrick	1827-42
Stephenson, John Burnaby	Cronk y Voddy	1880-2
Stevenson, Alexander	Santan	1571-5
	Braddan	1575-6
	Patrick	1576-80
	German	1576-80
	Arbory	1580-1
	Rushen	1581-8
Stevenson, John	Maughold	1576-80
	Arbory	1581-5
Stewart, Charles James	Cronk y Voddy	1854-7
Stockwood, Charles Vincent	St Olave	1918-27
	Douglas, St George	1927-48
	Cronk y Voddy	1948-58
	St John (the Baptist)	1948-58
Stowell, Hugh	Douglas, St Matthew	1797-1802
	Lonan	1802-14
	Ballaugh	1814-35
Stowell, Hugh Ashworth	Dhoon	1858-69
Stowell, John LaMothe	Douglas, St Matthew	1832-5
	German	1839-80
Stuart, James Orchard	Sulby, St Stephen	1859-60
Stubbs, Frederick William	Jurby	1895-1903
	Foxdale	1903-9
	Douglas, St Barnabas	1909-12
	Arbory	1912-37
Sturt, William	Ballure	1803-4
Sutton, Henry	Douglas, St Barnabas	1870-2
Swallow, Francis	Foxdale	1856-8
Swan, Sidney	Sulby, St Stephen	1889-90
Symeyn, Thomas	Arbory	1571-6
Symonds, William Charles Cato	Sulby, St Stephen	1929-33
	Cronk y Voddy	1933-6
	St John (the Baptist)	1933-6
Taggart, Hugh Selwyn	Douglas, St Matthew	1909-26
Taggart, Thomas Arthur	Douglas, St Matthew	1874-1909
Talbot, Theophilus	St Olave	1870-4
Taubman, John	Lonan	1686-1725
Taylor, Christopher Tennant	Cronk y Voddy	1857-8

Taylor, Thomas Whitehead	St Olave	1956-61
Thimbleby, Thomas	Castletown	1818-27
Thompson, John	Bride	1609-14
	Maughold	1614-24
	Braddan	1624-33
Thompson, John	Rushen	1652-60
	Lezayre	1660-7
Thompson, Matthew	Sulby, St Stephen	1851-3
Thompson, Nicholas	Ballaugh	1598-1640
Thompson, Patrick	Braddan	1633-89
Thompson, Richard	Rushen	1660-91
Thompson, William	Sulby, St Stephen	1853-5
Thomson, George	Baldwin, St Luke	1889-91
Thwaites, Thomas	Lonan	1674-86
Towndrow, Edwin James	Douglas, St Ninian	1928-32
Tracey, Frederick Francis	Rushen	1881-5
Turner, William Charles	Patrick	1959-63
Upton, Clement	Laxey	1993-6
Upton-Jones, Peter	Bride	2000-
	Andreas	2003-
Urquhart, William	Andreas	1669-87
Vaughan, Neville Shaw	Marown	1958-72
Wakeford, Robert	Onchan	1908-33
Walker, Samuel Sharpe	Sulby, St Stephen	1862-5
Walker, William	Ballaugh	1703-29
Walles, John	Andreas	1513
Walmsley, William Vernon	Ballaugh	1949-59
Ward, Joseph Preston	Sulby, St Stephen	1849-51
Warren, Mordaunt Laidlaw	Baldwin, St Luke	1891-4
Washington, Marmaduke	Douglas, St Thomas	1877-81
Waterhouse, Harry	Arbory	1969-72
Watson, Lewis Cecil	Douglas, St Matthew	1932-42
Watson, Robert William	Baldwin, St Luke	1894-9
Watterson, William	Rushen	1594-1606
	Malew	1606-8
Wattleworth, Charles	Arbory	1726-8
Wattleworth, Samuel	Michael	1672-7
	Patrick	1677-1703
	German	1682-1703
	Andreas	1703-18
Webster, Benjamin	Laxey	1926-30
	Patrick	1930-7
Weir, Peter	Lezayre	1955-8
Wells, Nicholas Anthony	Onchan	1997-2003

Wentner, Clarence Gordon Felix Justin	St John (the Baptist)	1930-3
Whalley, William	Dalby, St James	1898-1903
	Jurby	1903-5
White, Frederick Stanley	St Jude	1975-89
	Andreas	1978-94
White, Henry Grattan	Santan	1877-8
	Maughold	1878-94
White, Jack	Douglas, St George	1948-53
Whittaker, Frank	Baldwin, St Luke	1910-13
Whittaker, Henry Smith	Malew	1934-49
	Castletown	1949-55
Whitworth, Duncan	Douglas, St Matthew	1984-
Wilkinson, James Seely	St Jude	1872-88
	Lonan	1888-95
	Maughold	1895-8
Wilks, James	German	1744-52
	Michael	1752-71
	Ballaugh	1771-7
Willetts, William Henry	German	1922-5
William	Rushen	1408
Williams, George Ernest	Sulby, St Stephen	1936-9
	Foxdale	1939-46
Williams, James George	German	1881-9
Williams, Thomas	Dalby, St James	1903-7
Williams, Walter Whitfield	Douglas, St Ninian	1932-45
Willoughby, David Albert	Marown	1972-80
	Douglas, St George	1980-96
Wilson, David	St Jude	1934-7
	Patrick	1937-45
Wilson, Donald Albert	Lonan	1975-80
Wilson, George	Bride	1962-6
Wilson, Henry	Jurby	1891-5
Wilson, Peter Shepherd	Castletown	1978-83
Wood, William	Douglas, St Matthew	1943-54
Woodhouse, Disney Charles	Douglas, St Ninian	1913-15
Woods, John	Onchan	1650-80
	German	1680-2
	Braddan	1693-6
	Malew	1696-1739
Woods, John, jr	German	1730-40
Woods, Thomas William Joseph	Ballure	1747-54
	Maughold	1754-68
	Braddan	1768-86
Young, Ernest Andrew Stafford	Maughold	1920-7
Young, Halford William	St Olave	1930-50

BIBLIOGRAPHY

Bible chaserick yn lucht thie. The Manx family Bible, London, 1819. (Reprinted, Onchan, 1979.)

Bird, F. H., *An island that led - the history of Manx education*, 2 vols., Douglas, 1995.

Chaloner J., *A short treatise of the Isle of Man*, ed. J. G. Cumming, Manx Society Studies X, Douglas, 1864. (Originally published, London, 1656.)

Cheney, C. R., 'Manx synodal statutes, A. D. 1230(?)-1351', *Cambridge Medieval Celtic Studies* VII, 1984, pp. 63-89 and *ibid.*, VIII, 1984, pp. 51-63.

Dickinson, J. R., *The lordship of Man under the Stanleys. Government and economy in the Isle of Man, 1580-1704*, Douglas, 1997.

Gelling, J. D., *A history of the Manx church, 1698-1911*, Douglas, 1998.

Gumbley, K. F. W., *Manx church legislation*, second edition, Douglas, 1998.

Harrison, W., *The diocese of Sodor and Man*, Manx Society Studies XXIX, Douglas, 1879.

Moore, A. W., *The diocese of Sodor and Man*, London, 1893.

Quilliam, L., *Surnames of the Manks*, Peel, 1989. (Reprinted, Douglas, 1996.)

Statutes of Man, ed. J. Gill and others, Douglas, 1883-.

The works of the right reverend father in God, Thomas Wilson, D. D., 7 vols., Oxford, 1863.

INDEX OF REFERENCES TO HOLY SCRIPTURE

INDEX OF PERSONS AND PLACES

Names and places in the clergy indexes are not indexed here.

INDEX OF SUBJECTS